UNITED NATIONS DEVELOPMENT PROGRAMME
ARAB FUND FOR ECONOMIC AND SOCIAL DEVELOPMENT
ARAB GULF PROGRAMME FOR UNITED NATIONS DEVELOPMENT ORGANIZATIONS

THE ARAB HUMAN DEVELOPMENT REPORT 2004

Towards Freedom in the Arab World

REGIONAL BUREAU FOR ARAB STATES

Available through:
United Nations Publications
Room DC2-853
New York, NY 10017
USA

Telephone: 212 963 8302 and 800 253 9646 (From the United States)
Email: Publications@un.org
Web: www.un.org/Publications
Web: www.undp.org/rbas

Cover Design:
Walid Gadow

Layout and Production: SYNTAX, Amman, Jordan

Printed at: National Press, Amman, Jordan

ISBN: 92-1-126165-1

Printed in the Hashemite Kingdom of Jordan

The analysis and policy recommendations of this Report do not necessarily reflect the views of the United Nations
Development Programme, its Executive Board or its Member States. The Report is the work of an independent
team of authors sponsored by the Regional Bureau for Arab States.

This work was originally published in Arabic. In any cases of discrepancies, the original language shall govern.

Foreword by the Administrator, UNDP

The first two Arab Human Development Reports published by the United Nations Development Programme and written by an independent group of Arab scholars, policymakers and practitioners have, rightly, become landmarks in the broader debate and discussion over the future of the region. The key diagnosis of the first report that the Arab world is suffering three fundamental deficits – in political rights, in women's rights and in knowledge – that have, together, held back human development across the region has now become widely accepted. The second report then spelled out in compelling detail the first of these deficits, analyzing where Arab knowledge production and dissemination systems were falling short and articulating why Arab states need to turn outwards and engage with the outside world to make learning and research key drivers of social and economic innovation in the future.

Those two reports succeeded more spectacularly than we could have imagined in the scale of their impact. They were the talk of coffee shops and cabinets, boardrooms and world TV talk shows. More broadly, they were a media and publishing phenomenon, stimulating formal debate from the G8 summit at Sea Island, Georgia, to civil society meetings in Sana'a and Alexandria among many other gatherings. Above all, in a region where disagreement, sometimes violent, has been too often the norm of political discourse, longtime opponents found a lot to agree about in them. And that has been the real power of the Reports: starting to build a consensus around reform.

This report, the third in the series, seeks to focus on the thorny issues of freedom, good governance and political reform. Drawing on a mixture of survey data and other research it seeks to map out the challenges and constraints to moving forward on a path of democratic progress. In two key ways, however, the report has been more difficult to prepare than its predecessors. First has been the limitation of the data. One of the central sources of information was a specially designed survey to map out public attitudes to key aspects of reform. Regrettably several countries declined permission for the survey to be carried out, resulting in only a partial snapshot. Though most of the analysis in the report is not dependent on the survey this shortcoming inevitably hampered analysis of public attitudes and perceptions in the region.

A second problem has been the exceptionally rapid pace of events in the region itself. This is not in itself new – the first two reports were prepared in the shadow of continued violence in the occupied Palestinian Territory and then the invasion of Iraq, both of which have had broad repercussions throughout the Arab world. However, given the central conviction of the authors across all the reports that lasting and sustainable reform in the Arab world needs to come from within, the intensification of both conflicts over the past year and the fierce reactions they have provoked across the region have led to a deep concern on the part of the authors that the broad agenda of reform, and enhanced human development, was being retarded rather than accelerated.

At the same time, as a result of the high visibility of the reports, the very process of writing this AHDR has been a source of significant public, and, unfortunately, highly politicized and often inaccurate speculation. While reflecting the tremendous difficulty of writing a neutral, fact-based report in such an environment, this has inevitably created some tensions for UNDP given its fundamental character as a development rather than political institution. As a result, while the process has clearly demonstrated the need for a neutral, international platform of the kind UNDP is able to provide, it has also shown the limitations of such an approach and the need for a longer-term formula that would, in time, allow for wider ownership and institutionalization of the Reports as a representative voice of Arab civil society - a report written in the region and owned by the region.

In this context, as we have made clear since launching this initiative and other discussions of this kind, the AHDRs are, deliberately, not formal UN or UNDP documents and do not reflect the official views of either organization. Rather, they have been intended to stimulate and inform a dynamic, new public discourse across the Arab world and beyond. In the case of this year's report, however, I feel it necessary to state that some of the views expressed by the authors are not shared by UNDP or the UN. Nevertheless, the very strength of this report and the success of its predecessors has depended on their being seen as an authentic reflection of views and analysis of many of the most thoughtful, reform-minded intellectual figures in the Arab region. In that sense, this report clearly reflects a very real anger and concern felt across the region that needs to be urgently addressed if we are to reach our shared goal of helping to build a peaceful, democratic region able to meet the needs and aspirations of its citizens.

Mark Malloch Brown.
Administrator, UNDP

Foreword by the Regional Director, UNDP Regional Bureau for Arab States

The Arab Human Development Reports continue to examine the factors that prevent an Arab renaissance from taking off, and to search for those that could empower it to advance and progress. In this third installment in the series, the Report focuses on the issue of freedom in the Arab world and its relationship to good governance and human development.

The road to AHDR 3 has been long, eventful and lined with several obstacles. No subject excites stronger feelings in the region than that of freedom, whether among those denied it or among those who violate and confiscate it. No public discourse on any issue is more watchfully invigilated by the authorities, or more tightly encircled by penalties that push some to exercise self-censorship, in speech and thought, wherever the discussion relates to freedom. The difficulties are magnified when the definition of freedom is expanded, as in the case of this Report, to include the freedom of society and nations where liberty is confronted by powers intolerant of dissent, diversity and independent thinking.

Those in our region who demand freedom, and who struggle for it, may be in the majority; however, those who stifle it are stronger, more powerful and have better means. They not only possess the means to oppress, marginalize and impoverish, but they also control key forums and are able to recruit those adept at twisting various texts to perpetuate their interests and at bending intellectual norms and theories in order to prohibit freedom and permit its confiscation.

There were those who genuinely feared that the Report might be used to serve the interests of powers willing to transform causes honourable in their intent, design and aims into goods in political bargains. The Report team, however, felt that the best way forward was not to turn a blind eye to reality, but to show that Arabs can recognize and overcome their own weaknesses. Self-reform originating in balanced self-criticism is the only viable path towards a robust and independent region.

Despite such difficulties, or perhaps because of them, the authors remained convinced that their vision of this Report, in all essentials, was correct. They studied the scene of freedom in different theatres in the Arab world, and found them deficient in some areas and seriously deficient in others, such as political and civil liberties. Generalized violations, moreover, become harsher when they concern those religious or ethnic groups that are excluded from citizenship or rights. While some foreign factors including occupation which usurps the roots of freedom, helped to establish a climate of oppression in some Arab countries, there are legal, economic and political structures within Arab societies that continue to prevent Arabs from enjoying rights and freedoms that were enshrined in their values, culture and religion well before the promulgation of the International Declaration of Human Rights. Sadly, what Arab constitutions grant, Arab laws frequently curtail. And what laws render legal, actual practice often violates. People are thus besieged in their own country, their takeoff is held back, their development is blocked, and their nation is weakened.

There are, however, enlightened contemporary movements working for a transformation to societies where human rights reign supreme, freedoms flourish and the rule of law strikes deep roots. In the past year the Arab world witnessed unprecedented initiatives aimed at changing the status quo. Some, such as the resolutions of the Arab Summit, were formal while many others came from civil and political society. The report also notes a number of positive developments particularly in the field of education and the empowerment of women.

As part of its now-customary method, the Report does not stop at diagnosing obstacles to rights and freedoms. It outlines a broad-based strategic vision of how to rationalize efforts to strengthen freedom in the Arab world and to reinforce the pillars of good governance.

This vision focuses on widening the political space in order to move societies towards the peaceful alternation of power and on creating a strong legal and institutional structure in support of freedom, The first step in this direction is to launch the key freedoms of opinion, expression and organization, to put an end to all forms of discrimination against social groups, to abolish emergency rules and to ensure the independence and fairness of the justice system.

No matter how hard I try, I will not be able to do justice to the collective effort that this Report represents. But like any human endeavour, however true and worthwhile, this effort remains open to refinement and correction. The authors do not claim to have arrived at any form of final truth about the state of freedom and governance in the region. Their goal has been to promote, within the limitations of this sensitive arena, as thorough and objective a discussion on the challenges facing Arab societies and the means to overcome them.

It is especially important to make the issue of freedom the subject of a constructive debate in our societies. Important and urgent, for freedom is not only the most instrumental of enabling human rights anywhere in the world, but in our region, it is also, increasingly, the most fragile.

Lastly, I hope that readers will excuse us if, because of the delay in issuing this Report, they find that some events reported in Part I have been outpaced by fast-moving developments in the region. Hopefully, the next report in the series, on the empowerment of Arab women, will be an opportunity to make amends.

I wish to express my sincere thanks to those Arab states that allowed the Report team to carry out our field survey on freedom, which raised the standard of this aspect of our research: I salute here Algeria, Jordan, Lebanon, Morocco and Palestine.

I am especially grateful to all who participated in the preparation, review, translation and editing of AHDR3. I would like also to express my sincere thanks to a number of Arab intellectuals, whose joint concern for Arab advancement prompted them to make enriching contributions to the Report. My gratitude also goes to the Core Team for its innovative efforts and to its leader, Dr. Nader Fergany for his distinctive work and persistent follow-up through all its stages. I owe a sincere vote of thanks to the Advisory Board for its expert direction and informed advice, which - as usual - added depth and originality to the Report.

I am particularly grateful to Mr. Mark Malloch Brown, the Administrator of the United Nations Development Programme (UNDP), for his courageous decision to allow a publication attended by obvious political risks to appear bearing the emblem of the organization. In upholding the authors' right to an uncensored international platform while reserving his right to disagree with them on some matters, he has provided an immaculate example of what free expression truly means. I would also like to thank my colleagues in the Regional Bureau for Arab States, and in particular Mr. Zahir Jamal, Chief of the Regional Programme Division, for their dedication, hard work, and untiring support to the production of the Report series. Finally, I would like to express my great appreciation of our enduring partnership with the Arab Fund for Economic and Social Development. It is also a great pleasure to welcome to the series our new regional partner, AGFUND, and to extend my warm appreciation to its President, His Royal Highness, Prince Talal Bin Abdul Aziz, for his vision in electing to co-sponsor these efforts on behalf of the Arab peoples.

Rima Khalaf Hunaidi
Assistant Secretary General and Assistant Administrator, Regional Director,
Regional Bureau for Arab States, United Nations Development Programme

Foreword by the Director General and Chairman The Arab Fund for Economic and Social Development

The first Arab Human Development Report diagnosed the crisis facing human development in the Arab world and highlighted key deficits in the fields of knowledge acquisition, freedom and women's empowerment. The Second Report elaborated in details the issues of knowledge and the establishment of a strategic vision to develop it. Both reports were highly appreciated at the Arab and international levels, for their contribution to the revival of a deep and constructive dialogue with a vision to develop and advance our Arab society.

The Report at hand is the third in this series of Human Development Reports. It addresses the issue of freedom from several perspectives, its dimensions, intellectual foundations, legal and political structures, its regional and international and the future vision.

Effective participation and positive action at all economic and social spheres is known to increase people's capabilities and potentials. Exercising freedom within institutional frameworks and good governance is the most catalytic factor for achieving these capabilities and potentials. Therefore, the goal of this report, in our opinion, is to review elements of Governance, as one of the pillars of reform that will result in achieving progress in every respect.

The basis and programs of reforming the institutional structure and good governance must come from within and in harmony with the history and heritage of each country. These reforms must affect all social structures starting from the individual, the family to the social groups that constitute the whole national society. Several country level experiences demonstrate that success was achieved only when commitments to the principles of development extend to include the whole of society.

Emphasizing the rule of law, enhancement of freedom, independence of the judiciary, equal opportunities, at all levels, will enhance the prospects of successful development in the Arab states. This will be an essential factor to accelerate the regions integration in the global trends of political, economic, human and cultural development.

Although this report may not necessarily represent the views of the Arab Fund for Economic and Social Development, it decided to participate with the United Nations Development Program in issuing this report out of a sense of conviction in the importance of free dialogue in building societies, and towards achieving economic and social advancement.

Despite the serious obstacles and challenges that are facing Arab development at the present time, this air of pessimism should not dominate our minds and visions for the future. The Arab states nonetheless have made important economic and social achievements during the past few decades. In this regard, one should also recall the dark periods of colonialism, poor economic, financial and social situations in which the countries of the region were at the eve of independence.

We have great confidence in the ability of the Arab states to enhance their progress in confronting the major challenges facing their citizens. We may differ in the methodologies and visions, but we should never differ over the fact that serious efforts towards more openness, freedom and physical and human development is the key to progress in all societies.

Finally, I extend my sincere thanks and

appreciation to all those who participated in the preparation, discussion, revision and issuance of this report in the form that we see it today. I would like also to express my highest appreciation and consideration to the United Nations Development Programme for sponsoring this distinguished effort and to the Arab Gulf Programme for the United Nations Development Organizations (AGFUND) for its contribution to this serious work.

We pray to Allah to guide to the right actions and lead us greater success.

Abdel Latif Youseff El Hamed
Director General / Chairman of the Board of Directors
Arab Fund for Economic and Social Development

Foreword by HRH The President of the Arab Gulf Programme for United Nations Development Organizations (AGFUND)

The transparency we believe in and subscribe to prompts me to admit a sense of tension when we agreed to contribute to the funding of this edition of the Arab Human Development Report. This conflict was in no way personal in nature. For the content of the Report and its pivotal theme – Freedom and Good Governance – are core issues that have been of great interest to us for decades at the personal, institutional and public levels. The positive momentum caused by the First and the Second reports led us to contribute to the launch of the third, which gives an in-depth analysis of the call for freedom and the indispensable governance institutions and strengthens their significance in our societies.

The conflict stems mainly from differences between longtime convictions on the one hand, and the attitudes, whether favorable or guarded, toward the Report's content, its rigorous scientific methodology and statistical data on the other. What we and all sincere people hope for is that such conflict be resolved in a manner consistent with the spirit of transparency and self-criticism. Since we have rejected all the pressures exercised from all directions to obstruct the launch of this Report, we should at least avoid making similar mistakes. As the conventional wisdom says, "it is greatly disgraceful and discreditable if you advise against a particular conduct and allow yourself to do it all the same!" Although we do not agree with some of the items in this Report and have our own views about them, we would still support its launch in order not to lock away the other point of view.

The comprehensive first Arab Human development Report came to the conclusion that three fundamental deficits stand in the way of Arab development in the Arab countries; in the areas of knowledge, freedom and good governance, and enabling women. The second report dealt in some detail with the various dimensions of the first issue, i. e. the acquisition, reproduction and dissemination of knowledge. The third report comes in the same scientific context, taking the question of consolidating freedom and safeguarding it by good government as a pivotal theme for thoughtful investigation and prudent and perceptive analysis. The Report examines the status of freedom and rights in our Arab homeland, and scrutinizes its institutional structures in the legislative, legal and political areas in their national, regional and international frameworks. It also suggests guidelines for a strategic vision for desired and possible alternative prospects for freedom and governance in the Arab states.

Freedom, and its various facets and manifestations, and the ways in which it could be protected and strengthened by good governance, represents one of the motives that encouraged us, decades ago, to put in our modest share and contribution to bring about reform in the Arab World. Our mission has centered on providing support to sustainable human development efforts, targeting the neediest groups in the developing countries, including the Arab region. Our support efforts have covered a wide range of deprived communities, particularly women and children, in cooperation with the international development organizations, local associations and other institutions active in the field of human development. These efforts, we hope, have left their impact on the quality of life of tens of thousands of people in disadvantaged segments of society, and helped save them from dire need, severe disease and dismal ignorance.

One of our prime concerns has been the promotion of serious studies that shore up the development process and examine both the incentives and the obstacles in its way. We therefore believe that the successful launching of the third issue of the Arab Human Development Report series tones with and complements our call for bridging the gaps in strategic studies in the Arab region. Sustaining this venture poses great challenges and requires resolute determination and unshakable will.

We have often stated and on various occasions that human rights go hand in hand with human dignity, and that citizenship remains incomplete unless it is enhanced by human rights. We have furthermore stressed that democracy is an essential component of the human heritage, and an indispensable mechanism for reform. No serious dialogue could be initiated and maintained and brought to fruition outside an environment of political, economic and social reform, and without democratic practices and cultural open-mindedness. We have also emphasized that rational dialogue and debate inside and amongst us is an essential prerequisite for a credible dialogue with the outside world.

The authors of this Report who represent a team of competent scholars and intellectuals from all over the Arab World, recognize that the way out of the grim status quo towards a peaceful entry into the gates of freedom and good governance is an arduous, protracted process that cannot be accomplished overnight. However, we are fully aware of the consequences of any delay or obstruction of the desired reform,

and any attempt to substitute this process by cosmetic touches that do not touch upon the essence of the pressing issues, and do not respond to the grave challenges at hand. The result will extend yet another invitation to foreign forces and schemes bent on exercising further control of the resources and destinies of people in the Arab World.

Much like its predecessors, this Report will perhaps stimulate debate with a view to evolving development and reform visions. The need for such strategy is all the more pressing now if the Arab World wishes to join the development-oriented efforts and, specifically, move closer to the Millennium Development Goals in order to fulfill the aspirations of our societies. The first step is to draw up strategies based on a rigorous analysis of the situation and guided by science, knowledge and good governance, through support generated by local, regional and international partnerships. The Arab world must also embark on bold reforms in the main pillars of the state on the basis of transparency, accountability and sound and proper policies.

We have great expectations of the growing, confident and forward-moving forces of change in Arab life. High hopes for a better future are also pinned on the enlightened initiatives and trends that are unfolding and emerging among officials and reformers in government institutions in our contemporary societies, and among civil society activist alike.

طلال بن عبد العزيز

Talal Bin Abdul Aziz
President
The Arab Gulf Programme for United Nations
Development Organizations AGFUND

Report Team

Advisory Board

Rima Khalaf Hunaidi (Chair), Ahmed Kamal Aboulmagd, Farida Allaghi, Nabil Alnawwab (Economic and Social Commission for Western Asia), Mustafa Omar Attir, (the late) Mervat Badawi* (Arab Fund for Economic and Social Development), Mustafa Barghouthi, Farida Bennani, Mohamed Cherfi, (the late) Mamdouh Edwan**, Munira Fakhro, Ziad Fariz, Mohammed Fayek, Burhan Ghalioun, Fahmy Howeidy, Nasser Kahtani (Arab Gulf Programme for United Nations Development Organizations), Taher H. Kanaan, Atif Kubursi, Clovis Maksoud, Amin Medani, Abdelouahab Rezig, Ghassan Tuéni.

Core Team

Nader Fergany (Leader), Abdelwahab El-Affendi, Mohamed Nour Farahat, Marie Rose Zalzal.

Contributing Authors

Marie-Thérèse Abdel-Messih, Ali Abdel Gadir Ali, Mustapha K. Al Sayyid, Abdallah Al Ashaal, Amna Rashed Al-Hamdan, Habib Al-Jenhani, Majid A. Al-Moneef, Nabil Alnawwab, Siham Abdulrahman Alsuwaigh, Mohsen Awad, Azmi Bishara, Hafidha Chekir, Georges Corm, Abdelwahab El-Affendi, Jalila El Ati, Mohamed Mahmoud El-Imam, Khalida Sa'id Esber, Mohamed Nour Farahat, Rafia Obaid Ghubash, Abdelaziz Guessous, Salah El-Deen Hafez, Mustafa S. Hijazi, Fahmi Jadaan, Taher H. Kanaan, Abdalla Khalil, Mohammad Abdalla Khalil, Atif Kubursi, Jonathan Kuttab, Amina Lemrini, Maryam Sultan Lootah, Mohammed Malki, Khadija Marouazi, A.Hussain Shaban, Alla Eldin Shalaby, Marie Rose Zalzal.

Readers Group

(Arabic)

Khalid Abdalla, Farid Abdelkhalek, Kamal Abdellatif, Madawi Al-Rasheed, Abdulkarim El-Eryani, Haytham Manna, Mohamed Sid-Ahmed, Naila Silini.

(English)

Ziad Hafez, Michael Hudson, Santosh Mehrotra, Omar Noman, Mary Rose Oakar, Marina Ottaway, John M. Page, Alan Richards, Ngaire Woods.

UNDP RBAS / UNOPS

Uzma Ahmed, Dena Assaf, Moez Doraid (Report Coordinator), Jacqueline Estevez-Camejo, Melissa Esteva, Ghaith Fariz (Report Coordinator), Oscar Fernandez-Taranco, Jacqueline Ghazal, Randa Jamal, Zahir Jamal, Mary Jreidini, Azza M. Karam, Madi Musa, Maen Nsour, Win Min Nu, William Orme, Ahmad Ragab, Gillman Rebello, Nadine Shamounki, Amal Tillawi.

Editorial Team

Arabic Version: Fayiz Suyyagh
English Version: Barbara Brewka, Zahir Jamal

Implementation of the freedom survery

- Middle East Marketing and Research Consultants (MEMRC) / Amman, Jordan (Coordination + Questionnaire Design & Unifying Data Files).
- Societe D'etude De Realisation De Consultants (SEREC)/ Casablanca , Morocco.
- Jerusalem Media and Communication Center (JMCC) / East Jerusalem, Palestine.
- Statistics Lebanon Ltd. / Beirut, Lebanon.
- Cabinet Tiers – Consult / Alger.

Statistical tables on human development in Arab countries

Mohamad Baquer

Translation Team

June Ray (Coordinator), Sara Ansah, Marilyn Booth, Humphrey Davies, Shohrat el-A'alem, Bruce Inksetter, Nehad Salem.

Cover Design

Designer: Walid Gadow,
Calligraphy and Graphics: Mamoun Sakkal.

Technical Consultant for Design and Printing

Hassan Shahin

---

* Mervat Badawi: Exceptional lady who bestowed profound knowledge and care on the Arab Human Development Report since its inception but departed our world when this report was about to appear.

** Mamdouh Edwan: Distinguished Arab poet who has not been dettered by terminal illness from actively participating in the deliberations of the AHDR 3 Advisory group.

Contents

Foreword by the Administrator, UNDP   I
Foreword by the Regional Director, UNDP/Regional Bureau for Arab States   III
Foreword by the Director General and Chairman, Board of Directors, Arab Fund for Economic and Social Development   V
Foreword by HRH The President of the Arab Gulf Programme for United Nations Development Organizations (AGFUND) VII

PREFACE   1
THIS REPORT   1
    Introduction   1
Freedom and Human Development   1
The Main Conclusions of the First and Second Arab Human Development Reports   3
Contents of this Report   3

EXECUTIVE SUMMARY   5
    Introduction   5

Changes In Human Development Since The Launch Of AHDR 2003   5
  Calls For Reform Intensify   5
  A Constraining Regional and International Environment   6
    Israeli occupation of Palestine continues to impede human development and freedom   6
    The impact of the occupation of Iraq on human development   7
  Addressing The Three Deficits: Progress and Reversals   7

The State Of Freedom And Good Governance   8
  The State Of Freedoms and Rights   8
  Civil and Political Freedoms: From Deficient to Seriously Deficient   9
    The denial of individuals' fundamental freedoms   9
    Exclusion from citizenship   10
    Abusing minority rights   10
    Women doubly excluded   10
  Unmet Economic and Social Rights   10
  How Far Do Arabs Believe That They Enjoy Freedom?   11

Structures Impeding Freedom   11
  Region-Specific Problematic Issues   12
    The contradiction between freedom in Arab countries and narrow global interests   12
    Freedom shorn of effective advocates   12
    Appropriating religion to perpetuate tyranny   12
    "The trap of the one-off election"   12
    Specificity as a pretext for slighting human rights   13
  The Legal Architecture   13
    Constitutions granting rights and laws confiscating them   13
    And constitutions flatly violating rights   14
  The Political Architecture   15
    The "black-hole" State   15
    The crisis of legitimacy   16

Repression and political impoverishment   16

The vicious circle of repression and corruption   17

Societal Structures   17

The chain that stifles individual freedom   17

A mode of production that strengthens authoritarian governance   18

A longing for freedom and justice in popular culture   18

An Inhospitable Global and Regional Environment For Freedom   18

A Strategic Vision: Alternative Futures For Freedom And Governance In Arab Countries   19

Alternative Scenarios   19

The impending disaster scenario   19

The "Izdihar" alternative   19

The "Half Way House" scenario: the accommodation of external reform   20

Reforming Arab Societal Structures to Guarantee Freedom   20

Internal reform   20

Changes at the pan-Arab level   21

Governance at the global level   21

Achieving Peaceful Political Alternation in Arab Countries   22

Epilogue: the furthest lotus tree   22

PART I
CHANGES IN HUMAN DEVELOPMENT SINCE THE LAUNCH OF AHDR 2003

    25

Introduction   25

Arab Initiatives To Promote Region-wide Reform   25

Official Arab Reform Efforts   25

Formal initiatives   25

Civil Society Reform Initiatives   26

The Struggle Waged By Civil and Political Forces in The Arab World   26

Freedom and respect for human rights   26

Stronger grass-roots participation   27

Towards political reform   27

Towards peace   28

External Attempts At Change: The Broader Middle East Initiative   29

The Regional and International Context   29

Israeli Occupation of Palestine Continues to Constrain Human Development and Freedom   30

Violations of the right to life   30

Violations of human rights and individual and collective freedoms   31

Social and economic losses   31

The separation wall undermines human development   32

Looking to the Future   33

The Impact of the occupation of Iraq on Human Development   33

Absence of security and violations of the right to life   33

The right to freedom   34

Mis-treatment of prisoners of war and detainees   34

Dismantling the Iraqi State structure   35

Looking to the future   35

The escalation of terrorism 35

Addressing the Three Deficits: Gains and Setbacks 36
Knowledge Acquisition 36
Freedom and Governance 38
Signs of political openness 38
Indications of a regression in popular participation 39
Freedoms constrained 39
Freedom of civil society organizations 40
Restrictions on the media 40
Rights of subgroups: Darfur 41
Protest by intellectuals 41
The Empowerment of Women 41

Conclusion 43

PART II - REINFORCING FREEDOM AND ESTABLISHING GOOD GOVERNANCE 45
Section 1: Analytical Framework: Freedom, Good Governance and Human Development 45

CHAPTER ONE
THE INTELLECTUAL BASIS AND CONCEPT OF FREEDOM AND GOOD GOVERNANCE 47
Introduction 47

Freedom in Western Liberal Thought: From Individual Freedom to Human Development 47
The Primacy of Individual Liberties 47
Individual Freedom and Societal Regulation 48
The essence of democracy and democratic transition 48
Problematic Issues of Freedom: Liberalism and Democracy, Attributes of Majority Rule 49
The danger of tyranny of the majority 49
Tension between Freedom and Democracy? Or Democracy without Freedom? 50
Freedom and the Other Ultimate Human Goals 50
Freedom as Human Development: Reconciling Individual Freedom with Institutional Arrangements 51
Corporate governance and human development 52

Freedom in Arab Culture 53
Freedom in Arab History 53
Religious Freedom 53
Political Freedom 54
Social Freedom 54
Economic Freedom 54
Freedom in the Modern Context 54
From Freedom to Emancipation 55
Freedom From an Islamic Perspective 56
Freedom and Liberation 58
The Rights of Freedom 59
The Arab Renaissance and the Challenge of Freedom 60

The concept of freedom and good governance in this Report 61

CHAPTER TWO

FREEDOM AND GOVERNANCE IN ARAB COUNTRIES AT THE BEGINNING OF THE THIRD MILLENNIUM:
   SOME PROBLEMATIC ISSUES.   65
     Introduction   65

The Tension Between Freedom and Democratic Institutions in the Arab World   65

The Contradiction Between Freedom in Arab Countries and the Interests of Dominant Global Powers   65
   The Crisis of Democracy After September 11   67

Freedom Bereft of Organized Support   67

"Oriental Despotism" and the Arab Societal Context   68

Democracy and Religion   68
   Democracy and Islam: Potential for Harmony   69

Democracy and the Arab Region: The Trap of the One-off Election   71

Freedom and Human Rights   71
   The Importance of the Human Rights System   71
   International Human Rights Law   72
   The Applicability of International Human Rights Law to Arab Countries   74

The Challenge of Peaceful Transition to a Society of Freedom and Good Governance in the Arab Countries   77

PART II, Section 2: The State of Freedom and Governance in Arab Countries   79

CHAPTER THREE
THE STATE OF FREEDOMS AND RIGHTS   81
     Introduction   81
                                                                                      81

Freedoms and Human Rights   81
   Structural Constraints on Freedom   82
     Flawed structure of Arab nation-states   82
     Political constraints on the authority of the human rights system   82
     The crisis of citizenship   83
   National Freedom   83
   Civil and Political Freedoms in Arab States   84
     Freedom of opinion, expression and creativity   84
       Stifling creativity   85
     Freedom of association: civil society institutions   87
       Freedom to form political parties   87
       Freedom to form associations and surveillance of their activities   87
       Trade unions and professional associations   88
     The right to participation: 88
   Individual Freedoms   89
     Freedom of opinion and belief   89
     Freedom of privacy and personal life   89

Denial of Fundamental Individual Freedoms   90
   Violation of basic rights   90
     The right to life   90
     The right to liberty and personal safety   90
     The right to a fair and impartial trial   91
   Exclusion from citizenship   91
     Deprivation of citizenship   91
     Abusing the rights of minority groups.   91
     Women doubly excluded   92

Social and Economic Rights   93
   The Right to Lead a Long, Healthy Life   94
     The right to food and adequate nutrition: 94
     The right to a healthy life   95
       Physical health   95
       Psychological health   96
     The right to acquire knowledge   96
     The quality of education and health services in Arab countries 96

Perceived Enjoyment of Freedom in Contemporary Arab Opinion, Freedom Survey 2003   97
   The Perception of Freedom Among Contemporary Arabs   97
   Extent of Enjoyment of Freedom at the Time of the Survey (2003)   100
   Perceived Change in the Enjoyment of Freedom in Contemporary Arab Opinion 100

PART II, Section 3: The Societal Context Of Freedom And Governance   105

CHAPTER FOUR
THE LEGAL ARCHITECTURE   107
   Introduction   107

The Institutional Architecture of Freedom and Governance   107

Arab States and International Human Rights Standards   107

Legislative Regulation of Freedoms in Arab Constitutions   109
   Law and Justice, Public Order and National Security as Excuses to Limit Freedom 109
   Overview of Arab Constitutions   109
   Freedom of Opinion and Expression   109
   Freedom to Form Associations and Freedom of Peaceful Assembly   110
   Freedom to Form Political Parties   110
   The Human Right to Litigation and the Principle of the Independence of the Judiciary 111
     The international perspective and the Arab constitutional reality 111
     The legal profession and public freedoms   113
   Right of Nationality   114
   Personal Rights   114
   Constitutional Violations of Human Rights   115

Legislative Restrictions on Human Rights in Arab Legislation   116
   Legislative Restrictions on the Right of Peaceful Assembly   116

Legislative Restrictions on the Right of Political Organization 117

Legislative Restrictions on Freedom to form Associations 118

Restrictions on Freedom of Opinion, Expression and the Press in Arab Legislation 118

Pre-censorship and suspension by administrative decision 119

Curtailment of freedom on the pretext of security 119

Denying the right to obtain information 119

Harsher conditions for newspaper publication 120

Legal Restrictions on Public Freedoms During a State of Emergency 120

Legislative Regulation of the Role of the Judiciary in Protecting Human Rights and Freedoms 121

Independence of the judiciary (legislative regulation and practice) 121

Exceptional courts 123

The Impact of Authoritarian Power Relations on Freedom and Human Rights 123

CHAPTER FIVE

THE POLITICAL ARCHITECTURE 125

Introduction 125

The Crisis of Governance in Arab Countries 125

Characteristics of Authoritarian Governance 125

The "black-hole" State 126

Extra-judicial Controls 127

Tracing the Flaw 128

The Crisis of Legitimacy 129

Repression and Political Impoverishment 131

Weakening of Political Parties 131

The Marginalization of Civil Society 132

The status of Arab civil society 132

The State of Corporate Governance in the Arab World 133

Transparency 133

Accountability 134

Inclusiveness 134

Corporate governance and Arab stock markets 135

The vicious Circle of Repression and Corruption 135

Contours of Corruption in Arab Countries 137

Petty Corruption 137

The Arab Countries in the Global Context of Governance, 2002 138

The Debate on How to Reform 140

The Discourse on Reform 141

Change from the top or at grass-roots? 141

External versus internal 141

The Optimum Choice 142

Bridging the gap between political forces 143

CHAPTER SIX

ARAB SOCIETAL STRUCTURES AND THE REGIONAL AND INTERNATIONAL ENVIRONMENTS — 145
    Introduction — 145

Societal Structures — 145
  The Chain that Stifles Individual Freedom — 145
    Clannism (al-'asabiya) in Arab Society—the Authoritarian Paternalist System and the Family — 145
    Education — 147
      Freedom in the content of education in three Maghreb countries — 148
    The World of Work — 149
    The Political Realm — 150
    Poverty and the class structure — 150
    Is this stranglehold eternal? — 151
  A Mode Of Production that Reinforces Authoritarianism — 151
  The Longing For Freedom and Justice in Popular Culture — 153

The Global and Regional Context — 154
  Globalization and Freedom — 154
  Governance at the Global Level — 155
  The Impact of the "War on Terror" on Freedom — 156
  Governance at the Regional Level — 157

PART II, Section 4: Towards Reinforcing Freedom and Establishing Good Governance in the Arab Countries — 161

CHAPTER SEVEN

A STRATEGIC VISION OF FREEDOM AND GOVERNANCE IN ARAB COUNTRIES – ALTERNATIVE FUTURES — 163
    Introduction — 163

Grounds for Peaceful and Deep Political Alteration, Alternative Futures — 163
  Reasons for Change — 163
  Alternative Arab Futures — 164
    The impending disaster scenario: maintaining the 'Status Quo' — 164
    The ideal scenario: the "Izdihar" alternative — 164
    The "Half Way House" scenario: the accommodation of external reform — 165
  How to Deal with Reform Initiatives from Outside? — 165

Universal Features and Aims of the Desired System of Governance — 166

Reforming Arab Societal Structures to Guarantee Freedom: — 166
  The Internal Challenge — 166
    Enhancing the legal and institutional foundations that underpin freedom — 166
    Adherence to international human rights law — 167
    Binding the ruling authority to the rule of law — 167
    Guaranteeing freedoms and rights at the heart of the constitution — 167
    Strengthening civil and political rights in law — 168
    Guaranteeing the independence of the judiciary — 169
    Abolishing the state of emergency. — 169
    Guarantees for personal freedom — 169
    Ending discrimination against societal groups — 170

The Political Architecture   170
    Problematic issues in guaranteeing sound democratic arrangements   170
Code of Conduct for Societal Forces on the Path to Reform   171
    Obligations of the State: 171
    Obligations of the political élites: 171
    Obligations of civil society: 171
    Parliamentary representation: 172
    Reforming Arab Institutional Performance   172
    Correcting the Arab Development Trajectory   173
    The Reform of Corporate Governance   173

At the Pan-Arab level   174
    Liberation from Occupation   175

Governance at the Global Level   176
    A Role for the UN and Other International Agencies   177

Achieving Peaceful Political Alternation in Arab Countries in Order to Build Freedom and Good Governance: the 'Izdihar' Scenario. 177
    Act 1: Liberation of Civil Society, Laying the Foundation for Comprehensive Legal and Political Reform 178

Epilogue: the Furthest Lotus Tree   179

REFERENCES   181

ANNEX 1: MEASUREMENT OF FREEDOM IN ARAB COUNTRIES   191

ANNEX 2: SELECTED DOCUMENTS   215

ANNEX 3: LIST OF BACKGROUND PAPERS   233

ANNEX 4: STATISTICAL TABLES ON HUMAN DEVELOPMENT IN THE ARAB COUNTRIES   234

LIST OF BOXES

P1	Freedom and good governance: an historical legacy	2
1	Declaration on the Process of Reform and Modernisation in the Arab World (excerpts)	26
2	The Arab people's views on the importance of the Palestinian question	30
3	Unnoticed Losses	31
4	World Bank President Finds Israel's Conduct Shameful	31
5	By Law, This Wall Should Come Down - Findings of the International Court of Justice (ICJ).	32
6	Israel's Restrictions on Churches in the Holy Land	33
7	Conclusion of the Taguba Report	35
8	Quality Assessment of Primary and Middle Education in Mathematics and Science (TIMSS 2003) in the Arab World RAB01/005/A/01/31	36
9	"Development" of the University of the United Arab Emirates	36
10	An Assessment of Business Administration Programmes in Arab Universities	37
11	The Moroccan Family Code	42
1-1	Natural Human Rights	47
1-2	Freedom of opinion as a sacred right	48

1-3	Ahmed Kamal Aboulmagd: The principle of equality	51
1-4	Al Kawakibi: Freedom and Dignity	55
1-5	Naseef Nassar: The Reconstruction of Liberalism	60
1-6	Freedom for its own sake	61
1-7	The Charter of Medina	62
1-8	Setting the deviant ruler straight	63
1-9	Al-Kawakibi: Importance of holding the ruling authority accountable	63
1-10	Corporate governance	63
1-11	Taha Hussein: Freedom and Independence	64
2-1	The Reasons behind the Failure of Democracy in Arab Countries: Perceptions of a Western Scholar	66
2-2	Abdallah al-Arawy: Freedom and Liberalism in the Arab Context	67
2-3	Ibn al-Qayim al-Jawziya: On welfare	69
2-4	Imam Muhammad Abdu: The Legitimacy of Elections	70
2-5	Ayatollah al-Mohaqiq al-Naeeny: An Opinion Concerning Conditionality or Constitutionality	70
2-6	Boasting about human rights while destroying them	71
2-7	Declaration on the Right to Development Adopted by General Assembly Resolution 41/128 of 4 December 1986(excerpts)	71
2-8	Muhammad Shahrour: A Word About Freedom	73
2-9	The Pact of the Virtuous (Hilf al-fudul)	74
2-10	Human rights: universality and specificity	74
2-11	The Contribution of Arab States to the Universal Declaration of Human Rights and the Two International Covenants	75
2-12	Haytham Manna'a: The Books of Tribulations	76
2-13	Freedom and Emancipation	77
2-14	Timing the call for freedom	77
3-1	Ali Ibn Al Hussein: The Epistle on Rights	81
3-2	Marwan al-Barghouti (from his prison cell): I will overcome the cell and the occupiers	84
3-3	Al-Manfaluti: The value of freedom that has been stolen	86
3-4	Khalida Said: Creativity - Between Consciousness and Dreams	87
3-5	Declaration on the Right and Responsibility of Individuals, Groups and Organs of Society to Promote and Protect Universally Recognized Human Rights and Fundamental Freedoms, 1999 (excerpts)	89
3-6	Freedom Survey, Arab Human Development Report	98
4-1	The right to form political parties	110
4-2	Constitutional restrictions on rights	115
4-3	Restrictions on the rights to assembly and association	117
5-1	Muhammad Al-Charfi: Arab democracy - form without substance	130
5-2	Capital market legal reforms	135
5-3	Moncef Al-Marzouqi: Giving democracy every chance	142
6-1	Education and Human Rights in Arab Countries	147
6-2	Educational Development in Tunisia	150
6-3	Omar ibn Abd al-Aziz: Justice and the law, not the sword and the whip	150
6-4	Counsellor Yahya al-Rifai: Justice Above Might	156
6-5	The UN Special Rapporteur on Terrorism and Human Rights: The Root Causes of Terrorism	157
6-6	Adib al-Jadir: Hussein Jamil, An Iraqi Arab Activist Who Pursued Freedom	160
7-1	Mahdi Bunduq, Post-Bourgeois Society	166
7-2	Perpetuating power in the name of democracy and the people	167
7-3	Ten Principles for a Constitution of Freedom and Good Governance	168
7-4	The Supreme Constitutional Court in Egypt	168
7-5	Recommended Good Governance Institutions at the Pan-Arab Level	175
7-6	Excerpts from the Address by the UN Secretary General, Kofi Annan, at the Opening Session of the General Assembly, New York, 21 September 2004.	176
7-7	Guaranteeing freedom for civil society	178

LIST OF FIGURES

3-1   Percentage agreeing that women should have equal rights, five Arab countries, Freedom Survey, 2003   93

3-2   Estimate of the extent of deprivation of human capabilities, five Arab countries, Freedom Survey, 2003   94

3-3   Years of life expectancy lost to disease, by gender, Arab countries and comparator countries, 2002   95

3-4   Extent of satisfaction with the level and cost of education and health services by sector (public/private), five Arab countries, Freedom Survey, 2003   97

3-5a   Percentage of interviewees considering the elements of freedom part of their concept of freedom (%) Average of five Arab countries (weighted by population), Freedom Survey, 2003   98

3-5b   Percentage of interviewees considering the elements of freedom constituents of their concept of freedom Five Arab countries, Freedom Survey, 2003   99

3-6a   Extent of enjoyment of the elements of freedom (%), average of five Arab countries (weighted by population), Freedom Survey, 2003   100

3-6b   Extent of enjoyment of the elements of freedom (%), average of five Arab countries, Freedom Survey, 2003   101

3-7a   Perceived change in the enjoyment of elements of freedom (net %) during the five years preceding the survey, average of five Arab countries (weighted by population), Freedom Survey, 2003   102

3-7b   Perceived change in the enjoyment of elements of freedom (net %) during the five years preceding the survey, average of five Arab countries, Freedom Survey, 2003   103

4-1   Extent of willingness to go to court, Five Arab countries, Freedom Survey, 2003   122

5-1   Perceived absence of government accountability and lack of freedom of opinion and expression, five Arab countries, Freedom Survey, 2003   128

5-2   Extent of confidence in political institutions, five Arab countries   132

5-3   Corruption Perception Index, World and Arab Countries, 2003   136

5-4   Areas in which corruption is perceived to be widespread, five Arab countries, Freedom Survey, 2003   137

5-5   Extent to which different societal groups are believed to be involved in the spread of corruption, five Arab countries, Freedom Survey, 2003   137

5-6   Knowledge of acts of bribery or "favouritism" (wasta*) during the 12 months preceding the survey, five Arab countries, Freedom Survey, 2003   138

5-7   Reason for paying a bribe or using wasta during the 12 months preceding the survey, five Arab countries, Freedom Survey, 2003   139

5-8   The best way to obtain a favour or to avoid a penalty, five Arab countries, Freedom Survey, 2003   139

5-9   Voice and accountability, the Arab region compared to other world regions, 2002   140

5-10   Political stability, the Arab region compared to other world regions, 2002   140

5-11   Government effectiveness, the Arab region compared to other world regions, 2002   140

5-12   The rule of law, the Arab region compared to other world regions, 2002   141

5-13   Control of corruption, the Arab region compared to other world regions, 2002   141

6-1   The share of taxes in public revenues and the share of income taxes in total tax revenues (%), Arab countries, 1992-2002   153

6-2   Credibility of the Arab League and the United Nations: Estimates by five Arab states and comparator countries   158

6-3   Extent of satisfaction with the current level of Arab cooperation, five Arab countries, Freedom Survey, 2003   160

7-1   Extent of dissatisfaction over the presence of foreign military bases, five Arab countries, Freedom Survey, 2003   164

7-2   Preferred forms of stronger Arab cooperation, five Arab countries, Freedom Survey, 2003   174

7-3   Perception of just solutions to the Palestinian question, five Arab countries, Freedom Survey, 2003   175

LIST OF TABLES

4-1   Status of Ratifications of the Principal International Human Rights Treaties, January 2005   108

This Report

Introduction

The first Arab Human Development Report (AHDR 2002) provided a comprehensive, first hand overview of the situation in the Arab region from the perspective of human development. Its goal was to provide an objective analysis based on serious self-criticism and aimed at assuring freedom and dignity for all Arabs[1]. The Report diagnosed three cardinal deficits impeding human development in Arab countries: in knowledge acquisition, freedom and good governance, and women's empowerment. As a broad overview, that first Report did not explore these deficits in depth. Rather, it made the case for an extended analysis of each in order to promote a discussion about how to overcome them.

Accordingly, the second Report analysed the knowledge acquisition deficit in the Arab world in some depth, ending with a strategic vision for establishing a knowledge society in the region.

Continuing such extended treatment, this third Report provides a thorough examination of the deficit of freedom and good governance, a topic that dominates current discourse within the region and abroad. It is hoped that this detailed analysis will stimulate a dialogue in Arab societies on how to expand freedom and establish good governance. A serious and objective debate around the substance of this Report would pave the way for a process of social innovation leading to a genuine project for an Arab renaissance.

The first two Reports prompted a wide public response, for and against their findings, both inside and outside the Arab world, which underlined the sharp relevance of the issues raised, and the importance of addressing them at this critical period in the course of the region.

Unfortunately, as with other Arab reform initiatives, some forces outside the Arab world have used these Reports for their own purposes. This has led some Arabs to call for a halt to self-criticism in order to avoid giving others a pretext for interfering in Arab affairs. This call, however, rests on flawed logic. It assumes that others have sought to interfere in the region's affairs in response to such self-criticism by Arabs and not because of their own interests.

These interests and ambitions have turned into interventions for two reasons. The first is active: it reflects the considerable capabilities that foreign powers can muster to pursue their own ends. The second is passive: it relates to the weakness of the region, which makes it an easy target for outside intervention.

The only way for Arabs to deal with the ambitions of others is to recognize and overcome their own weaknesses and thus grow strong enough to prevent foreign objectives from taking hold. Self-reform originating in balanced self-criticism is the only viable way forward towards a robust and independent region. All committed actors in Arab societies should be able to rise to the occasion of their historic mission, which is to stimulate a renaissance movement. They can best do so by diagnosing the present regional situation in human development terms and proposing ways forward.

FREEDOM AND HUMAN DEVELOPMENT

Human development is most profoundly seen as a process of expanding "the range of human

A serious and objective debate around the substance of this Report would pave the way for a process of social innovation.

Self-reform originating in balanced self-criticism is the only viable way forward towards a robust and independent region.

---

[1] The term "Arab" is used in this report to denote all citizens of Arab countries inclusively.

Freedom is pivotal in human development.

choice". If human development means increasing people's choices, then people must have the freedom to choose among alternatives. This becomes an absolute priority. Freedom is pivotal in human development. Indeed, recent theoretical writings on this subject see development as synonymous with freedom (Sen 1999).

BOX P1

Freedom and good governance: an historical legacy

"Since when have you compelled people to enslavement, when their mothers birthed them free? [2]"

Omar bin al-Khattab

"If the king has treated the people unjustly
We refuse to condone humiliation among us"

Amr bin Kulthum

"The tyrant is the enemy of rights and of freedom; indeed their executioner. Right is the father of humanity and freedom their mother."

Abdel-Rahman al-Kawakibi

Thus, in human development terms, simply by virtue of belonging to humankind, people have an *a priori* right to a dignified life, materially and morally or spiritually, in body, self and soul. From this starting point two key conclusions follow:

- First: Human development is incompatible with any type of discrimination against any groups of human beings whether defined by gender, social origin, creed or colour.
- Second: In human development, the concept of well-being is not limited to material comfort. It includes the non-physical, non-material aspects of a dignified human life: freedom, knowledge, aesthetic pleasure, human dignity and self-fulfilment. These broader aims can only be achieved through the individual's effective participation in all endeavours of society.

Human entitlements, in principle, are infinite, and they develop and change continuously in accord with human advancement. At any level of development, though, the three basic human entitlements, according to the global Human Development Report, are: "to lead a long and healthy life, to acquire knowl-

The effective development and use of human capabilities enlarges people's choices and enables them to enjoy freedom in its comprehensive sense.

edge, and to have access to resources needed for a decent standard of living". Yet, human development does not end at this minimal level of entitlements. Rather, it goes beyond this minimum to encompass other additional entitlements, ranging from "political, economic, and social freedom to opportunities for being creative and productive, and enjoying self-respect and guaranteed human rights" (Human Development Report 1990).

The process of human development is founded on two principal axes. The first relates to building those human capabilities that make it possible to achieve a higher level of human welfare. These capabilities comprise, first and foremost, the ability of all people to enjoy a long and healthy life and to acquire knowledge and freedom without discrimination. The second axis relates to the efficient and appropriate utilization of human capabilities in all spheres of human endeavour, including production, and through people's active participation in civil society and politics. The effective development and use of human capabilities enlarges people's choices and enables them to enjoy freedom in its comprehensive sense.

Thus, human development in the full sense that we have adopted, is not merely about developing "human resources," neither is it a "development," *tout court*, of human beings, nor is it a matter solely of striving to fulfil the basic needs of people. It is much more a humanist and humanitarian blueprint for the comprehensive, total, and mutually reinforcing development, of people and social institutions, that aims to realize higher human goals and aspirations: freedom, justice, and human dignity.

Narrower definitions of development, whether limited to 'economic development' or to a restricted sense of human development, lack the rich possibilities of this fuller concept. In human development thinking, a wealthy person is not considered to enjoy an advanced state of well-being so long as that person is prevented from exercising freedom. Likewise, history, ancient and contemporary, teaches us that societies barred from experiencing free-

---

[2] In this saying, Khalifat Omar is addressing the son of his Wali (representative ruler) in Egypt. Of particular note is that the adversary referred to in the text had a different religion from the Khalifat himself…the adversary was a Christian Coptic. This conflict ended with the Khalifat Omar inflicting severe punishment on the son of his Wali in Egypt.

dom are unable to preserve whatever economic and other gains they may make in a more narrow definition of development; and thus, they cannot attain the higher rungs on the ladder of human advancement.

THE MAIN CONCLUSIONS OF THE FIRST AND SECOND ARAB HUMAN DEVELOPMENT REPORTS

The first AHDR (2002) concluded that "although Arab countries have made significant strides in more than one area of human development in the last three decades...the predominant characteristic of the current Arab reality seems to be the existence of deeply rooted shortcomings in the Arab institutional structure [which] are an obstacle to building human development." As noted earlier, the Report summarized these shortcomings as three deficits relating to knowledge acquisition, freedom and good governance and the empowerment of women. Taking into account these deficit areas in an alternative human development index, reduces the ranking of the Arab countries on the standard index. This new view underlined that the challenge of building human development, for most Arabs, is still very serious.

The first AHDR also affirmed that the Israeli occupation of Palestinian land is one of the most significant impediments to human development in Arab countries, in that it constitutes an obvious threat to security and peace across the region. Occupation has also given Arab regimes a pretext for postponing internal reform and has embarrassed Arab reformists by making the confrontation of external threats to the region a higher priority than internal reforms.

The second AHDR (2003) reviewed the most important global, regional and country-level developments after the completion of the first Report. It concluded that challenges to Arab human development remained grave. Indeed, it saw unfavourable developments at the regional and global levels as intensifying the challenge - or the threat - to human development notably in the realm of freedoms. These developments included the deteriorating state of civil and political freedoms for Arabs and Muslims in the West following the events of

September 11 and the consequent clampdown on freedoms in Arab countries; Israel's re-invasion of Palestinian cities, causing destruction and human suffering; and the invasion and occupation of Iraq by the US-led Coalition.

Looking into the state of knowledge acquisition at the beginning of the 21st century, the second Report concluded that the dissemination and production of knowledge in Arab countries remain weak despite the presence of significant Arab human capital. It noted that, under different circumstances, such capital would constitute a strong foundation for a knowledge renaissance.

The Report culminated in a strategic vision for establishing a knowledge society in Arab countries organized around five pillars:
1. Guaranteeing the key freedoms of opinion, expression and association, safeguarded by good governance.
2. Disseminating high quality education for all, particularly through higher education, learning in early childhood, continuous education and life-long learning.
3. Embedding and ingraining science in society, building and broadening the capacity for research and development across societal activities and catching up with the "information age".
4. Shifting Arab socio-economic structures rapidly towards knowledge-based production.
5. Developing an authentic, broadminded and enlightened Arab knowledge model based on:
• Returning to pure religion, free from political exploitation, and centred on ijtihad (independent interpretive scholarship); advancing the Arabic language; reclaiming the positive achievements of Arab heritage; enriching, supporting and celebrating cultural diversity in the region; and opening up to other cultures.

CONTENTS OF THIS REPORT

The Arab development crisis has widened, deepened and grown more complex to a degree that demands the full engagement of all Arab citizens in true reform in order to spearhead a human renaissance in the region. The strategic vision for establishing the "knowl-

The Israeli occupation of Palestinian land is one of the most significant impediments to human development in Arab countries.

Occupation has also given Arab regimes a pretext for postponing internal reform.

edge society" in the Arab states clearly showed that required reforms extend to the current socio-economic structure and, critically, to the political context at the national, regional and international levels. It indicated that partial reforms can not work in the absence of an appropriately positive social environment; however, in the present situation, this kind of reform is no longer effective or even possible. Vested interests can no longer be allowed to delay or slow down comprehensive societal reform in Arab countries.

Of all the impediments to an Arab renaissance, political restrictions on human development are the most stubborn. For that reason, this Report focuses on the acute deficit of freedom and good governance in the Arab world.

As is now the practice in this series, the Report opens by recounting events at the national, regional and global levels that have affected the overall course of human development in the Arab world during the period in review. This opening section (Part I) is followed by an in-depth analysis (Part II) of the main subject.

The Report complements the first two in the series and does not aim to go over ground previously covered.

Part II commences with an analytical framework that sets forth the concept and definition of freedom and good governance, focusing on both Western and Arab culture (Chapter 1). It then discusses some key problematic issues undermining freedom and governance in Arab countries at the start of the third millennium (Chapter 2).

Applying its analytical framework and its definition of freedom, the Report next looks at the state of freedoms and economic and social rights in Arab countries and evaluates how far they are enjoyed in practice (Chapter 3). It continues by analysing the factors that determine the extent to which Arabs enjoy freedoms and rights starting with the impact of institutional, legal and political structures (Chapters 4 and 5).

The Report then examines the impact of societal structures on freedom and governance in Arab countries. Since external events have increasing and palpable impacts on freedom in the region, the Report subsequently discusses the global and regional environment and its relationship to the main theme (Chapter 6).

Drawing on previous chapters, the Report concludes by offering an analytical overview of alternative prospects for freedom and good governance in Arab countries. The objective is to stimulate a broad discussion on action for enhancing and protecting freedom in the region through good governance (Chapter 7).

Of all the impediments to an Arab renaissance, political restrictions on human development are the most stubborn.

External events have increasing and palpable impacts on freedom in the region.

EXECUTIVE SUMMARY

Introduction

This Report, the third in the Arab Human Development Report (AHDR) series, sets out to provoke a spirited, considered debate among all dynamic societal forces in the Arab region to prepare the way for an Arab renaissance. It provides a thorough examination of the deficit of freedom and good governance, a topic that dominates current discourse within the region and abroad.

The Arab development crisis has widened, deepened and grown more complex to a degree that demands the full engagement of all Arab citizens in comprehensive reform in order to spearhead a human renaissance in the region. Partial reforms, no matter how varied, are no longer effective or even possible; perhaps they never were, since reform requires a responsive and supportive social environment. Comprehensive societal reform in Arab countries can no longer be delayed or slowed down on account of vested interests.

Of all the impediments to an Arab renaissance, political restrictions on human development are the most stubborn. This Report therefore focuses on the acute deficit of freedom and good governance.

CHANGES IN HUMAN DEVELOPMENT SINCE THE LAUNCH OF AHDR 2003

In line with the methodology established in this series, the Report opens by recounting

Freedom and good governance: an historical legacy

"Since when have you compelled people to enslavement, when their mothers birthed them free?"
Omar bin al-Khattab

some of the events at the country, regional and global levels that most influenced the overall course of human development in the region during this period.

CALLS FOR REFORM INTENSIFY

Since the publication of AHDR 2003, Arab governments and civil society organisations have proposed various reform initiatives to address some of the challenges facing the Arab world. The most significant official initiative was the "Declaration on the Process of Reform and Modernisation" issued by the Arab Summit held in May 2004. The Declaration called for the continuation and intensification of political, economic, social and educational change initiatives that reflect the will and aspirations of Arabs.

The Declaration specifically called for action "to deepen the foundations of democracy and consultation, and to broaden participation in political life and decision-making, in tandem with the rule of law, equality among citizens, respect for human rights, freedom of expression and ... safeguards for the independence of the judiciary".

Civil society organisations also spearheaded several reform initiatives as this Report was being prepared. Amongst the most significant of these are the "Sana'a Declaration", emerging from the Regional Conference on Democracy, Human Rights and the Role of the International Criminal Court (Sana'a, January 2004), and "The Alexandria Charter", the result of a conference of Arab civil society organisations entitled "Arab Reform Issues: Vision and Implementation" (Alexandria, March 2004).

Independent political and civil forces in the Arab world also stepped up their struggle

Partial reforms are no longer effective.

Of all the impediments to an Arab renaissance, political restrictions on human development are the most stubborn.

Reform initiatives, both those originating in and outside the region, were launched in an international and regional context that hampered progress.

Palestinians have sustained enormous social and economic losses. Some 58 per cent of the population subsists below the poverty line.

for political reform in Arab countries, resulting in some notable successes. In Morocco, human rights and political organizations persuaded the Government to acknowledge earlier violations, in particular relating to the disappearances of political opponents, and to begin to address the issue.

In Bahrain, the National Committee for Martyrs and Torture Victims began demanding compensation for the families of those killed and tortured by the security forces. It also called for those responsible for human rights violations in Bahrain to be brought to justice.

In Syria, civil society organizations asked for the state of emergency to be lifted and freedoms expanded. In Egypt, the Muslim Brotherhood announced an initiative for general reform.

At the beginning of 2004, Saudi Arabia witnessed an unprecedented number of civil initiatives, distinctive insofar as they were relatively acceptable to the government. A number of petitions and documents were addressed to the Crown Prince, some of which contained the demands of minority groups, such as the Shias, for religious freedom, civil rights, and equality among citizens. Others criticized acts of violence and called for political openness as a means out of the present crisis. Still other demands centred on improvements in the status of women, including guarantees of their full participation in public life. One petition called for a constitutional monarchy and fundamental political reforms, including elections, control of public funds and reform of the judiciary.

In Palestine, civil society organizations were active in many areas, from resisting occupation and defending human rights to assisting in relief and humanitarian aid operations and calling for reform.

World Bank President: The shame of Israel's demolition of homes

"Israel's military operations which demolish thousands of homes in Rafah are reckless, and leaves tens of thousands of people without a roof over their heads ....As a Jew, I am ashamed of this kind of treatment of people".

The Wall violates international law: International Court of Justice (ICJ).

"The construction of the wall being built by Israel, the occupying Power, in the Occupied Palestinian Territory, including in and around East Jerusalem, and its associated régime, are contrary to international law."

This period also witnessed external attempts to encourage reform, beginning with the "Greater Middle East Initiative", which the US Administration presented to the G8 countries. After Arabs and some European countries expressed reservations on its first draft, the US put forward an amended project called the "Broader Middle East Initiative", with more limited objectives. It was adopted at the G8 summit in June 2004.

Reform initiatives, both those originating in and outside the region, were launched in an international and regional context that hampered progress, as illustrated in the following:

A CONSTRAINING REGIONAL AND INTERNATIONAL ENVIRONMENT

The continued occupation of the Palestinian territories by Israel, the US-led occupation of Iraq and the escalation of terrorism adversely influenced Arab human development.

Israeli occupation of Palestine continues to impede human development and freedom

Israel continued its violation of the Palestinians' right to life through direct assassinations of Palestinian leaders and the killing of civilians during raids and incursions into, and re-occupation of cities and villages in the West Bank and Gaza. Between May 2003 and June 2004, and as a result of repeated invasion and bombing, a total of 768 Palestinians were killed and 4,064 injured. 22.7 per cent of Palestinians killed during that period were children under 18.

In the past year, Israel has continued its violations of individual and collective freedoms of Palestinians. This is evident in the many forms of collective punishment, including arbitrary arrest and detention, and repeated restrictive closures.

Israel also continued its policy of demolitions, destroying property and land. Its incursion into Rafah in May 2004 alone left some 4,000 Palestinians homeless after the Israeli army demolished their homes.

Palestinians have therefore sustained enormous social and economic losses. Currently 58.1% of the population subsists below the poverty line.

Israel continued constructing the separation wall, which does not follow the boundary between the Occupied Palestinian territories and Israel but incorporates Palestinian land. The International Court of Justice, in response to a General Assembly request, issued a decisive advisory opinion on July 9, 2004 on the legal consequences of constructing the Wall. The Court ruled that the Wall violates international law, declared that it should be removed and called on Israel to compensate Palestinians harmed by the structure.

The impact of the occupation of Iraq on human development

As a result of the invasion of their country, the Iraqi people have emerged from the grip of a despotic regime that violated their basic rights and freedoms, only to fall under a foreign occupation that increased human suffering.

A scientific study estimated the number of deaths associated with the invasion and the accompanying violence at around 100,000 Iraqis.

As the occupying powers proved unable to meet their obligations under the Geneva Conventions to protect citizens, Iraq witnessed an unprecedented loss of internal security, with killings and acts of terrorism in most parts of the country, including attacks against Iraqi and foreign civilians, international organizations and humanitarian organizations.

Women suffered the most. They were, and still remain, at risk of abduction and rape by professional gangs. In some cases, coalition soldiers reportedly also sexually abused female prisoners.

Thousands of Iraqis were imprisoned and tortured. Prisoners, mostly civilians, were subjected to inhumane and immoral treatment in Abu Ghraib and other occupation prisons. Such mistreatment is a clear breach of the Geneva Conventions.

The occupation forces struggled to restore basic facilities but were unable to bring electricity, water and telephone services back to their pre-war levels. A US report showed that, by the end of October 2004, the occupation authority had spent only US$ 1.3 billion on reconstruction out of the US$ 18.4 billion allocated for this purpose by the US Congress, i.e. less than 7 per cent.

ADDRESSING THE THREE DEFICITS: PROGRESS AND REVERSALS

During the period in review, some Arab countries took steps to deal with their capability gaps in freedom, the empowerment of women and knowledge. However, progress was uneven, particularly in the area of freedoms where many countries experienced setbacks.

There were a number of positive developments in education, the most important of which was increased attention to quality issues at the different levels of the education system. Nine Arab states have participated in an international study designed to evaluate the quality of basic education in science and mathematics. Also, the Union of Arab Universities has taken a decision to set up an independent institute tasked with evaluating the quality of higher education.

Moving towards good governance, some Arab governments have begun to open themselves cautiously and selectively to opposition forces and have started expanding the public sphere. Nevertheless, there are indications of a regression in popular participation, and human rights violations have continued.

Civil society organizations and the media continued to suffer increasing restrictions. According to a 2004 international report, the Middle East was the region that enjoyed the least press freedom during the previous year. Several journalists were killed, particularly at the hands of occupying forces. As many as 14 journalists were killed during 2003 - 12 in Iraq, of which 5 were killed by US-led occupation forces. Two correspondents were killed by the Israeli occupation forces in Palestine.

In Darfur, violations of minority rights continued. Conflict and human suffering increased, despite the cease-fire agreement and the interventions of the international community.

On the empowerment of women, Morocco achieved a distinctive success with a new family law that met the demands of the women's movement to safeguard women's rights, notably with respect to marriage, divorce and childcare. Women have continued to rise to senior executive positions in Arab countries,

A scientific study estimated the number of deaths associated with the invasion (of Iraq), and the accompanying violence, at around 100,000 Iraqis.

Some governments took steps to deal with their capability gaps in freedom, the empowerment of women and knowledge. However, progress was uneven.

and there is steadily broader scope for participation by women in legislative assemblies.

Yet careful scrutiny of developments in this period indicates that, overall, there has been no significant easing of the human development crisis in the Arab region. Certainly, incipient reforms are taking place in more than one of the priority areas identified in this Report, but for the most part those reforms have been embryonic and fragmentary. Some gains are undoubtedly real and promising, but they do not add up to a serious effort to dispel the prevailing environment of repression.

THE STATE OF FREEDOM AND GOOD GOVERNANCE

No Arab thinker today doubts that freedom is a vital and necessary condition, though not the only one, for a new Arab renaissance, or that the Arab world's capacity to face up to its internal and external challenges, depends on ending tyranny and securing fundamental rights and freedoms.

The scope of the concept of freedom ranges between two poles. The first is a narrow definition that restricts freedom to civil and political rights and freedoms. The second is comprehensive, and has been adopted in this Report. This comprehensive definition incorporates not only civil and political freedoms, including freedom from oppression, but also the liberation of the individual from all factors that are inconsistent with human dignity, such as hunger, disease, ignorance, poverty, and fear.

> In human rights terms, the understanding of freedom in this Report covers all realms of human rights: economic, social, cultural and environmental rights as well as civil and political rights.

Freedom, however, is one of those superior human culmination outcomes that must be guaranteed, sustained and promoted by effective societal structures and processes. These societal guarantees are summed up in the order of good governance that:

• Safeguards freedom to ensure the expansion of people's choices (the core of human development)

• Rests upon effective popular participation and full representation of the public at large.

• Is buttressed by first-rate institutions (in contrast to the tyranny of the individual), which operate efficiently and with complete transparency. These institutions are subject to effective accountability among themselves, protected by the government's separation of powers, and by a balance among those powers; they are also directly accountable to the populace through popular selection processes that are regular, free, and scrupulously fair.

• Ensures that the rule of law is supreme; and the law itself is fair, protective of freedom, and applies equally to all;

• Sees that an efficient, fair and strictly independent judiciary upholds application of the law and the executive branch duly implements judicial rulings.

> ### Al-Kawakibi: Importance of holding the ruling authority accountable
>
> In sum, we have said that government, of any sort, is not absolved of being described as oppressive as long as it escapes rigorous oversight and is not made to answer for its actions without fail.

The individual is free only in a free society within a free nation.

> ### Taha Hussein: Freedom and Independence
>
> We want to be free people in our country, free of foreigners such that they cannot oppress us or treat us unjustly; and free with respect to ourselves, such that no one of us can oppress or treat another unjustly.

With this model as its yardstick, AHDR 2004 asks: what is the status of freedom and governance in the Arab countries?

THE STATE OF FREEDOMS AND RIGHTS

Despite variations from country to country, rights and freedoms enjoyed in the Arab world remain poor. Even disregarding foreign intervention, freedoms in Arab countries are threatened by two kinds of power: that of undemocratic regimes, and that of tradition and tribalism, sometimes under the cover of

For the most part, reforms have been embryonic and fragmentary.

Freedom ...must be guaranteed, sustained and promoted by effective societal structures and processes.

religion. These twin forces have combined to curtail freedoms and fundamental rights and have weakened the good citizen's strength and ability to advance.

CIVIL AND POLITICAL FREEDOMS: FROM DEFICIENT TO SERIOUSLY DEFICIENT

With limited exceptions in some countries and certain areas, freedoms, particularly those of opinion, expression and creativity, are under pressure in most Arab countries.

During the three-year period 2001-2003, journalists were repeatedly targeted for prosecution on the grounds of opinions they had expressed. Some of them were physically attacked or held and given harsh sentences.

Early in 2003, Arab Ministers of the Interior agreed to an anti-terrorism strategy, leading to further restrictions on freedom of opinion and expression and other human rights.

Violations of freedom of opinion and expression have included attacks on outspoken political activists and human rights advocates.

The curtailment of freedom of opinion and expression, in the form of officially imposed censorship, extends also to literary and artistic creativity. Some Arab states have gone as far as to ban circulation of some of the most treasured works in the Arab literary heritage, such as *The Prophet*, by Gibran Kahlil Gibran, and *A Thousand and One Nights*.

Al-Manfaluti: The value of freedom that has been stolen

Man lives in two prisons, the prison of his own soul and the prison of his government, from cradle to grave.

A man who stretches out his hands to ask for freedom is not begging; he is seeking a right that has been stolen from him by human greed. If he obtains it, it will not be as a favour from anyone, and he will not be beholden to anyone.

The freedom to form associations is often violated by denying organisations permission to operate, or by dissolving existing ones. Most restrictions have been directed against grassroots human rights organizations.

With a few exceptions, some of which are cosmetic, free presidential elections involving more than one candidate do not occur in Arab countries. In only three Arab countries (Algeria, Sudan and Yemen), and in a fourth under occupation (Palestine), are presidents elected through direct elections with more than one candidate and with presidential term limits. Syria and Egypt depend on referendums where the president is nominated by the parliament, after which a national referendum is held. In presidential referenda the outcome varies between an absolutely majority and total unanimity.

Totally or partially elected parliaments now exist in all Arab countries except Saudi Arabia and the United Arab Emirates. However, the right to political participation has often been little more than a ritual, representing a purely formal application of a constitutional entitlement. In most cases, elections have resulted in misrepresenting the will of the electorate and in low levels of representation for the opposition. Hence, elections have not played their designated role as a participatory tool for the peaceful alternation of power. These elections have generally reproduced the same ruling elites.

Personal life is also violated in some Arab countries. Political authorities sometimes breach the inviolability of the home at any hour, monitoring private correspondence and tapping telephones. Dominant social groups can similarly usurp the personal freedom of citizens in the name of norms and traditions.

The denial of individuals' fundamental freedoms

Some Arab governments also violate the right to life extra-legally and extra-judicially. Human rights organizations have observed that official reports on killings tend to be short on facts. In most Arab states, the names of the victims are not mentioned, and no public investigation is conducted.

Extremist groups which perpetrate assassinations and bombings and espouse the use of violence also violate the right to life. Armed confrontations between security forces and armed groups result in civilian casualties that can outnumber victims in the ranks of the combatants.

Violations of freedom of opinion and expression have included attacks on outspoken political activists and human rights advocates.

Official reports on killings tend to be short on facts.

With the advent of the global "war on terror", there have been unprecedented numbers of arrests. Legal safeguards have been violated, and people have been deprived of their liberty and, in many instances, tortured and ill-treated in prisons, camps and detention centres where their personal safety is uncertain. Perhaps one of the greatest menaces facing any Arab citizen is the frequent disappearance of suspects in detention.

Safeguards surrounding the right to a fair trial are also being eroded. In several Arab countries, civilians are being referred for trial to military courts or other exceptional tribunals such as the emergency, state security, and special courts, as well as martial law tribunals.

Exclusion from citizenship

The withdrawal of nationality from an Arab citizen, as permitted under certain legislation through an administrative decision by a government official of less than ministerial rank, is one the most extreme forms of exclusion from citizenship.

Abusing minority rights

Violations of human rights in Arab countries are more pronounced when cultural, religious or ethnic dimensions are present. In areas of protracted conflict in Iraq and the Sudan, minority groups have suffered overt or covert persecution.

This kind of double subjugation affects a number of other social groups, notably *bidun* and naturalized citizens in Arab Gulf countries. The former, being stateless, have nowhere to go and are regarded as foreigners, while the latter are treated as second-class citizens; they are denied the right to stand for election to representative bodies or to vote.

"Card holders" in the border areas of Saudi Arabia, Kurds deprived of citizenship following the 1962 census in Syria, and "akhdam" in Yemen encounter much the same treatment.

Migrant workers in oil-producing Arab states, including Arab workers, suffer certain forms of discrimination according to international standards. The most notorious cases stem from the "guarantor system" and the abuse of domestic servants, chiefly women.

Socio-economic and military circumstances are creating bizarre situations in Mauritania and the Sudan. In the former, members of the group known as "haratin" (emancipated slaves) are not much better off than when they were slaves. In the Sudan, different tribes involved in the military conflict have abducted one other's women and children; here again, the victims' condition is tantamount to slavery.

Women doubly excluded

In general, women suffer from inequality with men and are vulnerable to discrimination, both at law and in practice.

Despite laudable efforts to promote the status of women, success remains limited. Greater progress is required in women's political participation, in changes to personal status laws, in the integration of women in development, and in the right of a woman married to a foreign husband to transmit her citizenship to her children. The inability of existing legislation to protect women from domestic violence or violence on the part of the state and society is another deficit area. Violence against women peaks in areas of armed conflict, especially in the Sudan, Somalia and Iraq.

UNMET ECONOMIC AND SOCIAL RIGHTS

Results of a study of 15 Arab countries found that 32 million people suffer from malnutrition. This figure represents nearly 12 per cent of the total population of the countries concerned, In the 1990s, the absolute numbers of those suffering malnutrition in the Arab world increased by more than six million. The worst results were observed in Iraq and Somalia.

However, physical illness still takes years off the life of the ordinary Arab. When years of illness are deducted from the estimate of life expectancy at birth, average healthy Arab life expectancy falls by ten years or more.

The spread of education is restricted by the prevalence of unacceptable rates of illiteracy (about one third of Arab men and half of Arab women in 2002) and the denial of the basic right to education of some Arab children – low as this percentage may be. The value of educa-

With the advent of the global "war on terror", there have been unprecedented numbers of arrests.

Despite laudable efforts to promote the status of women, success remains limited.

tion is also diluted by its low quality and the resulting failure to instil the basic capabilities of self-learning, critical analysis and innovation among those educated.

HOW FAR DO ARABS BELIEVE THAT THEY ENJOY FREEDOM?

The report team, in collaboration with reputable polling institutions, designed and conducted a field survey on what Arabs believe are the most important components of freedom. The study also explored the extent to which Arabs thought that they enjoyed those components of freedom in their own countries. The survey covered five Arab countries (Algeria, Jordan, Palestine, Lebanon, and Morocco) that represent about one quarter of the Arab population.

Interviewees in all five countries indicated that, in their view, the level of enjoyment of individual freedoms was comparatively high, whereas the enjoyment of 'public' freedoms was relatively low, especially regarding good governance.

For most interviewees, freedom of movement, marriage and ownership of property, and the freedom of 'minorities' to practice their own culture, topped the list of freedoms enjoyed in their countries. The existence of effective political opposition, an independent media and judiciary, transparent and accountable governance, and successful anti-corruption measures were put at the low end of the scale of enjoyment.

Asked how far they had seen an improvement or deterioration in the enjoyment of the elements of freedom during the five years before the survey, interviewees singled out individual freedoms in gender equality and marriage, freedom of thought, freedom from ignorance and disease, freedom of 'minorities' to practice own culture, and freedom of civil and co-operative organisations as areas of greatest improvement. The greatest deteriorations were thought to have occurred in the areas of corruption, lack of transparency and accountability in governance, lack of independence of the judiciary, inequality before the law and mounting poverty.

STRUCTURES IMPEDING FREEDOM

Why, do Arabs enjoy so little freedom? What has led Arab democratic institutions (where they exist) to become stripped of their original purpose to uphold freedom?

Some analysts seek answers in the fraught and ambiguous relationship between "East" and "West," portrayed as a stark split. The first pole is usually associated with "despotism" as a supposedly inherent characteristic of "the East" and "Eastern" civilization, while the second is linked to freedom, purportedly a fundamental quality of "Western" civilization. A few have claimed that Arabs and Muslims are not capable of being democrats, for the very reason of being Arab ("the Arab mind") or Muslims. However, a recent research effort, the World Values Survey (WVS), has exposed the falseness of these claims by demonstrating that there is a rational and understandable thirst among Arabs to be rid of despots and to enjoy democratic governance. Among the nine regions surveyed by the WVS, which included the advanced Western countries, Arab countries topped the list of those agreeing that "democracy is better that any other form of governance". A substantially high percentage also rejected authoritarian rule (defined as a strong ruler who disregards parliament or elections).

Undoubtedly, the real flaw behind the failure of democracy in several Arab countries is not cultural in origin. It lies in the convergence of political, social and economic structures that have suppressed or eliminated organized social and political actors capable of turning the crisis of authoritarian and totalitarian regimes to their advantage. The elimination of such forces has sapped the democratic movement of any real forward momentum. In addition, there are region-specific complexities that have deepened the crisis, the most significant of which are:

What has led Arab democratic institutions (where they exist) to become stripped of their original purpose to uphold freedom?

The real flaw behind the failure of democracy in several Arab countries is not cultural in origin.

Thus indulged, the Arab despots of the day ruled oppressively, restricting their countries' prospects of transition to democracy.

Political rulers, in power and in opposition, have selectively appropriated Islam to support and perpetuate their oppressive rule.

The Contradiction Between Freedom In Arab Countries And Narrow Global Interests

In the first half of the twentieth century, two factors emerged which were fated to have a far-reaching impact on the attitudes of the major powers towards freedom in the Arab region: the discovery of oil and the establishment of the state of Israel. The existence of large reserves of oil in the region and the dominant role of oil in the advanced economies, made continued supplies at reasonable prices the chief concern of global powers. Additionally, as vested interests in Israel grew, some global powers, especially the US, increasingly took any Arab country's attitude toward Israel and its practices as one of the most important yardsticks by which to judge that country.

Consequently, major world powers tended to gloss over human rights violations in their Arab client states so long as the countries concerned did not threaten these interests. Thus indulged, the Arab despots of the day ruled oppressively, restricting prospects of their countries' transition to democracy.

The events of September 11 have added a more recent dimension to this tension after the US Administration moved to curtail civil and political rights, especially those of Arabs and Muslims, in the fight against "terrorism" as it defined the term. The fact that some Western countries, which Arab reformers had long held up as models of freedom and democracy, have taken steps widely perceived to be discriminatory and repressive, has weakened the position of those reformers calling for Arab governments undertaking similar actions to change their course.

Ayatollah al-Mohaqiq al-Naeeny: An Opinion Concerning Conditionality or Constitutionality

The conduct of the ruler is bounded by the limitations of his prerogatives ... it is conditioned not to exceed them, the people are his partners in all that concerns the destiny of the country to which they all belong on an equal footing. Those in charge are but loyal trust bearers of the people, not owners nor servants. Like other trust bearers, they are responsible to each and every individual of the nation, they are accountable for any trespass they commit, and every single person has the right to question and to object in an environment of security and freedom, without being bound by the Sultan's will or preferences.

Freedom shorn of effective advocates

The cause of Arab freedom has suffered in the absence of effective, broad-based political movements capable of rallying people to the struggle. Popular political forces, such as the Arab nationalist and, later on, the Islamist movements, did not make comprehensive freedom their priority. When they did turn to the question, their more limited goal, understandably, was national freedom, which they made their public rallying point in the struggle against colonial powers at the regional and global levels.

Appropriating religion to perpetuate tyranny

The dominant trend in Islamic jurisprudence supports freedom. Enlightened Islamic interpretations find that the tools of democracy - when used properly – offer one possible practical arrangement for applying the principle of consultation (al-shura). The fundamental principles in Islam which dictate good governance, include the realization of justice and equality, the assurance of public freedoms, the right of the nation to appoint and dismiss rulers, and guarantees of all public and private rights for non-Muslims and Muslims alike

Notwithstanding these key theological and philosophical interpretations, political forces, in power and in opposition, have selectively appropriated Islam to support and perpetuate their oppressive rule.

"The trap of the one-off election"

This phrase refers to a ploy used by Arab regimes in Islamic societies to keep those apprehensive about the accession to power of Islamist groups on their side. It is also cited to justify foreign interference to prop up authoritarian Arab regimes. Essentially, it is contended that opening up the public sphere to all societal forces - among the most active of which is the Islamic movement - will end with these forces assuming power, followed by oppression, such that democratic competition becomes history after the one and only election.

Specificity as a pretext for slighting human rights

In contemporary jurisprudence, human rights constitute the collection of rights incorporated in international agreements and treaties that guarantee all people, irrespective of their nationality, ethnicity, language, sex, religion, ideology and abilities, the fundamental rights to which they are entitled by virtue of being human. However, in Arab countries the issue of 'specificity' is frequently raised to weaken international human rights law.

In spite of the existence of several interpretive texts which assert the congruence between international human rights law and Islamic law (Shari'a), traditional interpretations of Shari'a that stress differences between the two, are used to argue that international human rights laws are not applicable in Arab countries.

THE LEGAL ARCHITECTURE

Two sets of discrepancies commonly mar Arab legislation concerned with different levels of freedom and human rights. The first set reflects a gap between international norms and national constitutions, and one between national constitutions and national laws. The second set reflects a breach between international norms, national constitutions, and national laws on the one side, and actual practice on the other.

Constitutions granting rights and laws confiscating them

Freedom of thought, opinion and association: Many Arab constitutions contain special provisions on freedom of thought, opinion, and belief, and freedom of peaceful assembly, association and affiliation. However, the constitution may also stipulate numerous restrictions on the right of association under the pretext of safeguarding national security or national unity. Political parties are permitted in 14 Arab countries. Libya and the member states of the Gulf Cooperation Council (Saudi Arabia, the United Arab Emirates, Qatar, Bahrain, Kuwait and Oman) prohibit the formation of political parties.

Arab constitutions assign the regulation of rights and freedoms to ordinary legislation, which tends to restrict the right in the guise of regulation. As a result, many constitutional texts addressing rights and freedoms, whatever their own shortcomings may be, lose much of their worth, turning into an empty facade for the benefit of the international community. Examples include provisions that prohibit or restrict the exercise of the right to strike, demonstrate, hold mass gatherings or assemble peacefully.

In countries whose constitutions prescribe the multiparty system, there are legislative restrictions limiting the right to form political parties, requiring prior authorization from

> *Arab constitutions assign the regulation of rights and freedoms to ordinary legislation, which tends to restrict the right in the guise of regulation.*

Restrictions on the rights to assembly and association

The holding or organization of a public meeting is not permitted without previously obtaining a permit for that purpose from the Governor in whose area of authority the meeting will take place, and all public meetings that are held without a permit will be prevented and dispersed.

(Article 4, Decree Law concerning the holding of public meetings and assemblies, Kuwait)

---

predominantly governmental committees. Other laws contain conditions concerning party activity, allowing the state to dissolve a party whenever it considers the conditions have been breached.

Moreover, both the establishment of civil associations and their activities are heavily circumscribed and subject to rigorous control in Arab countries, with a few exceptions in dealing with civil society more liberally, as in Morocco and Lebanon.

Press freedom in 11 Arab countries can be blocked or curtailed by regulations that permit prior or post-printing censorship. Laws impose restrictions on the right to publish newspapers by requiring a licence whose withdrawal, or threat of withdrawal, is used by the executive to deter newspapers from crossing set boundaries of freedom of expression. Journalists' right to obtain information and news is assured in law in only five Arab states: Algeria, Egypt, Jordan, the Sudan and Yemen.

When regulating freedom of opinion and expression, including the media and mass communications, the Arab legislator prioritizes what s/he perceives as security and public interest considerations above freedom, diversity

> *Press freedom in 11 Arab countries can be blocked or curtailed by regulations that permit prior or post-printing censorship.*

and respect for human rights. The result is that Arab legislation is armed with provisions that regard newspaper publication, audio-visual broadcasting and free expression in general as dangerous activities warranting a panoply of bans, restrictions and deterrent sanctions.

The human right to litigation: Arab constitutions take a consistent line on upholding the independence and inviolability of the judiciary. But most maintain the executive presence within the judiciary and its institutions. Hence, not only are judgements delivered and enforced in the name of the head of state, but the latter is also vested with the right to preside over the constitutional bodies that oversee the judiciary. This can often nullify other constitutional provisions.

While many Arab constitutions stipulate safeguards for fair trial in criminal laws and trial systems, scholars and human rights activists frequently note a disparity - usually for political reasons - between such guarantees on paper and reality.

Consequently, independence of the judiciary as an institution, and of judges as individuals, is jeopardized. Ideological and autocratic regimes frequently interfere, in the name of "protecting the ideological foundations" of their authoritarian regimes. In addition, where the executive controls the finances, and intervenes in the appointment, transfer and dismissal of judges, judicial independence suffers. Material and moral temptations for underpaid and unprotected judges are sometimes a factor as well. Many are sometimes fearful in delivering their judgements, particularly when the State has a direct or indirect interest in the case in question.

Justice and the right to litigation are also obstructed by the vast case-load in the courts of some Arab countries and consequent delays in hearings and justice delivered. The absence of an authority capable of enforcing the law fairly and promptly can encourage recourse to violence and individual reprisals, and deter the public from resorting to courts for solutions.

Right of nationality: Nationality gives a person the legal status that confers rights and duties and helps her/him to acquire full citizenship. There is a noticeable difference between the constitutional status of this right and the situation of those who benefit from it in Arab countries; some constitutions remain silent on the subject, while others refer the matter of its regulation to the law, as in Egypt, Lebanon, Jordan, Saudi Arabia and Algeria. Still other constitutions allow for its forfeiture and provide for the conditions required, as in Qatar, Oman, the United Arab Emirates and Kuwait.

In some Arab countries, a new trend is emerging of granting nationality to the children of a mother bearing the nationality of the state. This is commendable, as it recognizes the principle of equality between mother and father in securing the nationality of their children and ends the misery that arises from the state denying nationality to the children where the mother is married to a foreign national.

And constitutions flatly violating rights

A number of Arab constitutions contain provisions that conflict with international human rights principles by assuming an ideological or religious character that removes public rights and freedoms or permits their removal. An example is the amendment introduced by the Yemeni legislators to an article which originally provided that "there shall be no crime and no punishment other than as stipulated by law." The amendment states that "there shall be no crime and no punishment other than on the basis of a provision of religious law (Shari'a) or law."

Taking the provisions of Shari'a as a source of legislation is not itself a violation of human rights. The objection is that, in Arab countries that do so, the discourse is directed to the judge, instead of the legislator. Investing discretionary powers in the judge to interpret the Shari'a text and to choose among the multiple opinions of jurisprudence entails a lack of legal precision. In order to harmonise Shari'a with the law, the constitutions of those states which adopt it must therefore stipulate the principle that there is no crime or punishment other than that prescribed by law.

The constitutional violation of human rights may assume a confessional shape, as illustrated in the Lebanese law, which provides that parliamentary seats in the Council of Deputies shall be divided on a religious and confessional basis.

Constitutional violations of human rights can also take the form of an ideological bias, which excludes differing opinions or political affiliations. For example, the Syrian Constitution affirms the Ba'th party as the leadership of

> The confusion between religion and state is nowhere more clearly demonstrated than in the Sudanese Constitution, which provides that God, the Creator of humankind, holds supremacy over the State, without specifying the meaning of supremacy. Governance practices apparently sanctioned by God are likely to be immune to criticism and opposition.

society and the state, meaning that the multiparty system has no constitutional legality.

One of the most serious legislative violations of human rights in the Arab world occurs where the Arab legislator permits the executive to declare a state of emergency and abuse all safeguards for individual rights and liberties. In some Arab countries, the state of emergency has become permanent and ongoing, with none of the dangers to warrant it. What was the exception has now become the rule (e.g. in Egypt, Syria and the Sudan). Emergency Laws (or rules of martial law), strip the citizen of many constitutional rights, such as inviolability of the home, personal liberty, freedom of opinion, expression and the press, confidentiality of correspondence, rights of movement and assembly. They remove key legislative powers from the elected parliament and transfer them to the executive or military governor (emergency authority).

THE POLITICAL ARCHITECTURE

It may at first seem difficult to talk about the common features of governance in the Arab world owing to the wide diversity of its regimes, ranging from absolute monarchies to revolutionary republics and radical Islamic states. Closer scrutiny, however, reveals an interesting affinity in the architecture and methods of Arab systems of governance.

The "black-hole" State

The modern Arab state, in the political sense, runs close to this astronomical model, whereby the executive apparatus resembles a "black hole" which converts its surrounding social environment into a setting in which nothing moves and from which nothing escapes.

This increasing centralization of the executive is guaranteed in the constitutional texts of certain states, which vest wide powers in the head of state. The latter becomes the supreme leader of the executive, the council of ministers, the armed forces, the judiciary and public services.

In addition to the absolute powers of the executive body, there are additional mechanisms that increase the concentration of power in its hands. For example, the so-called ruling parties (where they exist) are, in reality, simply institutions attached to the executive, since party officials (or electoral candidates) are designated by the president, who is also regarded as the party leader. In practice, this means that parliament is a bureaucratic adjunct of the executive that does not represent the people whose mistrust in it continues to grow.

Furthermore, the executive uses the ordinary and exceptional judiciary to eliminate and tame opponents, rivals and even supporters who step out of line. This is linked with what is known as "unspoken corruption" where close supporters are allowed to exploit their positions for unlawful gain, while "enforcement of the law" against them remains a weapon to ensure their continuing and total loyalty.

The key support buttressing the power of the executive is the intelligence apparatus, which is not responsible to the legislature or to public opinion, but is directly under the control of the president or king and possesses powers greater than those of any other organ. The security apparatus has substantial resources and intervenes in all the powers of the executive, particularly in regard to appointment decisions and the legal regulation of associations, to the point where the modern-day Arab state is frequently dubbed "the intelligence state"

Arab states vary in their embodiment of these general traits, particularly in the margin of freedom that is considered unthreatening.

In some Arab countries, the state of emergency has become permanent and ongoing, with none of the dangers to warrant it.

The executive apparatus resembles a "black hole" which converts its surrounding social environment into a setting in which nothing moves and from which nothing escapes.

However, what they have in common is that power is concentrated at the tip of the executive pyramid and that the margin of freedom permitted (which can swiftly be reduced) has no effect on the state's firm and absolute grip on power.

The crisis of legitimacy

Without the majority of people behind them, most Arab regimes resorted to other sources of legitimacy: traditional (religious/tribal), revolutionary (nationalist/liberation), or patriarchal, claiming authority based on the wisdom of the 'family head'. However, the failure to tackle major issues such as the question of Palestine, pan-Arab cooperation, foreign intervention, the advancement of human development and popular representation, drove Arab states into a crisis of legitimacy. Hence, in addressing the masses, the regimes resorted to a new tactic: they linked legitimacy to achievements, actual or promised, in specific areas such as the economy, peace, prosperity, stability, or safeguarding values and traditions. Sometimes the mere preservation of the state entity in the face of external threats was considered an achievement sufficient to confer legitimacy.

Some regimes now bolster their legitimacy by adopting a simplified and efficient formula to justify their continuation in power. They style themselves as the lesser of two evils, or the last line of defence against fundamentalist tyranny or, even more dramatically, against chaos and the collapse of the state. This formula is what some have dubbed "the legitimacy of blackmail".

The "legitimacy of blackmail" has been eroded by the growing realization that the absence of any effective alternative is itself one of the outcomes of the policies that block all avenues for political and civil activity, and so prevent other alternatives from materializing. Hence, the survival of "the black-hole State" has become more dependent on control and propaganda; on marginalizing the elites through scare-and-promise tactics; on striking bargains with dominant global or regional powers; and on mutually supportive regional blocs to reinforce the status of the ruling elites against emerging forces.

The absence of any effective (political) alternative is itself one of the outcomes of policies that block all avenues for political and civil activity.

Opposition parties suffer from internal problems that are no less serious.

> ### Muhammad Al-Charfi: Arab democracy - form without substance
>
> A citizen no longer has any guaranteed right unless s/he wishes to cheer the ruler, voice gratitude for his accomplishments and extol his qualities and wisdom.

Repression and political impoverishment

The Arab political scene today is quite varied. Some states categorically prohibit any political organization. Other states allow conditional political pluralism and, as a rule, ban the strongest and most important opposition party, while favouring the party established by the ruling authority. States which allow party activity nonetheless try to trip up the opposition parties, by depriving them of resources and media coverage, controlling nomination and election procedures, using the judiciary, the army and security services to curtail their activities, hounding their leaders and activists and tampering with election polls.

In addition to official repression, opposition parties suffer from internal problems that are no less serious. Despite theoretical references to democracy in their charters, their practices show that the influential political élite holds sway in most of these parties, resulting in immovable leaders who, with rare exceptions, only leave their posts when they die, casting doubt on their claims to modernity and democracy.

Beyond that, there is an acute "sectarian split" in the political community between the Islamic parties on the one hand and the liberal and nationalist secular parties on the other (as well as other sectarian divisions along doctrinal, ethnic, tribal and regional lines). As a result of this sectarian fragmentation some parties and political forces have preferred to co-operate with undemocratic governments rather than work with their rivals to lay the groundwork for a democratic rule open to all.

Restrictions on opposition parties have led to the marginalization of some parties and hastened their demise, and generated a lack of confidence in the political process as a whole. This contraction has pushed some towards clandestine political activities adopting violent and terrorist means, and others into political passivity. Constraints on political space have led some activists and scholars to rely on civil society organizations, especially trade unions and professional organizations, on the grounds that they are better equipped than Arab political parties to lead Arab society towards development and democracy.

Yet, civil society faces the same problems as the political community vis-à-vis the authorities who seek to control civil organizations, directly or indirectly, by using a dual strategy of containment and repression. In addition, many CSOs become extensions of political parties, which use them as fronts through which to expand their political influence at the popular level. This, in turn, limits the CSOs' initiative and independence of action. Consequently, civil society organizations have not been significant actors in resolving the existing political crisis, as they too have been caught up in its vortex.

The vicious circle of repression and corruption

Economic corruption is the natural result of political corruption. In some countries corruption may be characterised as "structural" because personal abuse of public office and misuse of public finances are considered normal according to prevailing custom (such as obtaining commissions for government deals). It also takes the form of "petty corruption" in some countries. Petty corruption refers to situations where Arab citizens have to rely on personal contacts (wasta) or pay a bribe to obtain services that are legitimate and to which they are entitled, or to avert a punishment by the authorities. If ending corruption entails, among other measures, deep economic reform, active laws and mechanisms of accountability, and transparent governance, "structural corruption" can be overcome only by radical reform of the political architecture.

SOCIETAL STRUCTURES

The chain that stifles individual freedom

The crisis in political structures is reflected in Arab societal structures that consist of em-bedded links in an interconnected chain constricting freedom. Starting with the child's upbringing within the family, passing through educational institutions, the world of work, and societal formation, and ending with politics - both internal and external - each link in the chain takes its portion of freedom from the individual and delivers her or him to the next, which, in turn, steals a further share.

In varying degrees, the family, the primary unit of Arab society, is based on clannism, which implants submission, and is considered the enemy of personal independence, intellectual daring, and the flowering of a unique and authentic human entity.

Clannism flourishes, and its negative impact on freedom and society becomes stronger, wherever civil or political institutions that protect rights and freedoms are weak or absent. Without institutional supports, individuals are driven to seek refuge in narrowly based loyalties that provide security and protection, thus further aggravating the phenomenon. Tribal allegiances also develop when the judiciary is ineffective or the executive authority is reluctant to implement its rulings, circumstances that make citizens unsure of their ability to realize their rights without the allegiances of the clan.

Once children enter school, they find an educational institution, curricula, teaching and evaluation methods which tend to rely on dictation and instil submissiveness. This learning environment does not permit free dialogue and active exploration and consequently does not open the doors to freedom of thought and criticism. On the contrary, it weakens the capacity to hold opposing viewpoints and to think outside the box. Its societal function is the reproduction of control in Arab societies.

For all its deficiencies and flaws, education, particularly at the higher levels, remains a vital source of knowledge, enlightenment and leavening for the forces of change.

Even so, outside the academy, the world remains harsh on the young. After a student graduates, and when fate or chance ends the period of unemployment, s/he steps onto the lowest rung of a rigid, restrictive hierarchy, especially if the job is with the civil service.

The chain constricting freedom completes

Many civil society organizations have become extensions of political parties, which use them as fronts.

Each link in the chain takes its portion of freedom from the individual and delivers her or him to the next, which, in turn, steals a further share.

its circle in the political realm, squeezing Arab public life into a small and constricted space. The limited dimensions of this space do not enable civil society institutions to provide effective group protection to citizens who are vulnerable to oppression as individuals. Such weakness affords oppressive powers, both at home and from abroad, free sway to suppress individual freedoms.

As they tighten and grow, the constrictions of the chain on freedom, in time, become internal constraints on the self. Suppression leads individuals to become their own censors and to contain every urge to speak or act. This complicated process has led Arab citizens, including some among the intelligentsia, to a state of submission fed by fear and marked by denial of their subjugation. Yet - even among segments once considered pillars of the restrictive status quo - there are signs that this state of affairs cannot continue and that the human urge to claim freedom will re-surface in society.

A mode of production that strengthens authoritarian governance

The rentier mode of production opens cracks in the fundamental relationship between citizens as a source of public tax revenue and government. Where a government relies on financing from the tax base represented by its citizens, it is subject to questioning about how it allocates state resources. In a rentier mode of production, however, the government can act as a generous provider that demands no taxes or duties in return. This hand that gives can also take away, and the government is therefore entitled to require loyalty from its citizens invoking the mentality of the clan.

A longing for freedom and justice in popular culture

There is no stronger indication of the thirst for freedom and justice in the Arab conscience than the way these concepts recur in a popular culture rich in depictions of struggles against oppression and injustice.

The greatest literary manifestations of that tradition are glowing examples of the elevation of the "dream of freedom". The siras (life stories) profoundly expressed popular anger against injustice, oppression and, tyranny in the Arab dark ages of disintegration and weakness. In calling for unity and liberation of the land, in voicing the dream of a better world, in nourishing the popular spirit by creating popular or epic heroes capable of overcoming adversity, they lifted people's souls and minds above their trials.

Popular aspirations for freedom are abundant as well in the myriad folk songs and poetry of the Arab world.

AN INHOSPITABLE GLOBAL AND REGIONAL ENVIRONMENT FOR FREEDOM

It is not possible to understand the problem of freedom in Arab society without also considering the effects of regional factors and of influences coming from outside the region, particularly those related to globalization and global governance.

Globalization has the potential to buttress the freedom of the individual as a result of minimising the State's capacity to repress people, particularly their ideas and aspirations. It can also, expand people's opportunities to acquire knowledge and broaden their horizons by facilitating communication and the circulation of ideas.

In particular, globalization can support freedom by strengthening civil society through wider networking among its actors, using modern information and communication technology. Yet globalization also entails the selective restriction of certain liberties world-wide through restrictions of vital knowledge flows and on the free movement of people.

With globalization, the State lost part of its sovereignty to international actors, such as trans-national corporations and international organizations, notably in the areas of economic activity. It has thus become critical to strengthen global governance, as embodied in the United Nations. However, this has yet to come about. The advent of a uni-polar world has resulted at times in the weakening and marginalization of the world organization. This has had adverse consequences for freedom in the Arab world. The US's repeated use, or threat of veto, has limited the effectiveness of the Se-

The rentier mode of production opens cracks in the fundamental relationship between citizens as sources of public tax revenue and government.

It has become critical to strengthen global governance as embodied in the United Nations.

curity Council in establishing peace in the region. Such marginalization has been among the factors contributing to continuing or increased human suffering and to the creation of new facts on the ground, such as the establishment of new settlements by Israel in the Occupied Territories and the construction of the separation wall that incorporates additional Palestinian land, all of which militate against a just and lasting peace. This has pushed many people in the region to lose hope of obtaining justice from global governance and could exacerbate a tendency towards extremism.

The "war on terror" has also cut into many Arab freedoms. Western leaders have strongly asserted their support for freedom and democracy as the best long-term solution to terrorism; in practice many have also understandably sought to tighten their own security legislation. An unfortunate by-product in some countries has been that Arabs are increasingly the victims of stereotyping, disproportionately harassed or detained without cause under new restrictions. At the same time, in the Arab world, several Governments have cited fear of terrorism as justification for steps to impose even tighter restrictions on their citizens.

At the regional level, current institutional arrangements for regional co-ordination have failed to give substantive support to Arab development, and to maintain security and peace in the Arab world.

A STRATEGIC VISION: ALTERNATIVE FUTURES FOR FREEDOM AND GOVERNANCE IN ARAB COUNTRIES

Modernization in Arab countries has yielded notable achievements, especially in combating morbidity and mortality, building infrastructure, the quantitative expansion of education and in increasing the integration of women in society. Yet by 21st century standards, Arab countries have not met the Arab people's aspirations for development, security and liberation despite variations between one country and another in that respect. Indeed, there is a near-complete consensus that there is a serious failing in the Arab world, and that this is located specifically in the political sphere.

Counsellor Yahya al-Rifai: Justice Above Might

There are two, and only two, ways of settling disputes: with the bludgeon of force or the justice of law, there is no third possibility. With force, a person's life, honour and property are never safe; he lives like a wild animal, hunting his prey without ever being sure that he will be able to keep any of it, never planting a crop because the harvest will go to the strongest, never building a house because there is no certainty that he will be able to live in it, and, indeed, afraid to settle anywhere.

The UN Special Rapporteur on Terrorism and Human Rights: The Root Causes of Terrorism

Some of the actions undertaken in the cause of the global war against terrorism have been the cause of consternation also for the highest officials in the UN system. For instance, the UN Secretary-General has pleaded on a number of occasions for States to uphold all human rights, stressing that greater respect for human rights, not their curtailment, is the best means of preventing terrorism.

ALTERNATIVE SCENARIOS

Since present-day regimes have not achieved fundamental reforms from within through which they could correct their course and improve hopes for a better future, Arabs anticipate a number of future scenarios, some of which are catastrophic, while others are hopeful.

The Impending Disaster Scenario

If the repressive situation in Arab countries today continues, intensified societal conflict is likely to follow. In the absence of peaceful and effective mechanisms to address injustice and achieve political alternation, some might be tempted to embrace violent protest, with the risk of internal disorder.

This could lead to chaotic upheavals that might force a transfer of power in Arab countries, but such a transfer could well involve armed violence and human losses that, however small, would be unacceptable. Nor would a transfer of power through violence guarantee that successor governance regimes would be any more desirable.

The "Izdihar" Alternative

Disaster can be averted. The alternative is to pursue an historic, peaceful and deep process of negotiated political alternation adopted by all pro-reform segments of Arab society,

By 21st century standards, Arab countries have not met the Arab peoples' aspirations for development, security and liberation.

Disaster can be averted.

whether in power or not, on all fronts and by all democratic means, to guarantee rights and freedoms. The desired outcome is a redistribution of power within Arab societies, restoring sovereignty to its rightful owners, the vast majority of people in the Arab world. The process would also establish good governance as a solid foundation for a human renaissance.

The "Half Way House" Scenario: the Accommodation of External Reform

Realistically, a third alternative may well lie in between these two scenarios in the form of a programme endorsed by external forces that would induce a series of internal reforms in Arab countries.

This third or "half way" alternative, falls short of the "ideal" (izdihar) scenario. Measures imposed from outside according to the vision of foreign powers are not necessarily consistent with the concepts of freedom and good governance, particularly those relating to liberation, self-determination and independence.

The challenge facing the advocates of an Arab renaissance is how to harness this alternative such that it enhances internal reform initiatives while the impact of its most critical defects is minimised.

Under all circumstances, co-operation with external non-governmental and governmental actors can be rewarding if all parties respect key principles:

- freedom for all and complete adherence to international human rights law, in particular the right to national liberation
- absolute respect for the tenet that Arabs should find their own way to freedom and good governance through innovation by Arab social forces, without pressure to adopt ready-made models
- inclusion of all societal forces in Arab countries in a system of good governance to ensure popular representation
- full respect for the outcomes freely chosen by the people
- dealing with Arabs in a partnership of equals free from patronage.

REFORMING ARAB SOCIETAL STRUCTURES TO GUARANTEE FREEDOM

Establishing a society of freedom and good governance requires comprehensive reform of governance at three interactive levels: internal, regional and global.

Internal Reform

Internal reform requires a structural reform of the state, civil society and the private sector to enhance the principles of sound administration. Also required is a correction of the region's present development trajectory by moving from rent-based economies to more diversified production systems, and thoroughgoing political reform. The latter should consist of:

The reform of practices: immediate action must be taken to address three priorities:
- Abolishing the state of emergency.
- Ending all forms of discrimination against any minority group.
- Guaranteeing the independence of the judiciary.

Legislative reform: There is a compelling need to modernize Arab legal systems, to make them compatible with international human rights standards and effective in protecting human rights and freedoms in practice. Constitutions need to be reformed to end the permanency of political power and to hold ruling authorities responsible for their actions before the judiciary and elected representational bodies. Political pluralism should be guaranteed by an effective system based on the principle of equality.

It is equally critical that Arab constitutions must guarantee fundamental rights and freedoms. The constitution should clearly provide that it is unlawful to enact any legislation that restricts rights and freedoms.

It is equally critical to reform laws regulating political rights, such that they affirm the principle of equality, and ensure that the principles of citizenship and equality apply to all constituent elements of national society.

Legislation must guarantee that citizens are free to set up civil society organizations and to enact parties, as well as to protect the right of parties to carry out peaceful political activities. Also necessary is a reform of Arab laws to ensure the protection of personal freedoms, the prevention of illegal arrest, torture, administrative detention and disappearances.

Political reform: The way to achieve good governance in the Arab region is through fundamental reform of its political architecture. This means, in particular, ending the executive's monopoly of power, and the marginalization of other state organs, which obstructs the free and healthy development of society's capabilities and potential. In some countries, this requires a clear distinction in both law and practice between the state apparatus and the party in power, so that the party concerned does not enjoy the prerogative of using state services to strengthen its presence, in breach of the principle of equality before the law.

The achievement of these desired reforms confers duties and responsibilities on the state and all societal forces.

The obligations of the State include allowing freedom of expression and organization, starting a direct dialogue with all active forces in society, safeguarding the independence and integrity of governance institutions, as well as carrying out comprehensive structural and functional reform of the security services. All service branches must obey the law, and should be at the service of the people and the nation, and not the ruler, party, sect or tribe.

The élites of political society need to develop a constructive discourse and reject policies of exclusion. They must also strive to find common ground among political forces and create a new mould for the political scene, clearly distinct from past trends of polarization and fragmentation, which could seriously hamper genuine democratic transformation in the Arab region. In addition, the political élites must demonstrate adherence to their own principles, seeking democratic solutions to settle differences.

Civil society has its obligations as well. They include developing appropriate methodologies and conceptual frameworks to adapt civil and human rights work to the local Arab environment; reaching out to include the widest possible social spectrum; securing their

Perpetuating power in the name of democracy and the people

Article 77 of the Egyptian Constitution of 1971 limits the maximum term in office of the President of the Republic to two consecutive terms.

Towards the end of President Sadat's second term of office, this constitutional provision was amended, on 30 April 1980, to permit the President of the Republic to be re-elected for further terms of office with no upper limit prescribed.

The stated reason for the amendment was that the President's term "began before the Constitution was promulgated, and in accordance with article 190 and article 77, his term of office concludes in November 1983. This outcome, resulting from the application of this provision, is not consistent with the democratic principles which our society safeguards."

own independence; and creating networks of associations and organizations with similar goals.

In terms of parliamentary representation, it is essential to establish the principle of total equality among citizens and provide safeguards against disqualifying candidates from parliamentary representation on any basis. Also required is the adoption of affirmative action policies targeting marginalized groups. These include allocating a quota of posts in government and the legislature for minorities, and for women while maintaining the principle of competition within quotas. It remains necessary to establish ethics committees for fairness in parliaments to prevent deputies from abusing their political standing.

Changes at the Pan-Arab level

Establishing good governance at the pan-Arab level entails transforming the ineffective regional set-up of the present day into a variety of structural arrangements aiming at integration.

It is suggested that regional mechanisms are set up to settle disputes and support preventive diplomacy between states. It has become necessary for Arab countries to conclude a new Arab Human Rights Convention, fully conforming to the human rights system. The convention should provide the mechanisms necessary to stop violations at the country and pan-Arab levels. Perhaps the most important of these would be an Arab Council of Human Rights and an Arab Court of Human Rights, which would allow individuals to bring action directly against their own governments.

Governance at the Global level

The global system will need to be reformed

The elites of political society need to develop a constructive discourse and reject policies of exclusion.

Establishing good governance at the pan-Arab level entails transforming the ineffective regional set-up of the present day into structural arrangements aiming at integration.

to provide effective and peaceful channels for settling disputes and a framework of fair rules that are subscribed to, and implemented by all. The system has to uphold the rule of law on the strong and the weak alike. This would require the development of an international instrument that can serve as an unbiased arbitrator, and provide peace, security and advancement for all humankind on a strong human rights basis, as well as on justice and prosperity for all.

The UN's credibility, which would be enhanced through its development, can enable it to play a crucial role in the process of transformation towards good governance and freedom in Arab countries. The organization can ensure the completion of initial legal reforms assuring civil society organizations the freedom to exist and operate; and guarantee that conditions are met for holding free and fair elections.

The (global) system has to uphold the rule of law on the strong and weak alike.

ACHIEVING PEACEFUL POLITICAL ALTERNATION IN ARAB COUNTRIES

The sequence of events leading to a transformation of the present political context passes through several stages. Vision dims the further one peers into the future, and prospects for alternatives multiply. In this light, the first act of this transformation is so crucial that it represents, in our view, the yardstick by which to judge the seriousness of governance reform in Arab countries.

The reform required in Arab countries will be marked by the total respect of the key freedoms of opinion, expression and association in Arab countries and the ending of all types of marginalization of, and discrimination against social groups. It will eliminate all types of extra-legal arrangements such as emergency laws and exceptional courts. It will lay down

foundations for the principles of transparency and disclosure in all organizations throughout Arab society.

As such, this act requires an initial far-reaching legal and organizational reform the crux of which is the guarantee of key freedoms and independence of the judiciary and changes that bind ruling authorities to the law and security forces to their original mandate in protecting the security of citizens and the nation

The climate of freedom created by unleashing these key freedoms can be expected to secure the remaining conditions for systemic change: high quality institutions within civil and political societies at the national and regional levels; and a political, legal and social basis for subsequent acts in the "izdihar" scenario to unfold.

Epilogue: the furthest lotus tree

Formidable obstacles stand in the way of a society of freedom and good governance in Arab countries. And this is an undeniable truth. But at the end of this difficult journey, there lies a noble goal, worthy of the hardships endured by those who seek it.

The time has come to make up for the missed opportunities of the past. It is to be hoped that the Arab people will not again fail to take the historic road leading it to its appropriate place in a better, fairer and freer world, one that it will have contributed to bring into being, and in whose benefits it will share.

Address by the UN Secretary General, Opening Session of the General Assembly, New York, 21 September 2004

All states – strong and weak, big and small – need a framework of fair rules, which each can be confident that others will obey...yet this framework is riddled with gaps and weaknesses. Too often it is applied selectively, and enforced arbitrarily. It lacks the teeth that turn a body of laws into an effective legal system...Those who seek to bestow legitimacy must themselves embody it; and those who invoke international law must themselves submit to it.

Part I

Changes in Human Development Since the Launch of AHDR 2003

Changes in Human Development Since the Launch of AHDR 2003

Introduction

This opening section of the Report reviews changes influencing human development in the Arab world dating from the completion of the second AHDR up to mid-2004. These changes are reflected in certain national, regional and international developments that, in the view of the Report team, had the greatest impact, for good or ill, on countries of the region. Readers may thus be able to form an overall view of the human development situation in Arab countries.

Prospects for human development in the Arab world have been affected by domestic and international attempts at promoting reform; they have also been influenced by developments at the regional and international level. Many of these trends have had a negative impact on Arab human development.

ARAB INITIATIVES TO PROMOTE REGION-WIDE REFORM

OFFICIAL ARAB REFORM EFFORTS

Since the publication of AHDR 2003, Arab governments and civil society organisations have undertaken a variety of reform initiatives to address some shortcomings in the Arab world.

Formal initiatives

The "Charter for Reform of the Arab Situation", proposed by the Crown Prince of Saudi Arabia, was the first in a series of such internal reform initiatives. The draft Charter was to have been submitted to the summit conference held just before the invasion of Iraq in 2003, but under the circumstances it

was postponed to the next meeting.

Calls for the reform of the League of Arab States grew more insistent through this period. The Government of Yemen put forward a draft document entitled "Development of the Joint Arab Action Mechanism". The Government of Egypt also tabled an initiative aimed at "developing the League of Arab States and activating the Joint Arab Action mechanism".

Against the backdrop of a rising tide of reform initiatives from outside the region, these various initiatives coalesced into a single joint draft document that has been adopted by the Governments of Egypt, Saudi Arabia and Syria. The text was laid before the meeting of Arab Ministers for Foreign Affairs held in Cairo early in March 2004.

At the same time, the Secretary-General of the League of Arab States unveiled a draft proposal for reforming the League and putting the Joint Arab Action mechanism into effect. The proposal contained nine main annexes. They dealt respectively with: the establishment of an Arab Parliament, the establishment of an Arab Security Council, the basic statute of an Arab Court of Justice, strengthening joint Arab economic action, development of the Economic and Social Council, the establishment of an Arab Investment and Development Bank, a procedure for the adoption of resolutions within the League, a mechanism for monitoring the implementation of resolutions, and the establishment of a High Council for Arab Culture (Al-Ahram, in Arabic, Cairo, 2 March), (selected documents, Annex 2).

On 24 May 2004, the Arab summit was finally held in Tunis. While almost half the Arab leaders were absent and though the meeting faced other difficulties, it produced a "Pledge of Accord and Solidarity", which was initialled by Ministers for Foreign Affairs. The

Prospects for human development in the Arab world have been affected by domestic and international attempts at promoting reform.

Calls for the reform of the Arab League grew more insistent in this period.

summit also issued a "Declaration on the Process of Reform and Modernisation". Although it included many constructive positions, the document, in the view of this Report, did not venture sufficiently into the essence of freedom and good governance.

These various declarations were also short on details concerning the effective implementation of principles adopted. The substance of the reform of Joint Arab Action mechanisms was postponed to the Algiers summit, which is scheduled for 2005.

CIVIL SOCIETY REFORM INITIATIVES

Civil society organisations were spearheading several reform initiatives as this Report was being prepared.

The Regional Conference on Democracy, Human Rights and the Role of the International Criminal Court (Sana'a, January 2004) resulted in " The Sana'a Declaration".

In March 2004, a conference of Arab civil society organisations was held at the Bibliotheca Alexandrina on "Arab Reform Issues: Vision and Implementation". The President of the Republic of Egypt inaugurated the conference and the participants issued "The Alexandria Charter".

On 1-3 June 2004 the "Arab Regional Conference on Education for All" took place and issued "The Arab Vision for the Future".

In December 2003 an Arab Business Council Meeting was organized in Aqaba, which called for reform.

Excerpts from some of these documents can be found in Annex 2.

THE STRUGGLE WAGED BY CIVIL AND POLITICAL FORCES IN THE ARAB WORLD

Despite the many hurdles in their way, independent political and civil forces in the Arab world are taking firm steps to pursue political reform in Arab countries. Their efforts in individual countries contribute to the broader reform movement in the region.

Freedom and respect for human rights

In Morocco, where civil activity has been vigorous for years, human rights and political organizations persuaded the Government to acknowledge earlier violations, in particular relating to the disappearances of political opponents, and to take steps to address the issue. Civil society movements achieved perhaps their greatest triumph in January 2004,

---

BOX 1

Declaration on the Process of Reform and Modernisation in the Arab World (excerpts)

Continuation and intensification of efforts in pursuit of the political, economic, social and educational reform process with a view to the progress of Arab societies stemming from their own free will, consistent with their cultural, religious and civilizational values and concepts and the circumstances and potential of each State:

• Action to deepen the foundations of democracy and consultation, and to broaden participation in political life and decision-making, in the context of the rule of law, equality among citizens, respect for human rights and freedom of expression in accordance with the provisions of the various relevant international conventions and charters and the Arab Charter for Human Rights, and safeguards for the independence of the judiciary, with a view to strengthening the roles played by all components of society, including non-governmental organisations, and participation by all social groups, men and women alike, in public life, as a means of ensuring that the elements of citizenship are solidly grounded in the Arab world.

• Action to ensure the welfare of children and young persons, and continued action to enhance the role played by women in Arab society, strengthen their rights and promote their status, with a view to enabling them to contribute more effectively to the comprehensive development process through fuller participation in various areas of political, economic, social and cultural life.

• Preparation of a comprehensive Arab economic, social and human development strategy aimed at establishing the concepts of good governance, addressing the phenomena of poverty, illiteracy and environmental protection, creating jobs and providing health care in the Arab world.

• Action to modernize the social structure of our States, upgrade their education systems and develop data bases incorporating scientific, technical and technological progress in the world, thereby enabling our societies to cope with the demands of the spirit of the age while still retaining our identity and continuing to respect our basic traditions.

• Greater efforts to enlist the international community in the task of achieving a just, comprehensive and lasting settlement of the Arab-Israeli conflict, in accordance with the Arab peace initiative and the relevant UN resolutions, with a view to:
- the establishment of an independent Palestinian State in its homeland, having East Jerusalem as its capital,
- Israel's withdrawal from all the occupied Arab territories to the borders of 4 June 1967, including withdrawal from the occupied Syrian Golan and the Shaba Farms of Lebanon,
- the realization of a just, agreed solution to the issue of the Palestinian refugees pursuant to General Assembly resolution 194, one that excludes all forms of Palestinian resettlement that are incompatible with the distinctive situations of the Arab host countries
- and affirms that the commitment to peace is a strategic choice entailing a corresponding Israeli commitment to faithful implementation of the relevant UN resolutions,
- the convening of a UN conference aimed at ridding the Middle East region, including Israel, of weapons of mass destruction, thereby bringing about security and stability in the region, eliminating tension and distrust, and orienting the energies of the States of the region toward comprehensive development and a more secure and prosperous future for their peoples.

Source: Al-Ahram, Cairo, in Arabic, 24 May 2004

---

when the Family Code (Personal Status Act), which met many of the demands of women's movements, was approved by parliamentary consensus.

In Bahrain, the National Committee for Martyrs and Torture Victims began demanding compensation for the families of those killed and tortured by the security forces. It also called for those responsible for human rights violations in Bahrain to be brought to justice. This Committee has managed to collect signatures from 33,000 citizens (Bahrain has a population of 400,000) on a petition demanding the repeal of Decree-Law No. 56, according to which court proceedings cannot be brought against anyone responsible for previous wide-scale human rights violations.

In Tunisia, organizations that the Government does not recognize, or which face harassment or squeezes on funding, nonetheless waged active campaigns. One in particular included seeking a general legislative amnesty for political prisoners. Similarly, students acted in solidarity with political detainees on hunger strike for improved conditions by organizing their own hunger strikes and sit-ins, which were forcibly broken up by security forces. Some student leaders were also expelled from university by the authorities.

In Egypt, Algeria and the Sudan civil society forces and political parties, including banned groups, use what margins of media freedom are available to fight corruption and human rights violations and to call for democracy. Long-established trade union and professional associations continued their defence of freedoms, incurring official harassment; in Egypt, some were placed under surveillance, and attempts were made to incapacitate them or impose government controls. Civil society institutions organized a variety of initiatives, in particular demonstrations against the war in Iraq and in solidarity with the intifada in Palestine. The authorities, however, repressed these initiatives.

In Syria, where a state of emergency is still in effect, dozens of members of associations and organizations assembled in March 2004 in front of the Parliament building on the 41st anniversary of the accession to power of the ruling Ba'th party. They demanded that the state of emergency be lifted and freedoms expanded. Their peaceful demands however, met with a strong response from the authorities, which broke up the demonstration and arrested 30 demonstrators. At the beginning of the year, approximately 700 Syrian intellectuals and activists signed a note to demand greater freedoms and the introduction of political reforms. A group of opposition parties and human rights associations also launched a political reconciliation initiative based on a draft national charter establishing freedom of political action for all.

Stronger grass-roots participation

In all Arab countries that permit party activity, political parties continued their efforts to strengthen grass-roots participation in parliamentary and presidential elections. Such efforts were conducted in the face of numerous official obstacles; in Egypt, for example, the Muslim Brothers organization was refused official permission to constitute itself as a political party, and its members were denied the opportunity to run for election. Activists were detained and voters were restricted. Despite such difficulties, the Muslim Brothers announced an initiative for general reform in Egypt.

In Mauritania, the most prominent candidates for the presidency were arrested and in Algeria one candidate was forbidden to stand for election. In Morocco, some new parties such as the Justice and Development Party, which has moderate Islamist leanings, successfully acquired the legal right to operate openly and won the second largest number of votes in the parliamentary elections.

Towards political reform

In countries where party activity is not officially recognized, political movements continued to press for reform. In Kuwait, political movements and civil society organizations stepped up their calls for political change. Newspapers, which enjoy relatively greater freedom in that country, are a basic forum for the expression of civil and political demands. A campaign was led against a Government proposal to tighten the provisions of the Press and Publications Act and demands increased for amending the Assembly Act, under which it is a criminal of-

Civil society forces and political parties... use what margins of media freedom are available to fight corruption and human rights violations and to call for democracy.

Political parties continued their efforts to strengthen grassroots participation in parliamentary and presidential elections...in the face of numerous obstacles.

fence to convene a group of over 20 persons to discuss any subject. Political forces and civil society institutions continued to call for the rights of women to stand as candidates and vote, as well as for reducing the voting age to 18 years. They also campaigned for the participation by members of the military forces in elections and for measures to address the situation of the stateless Bidun and enable them to study, receive medical treatment, marry, relocate, travel and work. The Kuwait parliament is regarded as an important platform for expressing grassroots demands, monitoring the government and questioning government officials.

At the beginning of 2004, Saudi Arabia witnessed an unprecedented number of civil initiatives that were distinctive insofar as they were relatively acceptable to the government. The year began with a symposium, convened in London by a liberal opposition group, which called for the swift introduction of political and legal reforms.

In January 2003, 104 activists from different regions and with differing intellectual and confessional approaches signed a document, addressed to the Crown Prince and entitled "A vision for the present and future of the homeland". This was followed in April by the presentation of another document, "Partners in the homeland", signed by 450 Shi'ites (men and women). It contained their demands for religious freedoms and civil rights, including measures to tackle discrimination against them.

In June, followers of the Ismaili sect in Najran presented a manifesto entitled "The homeland for all and all for the homeland" to the Crown Prince. The document called for equality among citizens and an end to discrimination against Ismailis. This was followed in September 2003 by the submission of a petition entitled "Defence of the homeland", which criticized acts of violence and called for political openness as a solution to the prevailing crises. Over 100 people, mainly liberals and a number of Islamists from different regions of the Kingdom, signed the text.

In December 2003, a petition signed by 300 women and calling for improvements in the status of women, including guarantees

of their full participation in public life was submitted. Another petition, "Constitutional reform first", was signed by 116 national personalities, both Shi'ite and Sunni, most of them with religious leanings. The petition called for a constitutional monarchy and fundamental political reforms, including elections, control of public funds and reform and independence of the judiciary. In January 2004, after the second round of national dialogue in the holy city of Mecca, the official statement, "All for reform", was declared and signed by some 900 people, mainly liberals, from throughout the Kingdom. The Crown Prince met with a number of delegations to discuss their declarations and proposals. Such progress, however, suffered a setback after the authorities detained a group of reform leaders at the end of March 2004.

In Libya, civil and political movements continue to call for reform through the opposition abroad. At the beginning of 2004, a human rights organization (Watch) was established in London, which is also a base for various Internet publications that monitor developments in Libya.

Towards peace

In countries experiencing civil war, such as Somalia and the Sudan, civil society organisations operating under international and regional sponsorship remain pivotal in driving the peace efforts under way in Kenya. (These efforts have been proceeding for over a year in the case of Somalia and for over 10 years in the case of the Sudan). Significant breakthroughs were achieved in this period. Such organizations have strived to contribute to peace efforts by holding symposiums and workshops, by meeting with and pressuring the leaderships concerned and by expressing through the media and demonstrations their desire to see an urgent end to the state of war. Relief organisations have also started to draw up plans for dealing with the post-war situation, in particular reconstruction, the settlement of displaced persons and migrants and the delivery of immediate services to those in need.

In Palestine, civil society organizations are active in many areas, from resisting occupation and defending human rights to assisting

Saudi Arabia witnessed an unprecedented number of civil initiatives.

The Kuwait parliament is regarded as an important platform for expressing grassroots demands, monitoring the government and questioning government officials.

in relief and humanitarian aid operations and calling for reform.

To conclude, various networks are now springing up in order to promote the different causes pursued by Arab civil organizations, creating links among them and reaping the benefit of their joint resources. Such activities include meetings, such as the Alexandria Conference, which advocated speedy political reform in all Arab countries. In addition, Internet networks and Arab media establishments, including satellite channels and newspapers in the Arab diaspora, now offer wide opportunities for Arab political and civil forces to communicate with one another, publicise their activities and open the way to joint initiatives.

These developments underscore the vitality of civil and political life, energies all the more remarkable because, given the frequent hostility of the authorities, often the simplest public activism, such as providing services to disaster victims or the families of political prisoners, or even undertaking garbage collection, entails risks.

EXTERNAL ATTEMPTS AT CHANGE: THE BROADER MIDDLE EAST INITIATIVE

The US Administration presented to the G8 countries a reform project in the region. The project, initially called "The Greater Middle East Initiative", included a call to reshape the Middle East through economic and social reforms that preserve the security interests of the US and its allies in the region. The initiative called for promoting democracy and good governance, the establishment of a knowledge society and the enhancement of economic opportunities.

After the document was leaked to the newspaper Al-Hayat and its contents published on February 13, 2004, the initiative encountered strong criticism in Arab circles. Its critics said that the initiative did not acknowledge the role of Israeli occupation in impeding freedom and development in the region, and that it was drafted without consulting the Arab world. Moreover, they maintained that it gave Arabs no significant role in deciding their future course.

After reservations on the first draft by Arabs and some European countries the US embarked on consultations with its European allies and some Arab leaders. The result was put forward in an amended project called the "Broader Middle East Initiative", which proposed more limited objectives. It was adopted at the G8 summit in June 2004. Responding to Arab requests, the new initiative acknowledged the importance of resolving the Arab-Israeli conflict and of returning security and peace to Iraq. At the same time, it was reiterated that conflict should not stand in the way of reforms.

The cornerstone of this initiative is the "Future Forum", a consultative mechanism of interested nations under which ministers from both sides meet. Parallel forums for businessmen and NGOs were also to be established. Through these mechanisms, consultations are to be conducted around political reform (moving towards democracy, the rule of law and respect for freedoms and human rights); social and cultural reform (reform and development of education and respect for women's rights and the rights of expression); and economic reform (enhancement of trade and investment opportunities, financial resource mobilization and eradicating corruption).

Although the modified initiative acknowledges that reform should come from within Arab societies and meet the Arab people's aspirations, there remain questions around the effectiveness of its recommendations especially since the ceiling of such recommendations has been lowered and they have been incorporated into existing projects that have not achieved notable results.

Reform initiatives of the kind cited in this section, both those originating in and outside the region, were launched in an international and regional context that often held up progress. As the next section illustrates, that context also affected human development negatively.

THE REGIONAL AND INTERNATIONAL CONTEXT

The continued occupation of the Palestinian territories by Israel, the US-led occupation of Iraq and the escalation of terrorism had an adverse influence on prospects for Arab human

Various networks are now springing up to promote the different causes pursued by Arab civil organizations.

The simplest public activism…entails risks.

Occupation is the negation of freedom and the right to self-determination.

The protracted conflict in the occupied Palestinian territories has resulted in escalating human and economic losses to both sides, albeit disproportionately.

development.

The international human rights system condemns foreign occupation as a violation of a people's right to freedom. Freedom lies at the heart of the concept of human development. Occupation is the negation of freedom and the right to self-determination, and thus obstructs human development. This can be seen particularly in Palestine where occupation has given rise to significant violations of fundamental human rights, while eroding people's essential capabilities, frustrating the efficient use of those capabilities and cutting short many opportunities for human development.

The practices of occupation forces, particularly in Palestine, amounted to human development reversals for Arabs as the region experienced setbacks because opportunities for peace and security were not grasped.

Such practices sapped the struggle for freedom and good governance in Arab countries in several ways. They provided Arab regimes with pretexts to halt or postpone the process of democratization, citing external threats. They forced Arab reformers to focus their struggle on resisting occupation, leaving less space on their agendas for democratic reforms. And they strengthened extremist groups as violent as the occupiers, hence further narrowing opportunities to achieve greater freedom in the Arab public sphere and stifling emerging reform initiatives.

ISRAELI OCCUPATION OF PALESTINE CONTINUES TO CONSTRAIN HUMAN DEVELOPMENT AND FREEDOM

The protracted conflict in the occupied Palestinian territories has resulted in escalating human and economic losses to both sides, albeit disproportionately. However, since the scope of this Report is confined to Arab human development, this section naturally focuses on the impact of occupation on Arab development.

In the period under review, the UN Commission on Human Rights (Round 60, March 2004, Annex 2) condemned Israel's occupation of Palestine as a crime against humanity and a flagrant violation of human rights. The occupation resulted in the following:

Violations of the right to life

In 2003 and in early 2004, Israeli forces stepped up their raids and incursions into, and re-occupation of cities and villages in the West Bank and Gaza, inflicting significant human and material devastation.

Between May 2003 and end-June 2004, a total of 768 Palestinians were killed and 4,064 injured (Palestinian Red Crescent Society website, www.palestinercs.org, September 2004). 22.7 per cent of Palestinians killed during that period were children under 18 (B'Tselem website, www.btselem.org, September 2004). In the same period 189 Israelis were killed, 8.9 per cent of them children. The majority of Israeli civilians were killed when Palestinians blew themselves up in crowded locations inside Israel. It goes without saying that any loss of innocent life is unconscionable and unacceptable.

Actions of the Israeli Occupation army against civilians, particularly in Rafah, received widespread condemnation. The Security Council condemned the Israeli operations (SC resolution 1544, 19 May 2004) with 14 out of 15 members voting in favour and the US abstaining. Israeli citizens also protested against

---

BOX 2

The Arab people's views on the importance of the Palestinian question

A field study into Arab values, beliefs and concerns found that among issues that people in seven Arab countries considered of the greatest importance in the region, the Palestinian question was rated at between 69% and 97%. Four countries (Jordan, Egypt, Morocco and Saudi Arabia) said that it was among the top four priority issues. Both Morocco and Saudi Arabia said it was the most important issue.

(Source: Zogby, 2002, 34)

---

[1]For example, Avraham Burg, the former Speaker of the Knesset and current Member representing the Labour Party: "Israel's Failed Society Collapses, Zionism's End?", International Herald Tribune, Washington DC, September 2003.
Keren Yedaya, film director, on the occasion of receiving the Camera d'Or at the 2004 Cannes Film Festival: "I come from Israel and we are responsible for the slavery of three million Palestinians. Please, there are many people in Israel who are fighting this occupation. Help them. Help the Palestinians," (Agence France Presse, 1 June 2004).

these actions[1] while some members of the Israeli Army refused to serve in the Occupied Territories and to wear their military medals.[2]

Between September 2000 and September 2003, assassination operations by Israel escalated causing the deaths of 328 Palestinians. Targeting Palestinian leaders, Israel assassinated Dr. Abdel Aziz al-Rantissi (April 17, 2004) after killing Sheikh Ahmed Yassin, the spiritual leader of the Islamic Resistance Movement (Hamas) on 21 March 2004. Although the US used its veto to prevent the UN Security Council from condemning Israel for the assassination of Sheikh Yassin, the act was widely criticized around the world. It was also condemned by elements of Israeli society.

Violations of human rights and individual and collective freedoms

In the past year, this pattern has intensified reflected in collective punishment, including arbitrary arrest and detention, and repeated restrictive closures. Figures issued by the Palestinian Ministry of Detainees and Ex-Prisoners (July 8, 2004) indicate that 7,400 Palestinians were imprisoned in Israeli jails and camps at the end of June 2004. 470 of those incarcerated were children, of whom 206 spent their 18th birthday in prison. (Source: International Press Centre, July 2004).

Checkpoints and curfews have continued to restrict the free movement of people, services and goods within, to and from Palestine. At the beginning of 2004, an estimated 734 checkpoints were dividing Palestinian territories into enclaves. This forced fragmentation has precipitated a large-scale humanitarian crisis and adversely affected Palestinian economic and social rights.

Israel continued its policy of demolitions, destroying property and land.[3] More than 12,000 homes have been either demolished or damaged in the West Bank since 2000. Between September 2000 and through September 2004, more than 24,000 Palestinians living in the Gaza strip have been made homeless by Israeli house demolitions. In the first nine months of 2004, the Israeli Defence Forces demolished on average 120 residential buildings each month - or four each day.[4] Israel's incursion into Rafah in May 2004 alone left some 4,000 Palestinians homeless after the Israeli army destroyed their homes supposedly to prevent arms smuggling through tunnels.

Forced fragmentation has precipitated a large-scale humanitarian crisis (in Palestine).

BOX 3

Unnoticed Losses

Testimony of Peter Hansen, Commissioner-General of UNRWA
"It is the unfortunate lot of the Palestinians that the loss of their homes to the maws of Israeli military bulldozers or powerful explosive charges is now so commonplace that it fails to make the grade as news. After all, something that happens every day, usually more than once a day, eventually stops being news. But it doesn't stop being terrifying.

Source: International Herald Tribune, 23 June 2003

BOX 4

World Bank President Finds Israel's Conduct Shameful

"Israel's military operations pertaining to the demolitions of thousands of homes in Rafah are reckless, and leaves tens of thousands of people without a roof over their heads ....As a Jew, I am ashamed of this kind of treatment of people".

Source: World Bank Blasts Israel in Wake of Gaza Operations, David Lipkin quoting James D. Wolfensohn, Maariv International, 17 May 2004

Social and economic losses

Nutrition and health conditions have deteriorated in the Occupied Territories since September 2000. The number of anaemic children aged 6-59 months has increased to 37.9%[5]. Palestinian women have been most severely affected with 48% of women aged 15-49 suffering from anaemia.[6] Post-natal health care has also decreased while child birth rates

Israel has demolished 4,000 Palestinian homes in the past three years.

---

[2] "It is an organization that doesn't hesitate to drop bombs on the most densely populated areas in the world." Captain Alon, expressing his embarrassment over belonging to the Israeli Armed Forces, Newsweek.

[3] Amnesty international declared that the repeated practice by the Israeli army of deliberate and wanton destruction of houses and civilian property was a grave violation of international human rights, notably of Articles 33 and 53 of the 4th Geneva Convention, and constituted a "war crime." (Press Release 13 October 2003).

[4] Office for the Coordination of Humanitarian affairs. occupied Palestinian territory. Humanitarian Information Fact Sheet January 2005. www.Humanitarianinfo.org/opt/OCHA

[5] UNICEF, At a glance: occupied Palestinian territory.www.unicef.org/infobycountry/opt_1535.html.

[6] UNDP: Millennium Development Goals Report - Palestine.2002

at hospitals have decreased to 67%.[7] In 46 recorded cases, pregnant women who were held up at checkpoints were unable to reach a hospital in time and had to give birth on the spot. More than half the infants born under these conditions (27 of them) died during delivery.[8]

UNICEF notes that at the start of the school year 2002/2003, over 226,000 children and 9,300 teachers were unable to reach their schools. 580 schools have been closed as a result of Israeli curfews, checkpoints and restrictions on movement.[9]

The Palestinian economy has been debili-

tated resulting in increased poverty and unemployment. Currently 58.1% of the population subsists below the poverty line and unemployment is estimated to be 28.6% (UN/OCHA).[10]

Hesitating to carry out necessary institutional reforms and without the means to govern effectively at its disposal, the Palestinian National Authority proved unable to cope with meeting people's needs.

The separation wall undermines human development

Israel continued constructing the separation wall, which does not follow the boundary between the occupied territories and Israel but incorporates Palestinian land. The Wall is thus twice as long as the old boundary and represents an expansionist move by Israel. The building of the wall was condemned in a UN General Assembly resolution adopted in October 2003 by 144 votes (UN General Assembly Resolution ES-10/13). The Secretary-General also issued a statement on 28 November 2003 describing Israel's action as contrary to international law.

The International Court of Justice, in response to a General Assembly request, also issued a decisive advisory opinion on July 9, 2004 on the legal consequences of constructing the Wall. The Court ruled (by a substantial majority of 14 to 1) that the Wall violates international law, declared that it should be removed and called on Israel to compensate Palestinians harmed by the structure.[11]

Subsequently, on July 20, the United Nations General Assembly approved the Court's findings by a substantial majority of 165-6, with 15 abstentions. However, Israel announced that it would proceed with the construction of the Wall.

The first section of the Wall has been built. Completion of the three planned phases will result in the loss of 43.5% of Palestinian land to the Israeli side of the Wall (Palestinian submission to the International Court of Justice, 88-89, in Arabic), as well as the "balkanisa-

---

BOX 5

By Law, This Wall Should Come Down - Findings of the International Court of Justice (ICJ).

The International Court of Justice found, by 14 votes to 1, that:

"The construction of the wall being built by Israel, the occupying Power, in the Occupied Palestinian Territory, including in and around East Jerusalem, and its associated régime, are contrary to international law;"

By 14 votes to 1, the Court stated that:

"Israel is under an obligation to terminate its breaches of international law; it is under an obligation to cease forthwith the works of construction of the wall being built in the Occupied Palestinian Territory, including in and around East Jerusalem, to dismantle forthwith the structure therein situated, and to repeal or render ineffective forthwith all legislative and regulatory acts relating thereto;"

By 14 votes to 1, the Court further ruled that:

"Israel is under an obligation to make reparation for all damage caused by the construction of the wall...;"

On matters of human rights, the ICJ was of the opinion that: "the construction of the wall and its associated régime impede the liberty of movement of the inhabitants of the Occupied Palestinian Territory (with the exception of Israeli citizens and those assimilated thereto) as guaranteed under Article 12, paragraph 1, of the International Covenant on Civil and Political Rights. They also impede the exercise by the persons concerned of the right to work, to health, to education and to an adequate standard of living as proclaimed in the International Covenant on Economic, Social and Cultural Rights and in the United Nations Convention on the Rights of the Child."

In reaching its conclusions, the ICJ considered and set aside Israel's contention that construction of the wall was an act of self-defence and moreover rejected its claim that the structure was an unavoidable necessity: "The Court is not convinced that the construction of the wall along the route chosen was the only means to safeguard the interests of Israel against the peril which it has invoked as justification for that construction."

The Court concluded, 14 to 1, by urging that: "the United Nations, and especially the General Assembly and the Security Council, should consider what further action is required to bring to an end the illegal situation resulting from the construction of the wall and the associated regime."

Source: International Court of Justice, Legal Consequences of the Construction of a Wall in the Occupied Palestinian Territory, Advisory Opinion of 9 July 2004.

---

[7] *ibid*

[8] *ibid*

[9] UNICEF, At a glance: occupied Palestinian territory.www.unicef.org/infobycountry/opt_reallives.html

[10] Office for the Coordination of Humanitarian affairs. occupied Palestinian territory. Humanitarian Information Fact Sheet January 2005. www.Humanitarianinfo.org/opt/OCHA

[11] International Court of Justice, Legal Consequences of the Construction of a Wall in the Occupied Palestinian Territory, Summary of the Advisory Opinion of 9 July 2004.

tion" of the remaining Palestinian territories. When finished the Wall will divide the West Bank into cantons in three separated areas where life in some pockets will be extremely difficult. As box 6 illustrates, the Wall is also slicing through religious facilities and blocking pilgrimage routes, hampering people's right to practice their faith.

Looking to the Future

From a human development perspective, only the end of Israel's occupation of territories occupied in 1967 and the restoration of Palestinians' rights, formost among which is the right to self-determination, will bring about that lasting peace the absence of which so far has contributed to frustrating human development in the region.

THE IMPACT OF THE OCCUPATION OF IRAQ ON HUMAN DEVELOPMENT

As a result of the invasion of their country, the Iraqi people have emerged from the grip of a despotic regime that violated their basic rights and freedoms, only to fall under a foreign occupation that increased human suffering in the following ways:

Absence of security and violations of the right to life

Under occupation, the security of Iraqi citizens deteriorated, and their lives came under further threat. The end of major combat operations in May 2003 did not signal an end to the killing of Iraqi civilians. According to Amnesty International, at least 10,000 people were killed[12] between the start of the military intervention and March 2004. (Amnesty International, 18 March, 2004).

The largest number of victims fell during search-and-arrest operations, as a result of shootings at demonstrators, or at road-blocks

---

BOX 6

Israel's Restrictions on Churches in the Holy Land

Christian churches in the Holy Land are facing an unprecedented crisis that some say is jeopardizing their future, including their capacity to maintain the faith's holy sites and charitable institutions and to educate clergy.

The Israeli government has failed to renew visas or residence permits for hundreds of religious workers, and has begun sending tax bills to charitable groups that have long had tax-exempt status, some since the Ottoman Empire. At the same time the separation wall being built in Jerusalem and on the West Bank is slicing through religious facilities, in some cases taking land and blocking pilgrimage routes.

"All indications point to the fact that the church is slowly but surely being strangled," said an official at the Latin Patriarchate.

"The most difficult situation in living memory for the Church in the Holy Land", according to Bishop Wilton Gregory, president of the US Conference of Catholic Bishops in a letter he sent to President Bush.

"In the Catholic world there is a growing view that Israel has deliberately framed a policy to hurt the Church", the Rev. David Jaeger, representative of the Holy See told the Israeli newspaper Ha'aretz.

"It's hard to accept that it's a purely bureaucratic problem...renewing a visa used to take only half a day. They even are threatening to expel a sister who is 92 years old and has lived here for more than 50 years, and another who is 82", stated the Rev. Robert Fortin, a Catholic official.

Source: Christian Science Monitor, 4 May 2004.

and checkpoints and through the shelling of residential areas.

The occupying powers failed to meet their obligations under the Geneva Conventions to provide security to citizens. Iraq witnessed an unprecedented loss of internal security, with killings and acts of terrorism in most parts of the country, including a series of explosions during the religious celebrations of Ashoura and targeting some churches in Iraq, possibly intended to trigger ethnic and religious strife in the country. There were also attacks on religious leaders and imams of mosques. Other victims have included a number of nuclear scientists, outstanding scientific experts, university professors, judges, doctors and others of notable achievement in the arts and literature (Arab Organization for Human Rights). A survey conducted by a British organization showed that three-quarters of Iraqis in the Middle and the South do not feel safe (Oxford Research International, 2004).[13]

International organizations were not

The Iraqi people have emerged from the grip of a despotic regime that violated their basic rights only to fall under a foreign occupation that increased human suffering.

---

[12] An updated estimate of Iraqi casualties since the 2003 invasion, published after this Part was completed, puts the figures much higher. The study is based on a cluster sample survey covering Iraqi governorates, where the numbers, causes and circumstances of death were compared during the period of 14.6 months before the invasion, and 17.8 months after it. The study concluded that the death toll associated with the invasion and the violence accompanying occupation is about 100,000 Iraqis. See Roberts, L. et al.,"Mortality before and after the 2003 invasion of Iraq: cluster sample survey", The Lancet, vol. 364, pages 1857-1864, November 20,2004.

[13] Oxford Research International, National Surveys of Iraq, Oxford, 2004.

spared. The explosion at UN headquarters in Baghdad on 19 August 2003 killed 22 people including the Special Representative of the UN Secretary-General, Sergio Vieira de Mello. Another explosion took place at the International Committee of the Red Cross (ICRC) central office in Baghdad on 27 November 2003. A number of Arab and foreign civilians also fell prey to terrorist attacks, some savagely beheaded.

The right to freedom

Thousands of Iraqis have been imprisoned since the occupation began. The BBC reported on April 2004 that, according to the United Kingdom authorities, US and UK forces were holding more than 5,300 Iraqi prisoners. A large proportion of detainees were civilians who were arrested in the course of search operations and raids. As a rule, these persons were not told what the charges against them were, and were not held under any particular provision of the law. An ICRC report revealed, on the basis of information obtained from Coalition intelligence officials, that 70% – 90% of these detainees had been arrested in error in the course of night raids (ICRC report, February 2004).

The spread of chaos in the country also undermined Iraqis' security and freedom. Abductions and disappearances became commonplace. Some incidents involved kidnappings for ransom, others were acts of revenge, but the worst concerned political operations aimed at killing or removing intellectuals and scientists (Arab Human Rights Organisation).

Women suffered the most. They were, and still remain, at risk of abduction and rape by professional gangs. In a permanent state of fear, they avoided leaving their homes and families were reluctant to send their daughters to school (*ibid.*). In some cases, coalition soldiers also sexually abused female prisoners (*Taguba Report*).

Nonetheless, the situation did not prevent the revival of civil society. Numerous civil society institutions and more than 200 political parties representing a variety of orientations had been established, and 38 newspapers were in circulation by end-2003. Despite

this broader scope for freedom of the media, efforts to suppress views opposed to the occupation continued. Examples included a two-week ban by the Governing Council on the Al-Arabiyya and Al-Jazeera networks, and an order by the US-led authorities in March 2004 closing Al-Hawzah, the newspaper of the Shiite leader, Muqtada al-Sadr (news.bbc.co.uk). The interim Iraqi government has since lifted the ban on Al-Arabiya and Al-Hawza but not on Al-Jazeera.

Mis-treatment of prisoners of war and detainees

Towards the end of April 2004 the media published photographs depicting the inhumane and immoral treatment of Iraqi prisoners in the Abu Ghraib Prison under the US military. Many victims were civilians not charged with any offence. The exposé was shortly followed by reports of abuses by British troops. Such mistreatment is a clear breach of the Geneva Conventions. While the American-British Coalition leaders condemned the violations, they also claimed initially that they were isolated individual cases rather than the result of a deliberate policy or of a systemic problem.

However, Amnesty International reported that these were not isolated cases and that it had received numerous similar reports of torture and other ill-treatment of Iraqi prisoners by Coalition forces. The organization called for an independent and impartial investigation of these incidents (30 April 2004). An internal US army investigation report prepared by Major-General Antonio Taguba, in February 2004, which was leaked to the media, stated that such violations were part of an established, systematic pattern (The Antonio Taguba Report, The New Yorker, 4 April 2004). The International Committee of the Red Cross disclosed that it had reached similar conclusions and had made them available to the Coalition Forces. The ICRC noted that since the beginning of the conflict, it had "regularly brought its concerns to the attention of the Coalition Forces…[but] allegations of ill-treatment continued…and thus suggested that the use of ill-treatment …went beyond exceptional cases and might be considered as a practice tolerated by the Coalition Forces" (ICRC report, February 2004).

Women suffered the most.

Many victims were civilians not charged with any offence.

The revelation that crimes of torture were being committed in Iraqi prisons brought wide condemnation internationally and from within the US itself. Voices in the American media demanded that those responsible be called to account. The American Congress opened a series of investigations into the matter. It is noteworthy that the US media were the first to broadcast the photographs of violations in Abu Ghraib Prison.

Dismantling the Iraqi State structure

The dismantling of the structure of the State of Iraq, which was more than 80 years old, was one of the negative results of the occupation.

The first signals of this policy came when Coalition forces stood by as governmental institutions (with some exceptions including the Ministry of Petroleum) were looted and destroyed, followed by the disbanding of the Iraqi Army. The destruction of the infrastructure, material resources and documents of the various Ministries was accompanied by the disruption of functional structures in the obscure situation created by "de-Ba'thification" operations.

After dismantling the old state, the US-led authorities made little progress in building a new one. Despite the optimistic reports published by the Occupation forces and the US Administration their performance continued to be deficient. The occupation forces struggled to bring various services, such as electricity, water and telephones, back to their pre-war levels. As of end - October, 2004, out of the US$ 18.4 billion appropriated for Iraq's reconstruction by the US Congress, an estimated US$ 1.3 billion had been spent - only about 7 percent.[14]

Looking to the future

By midyear, with the help of the Special Adviser of the UN Secretary General, an interim Government had been appointed in preparation for holding elections and drafting a permanent constitution. Under an annex to the Law on the Administration of the Iraqi State, the interim Government is prohibited

> BOX 7
>
> ### Conclusion of the Taguba Report
>
> Several US Army Soldiers have committed egregious acts and grave breaches of international law at Abu Ghraib/BCCF and Camp Bucca, Iraq. Furthermore, key senior leaders failed to comply with established regulations, policies, and command directives in preventing detainee abuses at Abu Ghraib (BCCF) and at Camp Bucca during the period August 2003 to February 2004.
>
> Source: Report by Major-General Taguba, p 50

from undertaking any actions that will affect the future of Iraq after the specified interim period. The formal transfer of power to the interim government took place on 28 June 2004.

Iraq's future is still beset by dangers. From the standpoint of human development, freedom and good governance, it is difficult to see how lasting benefits can accrue from the grave events that have occurred in the country and the massive damage it has sustained after invasion and occupation, unless its territorial integrity is preserved and sovereignty fully resides with the Iraqi people under a system of good governance, and unless Iraq is unified on a firm basis of common citizenship and freedom.

THE ESCALATION OF TERRORISM

Arab countries have been subjected to a number of serious terrorist attacks, most notably bombings in Saudi Arabia, Morocco and Iraq. Attacks have also occurred in major neighbouring states: in Turkey, whose Prime Minister took a strong position in support of Arab human rights (May 2004), condemning violations, and in Spain, which can play an important role as a natural bridge linking Arab countries with Europe.

These are crimes that constitute flagrant, indiscriminate violations of the human rights of their victims, including such fundamental rights as the right to life and to physical and psychological health. These unacceptable acts affect children, women and old people who are innocent by any decent human standards, or any religious teaching.

In addition to the gross human costs, these events have undoubtedly undermined human welfare and economic activity especially in those Arab countries that depend on tourism

After dismantling the old state, the US-led authorities made little progress in building a new one.

These unacceptable acts (of terrorism) affect children, women and old people who are innocent by any decent human standards or any religious teaching.

---

[14] Third Quarterly Report to Congress: Appendix J, US Department of Defence Status Report on Iraq, October 30, 2004, cited in "Progress or Peril -Measuring Iraq's Reconstruction", Centre for Strategic and International Studies, December, 2004.

and foreign investment. They have also had negative impacts on internal stability in the region, on neighbouring countries and on the world as a whole.

Quality Assessment of Primary and Middle Education in Mathematics and Science (TIMSS 2003) in the Arab World RAB01/005/A/01/31

In the context of monitoring the quality of education and improvement of educational achievement, nine Arab countries participated in the project entitled: Trends in International Mathematics and Science Study (TIMSS 2003); these countries included Jordan, Bahrain, Tunis, Syria, Palestine, Lebanon, Egypt, Morocco and Yemen.

The United Nations Development Programme supported the participation of Syria, Palestine, Lebanon, Egypt and Yemen, in addition to the provision of coordination work amongst all Arab participants.

TIMSS 2003 is considered the largest international comparative and assessment study aimed at measuring fourth and eighth grade student achievement in Mathematics and Science in almost fifty countries. The 'Study' had also compiled extensive data relevant to the changes affecting student, teacher and school, with regards to their achievement in the afore mentioned disciplines.

The average performance in mathematics, for the participating eighth grade Arab students reached 392 in comparison to a 467 international average scale score. Whereas the average Arab student performance in science reached 416 in comparison to a 474 international average scale score.

It is noteworthy to mention that Lebanon ranked first in mathematics among the participating Arab countries, achieving an average scale score of 433; this being lower than the international average scale score in Mathematics. On the other hand, Jordan outperformed Arab participating countries in science achieving an average scale score of 475; only one score higher than the international average scale score.

These results indicate a need for undertaking serious developmental efforts in the Arab countries to improve the level of student achievement in mathematics and science, instruments for development and progress in this era.

"Development" of the University of the United Arab Emirates

The University of the United Arab Emirates—its Faculty of Humanities in particular—has undergone a radical restructuring in the course of the past year, with departments being abolished and new fields of specialisation added. The Departments of Islamic Studies, English Language and Literature and French Language and Literature have been merged into a single programme, the Departments of Political Science and Geography have been merged into a Political Science, Government and Cultural Studies Unit, and the Departments of Arabic Language and Literature, History and Heritage have been combined. Furthermore, the language of instruction has been changed from Arabic to English (although in the case of a very few subjects, faculty members may be allowed

to give their courses in Arabic, provided they are able to show adequate cause why that is necessary).

Certainly proficiency in English or other foreign languages is essential, as are computer skills; educational plans and programmes must, of course, take labour market requirements into account. But this should not lead to neglecting the Arabic language altogether, or discarding some fields of specialisation on the grounds that there is no market demand for them. Human knowledge is multifaceted; its various aspects interact with each other, and all of them contribute to the expansion of people's mental horizons, flexibility, creativity, and ability to contribute effectively to their society's development.

ADDRESSING THE THREE DEFICITS: GAINS AND SETBACKS

During the period in review some Arab countries took steps to deal with their capability gaps in knowledge acquisition, freedom and good governance and women's empowerment, the three cardinal deficits of the region identified in the first AHDR. However, progress was uneven in the area of freedoms particularly, where many countries experienced setbacks. The following section reviews these developments.

KNOWLEDGE ACQUISITION

There were a number of positive developments in the field of education, the most important of which was increased attention to quality issues at the different levels of education.

In an unprecedented development, 9 Arab states have now participated in an international study designed to evaluate students' performance in science and mathematics in basic education. UNDP's Regional Bureau for Arab States is enabling five of these countries to participate in the study. At the tertiary level, the Union of Arab Universities, targeting the advancement of higher education establishments, decided to set up an independent institution to evaluate the quality of higher education, in cooperation with the Regional Bureau for Arab States,

The Regional Bureau for Arab States plans to extend its programmes for assessing of the quality of higher education in Arab countries to two new fields, namely law and education.

In Egypt, the Ministry of Education is co-operating with UNICEF, civil associations and teachers to draw on local and international experience to set down national standards for excellence. The project covers various aspects of the educational process (efficacy of the teacher and school, societal participation, education outputs, etc) at all stages of pre-university education. This is a major step towards improving the quality of education, and has attracted international interest with a view to replicating the example in the rest of the region.

In Bahrain, a National Conference on Education was held in 2003 to produce a comprehensive approach to unifying secondary-level

BOX 10

An Assessment of Business Administration Programmes in Arab Universities

A second cycle of academic reviews, focused on the evaluation of the quality of Business Administration education, was completed this spring by the Regional Bureau for Arab States, as part of its ongoing project for enhancing the quality of education in Arab universities. The year long process was carried out with the participation of 17 Arab universities (14 public, 3 private) from 11 countries (Algeria, Bahrain, Egypt, Jordan, Lebanon, Morocco, Oman, Palestine, Sudan, Syria and Yemen). The first review cycle was completed last spring and resulted in the evaluation of Computer Science programmes in 15 Arab universities (AHDR 2003, 57).

The new reviews were completed on schedule for all participating programmes with the exception of that at Al-Azhar University, Gaza. This was because the external review team was unable to enter the city after the occupation army suddenly closed off its entry. As in the first cycle, the review was carried out in three stages (training, internal evaluation and external evaluation and reporting).

The results show that the academic standards of only two of the 16 programmes were judged to be "Good", that four were found to be "Unsatisfactory" and the remaining ten "Satisfactory". The reviews also showed that the internal mechanisms for quality assurance and enhancement were "Unsatisfactory" in 6 of the programmes, "Satisfactory" in 9 and "Good" in one. All this indicates that, in general, the universities need to raise per-

formance in order to achieve the levels of excellence that are normally expected from modern universities.

The picture looks somewhat better with regard to two of three aspects that characterise the learning opportunities that the programmes provide to their students, namely, Methods of Learning & Teaching and Student Progression: one fourth of the programmes were graded as "Good" in each case. But in respect of the third aspect within the same category, which is concerned with the standards of learning resources and facilities, only one programme was graded as "Good", six as "Unsatisfactory" and the remaining 9 as "Satisfactory". These ratings substantiate the reviewers' general conclusion that, while academic staff were, in the majority of cases, well qualified academically and diligent in performing their duties, the standards of learning resources available, including the numbers of available academic staff, were unsatisfactory in many cases and below the levels required for achieving excellence, in most of them.

Detailed analyses of the various strengths and weaknesses identified by the reviewers under each aspect of review and programme are presented in a final review report sent, in confidence, to each university.

The picture is further illustrated by a number of derived indicators that quantify some of the detailed aspects of each review. Thus, with regard to learning resources, the number of available academic staff was

not found to be "Good" in any of the programmes. Library, Internet and PC facilities were "Good" in about one fourth of the cases but "Unsatisfactory" in about half, a high ratio by any standards. The indicators also reveal major weaknesses with regard to the following specific academic aspects of the programmes

• Practical inputs to the curriculum and work placement experiences
• Support for independent learning and internship programmes
• Promotion of critical modes of thinking as opposed to didactic methods of teaching.
• Effective use of the "graduation project"
• Internal and external moderation of examinations and other student assessments

The review results clearly show that the situation varies between universities. A small minority of the participating group seems to have reached a good level of development while a larger group is moving in that direction. This is evidenced by a number of emerging good practices that were noted with satisfaction. These include: breadth of curriculum coverage, enhanced practical inputs to teaching, improved methods of student assessment, increased focus on graduation projects. Moreover, the reviewers strongly commended what they identified as a clear determination by the majority of participating universities and academics to meet the challenges of academic evaluation and to make full use of its outcomes to raise the quality of their programmes.

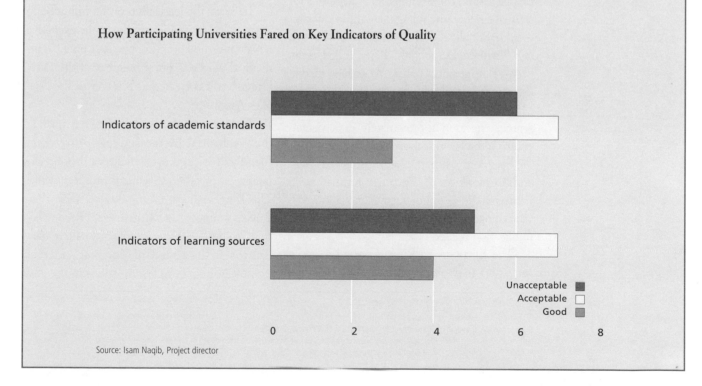

How Participating Universities Fared on Key Indicators of Quality

Source: Isam Naqib, Project director

academic programmes in order to bring them into line with the needs and requirements of society, while responding to the demands of the contemporary age. A related goal is to upgrade students' skills and capacities.

Kuwait is implementing a special programme to deal with why pupils drop out of, or fail at school and to develop assessment and evaluation methodologies.

Tunisia announced an initiative for addressing the causes of various forms of student failure and for achieving higher progress and success rates.

FREEDOM AND GOVERNANCE

Signs of political openness

Some Arab governments have begun to open themselves cautiously and selectively to opposition forces.

Some Arab governments have begun to open themselves cautiously and selectively to opposition forces and have started expanding the public sphere:

In Egypt, at the closing meeting of the first annual conference of the ruling party on 28 September 2003, the President of the Republic announced a number of democratic reforms that had been submitted by the party's Policy Committee. The reforms include the abolition of some military decrees promulgated under the Emergency Law[15], more freedom for political parties and trade unions, and safeguards for women's rights (including the right to transmit their nationality to their children). The ruling National Democratic Party called upon licensed opposition parties to engage in dialogue on political reform.

In the autumn of 2003 the Egyptian Government released approximately 1,000 detainees from the Islamist movement.

President Mubarak, addressing the General Conference of Egyptian Journalists in February 2004, announced a move towards abolishing imprisonment as a punishment for publication-related offences.[16]

The Egyptian Parliament passed a law in June 2003 to abolish state security courts, and

in January 2004 the formation of the National Council for Human Rights was announced.

In Oman, legislative elections took place in October 2003. 509 candidates competed for 83 seats. Fifteen of them were women. The right to vote was extended to those 21 years of age and above. As a result, the number of citizens eligible to vote rose to 822,000 compared to 114,000 in the year 2000 elections. 262,000 citizens registered as voters, of whom 95,000 were women. 74% of registered voters actually participated and voted in the elections. Two women who were members of the previous consultative council won seats in the election.

In Saudi Arabia, the intention to conduct municipal elections at the end of 2004 was announced and a journalists' association and a national commission for human rights were established. Scenes from sessions of the country's Consultative Council were shown on television for the first time. The founding of the "King Abd Al-Aziz Centre for National Dialogue" was also announced.

In Qatar, a new Constitution to take effect in June 2005 was promulgated after a referendum, and the country's first National Committee on Human Rights was established.

In Bahrain, a new Charter for "political" associations was issued.

In Syria, the leadership of the ruling Ba'th Party called for the separation of the executive power and the Party. For the first time, an individual who was not a member of the Party leadership was elected as Speaker of the People's Assembly.

In Morocco, the legal system was qualitatively enhanced by the addition of freedom-friendly provisions in the fields of: labour, the family, electoral arrangements and the media. The King granted an amnesty to more than 1,000 detainees. A "Justice and Reconciliation" commission was established with a mandate to heal the wounds of Moroccan society as a result of human rights violations in the past

---

[15] But not an end to the state of emergency itself.

[16] The next day, however, an opposition journalist reported that his case had been referred to the jurisdiction of the criminal courts under the provisions of the law prescribing imprisonment for journalists. It subsequently appeared that sentences of imprisonment had not been abolished altogether: the President of the People's Assembly announced that they would continue to be imposed in cases of "crimes" involving disrespect for the President of the Republic, military matters, espionage, and slander.

and 4,500 victims were given compensation. The "Special Court of Justice" was abolished.

In Algeria, house arrest on the leader of the Islamic Salvation Front was lifted. He and his Deputy remain unable to exercise political and civil rights. In the April 2004 presidential elections the incumbent in office contested five other candidates for the first time, and was elected by an overwhelming majority.

Indications of a regression in popular participation

In one Arab country, fewer men and women stood as candidates for election to the National Assembly.

In another, a low turnout marred the local elections in September 2003. Only 5% of the candidates were women, even though 35 women had won seats in the Parliamentary elections held approximately two years earlier.

In a third, 15 members of the People's Assembly were found ineligible to take their seats for having evaded their compulsory military service. In the view of some legal experts, by-elections that had been held in contravention of a Supreme Administrative Court ruling raised questions about the eligibility, not only of the winning candidates, but of the entire Assembly.

Freedoms Constrained

Obvious human rights violations have contin-.ued, notably in cases involving human rights activists in Arab countries. We have space here to mention only a few examples:

In one Arab country, the authorities detained 30 people demonstrating in support of abolishing the State of Emergency. Many people were detained for political reasons, among them at least 20 Kurds who were arrested during a peaceful demonstration after their return from exile. Hundreds of political prisoners, notably Islamists, are still in jail including prisoners of conscience while others, including some non-nationals, are missing.

In another country, on World Press Freedom Day 2003, the National Committee for the Defence of Freedom of Expression issued a statement condemning what it termed the muzzling of freedom of expression, the tyranny of uniformity of thought, the difficulties of journalists in gaining access to sources of information and the harassment they experienced while seeking to exercise their right to free speech. In addition, a number of human rights activists and prisoners of conscience embarked on a hunger strike in protest against harsh and degrading treatment by the authorities and the torturing of inmates in prison.

Human rights activists continue to report cases of torture and mistreatment at detention centres (including Ministries of the Interior). Since February 2004, 20 cases of detention have been recorded in the south of the country. The detainees were accused of surfing Islamic sites on the Internet. They were held at the Ministry of the Interior and prevented from contacting any one outside.

Defenders of human rights are frequently victims of harassment and threats. They share this with ex-political prisoners some of whom are not allowed to work or to obtain a health insurance card.

There are continuous accusations of torture and reports of unhealthy and inhumane circumstances in prisons. An Islamist died on March 22 after he was denied medical attention.

In a third country the People's Assembly decided in February 2003 that the emergency laws should remain in force for a further period of three years beginning in June of the same year. In 2003, the Islamic Research Council recommended that a book entitled Al-Khitab wa al-Ta'wil [preaching and interpretation] could not be sold in the country, on the grounds that it attacked "two fundamental tenets of the Islamic faith", namely the unity of God and preservation of the Qur'an. The book in question, which had been published in another Arab state, contains a prominent thinker's doctoral dissertation. In 2004, a novel by a famous writer, first printed 20 years ago, was recommended for confiscation.

A district regional Public Prosecution Office ordered the detention of the 51 year-old manager of a local contracting firm, with no history of political activism, on charges of "inciting hatred and disrespect for the Government". The man, who was released soon

Obvious human rights violations have continued, notably in cases involving human rights activists in Arab countries.

Human rights activists continue to report cases of torture and mistreatment at detention centres.

afterwards, had confessed to scrawling the words "No to rule by inheritance" on walls. While approximately 1,000 Islamists accused in the "Islamic Jihad" case have been released, a number of others remain behind bars even though they have served their sentences. Some of them are either seriously or chronically ill.

In one Mashriq country, 15 women were reported killed by family members in honour crimes. Meanwhile, political cases continue to be seen by the state security court whose laws are not in harmony with international standards.

In one Gulf country, authorities booked 24 citizens on criminal charges for collecting signatures on a political letter calling for constitutional changes that give wider authority to the elected parliament. The jailed are accused of "calling for changes in the political regime, inciting hatred and attempting to threaten national security". Three were released without being formally charged. In other cases, some journalists received prison sentences because they were connected with articles published in the foreign press.

In one Arab North African country, in July 2003, the National Union of Journalists launched a campaign against the imprisonment of journalists sentenced under the Anti-Terrorism Law and called for the release of all those detained.

In another Gulf country, a number of writers and intellectuals calling for reform were detained, apparently in a deliberately demeaning manner (a university professor was handcuffed in front of his students at the university) and some were forbidden to travel abroad. A journalist who criticized the arrests was himself detained.

In a country under occupation, a state of emergency was decreed and an emergency Government formed in October 2003.

In another Arab North African country, the former Prime Minister and Secretary of the former governing party was placed under house arrest.

Freedom of civil society organizations

In one country, several months after the new Law on Associations had come into force, civil society leaders complained of the arbitrary be-

haviour of the administrative body established under that law in refusing to approve new grassroots institutions. It had, for example, turned down an application from a centre for housing rights, claiming that the application contravened article 11 of the law. That article provides that "the establishment of secret associations, or associations the aims of which include the formation of military or paramilitary organizations or which present a threat to national unity, public order or morality or advocate discrimination among citizens, shall be prohibited."

Early in 2004, Organizations working in the area of human rights protested the arbitrary handling of the issue of foreign funding for Egyptian associations by the Ministry responsible for administering the Law on Associations.

In another country, the authorities proceeded to restrict voluntary and charitable work, in particular the collection of donations, influenced by the US Administration.

Restrictions on the media

According to the 2004 report published by Reporters sans frontières, the Middle East was the region that enjoyed the least press freedom in the world that year, with few independent media outlets. In a number of countries correspondents exercised strict self-censorship. The report added that the war in Iraq and the continuing Israeli/Palestinian conflict had placed both the freedom and safety of the media at risk. As many as 14 journalists were killed during 2003, 12 in Iraq, five of them at the hands of US-led occupation forces. Two correspondent were killed by the Israeli occupation forces in Palestine.

Foreign agencies have also participated in restricting Arab media freedoms. In Spain, a reporter for Al-Jazeera, Taysir Alouni, was charged by the government with being an al-Qa'ida member and arrested. The US Administration expressed dissatisfaction with Arab satellite TV channels, particularly Al-Jazeera, and informed the Qatari government of its views.

Some journalists received prison sentences because they were connected with articles published in the foreign press.

(In 2004), the Middle East was the region that enjoyed the least press freedom in the world.

Foreign agencies have also participated in restricting media freedoms in the Arab world.

Rights of subgroups: Darfur

In Darfur, western Sudan, thousands of civilians were killed or injured, and women subjected to rape, in attacks by the Janjaweed militia, reportedly with government support. Entire villages were laid waste, including through indiscriminate aerial bombing, forcing hundreds of thousands to abandon their homes and livelihoods, with around 120,000 fleeing to Chad (Amnesty International website, 29 June 2004). Though a ceasefire agreement was signed in April 2004, it continues to be violated by both the Government and the rebels, with the humanitarian toll continuing to mount.

In July 2004, the Security Council passed a resolution (Resolution 1556 of 30 July 2004) calling on the Government of Sudan to, inter alia, fulfil its commitments regarding: the facilitation of humanitarian access and assistance; the advancement of an independent investigation with the UN on violations of human rights and international humanitarian law; the establishment of credible security conditions for the protection of civilians; the resumption of political talks with the dissident groups; the disarmament of the Janjaweed militias; and the prosecution of Janjaweed leaders and their associates who have incited and carried out human rights violations. The resolution also urged the rebel groups to respect the cease-fire, end the violence immediately, engage in peace talks without preconditions and act in a positive and constructive manner to end the conflict. Finally, it called on the international community to support the efforts of the African Union (AU) for the deployment of international monitors and to provide additional assistance to mitigate the humanitarian catastrophe.

The Government has fulfilled its commitment to provide unimpeded access to the humanitarian community, which has allowed the latter to increase its level of assistance, and it has deployed additional security forces in camps for the protection of internally displaced persons. But at the time of writing, the Government had not fully complied with the requirement of disarming the militias. Furthermore it had taken minimal steps to prosecute the perpetrators of humanitarian law violations.

As these latter violations continued, conflict and human suffering increased despite the cease-fire agreement and the interventions of the international community. There remains an urgent need to stop the inflow of arms to the region and to arrive at a political solution to the problem. A massive aid effort is also required to assist the refugees in Chad and over one million internally displaced people within Darfur.

Protest by intellectuals

In one Arab country, a hotly contested election for seats on the executive of the journalists' union ended with the defeat of the government-sponsored candidate, for the first time in many years, and victory for an opposition candidate. This outcome was widely seen as an important development in the struggle for control of one of the country's leading professional associations.

At the Arab Novelists' Assembly organized by the Ministry of Culture, the novelist Sonallah Ibrahim refused to accept the Novelist of the Year award on the grounds that the Government offering it "did not have, in my view, the credibility to do so." He read a statement listing his reasons for declining the award and spoke of the deteriorating Arab situation. Ibrahim's gesture was widely acclaimed in the Arab world, although some criticised it, arguing that literature should not be mixed up with politics.

In January 2004, another Arab writer Ahmed Bouzfour, followed Ibrahim's example by turning down an award offered by the Government, citing various political, economic and cultural reasons. This gesture (Bouzfour's "sigh" [zefrat Bouzfour], as some called it) was another expression of the growing dissatisfaction among Arab intellectuals about the state of human rights.

THE EMPOWERMENT OF WOMEN

In Morocco, the governing authorities introduced wide-ranging reforms of the family law in response to demands by the women's movement to safeguard women's rights, notably with

Conflict and human suffering increased (in Darfur) despite the cease-fire agreement and interventions of the international community.

respect to marriage, divorce and childcare.

One of the most important provisions of the new family code is that it regards women as partners of men in matters relating to the care of the family and associated responsibilities. It also recognizes that they shall not be subject to guardianship upon reaching the age of majority, which the Code sets at the age of 18 years. Eighteen years is also made the minimum lawful age of marriage, and women are free to marry at their own discretion, the permission of a male family member no longer being required. In addition, under the revised Code, husband and wife may conclude an agreement, distinct from their marriage contract, concerning the management and disposal of assets acquired during the marriage.

Women have continued to rise to senior executive positions in Arab countries, and there is steadily broader scope for participation by women in legislative assemblies.

In Kuwait the government referred a draft law to the National Assembly, which would grant women their political rights, including the right to vote and stand as candidates in elections. This was the second time the government had taken such a move, as the Assembly had rejected a similar draft law in 1999.

In Jordan, six women from outside the capital won seats reserved for women at the parliamentary elections held in mid-2003, in the first application of a quota for women in elections of this kind. For the first time, the Cabinet formed early in 2003 included three women Ministers.

In Oman, a woman was appointed Minister of Higher Education, a first in that country. In yet another first, women were allowed to vote in the Shura council elections.

Saudi Arabia announced its own groundbreaking first: in a new move, women will be appointed to the police force under the Ministry of the Interior. 300 prominent citizens, 50 of them women, signed a petition to the Crown Prince requesting political and social reforms "for the sake of the nation". A women's association presented a petition asking for the reform of women's position in society and for guarantees for their full participation in public life.

In Mauritania, Aisha Bint Jeddane became the first woman ever to stand as a candidate (albeit unsuccessfully) for the position of President of the Republic.

In Algeria, Ms. Hanoune ran for the Presidency of the Republic. Ms. Burkan was promoted to the post of President of the Council of State, and Ms. Zermouni was appointed Governor of the province of Tibeze.

In Lebanon, Naila Mouawad offered herself as a candidate for President of the Republic.

In Bahrain, a woman was appointed Minister of Health.

In Tunisia, a woman was appointed Governor of the province of Zaghouane.

In Egypt, a woman was appointed, for the first time, as Mayor of the city of Al-Maragha, in the Sohag Governorate in Upper Egypt, long regarded as one of the most conservative parts of the country. The Minister of the Interior announced that Egyptian women married to non-Egyptians now had the right to transmit Egyptian nationality to their children. The Ministry of the Interior has already started to receive applications for recognition of the Egyptian citizenship of children of Egyptian women married to non-Egyptian men.

However, as a reflection of deeply rooted

Women have continued to rise to senior executive positions in Arab countries.

BOX 11

The Moroccan Family Code

• **Equality**
Husband and wife share responsibility for their family; a wife is no longer legally required to obey her husband; a woman who is of age is her own guardian, instead of being subject to the guardianship of a male family member, and she may exercise her guardianship freely and independently; the minimum age of marriage is 18 years for both men and women.

• **Divorce**
Both men and women possess the right of divorce, and may exercise that right under the supervision of a judge. The principle of divorce by mutual agreement is accepted.

• **Polygamy**
Polygamy requires a judge's authorization and is subject to stringent legal conditions that make it almost impossible in practice; a woman has the right to stipulate in her marriage contract that her husband shall not take other wives; in the absence of such a stipulation, the first wife must be informed of her husband's intent to take another wife, and the prospective second wife must be informed that her intended husband already has a wife. Furthermore, taking a second wife is grounds for divorce for the first wife.

• **Enforcement of the law**
The Family Code assigns a fundamental supporting role to the judiciary in enforcing the law. Inter alia, it states that the Public Prosecutor shall be a party to all legal actions in connection with the provisions of the Code.

• **Rights of children**
A woman is given the possibility of retaining custody of her children, even in the event of her remarrying or moving away from the area where her husband lives. The code also protects a child's right to acknowledgement of paternity in cases where the marriage has not been officially registered.

social factors, women continue to be sparsely represented in the Parliaments of those Arab Gulf countries that allow women to stand as candidates and to vote.

In general, women's accession to high levels of government, though moving in the right direction, will remain inadequate so long as the vast majority of women are not allowed to develop their capabilities and use them in various fields.

CONCLUSION

Careful scrutiny of developments in this period indicates that there has been no significant easing of the human development crisis in the Arab region. Serious human rights violations continue.

Unquestionably, incipient reforms are taking place in more than one of the priority areas identified in this Report, but for the most part those reforms have been embryonic and fragmentary. There is no dispute that some are real and promising but they do not add up to a serious effort to dispel the prevailing environment of repression. Some measures may have been merely cosmetic and superficial with the effect of delaying the advent of meaningful in-depth reform. This is the case especially with respect to good governance.

Finally, the human development crisis in the Arab world has become more acute with respect to self-determination especially with the prospects for a just peace in Palestine receding. As a result, the Arab people still risk being oppressed at home and violated from abroad.

The critical situation of the Arab region today is complex because of the interplay of internal and external factors. The Arab future is overshadowed by the gravity of possible developments.

Yet this series of Reports has repeatedly emphasized that hope abounds in those dynamic social forces in Arab countries that seek a human renaissance in the region. Mobilizing their potential in thought and deed can break through the thickening clouds gathering around their future.

There has been no significant easing of the human development crisis in the Arab region.

Part II

Reinforcing Freedom and Establishing Good Governance

Section 1: Analytical Framework: Freedom, Good Governance and Human Development

This section presents the analytical framework for Part II of the report, devoted to freedom and governance. The section starts with a brief survey of the intellectual basis of the topic that ends in the report's definition of freedom and good governance, and then turns to a discussion of some of the problematic issues of freedom and governance in Arab countries at present.

CHAPTER ONE

The Intellectual Basis and Concept of Freedom and Good Governance

Introduction

This chapter presents the analytical framework underpinning the Report's analysis of freedom and good governance.

The chapter starts by summarizing key postulates of freedom in Western thought. It traces how thinking shifted from stressing the primacy of individual freedom to underlining the harmonization of individual freedom with collective societal arrangements in order to reconcile individual freedom with other higher human goals. The latter formulation is close to the Report's concept of human development. The chapter next examines the place of freedom in Arabic culture, indicating its presence in various schools of thought. Drawing on the features of freedom in both Arabic and Western thinking, the chapter sets out the concept of freedom adopted in the Report and the elements of good governance guaranteeing its realization. This exposition frames the main discussion.

FREEDOM IN WESTERN LIBERAL THOUGHT: FROM INDIVIDUAL FREEDOM TO HUMAN DEVELOPMENT

THE PRIMACY OF INDIVIDUAL LIBERTIES

In Western thought, the Utilitarian philosophers, in particular, searched for a form of government capable of ensuring that those who hold power would not crush or endanger the liberty of those they governed. The solution upon which James Mill settled was "representative government," in which the interests of government and people would be-

---

> BOX 1-1
>
> ### Natural Human Rights
>
> "The end in view of every political association is the preservation of the natural and imprescriptible rights of man. These rights are liberty, property, security and resistance to oppression."
>
> Article II, French Declaration of the Rights of Man and The Citizen, August, 1789 (in French).

---

come congruent through a mechanism of representation by proxy: representatives would be accountable to the people through elections. Thus, the government would be an instrument for securing liberty rather than a source of oppression.

Accordingly, principles of "democracy" were developed, as a means to safeguard the freedom of the majority from oppression by any dominant minority, whether the latter's source of power was might or wealth. The fundamental principle at issue here is "democratic legitimacy," which denotes that the source of societal authority is the will of the majority.

For John Stuart Mill, the goal of freedom is "pursuing our own good in our own way," and this is the most important component of "happiness or human well-being." On this basis, he believed that happiness would accrue only to "someone who was capable of choosing an independent path and who had the public sphere available in which to exercise that capacity," through possessing "faculties of critical judgment and free choice." And thus the democracy that ensures liberty is the most fertile soil for social progress, and also for pursuing the aim of individual happiness.

However, Mill was not confident that democratic society would of its own accord safeguard the freedom of individuals and minorities. Moreover, fearful that the democratic process would subject all aspects of life to control by the ruling authority, thereby instituting "tyranny of the majority," he inquired

The source of societal authority is the will of the majority.

The democracy that ensures liberty is the most fertile soil for social progress.

into what properties were common to activities that would qualify for exemption from government control. His fears were not confined to the regulatory actions of government. They extended to "the government of popular opinion," or unofficial forms of coercion to which those who hold unpopular beliefs or practice unorthodox actions are subjected.

According to Mill, we have the right to discuss, to disagree, to attack, to reject, or even to forcefully condemn an opinion. But we have absolutely no right to obstruct or suppress that opinion, because to do so will destroy "the thin along with the fat" in equal measure. Indeed, to do so constitutes nothing less than collective suicide, both intellectual and moral. For without the right and ability to protest, there can be no justice and no end worth striving for. Without complete freedom of opinion and debate, the truth cannot emerge.

Without complete freedom of opinion and debate, the truth cannot emerge.

<table>
<tr><td colspan="2">BOX 1-2</td></tr>
<tr><td colspan="2">Freedom of opinion as a sacred right</td></tr>
<tr><td>If all mankind minus one were of one opinion, and only one person were of the contrary opinion, mankind would be no</td><td>more justified in silencing that one person than he, if he had the power, would be justified in silencing mankind.</td></tr>
<tr><td colspan="2">Source: Mill, 1978, 16</td></tr>
</table>

And so, in his view, even if we find our selves facing no actual opposition, we should devise arguments against ourselves simply in order to remain in a state of "intellectual fitness."

Thus Mill poses a very strong connection between freedom, especially freedom of thought and debate, creative expression, innovation, and human progress. For him the primary engine of progress is the coupling of "freedom and variety," which leads in turn to individuality and originality. This combination forestalls the mediocrity that necessarily arises when people remain in a state of conformity and compliance. And he made no exception for the issue of freedom itself. In the introduction to *On Liberty*, he proposes that issues of liberty must be presented anew to humanity whenever human conditions change.

Thus it is that we present here our recon-

Issues of liberty must be presented anew to humanity whenever human conditions change.

sideration of freedom with regard to the Arab world at the start of the third millennium.

Mill considered only two justifications for restricting individual liberty valid: to prevent the individual from harming others, and to prevent the individual from violating an obligation toward others, whether by a certain act or through inaction. In relation to the individual, her/his independence is absolute, since "over himself, over his own body and mind, the individual is sovereign" and "the individual is not accountable to society for his actions in so far as these concern the interests of no person but himself". The only exception would be a case of verified, and not merely possible, danger.

INDIVIDUAL FREEDOM AND SOCIETAL REGULATION

Safeguarding liberty, however, does not mean opposing societal organization per se; after all, such organization constitutes one of humankind's most important means of progress. But it certainly implies taking a determined stance against all forms of elite, monopolistic or coercive organization, all of which inhibit new discoveries and innovation. Thus, as long as it is based on voluntary participation in an atmosphere of freedom, the social order remains beneficial and effective (Hayek, 1978, 37).

Moreover, democratic rule is able to establish institutional guarantees to forestall flawed decisions arising from a democratic majority. A theoretical position evolved that some institutional arrangements can actively enable individuals to use their capabilities for the sake of progress, while minimizing any harm resulting from organizational restrictions. That position entails imposing restrictions on the decisions of the majority to prevent legislation that is unacceptable in principle.[1] Equally, it allows for courts and ombudsmen who have the authority to criticize or rectify such decisions.

The Essence of Democracy and Democratic Transition

Democracy, in essence, is a system for managing conflict that allows free competition over

---

[1] For example, the US Constitution includes a 'Bill of Rights' that defines activities that the government or Congress must not regulate. The First Amendment stipulates that Congress will not pass any legislation that restricts freedom of expression, at the federal level.

the values and goals that citizens care to preserve. On this basis, as long as there is a group that does not resort to violence, and does not transgress the rights of other citizens, it is accorded freedom to work to promote its interests in both civil and political society. This, in brief, constitutes the core of democratic institutional arrangements (Stepan, 2001, 216).

In the theory of democratic transition, elections - free and competitive - occupy a central position. In large societies, there are additional institutional arrangements charged with formulating preferences, expressing them, and making sure that they are taken into account in suitable fashion in the governance process (Dahl, 1971).

The recommended institutional guarantees (*ibid*) include the following seven elements:
- Freedom of expression
- The right to vote
- Freedom to establish and join organizations
- Eligibility for public office
- The right of political leaders to compete for support and votes
- Availability of alternative sources of information
- Policy-making institutions based on voting in free and fair elections and other means by which the people express their preferences.

Other theorists find these guarantees, if necessary, not sufficient (Linz and Stepan, 1996). In their view, political society must be protected in the form of a democratic constitution that respects fundamental freedoms including the rights of minorities. They also stipulate that the elected government govern democratically according to the constitution; that it adheres to the law and to a system composed of institutions, both horizontal and vertical, that guarantee accountability.

Implicit in the guarantees mentioned above is a strong and viable civil society, able to be critical, to check the State and to generate alternative policies. In order for these alternatives to be formulated properly and be viable, the relationships between political society, especially political parties, and with civil society must be absolutely free from control.

PROBLEMATIC ISSUES OF FREEDOM: LIBERALISM AND DEMOCRACY, ATTRIBUTES OF MAJORITY RULE

It is often acknowledged in Western liberal ideology that democracy can harbour flaws. If democracy can restrict liberty, then society cannot be considered free unless two related conditions are simultaneously present:

First, there can be no absolute powers, such that everyone has the right to reject inhuman behaviour.

Second, there must be a firmly established sphere of rights and freedoms within which a person's humanity cannot be violated. (Berlin 1969, 165)

In principle, therefore, democracy is an instrument and not an end in itself. It is judged by what it succeeds in realizing, the goal that it was instituted to accomplish, and which is summed up in "liberty, and the courage and industry which liberty begets" (17th century commentator John Culpepper, quoted in Hayek, 1978, 107).

The danger of tyranny of the majority

Those who give first and absolute priority to democracy, as a formal structure and as a value, have argued that the greatest possible number of issues must be decided according to majority opinion. For them, popular sovereignty signifies the unlimited authority of the majority, an authority that need not be subject to control in any way.

However, purist supporters of liberty believe it is essential to set limits on matters decided by majority rule. Indeed, they consider that the authority of any temporary majority should be restricted as regards principles that will prevail over the longer term. That is, the decisions of the majority express the wishes of the people -- as the majority -- at a particular time, but cannot determine what would be in their best interest if they had more knowledge at their disposal (as generally happens with the passage of time). Furthermore the decisions of the majority do not in fact come from absolute wisdom. They are usually the outcome of negotiations and compromises that might not sat-

Political society must be protected in the form of a democratic constitution that respects fundamental freedoms, including the rights of minorities.

Democracy can harbour flaws.

isfy anyone completely. In fact, such decisions might well be of less value than one taken by the wisest members of society after canvassing all opinions.

What is certain is that there is no moral justification for granting privileges to members of any majority that will distinguish them from, and give them advantages over, those not belonging to that majority. Indeed, progress may be epitomized by the majority's persuasion to a minority view.

And so the success of society in guaranteeing and protecting liberty —including safeguarding it from the tyranny of the majority — depends on the existence of a public sphere that is both extensive and independent of the control of the majority, in which individuals' opinions are formed and expressed. Hence there is an organic link between freedom, in its comprehensive sense, and the key freedoms of opinion, expression, and association. Freedom of opinion guarantees that a person can form a position on societal issues, while freedom of expression permits that person to express those positions and thereby stimulate and inform discussion. Finally, freedom of association guarantees that people can organize themselves through, and in, institutions that adopt positions on issues and actively promote them in society's public sphere.

What is undeniable, in any case, is that the benefits of democracy — indeed, of freedom itself — can be confirmed only in the long term.

Tension between Freedom and Democracy? Or Democracy without Freedom?

As noted, liberal democracy harbours potential flaws. Perhaps the most important of these, from the perspective of freedom, is that "democratic" arrangements can coexist with basic violations of freedom in its comprehensive sense. It is possible, for example, for poverty (however it is understood) to spread in a context of political democracy and without violation of property rights. Even as Sen insists that no widespread famine has occurred under democratic rule, he observes that considerable famines have indeed occurred in contexts where civil and political rights, including prop-

erty rights, were respected (Sen, 1999, 16, 66).

What is more serious is a situation where democratic regulation coexists with extensive violation of freedom in the narrow sense, that is, civil and political rights. In the contemporary world, moreover, this disjunction exists not only in developing countries where freedom and democracy are newcomers (and where elected governments may impose restrictions on the freedom of other sectors of society such as the judiciary, local communities the media, civil society organizations) but even in countries with a long tradition of freedom and democracy, as in the industrialized West. Some contemporary writers even argue the necessity of distinguishing between freedom and democracy. If we compare the two, they argue, we may find an excess of the second – democracy - and a deficit in the first - freedom. Indeed, "democracy" can be used to legislate restrictions on freedom (Zakaria, 2003). In other words, freedom leads to democracy (as in the case of the UK and the US where the enjoyment of freedom preceded the establishment of democracy in the 19th century), but the opposite is not necessarily true.

FREEDOM AND THE OTHER ULTIMATE HUMAN GOALS

Freedom is not the only supreme human goal. Freedom is not justice, equality or beauty, for example. Freedom might even be in conflict with other supreme human goals: some thinkers argue that it is a contradiction in terms to speak of perfect or complete human achievement. This means that a superior and enriching human existence might sometimes require preferring one value over another, or reconciling freedom with other ultimate human goals.

This possible clash among ultimate goals is one of the basic reasons for the insistence on the high value of the freedom to choose. If it were possible in a good society to realize all the ultimate human goals in concert, the agony of choosing between alternatives would vanish.

Freedom is not a blessing that comes without costs: freedom and responsibility go together. Freedom does not only imply the individual's enjoyment of opportunities, nor does it require simply that the individual shoulder the burden of choice. It also implies bearing the consequences of one's decisions; thus, to withdraw from responsibility means, in reality, to surrender freedom.

Equality before the law and with regard to prevailing norms of conduct is the sole type of equality to be guaranteed for preserving freedom. For freedom may ultimately entail the negation of equality in numerous spheres. While justice demands certain conditions or opportunities for people, which the government defines for all equally, it is possible that conditions of freedom will produce a minimum of equality in terms of results. Equality before the law and equality of opportunity can coexist with various forms of human hardship, such as hunger, disease, or poverty.

FREEDOM AS HUMAN DEVELOPMENT: RECONCILING INDIVIDUAL FREEDOM WITH INSTITUTIONAL ARRANGEMENTS

The notion of integrating individual liberty with societal organization in the service of human progress attains maturity in Amartya Sen's writings on human development, culminating in *Development as Freedom* (1999). For Sen, development consists of the "removal of unfreedom," or expansion of the scope of human freedom.

Sen observes that societal institutions play an essential role in securing or delimiting the liberty of individuals, considering them as active agents and not as passive recipients of benefits (*ibid.*, Introduction).

Many kinds of societal institutions play significant roles in this respect: (free) markets, government administration, legislatures, political parties, the justice system, nongovernmental organizations, and mass media. All of these share in the process of development precisely through their impact in strengthening and safeguarding individual freedom.

Sen outlines five types of instrumental freedoms: political freedoms, economic facilities, social opportunities, transparency guarantees, and protective security. These complement each other, in addition to making it possible for people to build human capabilities and to utilize them to realize the kind of

---

BOX 1-3

Ahmed Kamal Aboulmagd: The principle of equality

The principle of equality is one of those principles that hardly need to be explicitly mentioned in a contemporary constitution. Constitutional courts and administrative courts have deemed it to be one of a number of "general legal principles" which, in the words of the Council of State, "are firmly established in the general conscience and do not need to be spelled out".

When the principle first appeared in law and judicial practice in Europe, equality had to do with two fundamental matters, both of them related to the history of conflict between kings and peoples since the Middle Ages:
(1) Equality as it applied to financial burdens (taxes);
(2) Equality as it applied to judicial practice.

Most modern constitutions use the expression "citizens are equal before the law" or "equal under the law". Both phrases encompass all forms of equality, and are never restricted to the concept of equality as it applies to judicial practice.

Most constitutions, after stating that citizens are equal before (or under) the law, add one or both of the two following clauses:
• A clause specifying that citizens "are not subject to any discrimination based on colour, race or creed";
• A clause enunciating another principle that supplements the concept of equality, namely the principle of equality of opportunity.

The meaning of all these provisions is that the legislative power is debarred from enacting any law containing anything in its substantive text that is inconsistent with the principle of equality in terms of discrimination based on colour, creed or sex (gender).

In this framework, regardless of the wording of these various legal formulations in constitutional texts, legal theory and judicial practice have unanimously agreed that equality means the uniform application of the law in dealing with persons in comparable legal situations, and that differential treatment of such persons constitutes unlawful discrimination that is prohibited under the constitution. On the other hand, where differential treatment is based on objective or real factors reflecting differences in the legal situations of the persons concerned, it does not constitute unlawful discrimination, but rather a legitimate recognition of different categories or divisions.

There is a very fine line between unlawful discrimination and legitimate recognition of differences, and the task of determining where that line should be drawn is one of the most delicate issues arising in judicial practice. The standard that has come to be applied, especially by constitutional courts, is that differential treatment is deemed to be discrimination and unlawful under the constitution where there is no logical causal link between the discrimination and the result to which it leads, as in the case of a law prescribing lower wages for a woman worker than for a male worker doing exactly the same kind of work. In contrast, where there is a causal link between the differential treatment and the result, the law is not discriminating, but making a legitimate distinction. For example, the Civil Service Law may provide that every year worked by an employee assigned to a remote area shall count as two years for seniority purposes.

There is another important and equally delicate question, and that is the distinction in judicial practice between what are sometimes referred to as "positive discrimination" and "negative discrimination". Positive discrimination is acceptable as an interim measure, where the goal is to correct the cumulative effects of past negative discrimination, as, for example, in hiring quotas for women or black persons (as in the United States).

---

life they desire. While Sen emphasizes that civil and political freedoms are desirable for their own sake, he stresses that when it comes to economic facilities, income and wealth are not to be sought for their own sake but for the extent to which they make possible the freedom to live our lives according to our desires. People who enjoy economic facilities but are deprived

Development consists of the "removal of unfreedom".

of civil and political freedoms are being denied the essential freedom to choose the kind of life they want, to participate in shaping crucial societal decisions that impact on their well-being now and in the future (*ibid*, 16).

The ability to exercise basic political rights also secures respect for social and economic rights, and so the construction and strengthening of a democratic system of governance is considered a linchpin of the development process. The availability of social opportunities, especially in education and health care, has a direct role in strengthening human capabilities and enhancing the quality of life.

Sen distinguishes between the opportunities that freedom affords and the processes that allow freedom. Both, however, constitute legitimate subjects in studying freedom and working to promote it. To him, to understand development as freedom, means recognizing the importance of the processes and procedures that should be respected, and not restricting one's attention to ends and goals.

Thus, in concert with the numerous and interrelated freedoms there is a need for many societal institutions that intersect with the processes of supporting and strengthening freedom, such as those for democratic regulation, legal mechanisms, provision of educational services and health care, and means of communication between people and institutions.

Ultimately, Sen finds that the organizing principle for development - as freedom - is the indefatigable attempt to enhance individual freedoms and the social commitment to preserve them. These take form in, and develop through, societal institutions and processes that lead to and nurture these freedoms (Sen, 1999, 298).

It is precisely in the area of economics that this connection between individual freedom and institutional arrangements for serving the public interest carries us from the level of micro-economic analysis to that of political economy. The former concerns economic conduct at the level of the economic unit (the individual or the enterprise). The latter focuses on collective conduct in such areas as the allocation of resources, the distribution of economic surpluses among different social groups and the use of wealth at the level of society, particularly in consumption and investment. This underscores the need for economically rational societal institutions that protect freedom in the sense adopted here, in addition to guarantees of property rights and free economic activity at the individual level. Rational economic activity on this level is achieved by mobilizing resources, by encouraging investment in productive fields and by systematically enhancing productivity. The latter in turn necessitates efficiency to protect competitiveness, combat monopoly and ensure justice in the distribution of the economic surplus among societal groups.

Corporate governance and human development

In the context of enhancing the private sector's contribution to human development, corporate governance is a key dimension of responsible economic management. One broad definition of corporate governance refers to "the private and public institutions, including laws, regulations and accepted business practices, which together govern the relationship, in a market economy, between corporate managers and entrepreneurs ("corporate insiders") on one hand, and those who invest resources in corporations, on the other. Investors can include suppliers of equity finance (shareholders), suppliers of debt finance (creditors), suppliers of relatively firm-specific human capital (employers) and suppliers of other tangible and intangible assets that corporations may use to operate and grow"[2].

Good corporate governance ensures that the operations of firms, businesses and markets are transparent, accountable and inclusively responsive to the interests of all stakeholders. These principles matter for development because they can contribute greatly to achieving sustained productivity growth in developing countries, in addition to improving the efficiency of economic performance. Moreover, by increasing corporate social responsibility, corporate governance treats stakeholders within and outside firms and businesses in an

The ability to exercise basic political rights also secures respect for social and economic rights.

Corporate governance is a key dimension of responsible economic management.

---

[2] C. Oman, "Corporate Governance and National Development", OECD Development Centre, Technical papers No.180, September 2001

equitable and socially responsive way. Applying corporate governance principles empowers stakeholders and enables them to understand and take part in business management decisions as a result of their increased access to information and the greater transparency and accountability of owners and managers.

In order for societies to experience these benefits, sound frameworks and institutions need to be in place to provide guidelines, checks and balances within the system and ensure that firms, businesses and markets observe the principles of good corporate governance. In particular, a regulatory framework for the efficient, accountable and inclusive management of resources is necessary for spurring development of the Arab region.

FREEDOM IN ARAB CULTURE

FREEDOM IN ARAB HISTORY

Arab Islamic history provides both actual and practical experience of particular significance in the matter of freedom and its opposite, coercion. The fields of jurisprudence, ethics, logic and scholastic theology (kalam), the philosophy of Sufism and the open social space claimed by nomads and tribes, strongly indicate the presence of the concept of freedom in the Arab Islamic historical experience. Jurisprudence links the validity of acts to freedom. Ethics and theology link legal obligation to responsibility, to individual free will and to human choice with regard to divine will. There were however, differences in how this relation was perceived, as demonstrated by the dialectics of the 'Jabriya', the 'Qadariyya', the Mu'tazila and the Asha'ira. The nomadic way of life was a symbol of "breaking free from all contrived fetters", of "unimpeded life", of "space for living" and "space for action". Sufism is a personal, spiritual experience where the Sufi breaks away from external constraints and pressures – nature, society, the State and legislation - and experiences absolute freedom outside the realm of natural and man-made laws, away from oppression and slavery (Abdullah al-Arawy, in Arabic, 1993, 15-22).

Where political freedom is concerned,

early Arab history witnessed the upsurge of the "Umayyad coercive ideology" that attempted to exploit religion for overt political purposes. The Umayyad caliphs encouraged the pre-destination doctrine view that human actions are pre-ordained in order to claim that the many injustices for which they were responsible were fated acts ordained by God under their rule in the name of God. This ideology gave rise to the contrary position espoused by Hassan al-Basri and his school and the new enlightenment discourse. They advocated a discourse, supported by both text and reason, affirming that people do have a choice and are responsible for their actions. The Mu'tazila bolstered that current of enlightenment by giving the ontological concept of freedom an open political dimension. By so doing they greatly contributed to refuting the claims of the ideology of coercion and helped to place political freedom in Arab religious political thought on solid foundations (al-Habib al-Jenhani, background paper for this Report).

In general, expressions of freedom surface visibly across Arab history in all core domains: religion, politics, society and economics. These expressions were sometimes peaceful and sometimes not.

Religious Freedom

The religious "text" itself stresses that "there is no compulsion in religion" (Al-Baqara: 256), that "You have your religion and I have mine" (Al-Kafiroun: 6), thus allowing the free practice of religion and belief in the land of Revelation, particularly among the Jews, Christians and Sabians. If certain practices in jurisprudence and the political arena have not always followed such guidance, that is only one illustration of the difference between original 'thinking' and principle, i.e. the Revelation, and actual historical practice. Yet the scope of "religious freedom" developed considerably under both the Umayyads and the Abbasids. In literary and cultural circles, debate on religion and articles of faith between Muslims and Christians was free and rich, and it extended to other creeds and schools of thought. It is difficult to speak of persecution on the basis of religion or articles of faith, as such, since such

Expressions of freedom surface visibly across Arab history in all core domains: religion, politics, ethics and economics.

The religious "text" itself stresses that "there is no compulsion in religion".

cases[3] generally concealed a political element. However, members of some sects did not hesitate to accuse those of others, or sometimes their own kind, of heresy if they disagreed with them. Such attitudes undoubtedly cast their shadow on the state and fate of freedom.

Political Freedom

Opponents of the status quo exercised a form of political freedom by rejecting the principle of "obedience" to those in charge. Instead, they championed the text: "No obedience is owed to any creature if it means disobedience of the Creator", a position which can be enforced by several means: counselling, criticism, secret action, concealment of one's true creed, disobedience, struggle, and rebellion. The examples are many: The revolt of Al Qura' (the Readers), al-Fitna al-Kubra (the Great Sedition), the Khawarij movement, the movements of Al Zinj and of the Qaramita, the secret activities of Ikhwan al- Safa and the Abbasid coup d'état. Thanks to early proponents of freedom, tyrants and totalitarians who established themselves as "the shadow of God and His rule on earth" did not entirely succeed in forcing people to subscribe to the school of thought of the "Sultan's jurists" who claimed that "a century of injustice is better than one hour of chaos".

Social Freedom

The historic period of the great Arab renaissance witnessed obvious manifestations of moral, social and cultural freedom notwithstanding the stipulations of Islamic law regulating both moral and social conduct in Arab-Islamic regions and constraints imposed by Arab custom and tradition. In fact the 3rd and 4th Hijra centuries (9th and 10th centuries AD) represent 'the age of liberalism' of the time, evidenced by the cultural content and daily moral practices where "freedom often expressed itself in forms incompatible with 'traditional' rules".

Opponents of the status quo exercised a form of political freedom by rejecting the principle of "obedience" to those in charge.

Freedom in the modern sense of the word was introduced into Arab culture after contact developed between modern Arabs and Europe.

Economic Freedom

Freedom in the economic realm manifested itself through the recognition of property rights, free trade and profit-making, sometimes on the basis of a "text", and sometimes driven by the very logic of economic and daily activities. Economic activities in Arab Islamic history reflect a "capitalist" economic pattern, i.e. a pattern of freedom despite certain challenges and constraints. This was solidified by the expansion of the Islamic state to include vast territories whose prosperous economic relations were firmly based on the rule of freedom. This rule was evident in the Islamic jurisprudence's perception of the legal organization of economic transaction which is built on free consent and free acceptance and also on putting a condition that the contractual will should not be affected by any of the drawbacks of an unfree will.

FREEDOM IN THE MODERN CONTEXT

Freedom in the modern sense of the word was introduced into Arab culture after contact developed between modern Arabs and Europe, particularly France. The Egyptian scholar Rifaa al-Tahtawi (1801-1873) was the first to refer to the idea of freedom (Liberté) and to connect it with "justice and equity" in the Islamic heritage. He considered freedom a condition sine qua non for the progress and civilization of the nation (Rifaa al-Tahtawi, in Arabic, 1840, 73, 74, 80; Rifaa al-Tahtawi, in Arabic, 1872, 8, 127). His Moroccan contemporary, Ahmed bin Khalid al-Nasseri (1835-1897), however, declared that "the notion of freedom invented by the ferenja (foreigners or French) is, undoubtedly, the work of heretics. It requires disregard of the rights of God, the rights of parents and even the rights of humanity" (Ahmed bin Khalid al-Nasseri, in Arabic, 1956, 9, 114). Khayr al-Din al-Tounsi (1825-1889), associated freedom with a number of related rights and referred to personal freedom, political freedom and citizens' participation in managing the affairs of the State as well as freedom of the press. Thus he upheld freedom of

---

[3] E.g. Al Jahm Bin Safwan, Mebed al-Jahny, Ghilan al-Dimashqi, Al Hallaj, Malik bin Anas, Ahmed bin Nasr al-Khuzra'i, "testing of belief in the Revelation of the Qur'an" and Sahrawardy, who was killed.

opinion and expression, which he considered the equivalent of the Islamic principle of "enjoining what is right and forbidding wrong".

All these thinkers echoed the call for freedom in different contexts: whether in connection with Ottoman tyranny, and in its aftermath, the European colonization of Arab countries; or with the pressures of a history of prejudices and traditions. Elsewhere, freedom is related to its determining role in achieving European progress. The tyrannical nature of the Ottoman regime and the desire for freedom prompted Abdel Rahman al-Kawakibi's masterpiece: Tabai al-Istibdad (The Nature of Tyranny). The European "liberal example" inspired the pioneers of free social thinking, as reflected in Qassim Amin's great work, Tahrir al Mar'a (The Emancipation of Women), as well as in other works which followed in his footsteps. These include the writings of Bahet-hat al-Badiya (1886-1918), Tahir al-Haddad (1899-1935) and Nazira Zein al-Din. This same example gave birth to the liberal trend articulated by the Egyptian pioneer, Ahmed Lutfi al-Sayyid, who became the acknowledged leader of all liberals. The following sentence is a clear expression of his ideas: "Our spirits were created free, God having imbued them with the nature of freedom. Indeed our freedom is us, our very selves and the essence of our selves, it is what gives significance to a human being as being human. Our freedom is our very being and our being is our freedom" (Mabadi fi a- Siyasa wa a- Adab wa al-Ijtima [Principles in Politics, Literature and Sociology], in Arabic, 138; also Youssef Salama, Ishkaliyet al-Hurriya [Problematics of Freedom] in Arabic, 661).

Throughout the 20th century, freedom in Arab culture represents a strong desire, a vital need, a major demand and a powerful slogan promoted, most notably, by the proponents of "free thought" as well those of "national independence". The call for freedom seemed to represent a break with the past among the individuals, groups and parties that sought it; it was an aim to be pursued for the sake of life itself and for the future.

FROM FREEDOM TO EMANCIPATION

In the middle of the last century an overwhelming wave of interest in the philosophy of freedom inspired by existentialism swept the Arab cultural scene. The matter went beyond the mere study and emulation of existentialism for some Arab intellectuals, like Abdul Rahman Badawi, Zakariya Ibrahim and Mutaa' Safdi. This does not mean that there were no other remarkable works, nor does it underestimate the impact on the young generation of the translation into Arabic of Jean-Paul Sartre's plays and Simone de Beauvoir's works. However, one of the most important works that have appeared was the book by the Moroccan philosopher Mohammed Aziz al-Habbabi, entitled "Liberté ou Libération". The innovation introduced by al-Habbabi was what he termed 'realistic personalism', which he later described in an outstanding work first published in French in 1967: "Le Personnalisme Musulman" (Muslim Personalism) translated into Arabic under the same title in 1969.

Comparing philosophies inspired by existentialism with those by 'realistic personalism' reveals a progression in the concept of freedom that can be summed up in the phrase "from freedom to emancipation". This was a move from freedom as a psychological, spiritual, metaphysical experience and total independence of the self, to a "militant, practical and social experience which, in the outside world, in society, is embodied in emancipation from natural constraints and from all kinds of op-

Throughout the 20th century, freedom in Arab culture represents a strong desire, a vital need, a major demand and a powerful slogan.

pression, deprivation and exploitation. It is embodied in "real freedoms", social, economic and political (Mohammed Aziz al-Habbabi, in Arabic, 1972, 68, 90-91, 185-186). This development gave rise to related societal and civilizational orientations, such as are expressed by the nationalist thinker, Constantine Zurreq, and a group of social-minded intellectuals inspired by Marxism, the most outstanding of whom are Mahmoud Amin al-Alam, Samir Amin, Abdallah al-Arawy, Mahdi Aamil, Elias Murqus and Al-Tayyib Tizini.

Constantine Zurreq linked the question of freedom to that of "civilizational potential" or "civilization", which, he believed, distinguishes nations in terms of their progress or backwardness. He thought that the backwardness suffered by the Arabs in modern times was due to their weak and unbalanced standards of civilization. To overcome both the imbalance and the weakness, basic conditions for civilization must be guaranteed, for they alone can ensure progress. Zurreq believes that the eight most important yardsticks for determining the degree of civilization in a given society are: technical know-how, accumulated scientific knowledge, moral values, artistic and literary creativity, freedom of thought, the extent to which skills and values are to be found throughout society, the prevailing systems, institutions and traditions with the freedoms and rights they contain, and the persons whose lives and activities reflect those skills and values (Constantine Zurreq, in Arabic, 1981, 278). He gathered his arguments under two main headings: creativity and emancipation. Freedom of thought was the condition sine qua non for creativity and all else depended on it. Emancipation was the other facet of civilization and embodied the degree of a person's liberation from nature; from the illusions and desires of the self; and from other people, be they exploiting groups or classes or the hegemony of other societies (*ibid.* 279-281).

Emancipation also figures in the Marxist view of the freedom question. In their view, in the final analysis, the aim is to be liberated from man's arbitrariness, from the domination of nature, from exploitation by capitalism, from the power of private property, from poverty and conflict This view postpones the reali-

zation of freedom until such time that both the individual and society are socially, economically and politically liberated. For them "full individual freedom can only be realized when all its objective conditions become a reality in a free society" (Abdullah al-Arawy, in Arabic, 1993, 76). This can only be achieved through a comprehensive Arab liberation movement distant from the Arab bourgeoisie and prevalent colonial conditions (Mahdi Aamil).

FREEDOM FROM AN ISLAMIC PERSPECTIVE

At first glance, it would appear that contemporary Islamic thought is not particularly concerned with the question of freedom in its practical sense, concentrating, essentially, on the old question of whether human actions are the doing of God or man. However, Islamists do have a clear-cut theory and the old question of freedom, i.e. metaphysical or ontological freedom – is not their only concern. Freedom of opinion – one of "the external, societal freedoms – features prominently in the debate between Islamists and their adversaries, who question how far the latter tolerate such freedom among those who disagree with them and how far Islam guarantees freedom of opinion and belief for non-Muslims.

This challenge led to intensive efforts by Islamic thinkers to "defend" and "justify" their thesis that Islam guarantees freedom of opinion. They asserted that "freedom is instinctive" and that the "life of all the prophets" is an affirmation of the freedom of opinion. They insisted that both the Qur'an and the Sunna "recognize freedom of opinion" and that "political freedom is but a branch of a bigger, more general origin", namely "the freedom of man that stems from the fact that he is a man, as recognized in unequivocal texts of the Book and the Sunna (Mohammed Selim al-Awwa, in Arabic, 1989, 211-216; Hassan al-Turabi, in Arabic, 2003,162-174). At the same time, Islamists also stressed that "this freedom of the mind or freedom of opinion", recognized by Islam and guaranteed by the Qur'an, is subject to one limitation: commitment to Islamic law. An opinion expressed by a Muslim, in exercising this freedom, must not cast doubt on Islam or break its rules. That was considered as contrary to public order in the Islamic State, for which a person was liable to be declared incompetent and for which, in certain circumstances, he could be subjected to punishment (Mohammed Selim al-Awwa, in Arabic, 1989, 216). Such a position, which is held by the majority in Islamic literature, does not offer an Islamic theory concerning freedom; it would more fittingly come under "rights of freedom". This does not, however, mean that contemporary Islamic writings are devoid of any profound theory "defining freedom". Prominent representatives of the Islamic movement have indeed formulated such a theory despite their differences, such as Youssef al-Qaradawi, Allal al-Fasi, Hassan Saab, Hassan al-Turabi, Hassan Hanafi and Rashed al-Ghanoushi. "Emancipated Slavery" may well reflect their theory which signifies "slavery to God alone" and emancipation from slavery to any other but God (Radwan al-Sayyid, in Arabic, 2002, 565).

For these thinkers, the theory of Islamic freedom stems from their critique of the liberal concept of freedom. According to Youssef al-Qaradawi, this concept is based on a number of "extraneous" elements, such as secularism, the nationalist movement, capitalist economics and personal freedom as defined in the West, including women's freedom to wear practical modern clothing and mix with men, the implementation of foreign laws and a parliamentary system. Its major defect, in their view, is that it contains no "spiritual" element, which it deliberately neglects by "turning away from God and refusing to follow His guidance" (Youssef al-Qaradawi, in Arabic, 1977, 121).

Allal al-Fasi, an independent Moroccan political thinker, seems to be both more precise and profound, and more adept at developing theory on the question of freedom, than any other Islamic thinker. The concept of freedom, for Allal al-Fasi, starts with the will for the total liberation of the national personality from all constraints, whether external, such as colonialism, or internal such as social relations that negate freedom or certain remaining traditions that hamper people's freedom. The substance of his theory is political and aims at liberating humankind from all kinds and levels of aliena-

tion (Muhammad Waqidi, in Arabic, 1990, 146-148; Mostafa Hanafi, in Arabic, 2002, 336-337). The more restricted framework within which al-Fasi raises the problem of freedom remains, however, a religious Islamic one governed by the concepts of absolute divine freedom, and God's injunctions to human beings, His heirs on Earth, responsible for populating it and for ensuring justice and freedom. For him, freedom is part of humankind's personal nature, since human beings were not created free but were created to *become* free; freedom not being just a right but also an obligation that comes second to the interest of the society (Allal al-Fasi, in Arabic, 1997, 2-14; Muhammad Waqidi, in Arabic, 1990, 149-161). The essence of Al-Fasi's perception of freedom is that belief in God is the path to freedom, for God is absolute freedom or "true freedom" the belief in whom is the path towards the freedom of humankind.

The writings of the Lebanese intellectual, Hassan Saab, reflect precisely the same perception. He argues that the monotheistic Islamic creed is "synonymous with the process of liberation" (Hassan Saab, in Arabic, 1981, 28). Monotheism is "slavery to God alone". Such 'slavery' is humankind's emancipation from natural, historical and political constraints. It is emancipation from everything that is not God, it is what releases a person from the universe of necessity into the realm of freedom, away from all modern ideologies which are only new forms of slavery: economic liberalism, materialistic communism, natural scientism, Nietzsche's nihilism, Freudian sexualism, etc. (*ibid*, 10-11).

That is also the school of thought adopted by the leading Islamists, Hassan al-Turabi and Rashed al-Ghanoushi, who believe freedom to be a breaking free from mortal constraints, emancipation and slavery to God. Al-Ghanoushi quotes from a lecture by Al-Turabi on 'freedom and unity' to the effect that "Freedom is humankind's destiny, that which differentiates human beings from all other creatures, so he knelt to God voluntarily since God when He created mortals did not include any element that would force them to believe. Freedom is not an end but a means to worship God ... If freedom in its legal manifestation is

(For Allal al-Fasi), freedom is part of humankind's personal nature, since human beings were not created free: they were created to become free.

The essence of this perception... is that belief in God is the path to freedom.

licence, in its religious manifestation it is the path towards the worship of God. It is humankind's duty to emancipate itself for God and to be faithful in forming opinions and positions. From the Islamic viewpoint, such a freedom is absolute because it is an endless striving for the Absolute. The more faithful people are in their slavery to God, the greater will be their emancipation from all other creations in nature ... and the higher will be the levels of their achievement of human perfection" (Rashed al-Ghanoushi, in Arabic, 1993, 38).

This is how Islamic writings promote and consecrate the concept of freedom as being a voluntary human action, but also an emancipatory action, thus reconciling Islam with the "emancipation" movement and, ultimately, considering it to be synonymous with "slavery to God", i.e. removing it from human to divine space.

FREEDOM AND LIBERATION

In the 1950s the notion of Arab nationalism came to be embodied in political movements and regimes, as in Ba'thism in Syria and several neighbouring countries, and Nasserism in Egypt. These movements made freedom one of their basic tenets. In fact, it is one of the three cornerstones of the Ba'thist credo (unity, socialism, freedom), and a major element of democracy in Nasserism. Yet, the "revolutionary" nature of these movements and the surrounding conditions of international, regional and local struggle and conflict made the leaders of those movements postpone implementing the principle of freedom in favour of other principles: Arab unity in the party's ideology (Ba'thism) and socialism in Nasserism. They even justified certain formulations that curtailed freedom throughout "the revolutionary stage". This view was, however, linked to their concept of "liberation" and to defending the idea that the liberation of the Arab human being or individual was a pre-requisite for the establishment of complete freedom. All seemed to agree that "liberation" meant the liberation of the Arab individual from all kinds of exploitation, oppression, poverty, need, sickness, capitalism, feudalism, and everything that represents a "constraint" limiting man's

actions, and obstacles to the individual's real freedom. In other words, economic, political and social liberation were basic conditions for the real freedom of the people and citizens. (Munif al-Razzaz, in Arabic, 1985, 491, 583, 594).

One cannot approach the issues of freedom, emancipation and liberation without reference to what has, since the early 1950s, been termed "the Arab liberation movement". This was the name given to "progressive" political organizations and parties in the Arab arena, the organizations that were struggling for freedom, unity, development and progress. Despite the lofty aims, slogans and values espoused by the movement to justify its existence – liberation, unity, justice and development – in reality it was in a state of crisis and bitter failure. The explanation given by Kamal Abdel Latif and others is salient: "The historical awareness behind the Arab liberation movement, that reached the threshold of power, was unable to come to terms with the liberal gains achieved in the Mashriq between the two wars. All the intellectual and political values that arose in the first quarter of the 20th century were ignored, hence civil society was not established, and the State was unable to acquire legal, secular legitimacy. It donned the cape of charismatic power and resorted to masked tyranny" (Kamal Abdel Latif, in Arabic, 75).

From the foregoing analysis of the concepts of freedom, emancipation and liberation it would seem that ontological freedom was not considered to be a gateway to emancipation and liberation. Indeed, intellectuals concerned with emancipation openly criticized the old definition of freedom in terms of personal will, individual awareness and independence from external factors. While many realized that the attainment of freedom requires relentless struggle and effort, most of their ideas of emancipation and liberation revolved around issues of economic and social exploitation as well as political tyranny.

The experience of the Palestinian struggle, however, offered the Palestinian intellectual Sari Nusaiba an unusual philosophical opportunity, which enabled him to combine freedom in its ontological sense and liberation in its political sense. What is freedom? Freedom is

Islamic writings promote and consecrate the concept of freedom as being a voluntary human action, but also an emancipatory one.

The state was unable to acquire legal, secular legitimacy. It donned the cape of charismatic power and resorted to masked tyranny.

the absence of bonds or the removal of bonds or the emancipation from bonds (Sari Nusaiba, in Arabic, 1995, 33 onwards). Freedom means "the capacity for growth and development towards the better" and "the breaking of the fetters preventing such growth and development" (*ibid.*, 85). Such a capacity is achieved at the level of the "self" or at the level of the "will", i.e. at the level of the inner interaction within the self that engenders the victory of the positive over the negative by the determination to undertake a certain action, or the refusal to submit to undertaking it". This interaction "includes elements such as self-awareness, awareness of the reality outside the self and, most important, the clash or interconnection of the first and the second, leading to the domination of the self over the action so that a human being's action is in harmony with what he believes in" (*ibid*, 117). Sari Nusaiba illustrates his interpretation with the case of an imprisoned Palestinian militant subjected to questioning and torture. The militant's absolute determination, awareness of his personal identity, capacity to overcome inner bonds and unwavering resolve which embodies the collective resolve, enables him to overcome the external enemy's will that binds him, and to achieve freedom and independence for himself and for his people (*ibid*, 118-127).

THE RIGHTS OF FREEDOM

Ever since "freedom" acquired its right of citizenship as one of the values within the modern Arab cultural cluster, its proponents' main intention was not to adopt an abstract, absolute concept of freedom, but rather a concept that has practical, intellectual, political, social, religious and economic facets. It is true that those facets were considered forms of freedom, but in reality they were also the "rights" of every free human being. Freedom did not only mean freedom of action and behaviour, the lifting of constraints within the boundaries of law and of Islamic law; it also meant the free citizen's entitlement to enjoy a number of rights originally linked to freedom. Rifaa al-Tahtawy recognized this when he considered that freedoms - natural, behavioural, religious, political and

economic - were in fact the rights of citizenship (Wajih Kawtharany, in Arabic, 2002, 427-430). Khayr al-Din al-Tounsi stressed a person's right to free disposal of himself and his belongings – that is personal freedom – and the right of the constituency to "intervene in royal policies and to debate what is for the best". He also referred to the right to freedom of expression or what he termed "freedom of the printing press" (*ibid.*, 433).

The leading thinkers of the Arab age of renaissance followed suit. Throughout the 20th century, all political and social movements came to agree on the "necessity of freedom" as a slogan, a claim, a supreme value and a right. While they focused on different forms of freedom - national, political, social, economic and intellectual "freedom of opinion" - they were all in agreement that these were human rights for the citizen and for society (Muhammad Waqidi, in Arabic, 1990, 164-165). The fact remains, however, as Burhan Ghalioun notes, that such clear recognition of the rights and freedoms of the individual has been linked to the call for democracy which has become a concrete reality at more than one level, as well as "the uppermost value among political values and the first among Arab social claims" (Burhan Ghalioun, in Arabic, 1994,109). More recently, this recognition also became linked to the claims of those seeking to promote respect for human rights and to encourage backward societies along the path of democracy. As long as the task of the democratic political regime is to guarantee freedoms and as long as such freedoms represent vital demands for citizens, they end up by becoming rights, not to say obligations, to quote Allal al-Fasi.

In Arab culture, fundamental freedoms have in recent times become linked inextricably to the question of human rights and to an acute awareness of the oppressive nature of political regimes, particularly where political freedoms are concerned. Prominent Arab human rights advocates stressed the importance of human rights and fundamental freedoms. Munther Anabtawy, one of the foremost pioneering human rights activists, said that all the Arab military and political catastrophes, cataclysms and defeats were due to "the continuing deprivation of the Arab citizen

Throughout the 20th century, all political and social movements came to agree on the "necessity of freedom" as a slogan, a claim, a supreme value and a right.

In Arab culture, fundamental freedoms have become linked inextricably to the question of human rights and to an acute awareness of the oppressive nature of political regimes.

of his fundamental rights and freedoms". He believed that it had become imperative for intellectual élites to contribute to promoting the human rights of Arabs, that being one of the necessary conditions for the revival of the Arab national project and for overcoming the social, political and economic problems confronting Arab citizens and Arab countries today (Burhan Ghalioun, *ibid.*, 395-397).

The general call to respect human rights and to guarantee the fundamental freedoms of the Arab citizen is no longer voiced for its own sake in Arab intellectual circles; these principles have become the two vital conditions for an Arab renaissance. Arab nationalists, liberals, Islamists, Marxists and independents, unanimously proclaim the call. Not all agree on the limits of such freedoms and rights or on their scope and particular manifestations: some speak of personal freedom and freedom of belief, others speak of economic, social, political and other freedoms. There are differences, sometimes fundamental, in how the various groups perceive these issues.

For example, the liberal and the Islamist are unlikely to agree on the scope of personal and moral freedom, though they may be in agreement over freedom of ownership and work. The liberal, the nationalist and the Islamist want to see freedom implemented, while the Marxist's priorities are revolution, the struggle against capitalism and the victory of socialism before true freedom can be attained. Many criticize bourgeois liberalism for its superficiality, insignificance and lack of authenticity. Yet they also question whether the Islamists, if they ever came to power, would respect the human rights and freedoms of those with whom they disagree. Most remain sceptical about this despite the Islamists' assurances and reassurances to the contrary, and the recent efforts made by some to justify the right to differ (Fahmy Jadaan, in Arabic, 2002) and despite the guarantees provided in Islamic human rights declarations and charters elaborated over the past two decades.

No Arab thinker today doubts that freedom is a vital and necessary condition for a new Arab renaissance.

THE ARAB RENAISSANCE AND THE CHALLENGE OF FREEDOM

No Arab thinker today doubts that freedom is a vital and necessary condition for a new Arab renaissance, nor that the Arab world's capacity to face up to the problems and risks of globalization depends on ending tyranny and securing fundamental rights and freedoms.

Freedom is not the only, nor is it a sufficient, condition for this renaissance to take place, but it is a condition sine qua non. It is counterproductive to debate the prioritisation of values needed for such a renaissance: freedom, or development or justice. All are essential; the renaissance cannot work in the absence of any one of them; they are an interconnected and interrelated whole.

With the prevailing situation in the Arab world and with recent global developments, it is vital to think about freedom and the form it can take to embody the specificities of Arab societies, and the fundamental social and political aspirations of their people.

Reflecting on this subject, Naseef Nassar turns to liberalism as a social system based on the principle of individual freedom, noting

---

BOX 1-5

Naseef Nassar: The Reconstruction of Liberalism

The power of liberalism is not only that it raises the banner of individual freedom and counteracts the tendency to dissolve the individual within the group, but also that it claims freedom for all human beings without exception, men and women alike. History, however, teaches us that to organize social life in a practical, liberal manner is far from the mere application of a ready-made and final view, or a pleasant walk in a rose garden. It is an open process of struggle, one that requires an ever-developing awareness of the dimensions of freedom and of its problems, in the light of direct experience and in all the areas freedom touches. It also requires an associated theoretical understanding of the liberal orientation itself and a critical review of its achievements.

As a result of the principle of freedom of thought and belief, the liberal society does not lean towards a comprehensive and complete unity of thought, but rather towards a plurality of beliefs, or towards variety within one single belief. Taken to extremes, such a tendency leads to the exact opposite of dogmatic

unity of belief, i.e. to a kind of chaos that is no less dangerous than its opposite where human relations, understanding and development are concerned. That is why for a liberal society to remain viable and to progress, it needs to organize the processes of intellectual understanding among its members.

It also needs to set up mechanisms for sifting, comparing and selecting in order to make room for truths to surface, to agree on common truths and their link to the right institutions for them.

It goes without saying that the truths in question are not the ones related to the absolute and the eternal alone, but rather the social, the cultural, political, economic and moral truths on which hang the history of individuals as well as their destiny in this fleeting world. Despite its individualistic premises, the liberal society in the West has never ceased to try developing a response to this need, yet the challenge now imposes itself in new forms amid the rising tide of globalisation which requires a reconstruction of liberalism.

Source: Naseef Nassar, in Arabic, 2004, 77-78 and 107.

that liberalism is not limited to the forms it has taken in Western societies up to the present day; and that other countries – among them Arab countries – can seek "the form they deem best to promote freedom depending on their position on the map of civilization and without excluding the experiences of Western countries" (*ibid.*, 150-155).

Nassar believes that liberalism should be reconstructed, which requires "the assimilation of the principle of individual freedom within a new concept of the sociability of man", one that links reason to justice and to authority. Along the same lines, individualistic globalized liberalism should be excluded – since it neglects freedom of will in favour of unbridled capitalistic power. A new philosophy must be devised, based on a "social liberalism" which can be called "the liberalism of social solidarity", a liberalism founded on social reason, social justice and a political authority that establishes the frameworks and organizations conducive to protecting and safeguarding freedom (*ibid.* 158-159). Starting with this "liberalism of social solidarity" and within its space, the issues of unity, pluralism, stability, labour, social wealth, political system, knowledge, faith and education can all be reconstructed, along with the institutions and organizations they require, in a manner no less flexible or efficient than that followed by European states in their transition from the Europe we know to a new Europe that will give a new face to globalization (*ibid.*167). The great freedom we seek resides in this system based on "the liberalism of social solidarity" and not in "neo-liberalism".

The majority of Arab thinkers today are moving in the direction of a renaissance which combines the principles of freedom and justice with the additional principle of social and economic development, although they may differ as to which principle should come first. This trend should be entirely compatible with an Arab order of good governance of a humane nature, based on freedom, creativity, justice, welfare, dignity, fairness and the public good.

THE CONCEPT OF FREEDOM AND GOOD GOVERNANCE IN THIS REPORT

Freedom is one of the principal human goals and highest human values. It is cherished in itself and sought for its own sake.

BOX 1-6

Freedom for its own sake

A person's freedom can be seen as being valuable in addition to his or her achievements. A person's options and opportunities can be seen as counting in a normative evaluation, in addition to what the person ends up achieving or securing. Freedom may be valued not merely because it assists achievement, but also because of its own importance, going beyond the value of the state of existence actually achieved. If, for example, all the alternatives other than the one actually chosen were to be eliminated, this need not affect achievement (since the chosen alternative can be still chosen), but the person clearly has less freedom, and this may be seen as a loss of some importance.

Amartya Sen, 1988, 60

The concept of freedom accommodates two senses, negative and positive. The first concerns the domain in which an individual (or group) is able to exist and to act as s/he (or it) wishes without interference by others; it entails lifting any restrictions placed on the individual. The second, positive sense has to do with the source of interference or control over the being or action of the individual (or group), or the manners in which individual freedom is regulated for the purpose of avoiding chaos, (Berlin, 1969).

The importance of the second sense of freedom is that some freedoms can be incompatible with higher human goals. An oft-cited example is the "liberty" of someone to inflict pain on another by committing the crime of torture. Moreover, the natural, unimpeded spread of total freedom may on the one hand block the satisfaction of the basic needs of people at large; and, on the other, allow the strong to tyrannize the weak.

However, the individual's consent to the principle that freedom must be subject to control raises the possibility of oppression by a ruling individual or majority. Hence, the inseparability of freedom and good governance, defined in a specific societal context, constitutes the ideal position between absolute freedom (chaos) and oppression. For this reason, the present Report takes a broad purview that encompasses the negative and the positive dimensions of freedom.

Freedom is one of the principal human goals and highest human values. It is cherished in itself and sought for its own sake.

The scope of the concept of freedom ranges between two extremes. The first is a narrow one that restricts freedom to civil and political rights and freedoms, linking it to citizenship and democracy, and to the emergence of liberalism in Western thought since the 17th century. The second is comprehensive, and has been adopted in this Report. This comprehensive scope incorporates not only civil and political freedoms (in other words, liberation from oppression) but also the liberation of the individual from all factors that are inconsistent with human dignity, such as hunger, disease, ignorance, poverty, and fear. In human rights terms, the understanding of freedom in the present Report covers all realms of human rights, that is, economic, social, cultural and environmental rights as well as civil and political rights.

In this comprehensive definition, freedom is an ideal and persistently broadening goal. It is thus true to say that freedom is a goal ever sought but never reached.

As is the case with civil and political freedoms, the other freedoms are valued in themselves as human aspirations. A citizen who enjoys civil and political freedoms will still seek to avoid hunger or disease. While some may think that adversity or insecurity may distract people from such issues as, for example, freedom of expression and association, lack of these other freedoms may often spur demand for freedom and good governance. Ultimately, these other freedoms complement and complete civil and political freedoms, to form the core of human well-being. This core constitutes true freedom: the absence of even one of these other freedoms detracts from the value of civil and political freedoms. What, for instance, is the point of a person having the legal right to buy basic commodities, i.e. the right to economic transactions, if poverty precludes the effective exercise of that right?

In this comprehensive sense, freedom is considered both the ultimate goal of human development and its foundation.

Freedom, however, is one of those superior human culmination outcomes that must be guaranteed, sustained and promoted by effective societal structures and processes. These societal guarantees are summed up in the order of good governance embodied in synergy between the state, civil society, and the private sector as depicted in the first Report in our series. Such an order:

- Safeguards freedom to ensure the expansion of people's choices (the core of human development)
- Rests upon effective popular participation and full representation of the public at large.
- Is buttressed by first-rate institutions (in contrast to the tyranny of the individual),

Freedom is an ideal and persistently broadening goal.

BOX 1-7

The Charter of Medina

One of the most important acts with which the Messenger of God (the Prophet Muhammad) began his life in Medina was the writing of a missive in which he formally set out the relationship between Muslims and others in Medinan society. He referred to the groups collectively as "the people of this document [lit., page, sahifah]," that is, the missive he had written. This document is considered the equivalent to the constitution of the emergent Islamic state in Medina, and indeed many modern scholars refer to it as the "Constitution of Medina" or "Charter of Medina". Nearly a millennium and a half ago, this document articulated and established the principles of citizenship, equality and justice (combating oppression), and of freedom of belief, in a written pact.

This is possibly one of the earliest documents in history to appraise the relationship between governance and people on the basis of citizenship, rather than on any discriminatory basis (religion in this case)

Ibn Ishaq reported: The Messenger of God drew up a written document among the Emigrants[4] and the Medinans (Ansar) in which he made a pact with the Jews [in Medina], establishing their right to practice their religion and retain their property, and in which he made and accepted conditions of mutual co-existence in the city.

From the Text of the Charter:

"In the name of God the Beneficent and Merciful, this is a document from Muhammad the Prophet [to govern the relations] between the believers and Muslims of Quraysh and Yathrib[5] and those who followed and joined and strove with them. They are one community (umma), exclusive of all other people....

"The pious believers will stand against rebellious elements or those who promote oppression or injustice, enmity or sin and corruption, among believers. Every person's hand will be against such a one even if that one is the offspring of any one of him or her....

"The Jews have their religion, and the Muslims have theirs, and this applies to their freedmen as well as to themselves, except for the one who acts wrongly or unjustly. That person hurts none but himself and his family. The Jews of Bani Najjar will have the same rights as the Jews of Bani Awf, and the Jews of Bani Harth will be as the Jews of Bani Awf....

The Jews of al-Aws, both their freedmen and themselves, will have the same standing as the people of this document, in good and pure loyalty from the people of this document."

Sources: Abi Muhammad Abdulmalik ibn Hashim al-Mu'afari, in Arabic, 1998; Abd al-Rahman Ahmad Salim, in Arabic, 1999; Muhammad Salim al-'Awa, in Arabic, 1989

---

[4]Emigrants: those who had emigrated with the Messenger of Gods from Mecca to Medina to found a community of Muslims. The Ansar ("supporters," "helpers") were the Muslims of Medina who invited the Messenger of Gods to settle there.

[5]Quraysh: The Meccan clan from which Muhammad, the Messenger of God, came. Yathrib: the name of Medina before it became Medinat al-Nabi, "City of the Prophet," shortened form, Medina.

which operate efficiently and with complete transparency. These institutions are subject to effective accountability among themselves, protected by the government's separation of powers, and by a balance among those powers; they are also directly accountable to the populace through popular selection processes that are regular, free, and scrupulously fair.

- Upholds the rule of law; and ensures that the law itself is fair, protective of freedom, and applies equally to all;
- Ensures that an efficient, fair and independent judiciary applies the law impartially and that the executive branch duly implements judicial rulings.

A society distinguished by freedom and good governance requires an institutional architecture based on the synergy of three social sectors:

- The State, incorporating government, representative bodies, and the judiciary;
- Civil society, in the broadest sense, which embraces non-governmental organizations, professional associations and syndicates, mass media, and political parties;
- The (profit-seeking) private sector.

Good governance requires each sector to possess the following two characteristics:

- Respect for freedom and human rights, and adherence to the legal architecture that protects them.
- Observance of the principles of rational public administration. This calls for stable institutional structures in place of supreme individual authorities, and adherence to key principles: efficiency, separation of powers, transparency, disclosure, and accountability.

Beyond these general criteria for the institutional structure in a society of freedom and good governance, there are particular requisites for each of the three sectors, in the following respects:

- Judiciary: impartiality
- Representational bodies: efficacy of legislation and oversight
- Government: leadership directly selected by, and accountable to the people
- Private sector: creativity, efficiency and social responsibility
- Civil society: effectiveness, self-sustainability and social responsibility.

Undoubtedly, the institutional architecture, especially the legal and political architecture, occupies the pre-eminent position, as this is the foundation on which all else must build. Thus, the present Report puts the spotlight on these two cornerstones.

Similarly, the concept emphasises civil society, as characterized above, because the latter has a pivotal role to play in achieving a deep political alternation in society as countries make the transition from a status quo inimical to freedom, to the regime of good governance described here.

Economic and social freedoms are underpinned by efficient and sustainable economic growth in which corporate governance plays a major role.

Taha Hussein (1938): Freedom and Independence

We live in an era among whose more special attributes is the fact that freedom and independence are not so much a goal towards which peoples look and to which nations strive, as they are a means to achieve higher and more lasting goals, beyond freedom and independence in themselves—ends that are more broadly beneficial and more widely advantageous.

Many groups of people in many parts of the world once lived free and independent. Yet freedom availed them of nothing, and they found no further benefit in independence. Their own freedom and independence did not protect them from encroachment by other peoples who had freedom and independence but were not content to make these alone

suffice and did not regard them as their only long-term goal, but instead supplemented them with the civilization that is based on culture and knowledge, the strength that emerges from culture and knowledge, and the wealth that is produced out of culture and knowledge.

We want to be free people in our country, free of foreigners such that they cannot oppress us or treat us unjustly; and free with respect to ourselves, such that no one of us can oppress or treat another unjustly.

We want internal domestic freedom, and its foundation, the democratic order. We also want external freedom, and what it is based on, true independence and the strength that surrounds this independence.

Source: Taha Hussein, in Arabic, 1996, 15, 41

The individual is free only in a free society within a free nation.

Under such a system of good governance, it is virtually impossible to destroy freedom. On the other hand, freedom remains at risk, and the mode of government can become oppressive, where any of these cornerstones of good governance are absent or deficient.

It needs to be underlined, however, that the individual is free only in a free society within a free nation. Distinguishing between society and nation allows for an analysis of the freedoms of different groups in that social space between the individual and the nation. It thus facilitates consideration of minorities, whether ethnic or religious, and the important question of respect for their rights.

The paradigm of "good governance" discussed here and the collective societal process for its advancement are especially relevant because they enable different societies to represent their own particularities. This provides Arab countries with an opportunity to think creatively about how to achieve the best and most representative system of good governance in their respective contexts.

In the Arab region, national liberation is of particular importance because of the Israeli occupation of Palestinian Arab territories, which impedes human development in the area, and threatens peace and security in the region. There is also the more recent dimension posed by the US-led occupation of Iraq, along with the increasing foreign military presence and other external influences in many Arab countries.

Governance in Arab countries is undergoing a process of reform. We hope that these Reports will help to plant the seeds of good governance in the region by inspiring a society-wide process of creative thinking, innovation and collective work in which all dynamic societal forces in Arab countries will take part. And this includes, of course, governments of the day.

The pivotal question is: can the present Arab society accommodate this concept of freedom and good governance?. An answer is attempted in Chapter 2. The concept adopted raises another question of a historical nature: can the future unfold along a trajectory that will lead the Arab world to a society of freedom and good governance?.

Freedom and Governance in Arab Countries at the Beginning of the Third Millennium: Some Problematic Issues.

Introduction

In Arab countries, the model of comprehensive freedom and the model of good governance guaranteeing such freedom both face significant conceptual and practical challenges. A combination of global, regional and local circumstances accounts for this. Based on the adopted understanding of freedom, the present chapter briefly discusses some of these issues, examined in more detail in subsequent chapters. The first issue is the tension between freedom and democratic institutions as they exist today in the Arab world. The second concerns how the interests of dominant global powers in the region affect freedom and good governance in Arab countries. This chapter also examines claims that Islam and Arab culture are inherently incompatible with freedom and good governance. That scrutiny is followed by a discussion of international human rights law as a basic reference for good governance in Arab countries. The chapter concludes with a section on peaceful transition towards a society of freedom and good governance in the Arab region, addressed in more depth in Chapter 7.

THE TENSION BETWEEN FREEDOM AND DEMOCRATIC INSTITUTIONS IN THE ARAB WORLD

In Arab countries today, there seems to be a contradiction between freedom and democracy because many democratic institutions that exist have been stripped of their original purpose to uphold freedom, in its comprehensive sense. Moreover, such institutions are subordinate to the executive authority as part of a governance apparatus that does not protect freedom.

This contradiction, which varies in degree from one country to another, takes various forms: laws that actually violate rights and freedoms; parliamentary "representatives" who bend to the executive authority, instead of scrutinizing its performance and holding it accountable; non-governmental organizations that are run directly or indirectly by the government, or reflect corrupt governance; and "trade unions" that defend governmental or business interests, with little regard for those they are supposed to represent. Then there are some media outlets that are little more than mouthpieces for government propaganda, promoting freedom of speech only if it does not turn into political activity. Such captive outlets fail to stimulate intelligent and objective debate, enhance knowledge acquisition and advance human development among the public at large.

This is not to deny that, within such institutions, there are many sincere and committed parliamentarians, journalists and civil society representatives actively working for the good of the people.

A more recent form of this contradiction is the move towards the hereditary transmission of power in republican systems of governance. By portending dynastic trends, this new formula invalidates the very essence of the republican system.

THE CONTRADICTION BETWEEN FREEDOM IN ARAB COUNTRIES AND THE INTERESTS OF DOMINANT GLOBAL POWERS

Arab states grew up in the shadow of, and in some cases even because of, colonial arrangements such as the Sykes-Picot Agreement between the two Great Powers of that day, Britain and France, after World War I. Many

In Arab countries today…democratic institutions that exist have been stripped of their original purpose to uphold freedom.

Arab states grew up in the shadow of, and in some cases because of, colonial arrangements.

were subjected to a protracted period of colonialism, which, as in the case of Egypt in 1882, aided authoritarian regimes to start curbing national opposition.

Certain restrictions of freedom in Arab countries have their origins in the colonial period when the authorities handled popular resistance to occupation by introducing systems, laws and practices that curbed freedom. Both the British and French set up exceptional courts to try the opponents of colonial rule. In Egypt, for example, martial law was imposed for the first time under the British administration. Although by the mid 20th century occupation had come to an end, some of the legal structures and practices limiting freedom under occupation were to be adopted in the political and legal architecture of the newly independent Arab states.

In the internal-external equation in Arab countries, two factors emerged which were fated to have a far-reaching impact on the attitudes of the major powers towards freedom in the Arab region: the discovery of oil and the establishment of the state of Israel. The discovery of large reserves of oil in the region, combined with the dominant role that oil has

come to play in the advanced economies, made the Arab region of crucial strategic value to the industrialized countries whose main interest was to ensure continuing oil supplies at reasonable prices. The second factor was the creation of Israel in 1948. Any Arab country's attitude toward Israel and its practices has become one of the most important yardsticks by which that country is judged by some global powers, especially the US.

It was inevitable that a contradiction would arise between such interests and legitimate Arab aspirations for freedom and self-determination. It was generally feared that if freedom and democracy ever prospered in the Arab world, enabling the majority to freely express their will, this might not help, and could actively conflict with narrow interests in the region.

When expedient, global powers intervened in the affairs of Arab states, even if at times this involved suppressing freedom movements. This was sometimes achieved through direct military intervention, such as when Britain re-occupied Iraq in 1941 (Khalidi, 2004, 24), or else through intervening to destabilize any Arab State that presumed to oppose their interests or to resist Israel as was the case with the tripartite aggression against Egypt in 1956. To that end, the global powers set up alliances, sometimes with other Arab partners, to encircle and pressure the "upstarts".

Newly independent Arab states emerged weak and fragile. On a tense global battleground, the majority of them had to find a place for themselves, usually by associating themselves with one or the other of the two competing Cold War super-powers. Freedom in Arab countries thus succumbed to a polarized world. While one camp did not adopt freedom in its comprehensive sense, the other, while publicly proclaiming freedom, sometimes took pains to prevent it from spreading in Arab countries.

Consequently, major world powers tended to gloss over human rights violations in their Arab client states so long as the regimes concerned continued to serve their interests. Thus indulged, the Arab despots of the day ruled oppressively, postponing their countries' transition to democracy.

> *When expedient, global powers intervened in the affairs of Arab states, even if at times this involved crushing freedom movements.*

BOX 2-1

The Reasons behind the Failure of Democracy in Arab Countries: Perceptions of a Western Scholar

Seven reasons are suggested in this account: oil wealth, levels of income, the nature of the Arab state, the Arab-Israeli conflict, geography, outside support for friendly tyrants, and Islamism. Three can be tied to the context of this Report:

"Arab-Israeli tension: The creation of the state of Israel on Palestinian soil came at a time when most Arab states themselves were just gaining their own independence. The swift Arab rejection of the new Israeli State, and subsequent wars and Arab defeats have encouraged the development of military regimes and security-focused states that are readily exploited by dictators.

Geography: The location of the Arab world on a central East-West axis and the geopolitical reality of holding over half of the world's oil reserves made the Middle East a key focus of European colonialism in the nineteenth and twentieth centuries. Struggles between Arab states and colonial powers for control over their oil and its pricing have led to frequent Western military intervention that is still ongoing. These conditions and continuing regional tensions have not been conducive to democratic developments.

Long-standing Western Support for "Friendly Tyrants" in the Middle East: This phenomenon began with the Cold War and systematically weakened democratic forces within the region. After the end of the Cold War, the emergence of international terrorism and the Bush Administration's war on terror have continued to favour the maintenance of "friendly" authoritarian regimes. The Bush administration's call for democratization invariably takes a back seat to security considerations, perpetuating tolerance of cooperative dictators who support the war on terror".

Source: Fuller, G.E., Islamists in the Arab World, the Dance around Democracy, Carnegie Endowment for International Peace, Washington DC, September 2004, p.6.

FREEDOM BEREFT OF ORGANIZED SUPPORT

The events of September 11 have added another dimension to this tension between the interests of global powers and freedom in Arab countries. Western countries, especially the US, were considered by many democratic movements in the world to be premier examples of mature, free democracies. Relations with democratic Western societies stirred moves towards democratic change in many countries struggling for freedom. However, this stimulus began to wane after the events following 9/11 when the US administration moved to curtail civil and political rights, especially those of Arabs and Muslims, in the fight against "terrorism" as the former defined it.

According to some US citizens' groups and lawyers' associations, probably the most significant sign of the erosion of civil and political rights in the US is the Patriot Act issued in the wake of those events. To put this Act in a historical context, we refer again to The Bill of Rights, which restricts the authority of the federal government in matters of surveillance and the pre-emptive arrests of citizens. Under the provisions of the Patriot Act, the government obtained broader powers for tapping telephone conversations, screening private electronic mail and searching databases. Many immigrant rights, including those of legal immigrants, have been curbed. One example is the subjection of immigrants to "preventive administrative detention", on the order of the Attorney General, even when no charges have been proffered and the individual cannot be legally deported.[1]

Many of these new laws are the subject of vigorous internal debate and are being challenged in the courts. Nevertheless, the fact that some Western countries which Arab reformers had long held up as models have taken steps widely perceived to be discriminatory and repressive, especially with regard to foreigners, has weakened the position of those reformers calling for Arab governments undertaking similar actions to change their course.

In Arab political life, the cause of freedom faltered in the absence of effective, broad-based political movements capable of rallying people to the struggle and building systems of good governance. In most Arab countries, freedom thus remained a disembodied ideal.

Popular political forces, such as the Arab nationalist and, later on, the Islamist movements, did not make comprehensive freedom their priority. When they did turn to the question, their more limited goal, understandably, was national freedom, which they made their public rallying point in the struggle against colonial powers.

Meanwhile, advocates of larger theories of freedom refrained from practical political organization and consequently the struggle for freedom remained on paper, in books that were seldom read.

Relations with democratic Western states stirred moves towards democratic change in many countries struggling for freedom.

BOX 2-2

Abdallah al-Arawy: Freedom and Liberalism in the Arab Context

Whenever we speak of freedom, we have to take a stand vis-à-vis the intellectual system, which includes the word freedom in its very title, i.e. liberalism.

Liberalism considers freedom the principle and the ultimate, the source and the goal, the origin and the result in the life of the human being. Liberalism is the only intellectual system that aspires to nothing but to describe, explain and comment on aspects of free human activity.

Consequently, it is natural for modern Arab thinkers to have acquired the concept of freedom through their knowledge of liberalism. Yet the difficulty facing the political historian and analyst is that of determining the characteristics of liberal thought or, more precisely, diagnosing the components that were previously incomplete, and which later merged with other ideas that led to the loss of its specificity.

I reject the notion that Western liberalism automatically engendered Arab liberalism, and that the call for freedom in the Arab Islamic world is an exact replica of the European call for freedom, that the very word freedom is the translation of a foreign word. I say that the call for freedom is born, first and foremost, from a need within Arab society, a need felt by a number of people. The fact that the expression of this need benefited from similar foreign experiences, that Arab authors rushed to embrace the liberal system because it adequately expressed what they felt does not mean that it was foreign influence itself that triggered the need. The proof lies in the fact that Arab writers did not faithfully copy the European liberalism of their time; rather, they disregarded its awareness of its own contradictions. What they needed was an optimistic, firm and self-assured liberalism, so they projected their own wishes on the pale and pessimistic liberalism of which they were contemporaries.

Source: Abdallah al-Arawy, in Arabic, 1981, 36, 39, 59.

---

[1] It is significant to note here that hundreds of town councils in the US adopted resolutions opposing this law.

"ORIENTAL DESPOTISM" AND THE ARAB SOCIETAL CONTEXT

Some historians hold that, from the fall of Baghdad in the mid-13th century to the collapse of the Ottoman State, freedom left the Arab scene and an intellectual culture of reason receded before one that emphasized the metaphysical and the mythical. A state of intellectual inflexibility ensued, "closing the door on independent reasoning and (ijtihad) or interpretive scholarship (ijtihad)".

In the context of the fraught and ambiguous relationship between "East" and "West," presented as a stark split, the first pole was usually associated with "despotism" as a supposedly inherent characteristic of "the East" and "Eastern" civilization, while the second was linked with freedom, purportedly a fundamental quality of "Western" civilization.

Thus despotism came to be considered the principal factor in explaining slow progress or underdevelopment in "the East." This explanation was reinforced by the suffering imposed on the Arab East by despotic rulers and governors, by the dominant influence of obsolete customs and practices on people's lives, and by the lack of freedom. At the same time, freedom was spreading, to varying degrees, among countries of the West. As a result, we now face the dichotomies of "despotism/backwardness" and "freedom/progress", metonyms for the "East/West" duality (Mahir Hanandah, in Arabic, 2002).

The notion that "the East" is innately severed from freedom (or democracy) gained new currency with "the clash of civilizations" (Huntington, 1996), and efforts to play up and magnify this distinction after the catastrophic events of September 11 and the "war on terrorism." Many observed that Arab and Muslim states are not democratic, and one can hardly take issue with that. But altogether more questionably, a few claimed that Arabs and Muslims are not capable of being democrats, for the very reason of being Arab ("the Arab mind") or Muslims.

International studies such as the World Values Survey (WVS)[2] have exposed the falseness of these claims by demonstrating that there is a rational and understandable thirst among Arabs to be rid of despots and to enjoy democratic governance. That survey clearly showed that Arab attitudes and values strongly support knowledge and good governance. Among the nine surveyed regions, which included the advanced Western countries, Arab countries topped the list of those agreeing that "democracy is better that any other form of governance". A substantially high percentage also rejected authoritarian rule (defined as a strong ruler who disregards parliament or elections). These results are quite logical in comparative terms, since those who bear the scars of despotism and harsh rule naturally look forward to freedom and good governance more than others.

Erroneous and mechanical connections between Islam and despotism are similar to those that were sometimes made between Catholicism and oppression in certain Latin American countries, in Eastern Europe and in East Asia some thirty years ago. It is as wrong to link Islam and oppression now as it was to bracket Catholicism with oppression then.

DEMOCRACY AND RELIGION

In democratic thinking, institutions must be able to formulate policies freely and independently, within the boundaries set by the constitution and human rights. Specifically, there should be no privileged position for religious institutions that would permit them to dictate policy to a democratically elected government.

By the same token, individuals and religious groups must be guaranteed independence vis-a-vis both the government and other religious groups. This independent arena must protect the right of people and groups not only to worship as they wish, in private; but also to promote their values publicly in civil society.

That some Western countries which Arab reformers had long held up as models have taken steps widely perceived to be discriminatory... has weakened the position of those reformers calling for Arab governments undertaking similar actions to change their course.

Erroneous and mechanical connections between Islam and despotism are similar to those that were made between Catholicism and oppression in Latin American countries, in Eastern Europe and in East Asia thirty years ago.

[2] An extensive international study, the World Values Survey provides an opportunity to assess the relative preferences of Arab people, in comparison with people of other regions and cultures, on issues of freedom and governance.

The results presented in this study are based on field surveys in a large number of countries in the world, including five in the Arab region (Jordan, Algeria, Morocco, Egypt, and Saudi Arabia). The results cover approximately half the population of Arab countries. In addition to the Arab countries, the surveys provide data concerning eight other country groups: other Islamic countries (non-Arab), sub-Saharan Africa, Eastern Europe, South Asia, the US and Canada and Australia and New Zealand, Latin America, East Asia, and Western Europe.

They must be free to create organizations or movements within political society for the same purpose, provided that such activity has no negative impact on the freedom of other citizens or democratic rules and principles.

These institutional principles of democracy mean that it is unacceptable to prevent any societal group, including religious groups, from forming a political party. However, these groups should agree and adhere to all the guarantees of democratic practice in society (Chapter One) even when faced with the "tyranny of the majority", so that democratic principles remain the standard for correcting departures from democratic practice. It is only permissible to impose restrictions on political parties once their actual conduct has led to acts inimical to democracy, and where it is the judiciary, and not the ruling party, that makes the ruling (Stepan, 2001, 216-217).

Interestingly, in advanced Western countries that are incontestably democratic, religion is not distant from political society. Indeed, some theorists argue that no existing Western democracy can claim a hard-and-fast separation between Church and State, having reached the point where "freedom of faith" does not end with practicing religious rites in private life, but extends to the right to organize in civil and political society. Indeed, some theorists maintain that neither "secularism" nor "the separation of 'Church' from State" constitutes an essential property of democracy (e.g. Stepan, 2001, 223). What is always necessary is to assure the State's impartiality towards the beliefs of its citizens.

DEMOCRACY AND ISLAM: POTENTIAL FOR HARMONY

Our starting point here is that Islam, in the prevailing Sunni sects, has no "clergy" and no "church," and consequently the concept of religious authority or rule does not arise. Even in Shi'ism, contemporary ijtihad or interpretive scholarship favours "the authority of the umma (nation)," rather than "the authority of the faqih (jurisprudent)." Such is the opinion of Ayatollah Muhammad Mahdi Shamseddin,

Head of the Shi'ite Supreme Council of Lebanon, who ruled that "During the period of occultation, the umma, or nation of Muslims, reclaims governance authority (wilaya), and appoints the ruler or rulers by means of choice and election. Through its will the nation grants the ruler(s) authority whose duration or substance is limited" (Muhammad Selim al-Awwa, in Arabic, 1998, 61-63; Muhammad al-Mahdi Shamseddin, as quoted in Muhammad Selim al-Awwa, 1989).

Islam may not set out a detailed and comprehensive system for good governance in its sacred text. Yet that text ("bearer of multiple perspectives"), its interpretation (which is multiple), and Islamic history (which reflects great variety) all embody the core principles that sustain freedom and good governance as we understand them. These principles include obligatory consultation, respect for freedoms, questioning rulers and holding them accountable.[3] The dominant trend in Islamic jurisprudence supports obligatory consultation and freedom, without prejudice to the rights of others. Specifically, enlightened Islamic interpretations find that the tools of democracy - when used properly – offer one possible practical arrangement for applying the principle of consultation (al-shura).

These fundamental principles (from which governance systems and detailed regulations may be derived) provide for the realization of justice and equality, the assurance of public freedoms, the right of the nation to appoint and dismiss rulers, and guarantees of all public

Islam, in the prevailing Sunni rite, has no "clergy" and no "church".

BOX 2-3

Ibn al-Qayim al-Jawziya: On welfare

This is a difficult subject, so much so that some have given it up, asserting that the sacred law is deficient and is not concerned with human welfare. But those who hold this to be the case have excluded themselves and humanity at large from many right and beneficial courses of action, which in their opinion are incompatible with the law. By the life of the Almighty! Those courses of action are incompatible, not with the law, but with those individuals' understanding of the law. They have been led astray by a kind of defect in their knowledge of truth and their knowledge of reality, and the error of regarding the one as less important than the other.

Know that the law is all justice, all equity and all mercy. Every matter that deviates from justice toward injustice, and from equity toward oppression, and from mercy toward lack of mercy, is not of the law, though it may have been incorporated into the law through interpretation.

Source: Ibn al-Qayim al-Jawziya, Kitab al-turuq wa al-hikma

---

[3] This does not conflict with the fact that much of the traditional heritage leans towards "establishing the legitimacy of the existing state, even when it is one of oppression and tyranny" (Kamal Abdel-Latif, in Arabic, 1999, 67).

Imam Muhammad Abdu: The Legitimacy of Elections

"States that have built their power on the basis of consultation, entrust the nation to elect trustworthy people who will establish the public laws of the kingdom and monitor their implementation by the government. Such elections cannot be legitimate unless the nation has the full freedom to choose, without any pressure from the government or from others, with no temptation and no intimidation. Thus, the nation must be aware of its rights and their purpose. If different people are elected under the influence of the government or others, this is legally null and void and the chosen ones have not the authority to be in charge and, consequently, to obey them is not a legal obligation as ordained in the Qur'an, but enforced obedience. For example, if a man were forced to elect a so-called deputy of the nation to what is known as the legislative power, he would be like one who was forced to marry or to buy; he would be legally entitled to neither wife nor goods".

Source: Farid Abdel Khaleq, in Arabic, 1998, 47

and private rights for non-Muslims and Muslims alike, including the right to hold public office (Muhammad Selim al-Awwa, in Arabic, 1998, 58-59, 72).

Even in the Prophet's saying (hadith) on obedience to rulers, the utterance "Obey the person in charge," which is often exploited to support existing rule no matter how oppressive, and to illustrate "the Arab/Muslim mentality" on governance, is in fact only one part of the hadith. The text stipulates obedience only "in what accords with the truth"[4] and indeed goes beyond that to fault the bad ruler.

Notwithstanding these key theological and philosophical nuances, political forces, both those in power and in opposition, have selectively appropriated Islam to support and perpetuate their oppressive rule.

This underlines the importance of establishing political freedom in the public space and promoting enlightened explanations of Islam much more widely, as mutually supportive pillars of freedom and good governance in Arab countries.

Ayatollah al-Mohaqiq al-Naeeny: An Opinion Concerning Conditionality or Constitutionality

The conduct of the ruler is bounded by the limitations of his prerogatives … it is conditioned not to exceed them, the people are his partners in all that concerns the destiny of the country to which they all belong on an equal footing Those in charge are but loyal trust bearers of the people, not owners nor servants. Like other trust bearers, they are responsible to each and every individual of the nation, they are accountable for any trespass they commit, and every single person has the right to question and to object in an environment of security and freedom, without being bound by the Sultan's will or preferences.

Power of this kind is known as limited, bound, just, conditioned, accountable, constitutional; the reason for so naming it is obvious, and the person in charge of such power is called a protector and a guardian, a dispenser of justice, the responsible, the just. The nation enjoying such bounty is known as a nation that is worthy of reward in the hereafter, a nation proud, free and vital; the reason for such attributes is also clear!

This type of power is based on responsibility and honesty; that is why, like all other responsibilities and honest charges it is conditioned by the absence of excess and bound by the absence of waste. The one element that preserves this type of power and prevents it from turning into absolute power and from excesses is supervision, accountability and full responsibility.

That is why we of the Imamiyya school of thought consider virtuousness a condition of power; it is the highest imaginable degree of loyalty to one's charge and a safeguard against tyranny and subservience to one's desires. The most that can be reached as a natural, human substitute for such a virtuous custody - even by imposition - is a solution that is an approximation, a shadow of that perfect image.

Such a solution depends on two matters: a constitution that fully contains the above-mentioned limitations, so as to differentiate between the functions that the Sultan is committed to perform, and those wherein he has no right to intervene or act. The constitution must also state how such functions are to be performed, to what degree the Sultan may rule, the freedom of the nation and the rights of its different groups and classes in a way that is concomitant with the rulings of the doctrine and the requirements of law. In such a case, to exceed those functions and to put the trust to waste would be a betrayal - like all kinds of betrayal of confidence - necessitating removal from power, officially and forever, with all the sanctions entailed by betrayal.

Scrutiny and accountability are necessary. These functions are to be entrusted to a body composed of the wise and learned members of the nation, experts in international rights, well versed in the requirements and characteristics of the age. They are to monitor and call to account the persons in charge of the nation so as to ensure that there is no excess or waste. They are the representatives and spokespersons of the nation, the embodiment of its learned power. The people's assembly is but the official council composed of these persons. Their functions of supervising, calling to account, maintaining the limitations of power to prevent it from becoming absolute, can only be performed if all the state employees - as the country's executive power - are under the supervision of that body, which is in turn responsible to each and every member of the nation.

Both the Sunni and Ja'afari doctrines justify the legitimacy of the supervisory function of the nation's representatives and their right to intervene in matters of politics. According to the former, wherein matters are entrusted to decision-makers, election of representatives achieves the desired purpose and nothing else is required to confer legitimacy. According to our own doctrine, we believe that matters and politics of the nation are the responsibility of the public representatives, the desired legitimacy requires only that the elected body be composed of just people who strive to interpret or who have been entrusted to act. To correct expressed opinions and to approve their implementation is sufficient to confer legitimacy upon the supervisory function of the body of representatives.

Source: Al-Mohaqiq al- Naeeny, in Arabic, 1909

[4] For example: Hisham ibn Arwa related on the authority of Abu Salih who had it from Abu Hurayra that the Messenger of God, said, "Others will rule you after me. The pious will rule you piously and the impious impiously. Hearken to them and obey them in all that accords with the Truth. If they do good, the credit will be yours and theirs, and if they do bad, the credit will be yours and the discredit theirs." (Ali ibn Muhammad Habib al-Basri al-Mawardi, in Arabic, 1983, 5).

DEMOCRACY AND THE ARAB REGION: THE TRAP OF THE ONE-OFF ELECTION

The "trap of the one-off election" refers to a ploy used in relation to Islamic societies to alarm those apprehensive about the accession to power of fundamentalist Islamic groups. It has also been cited to justify foreign interference to prop up authoritarian Arab regimes. It is contended that opening up the public sphere to all societal forces - among the most active of which is the Islamic movement - will end with these forces assuming power, followed by oppression, such that democratic competition becomes history after the one and only election. Fear of this "trap" is undoubtedly real, and indeed finds some justification in contemporary Arab experience. For this reason, some schools of thought and some political forces in Arab countries have opposed the freedom of Islamic political movements to organize publicly, fearing that, if these forces ever came to power through elections, that would put an end to any chances for peaceful political alternation.

In line with the previous discussion on democracy and religion, we believe that the best insurance against this risk is to strengthen constitutional principles and clauses to safeguard society from abuses of majority power, and to secure at the outset the commitment of all political movements to respect those measures.

FREEDOM AND HUMAN RIGHTS

Freedom is a human being's primary right. It is a right conferred at birth, and because of this all human beings possess this right on an equal footing. This primary human right is the foundation on which human rights as a whole are built.

The human rights system in its present form developed through a number of stages and expanded to ever wider spheres, to the point where international human rights law is virtually a reference framework for human development and a criterion by which to judge the quality of life in societies.

> ### BOX 2-6
> ### Boasting about human rights while destroying them
>
> In the 1980s, there was an Arab country that was able to make rapid strides on the road to democracy. It was striving to achieve a society without great disparities, and it did not suffer from any great class differences. It was characterized by a civil society that included a strong human-rights movement, promising young opposition parties and a bold, responsible press.
>
> However, developments during the last decade have brought this country under scrutiny by Arab and international human rights movements and it has repeatedly been condemned for its use of torture, unfair trials, persecution of human rights activists, denial of freedom of opinion, and fraudulent elections.
>
> The importance of this situation does not derive from the gravity of the abuses, for, by comparison with what occurs in other Arab countries, they are less significant numerically and result in essence from the regime's successful destruction of the opposition. What is striking is that some democrats, following the regime's cosmetic adoption of their programmes, accorded it, at the outset, a degree of legitimacy, acceptance, and collaboration. This regime however duped civil society, causing a deep split between those naïve enough to believe promises whose emptiness became daily more apparent and those who refused to continue to collaborate with the regime that was fast transforming itself into a police state.
>
> More dangerous still, this regime started a wide destructive operation against democracy and human rights concealed by cosmetics. At time when torture was common practice, the regime was posting up the Universal Declaration in police stations. Even as it moved to muzzle the press, it claimed that it supported freedom of opinion. And as it undercut popular freedoms by interfering at times in elections, it would speak fulsomely about the sovereignty of the people.
>
> Arab and international organizations have published dozens of reports criticizing the regime. They emphasize not only such abuses but also the regime's facade of democracy and human rights now manifest to all.

THE IMPORTANCE OF THE HUMAN RIGHTS SYSTEM

The human rights system enjoys worldwide respect to an unprecedented degree - a respect that has grown steadily, especially as the concept of human rights has advanced over the years to comprise increasingly comprehensive standards for human well-being.

Strengthening and protecting human rights has thus become a defining quest of our time.

This quest gains additional legitimacy, and

> ### BOX 2-7
> ### Declaration on the Right to Development Adopted by General Assembly Resolution 41/128 of 4 December 1986 (excerpts)
>
> Recalling the right of peoples to self-determination, by virtue of which they have the right freely to determine their political status and to pursue their economic, social and cultural development.
>
> **Article 1**
> 1. The right to development is an inalienable human right by virtue of which every human person and all peoples are entitled to participate in, contribute to, and enjoy economic, social, cultural and political development, in which all human rights and fundamental freedoms can be fully realized.
> 2. The human right to development also implies the full realization of the right of peoples to self-determination, which includes, subject to the relevant provisions of both International Covenants on Human Rights, the exercise of their inalienable right to full sovereignty over all their natural wealth and resources.

is the more urgent, in those developing countries where human rights are seriously violated even as the peoples of these societies aspire to a better and more humane life. Respect for human rights has now become a key component in defining the concept of Arab human development and freedom.

In contemporary jurisprudence human rights constitute the collection of rights incorporated in international agreements and treaties that guarantee all people, irrespective of their nationality, ethnicity, language, sex, religion, ideology and abilities, the fundamental rights to which they are entitled by virtue of being human. The importance of the human rights system is that it guarantees the individual a collection of rights that cannot be surrendered. Human rights codified in international covenants and laws transcend national regulation and practices. They constitute supreme standards of a compelling legal nature against which other regulations and practices may be weighed. The contemporary international legal regulation of human rights originates in the Universal Declaration of Human Rights (UDHR) adopted by the UN General Assembly in 1948. However, such rights are the common inheritance of humanity and can be traced back to the religious and cultural norms, values and practices of many societies.

Human rights are generally classified into two groups, civil and political rights, and economic and social rights. The first group includes freedom of opinion and expression, religious freedom, freedom of assembly and association, the right to form political parties, the right of participation in public decision-making and the right to self-determination, among others. This group also covers legal rights such as equality before the law, the right to trial and defence, the right to presumption of innocence and impartial due process. Civil rights further uphold the independence of the judiciary and the right to protection from torture.

Economic and social rights include the individual's right to work, education, health care, adequate housing and to join a trade union. In addition, a new generation of collective rights has emerged relating to the right to development and the right to a clean environment. Moreover, several international organizations are engaged in promoting the rights of vulnerable groups such as children, women and minorities.

The relationship between human rights and human development was underlined in the first AHDR (Chapter One). Put simply, the two reinforce each other and their common denominator is human freedom. Human development, by enhancing people's capabilities, gives them the ability to exercise freedom. Human rights, by providing the necessary legal framework, guarantee the opportunity to exercise that freedom. This instrumental relationship defines the renaissance movement advanced through these Reports and understanding it is crucial for Arab countries where first, the human rights situation is deteriorating and may well grow worse, and second, work to promote and safeguard human rights is as yet under-developed.

The latter situation can be attributed to several factors. First, awareness of human rights principles is limited; such rights are not deeply rooted in the Arab cultural environment. Second, civil society is generally weak; and third, human rights organizations, such as the Arab Organization for Human Rights and the Arab Institute for Human Rights, are relatively new, with limited popular support and resources.

INTERNATIONAL HUMAN RIGHTS LAW

Perhaps no international document enjoys as much consensus as the Universal Declaration of Human Rights. The UDHR starts by affirming that "recognition of the inherent dignity and of the equal and inalienable rights of all members of the human family is the foundation of freedom, justice and peace in the world"; and, in adopting the Declaration, the UN General Assembly proclaimed it "a common standard of achievement for all peoples and all nations," (integral text, Annex 3)

The UDHR came about following the recognition of four international agreements, concerning slavery (1926), forced labour (1930), freedom to join unions and protection of the right to union organization (1948), and prohibition of the crime of genocide (1948).

Respect for human rights has now become a key component in defining the concept of Arab human development.

Human rights and human development… reinforce each other and their common denominator is human freedom.

The Declaration stimulated a growing body of international standards that seek to strengthen and protect human rights. From the date of its adoption through to 1986, more than 60 international human rights standards were developed, covering the range of declarations, conventions and protocols as well as UN General Assembly resolutions. Over time, international human rights treaties became more focused and specialized concerning both the issue addressed and the social group(s) identified as requiring protection; thus, such documents were defined more comprehensively and in greater detail.

But at the core of international accords on human rights remains what is termed the International Bill of Human Rights, (IBHR) consisting of the UDHR, the International Covenant on Economic, Social, and Cultural Rights (ICESCR), and the International Covenant on Civil and Political Rights (ICCPR), concluded in 1966, as well as the Optional Protocols.

International human rights law, or the IBHR in its widest sense, embraces not only

At the core of international accords on human rights remains the International Bill on Human Rights.

BOX 2-8

Muhammad Shahrour: A Word About Freedom

Sometimes words fall short of expressing one's intention, of explaining an emotion or a meaning or of defining something that one feels but cannot describe. Language, as a spoken, heard, written and read instrument for human communication and for the transfer of knowledge, more easily describes material objects. No two persons will disagree in defining dress or table for example. It is however not as efficient in the area of abstract things and meanings. The reason, as I see it, is simple. Language is a container and a container, however large, is limited, while meaning is absolute and infinite, however narrow or small; never will the limited contain the absolute, nor can the infinite be stuffed into the finite; the equation is basically impossible! Freedom – like a multi-faceted polished diamond – represents the most outstanding of those difficult to describe and define abstracts. For the Greek Aesop, freedom means liberation from slavery, for Schopenhauer it means liberation in the Sufi sense – of the fetters of earthly flesh, only achieved through death, a meaning shared by the Egyptian poet Salah Jahin who says in one of his quatrains:

The ducks have lifted to cross deserts and seas
Oh how I wish to go, to roam with birds and bees
Please God, by all that's dear, when I die one day
Send me not to heaven, it too has locks and keys!

Therefore, he who says that freedom is development is right, he who says that it is something within a human being that pushes him to refuse oppression, repression and tyranny is also right.

Freedom, in my view, is choice and the capacity to make a choice. A human being's capacity to choose his actions is what differentiates him from angels ("they do what they are ordered to do"), without it, accountability on judgment day has no meaning. That is why I have reservations when I hear someone say: "An individual can only be free in a free society/nation", because a free human being makes a free nation, not the opposite.

Freedom for me is destiny and divine decree; destiny is what the Almighty explained by saying "We have created all things as they were destined to be" (Al-Qamar, 49), divine decree is a human being's ability to deal voluntarily with what was decreed, the relation between the two is knowledge. The greater a human being's knowledge with what was decreed, the wider the margin of his freedom to deal with what is. That is why I consider the spreading of education and knowledge as a first priority in preparing a free individual, for he who knows nothing, chooses nothing.

There are limits to freedom that regulate and control it, be it at the level of the individual, society or the ruling power. If an individual exceeds the limits of his freedom, he falls into chaos (the freedom of your finger ends where the freedom of the other person's eye begins). If society exceeds these limits, it becomes occupied and colonized; if the ruling power does so, then it is repression and tyranny; even if that power is a paragon of faith and morality and came to power by a legitimate and democratic process, since it controls money, weapons, the media and the fora of science and learning. The situation is even worse if the rulers have not come to power through a democratic process! Napoleon said: "Injustice is inherent in the soul, only power brings it to the surface", and the Arab poet said:

"Injustice is one of the soul's realities
If a virtuous man you find
He may be just, but for a cause unknown".

They both meant absolute freedom that exceeds its limits, rather than injustice since practicing freedom requires constant observation and control at the level of the individual of the community in general and of the ruler in particular. The Almighty said: "Let there be from among you a nation that calls for good, enjoining what is good and forbidding wrong" (Al-Imran, 104), and went so far as to consider the latter as coming before faith in God by saying: "You were the best nation given unto people, enjoining what is right, forbidding wrong and having faith in God". (Al-Imran, 110).

In the light of knowledge prevailing today, little reflection is required to see that the Qur'anic verse refers to supervisory groups over which the State has no power. These are groups that enjoy freedom of expression and opinion within a framework of free information, freely supervising and regulating freedoms in society in general and, in particular, those of the ruling power, at the level of thought as well as at the political and economic levels.

But still we see some Muslim Arabs who understand freedom as being solely the opposite of slavery. We sometimes see Arab and Islamic thought governed by the principle that "a Sultan feared by his subjects is better than a Sultan who fears his subjects", and by the principle that "an informative consultative opinion is not one that is binding". We see that ordaining what is good and prohibiting what is evil can lead to an institution ruled by the State, one whose sole task is to consecrate what was and what is (the status quo), one that sees in "tomorrow" an image of "yesterday" and to whom ordaining what is good means no more than herding people to prayers with a stick. And we see educational curricula established on the basis of dictating knowledge, thus killing creativity and producing people who are educated but who have no opinion of their own, who will obey the ruler were he to beat them or take away their money. Yet even when all of this prevails, you will still find freedom firmly rooted in the collective psyche of the Arabs and Muslims. I say: Give me one single individual who understands freedom and believes in it, I shall then give you a community where there is no place for a tyrannical ruler.

The encounter between the global and the particular is especially sensitive when it comes to human rights.

all the above core instruments but also treaties, conventions, declarations, codes and principles, which deepen and elaborate the elements of the IBHR. Among the notable additional constituents of international human rights law are the following instruments: The Convention against Torture and Other Cruel, Inhuman or Degrading Treatment or Punishment (CAT), The Convention on the Elimination of All Forms of Racial Discrimination (CERD), The Convention on The Elimination of All Forms Of Discrimination against Women (CEDAW), The Convention on the Rights of the Child (CRC), and the International Convention on the Protection of the Rights of All Migrant Workers and Members of Their Families.

BOX 2-9

The Pact of the Virtuous (Hilf al-fudul)

The first public treaty on human rights, the Pact of the Virtuous[5] was concluded by Arab tribes sometime around 590 AD. The purpose was to defend any individual who had suffered injustice at the hands of another, regardless of the origin or position of either individual, until the wrongdoing was stopped and the wrong redressed. The Pact had been preceded by numerous treaties among the Arab tribes, especially those of Mecca, which had set up mutual assistance schemes to help the needy.

This Pact was ratified twenty years before God made Muhammad His Messenger. The Messenger of God witnessed its ratification, and later said of it: "I witnessed in the house of 'Abdallah ibn Jad'an the making of a pact dearer to me than the most abundant material blessings. If someone were to invoke it under

Islam, I would respond, [honouring it]." The content of this pact, as transmitted by 'Ibn Hisham' from 'Ibn Ishaq', was as follows: "They agreed on and concluded this pact that said that any individual in Mecca, whether a native of Mecca or someone from elsewhere, would receive their support; they would stand with him until the one who had wronged him gave him redress for the injustice." They named it the Pact of the Virtuous "because they made a pact that rights be honoured, and in order that a wrongdoer not assail or be victorious over one who had been wronged." It is said also that it resembled a pact that was ratified by "Jurhum" in earlier times in which three of its men made an accord: 'al-Fadl ibn Fadala', 'al-Fadl ibn Wadi', and 'al-Fadil ibn al-Harith', and it became known as the Pact of the Fadls[6]

Source: Ahmed Sidqi al-Dajani, in Arabic, 1988, 19-20.

BOX 2-10

Human rights: universality and specificity

The General Assembly session on the Millennium, resulting from the World Conference on Human Rights held in Vienna on 25 June 1993, agreed that:

All human rights are universal, indivisible and interdependent and interrelated. The international community must treat human rights globally in a fair and equal manner, on the same footing,

and with the same emphasis. While the significance of national and regional particularities and various historical, cultural and religious backgrounds must be borne in mind, it is the duty of states, regardless of their political, economic and cultural systems, to promote and protect all human rights and fundamental freedoms.

Source: Office of the United Nations High Commissioner for Human Rights, in Arabic, 2002, 61

THE APPLICABILITY OF INTERNATIONAL HUMAN RIGHTS LAW TO ARAB COUNTRIES

In many developing countries, the question of whether a global or a local approach to various aspects of life is more appropriate is often a controversial issue. Human rights are no exception. In general, we incline towards the local or the particular, a context that is conducive to supporting and encouraging an Arab identity, but with the caveat that we should not isolate ourselves or ignore the global environment of which we are a part. In other words, we support taking the local or particular approach in the context of a creative interaction with the achievements of human civilization, within the framework of a project to stimulate an Arab renaissance. Yet the encounter between the global and the particular is especially sensitive when it comes to human rights.

It is regrettable that in Arab countries 'specificity' is frequently raised with the aim of weakening international human rights law. Nevertheless we remain hopeful that considerations of Arab specificity will combine with universal human rights to enrich international human rights law from an Arab perspective, rather than to detract from it.

Human rights constitute a universal or global issue par excellence. After all, specific rights are assigned to a person purely because s/he is a human being, without regard to any special characteristics, because equality is the basic principle that organizes the concept of human rights. Some however maintain that applying existing universal definitions of human rights principles as embodied in international human rights law is unacceptable since these definitions were not shaped as a result of effective participation of all countries as equal partners in the endeavour. Rather, Western industrial countries held the upper hand in their development.

The UDHR was formulated immediately after the end of the Second World War under the aegis of the UN, which was dominated by the five permanent members of the Security Council. Up to the time when the two fun-

---

[5] This has also been translated as "the Alliance of Excellence."

[6] fadl, pl. fudul: virtue, favour, kindness, excellence, superiority.

damental international instruments of 1966 were in final form, only a small number of developing countries were members of the UN — and their influence was extremely limited. Some objectors observe that the representation of developing countries in the UN came about, in any case, through national élites who were not the most reliable representatives of their people. Thus, the argument goes, the circumstances surrounding the formation of human rights principles ensured that these instruments reflected Western values, values that were hegemonic with respect to the international order especially at the time when the UDHR was formulated. In this view, the International Bill of Human Rights contained the seeds of contradiction between certain cultural values prevailing in different regions of the world, and the particularities of these regions and the aspirations of their peoples.

Yet this point of view underestimates the extent of the Arab contribution, whether on the part of the Arab states that actively and effectively participated in debates on the substantive elements of human rights standards, or in the persons of distinguished Arab experts who helped shape international human rights law.

In any case, the Arab world remains in need of an Arab Bill of Human Rights that is acceptable to all in the region and that can draw on the values of the Arab-Islamic culture. This effort to assimilate both dimensions is all the more urgent in light of the cultural particularities of Arab societies and because of the complex and problematic nature of human rights in this part of the world.

Some think that it is crucial to acknowledge a disparity between human rights principles, according to international human rights law, and traditional interpretations of Islamic law (Shari'a) in some areas, such as capital punishment, total equality between men and women, and the treatment of religious minorities. International law considers the right to life the premier civil right; hence the global human rights movement seeks abolition of the death penalty, and pending abolition, seeks to set in place stringent limits. Likewise, the principle of complete gender equality means that international human rights law prohibits

---

BOX 2-11

The Contribution of Arab States to the Universal Declaration of Human Rights and the Two International Covenants

Omar Lutfi, Mahmoud 'Azmi (both Egyptian) and Charles Malik (Lebanese) were all involved in the different stages in the preparation of the Universal Declaration of Human Rights.

Omar Lutfi was responsible (despite opposition by some powerful states) for the inclusion of what Susan Waltz considers to be the strongest statement on universality, contained in article 2, paragraph 2:

"No distinction shall be made on the basis of the political, jurisdictional or international status of the country or territory to which a person belongs, whether it be independent, trust, non-self-governing or under any other limitation of sovereignty."

Throughout the 20-year process of developing the Universal Declaration of Human Rights and the two Covenants, at no stage did any Arab state withdraw from the debate.

The two Covenants were adopted at the General Assembly by unanimous vote. Arab states participating at the time were: Algeria, Iraq, Jordan, Libya, Mauritania, Morocco, Saudi Arabia, Somalia, Syria, Tunisia, the United Arab Republic (Egypt) and Yemen.

In the development of the two Covenants Badia Afnan, representing Iraq, was insistent that gender equality should be explicitly guaranteed in both Covenants at a time when such a provision was not favoured by several Western and other states. In the first drafts of the Covenants gender equality was absent. Afnan objected and fought for the inclusion of the present article 3 (ICCPR): "The States Parties to the present Covenant undertake to ensure the equal rights of men and women to the enjoyment of all civil and political rights set forth in the present Covenant."

Arab states, notably Syria and Saudi Arabia led the movement to include the right to self-determination in the legally binding Covenants.

In the long-standing debates on the development of the two Covenants both Egypt and Syria are on record as supporting effective measures of implementation. Syria proposed a UN investigation mechanism, and Egypt supported the rights of individuals, groups and non-governmental organizations to refer complaints of human rights violations directly to the UN. In 1950, for example, the Egyptian representative stated that the delegation of Egypt was "ready to accept the establishment of a permanent human rights committee, a court to sanction the committee's findings, or any other provision that might seem necessary".

Source: Susan Waltz, 2004

---

discrimination against women (for example, on inheritance) and minorities (for instance, acceding to the position of Head of State). Some argue that international human rights law and Islam can be harmonized only by applying the logic of ijtihad (interpretive reasoning) starting from the principle of the welfare of the Muslim nation, even if this transcends the current logic of jurisprudence (fiqh). In fact some such interpretations have already established congruence between international human rights law and Islamic law.

It may be appropriate to work towards a concept of human rights in the Arab context, that respects international human rights law in its entirety, while recognizing the Arab national identity and its aspirations as an historical legacy of critical importance in defining Arab reality, and in shaping the Arab future.

The Arab world remains in need of an Arab Bill of Human Rights.

Foremost among the rights of the Arab people is the legitimate desire to achieve such goals as national liberation and self-determination, unity, human development, and national security. These are intersecting goals that a project for an Arab renaissance must regard as necessarily integrated within a firmly conceived structure. The goals of national liberation and self-determination lead directly to that of liberating Arab territory--and liberating the agency of the Arab people. Specifically this means obtaining the guaranteed right of the people to determine what political forms and entities will constitute the Arab region; to conceive and achieve a desired cultural, social, political and economic blueprint for the homeland; and to formulate the means by which this can be achieved. This goal includes the specific guarantee of effective popular participation in determining people's futures, with the caveat that addressing these demands should not in any way conflict with the global human rights system.

> *The goals of national liberation and self-determination lead directly to that of liberating Arab territory.*

There was an important initiative to adapt international human rights law in order to arrive at an Arab Human Rights Charter. The document in question is the *Draft Charter for Human Rights in the Arab Homeland*, the outcome of a conference of Arab experts held at the International Institute of Higher Studies in Criminal Sciences in Siracusa, Italy, in 1986 (Mahmud Cherif Bassiouni et. al., in Arabic, 1989).

This draft was based on the idea of Arab specificity, represented as an ideological foundation governed by the general framework of the Shari'a, but within the framework of the global human rights movement. Its originators took as their mandate the formulation of a Charter that would represent the situation of the Arab people in today's global context. This is apparent in the nomenclature adopted. The draft organizes rights on the basis of a perspective that sees people as individuals first, members of society second, then thirdly as members of a political entity, and finally as Arabs belonging to the larger homeland (watan). Thus, the draft provides for civil rights, followed by social, political, and cultural rights, and then political rights, concluding with the collective rights of the Arab people. Beyond this, the draft made considerable advances with respect to human rights on the global level in that it included elements of a "third generation" of human rights, such as the right to a just distribution of income.

The rights included in that draft framework form an integrated platform of interlocking and coherent elements. They also constitute an Arab concept of development, as their elements provide criteria for judging the progress of human development in Arab countries, over time and across geographical space. Elements of this concept can be divided into two parts: the first global and the second devoted to the specific characteristics of the Arab region (Nader Fergany, in Arabic, 1992, 55-58).

A similar approach is to be found in the report of a group of Arab experts mandated to review an updated draft of the *Arab Charter for Human Rights*, (Annex 2) under the auspices of the Arab League.

While the updated draft of the Charter corrects many of the defects contained in the

---

BOX 2-12

Haytham Manna'a: The Books of Tribulations

The books of tribulations and ordeals were the first expression of the suffering entailed by affiliation to a religion, doctrine or political opposition party. They followed a methodology born of the era to which they belonged, which differs from contemporary approaches. Sometimes their topic was general, so that the book included political assassination, pursuit, arrest, abduction, murder and physical or psychological injury. Other books would deal solely with those who were killed and not touch on imprisonment or injury.

There were also books that dealt exclusively with certain families, such as "The Victims of Murder Among the Talibites" by Abul Farag al-Asfahany, which he devoted to the descendants of Ali Ibn Abi Talib who were murdered. Other works dealt with famous personalities and descendants of the Prophet (or nobles), while some researchers concentrated on poets, prophets or doctors. Some devoted a whole book to one single case, such as Imam Ali Ibn Abi Talib and his son, Hussein, or Ahmed Ibn Hanbal (for example, we have found six books on the ordeal of Ibn Hanbal).

The book on tribulation by Abul Arab Mohammad Ibn Ahmad Ibn Tamim Al Tamimi, verified by Dr. Yehia Wahib al Jabbouri in 1983, is the best illustration of this important phenomenon, wherein he identified 48 books on tribulations and ordeals. He goes to considerable lengths to introduce the book, and explain its style and purpose. What is important in his writing this comprehensive book of almost 500 pages is that Abul Arab himself experienced imprisonment, fear and threats. Here he explains his purpose in writing the book: "I speak hereafter of those who suffered from among the best of the nation, men of learning and noble men, those who were imprisoned, beaten, threatened or were tried in other ways. It is meant as a consolation for those who have undergone the same ordeals as the virtuous men of the early days of this nation." This explanation is to be found in most books on tribulations that suggest, in more ways than one, that the best of the best are those who suffer the most. For their authors, such books go beyond merely relating history or giving information, they serve to sow the seeds of a culture of resistance and opposition to injustice and arbitrary treatment.

previous version, it still falls short of providing for the comprehensive protections contained in international human rights law, particularly of freedom of expression, belief and association. It also omits specific texts on the elimination of all forms of discrimination against women and the rights of the child. The revised Charter further contains provisions to be defined by the law, which could allow laws to be used to curtail freedoms in Arab countries.

THE CHALLENGE OF PEACEFUL TRANSITION TO A SOCIETY OF FREEDOM AND GOOD GOVERNANCE IN THE ARAB COUNTRIES

Chapter One describes free societies, in their normative dimension, as fundamental contrasts with present-day Arab countries. The enormous gap that separates today's reality and what many in the region hope for, is a source of widespread frustration and despair among Arabs about their countries' prospects for a peaceful transition to societies enjoying freedom and good governance. Moreover, persisting tendencies in Arab social structures could well lead to spiralling social, economic, and political crises. Each further stage of crisis would impose itself as a new reality, producing injustices eventually beyond control.

Moreover, the Arab societal environment persistently reinforces individual inertia and resistance to change insofar as progress toward freedom and good governance would inevitably harm the interests of the minority that at present influences the shape of things to come in Arab countries.

Another concern relates to the many victims of injustice who are denied peaceful and effective political means to seek redress. This denial could become an invitation to resort to social conflict and perhaps violence. When the prospects of effective political action in Arab countries are foreclosed, this is effective warning of a period of social strife that could well prove destructive. While some believe that violence may be historically necessary to change a reality that has long suppressed the capabilities of these countries, freedom could well be its first victim. This is a fate that all of those who

care about the future of the Arab region must strive to avert.

If the Arab people are to have true societies of freedom and good governance, they will need to be socially innovative. Their challenge is to create a viable mode of transition from a situation where liberty is curtailed and oppression the rule to one of freedom and good governance that minimises social upheaval and human costs, to the fullest extent possible,. History will judge this a transcendent achievement through which the region finally attained its well-deserved freedom.

This challenge concerns, first and foremost, the intellectual and political vanguards of the region, those who have until now seemingly neglected to take up their societal role as the conscience and leaders of the nation, hesitating to play their inescapable part in steering their people towards human progress. Facing this challenge squarely requires a new kind of thought and a new discourse consistent with that thought. For, to cast off oppression requires a new language far removed from the vocabulary of oppression and the moulds into which it forces reality. It also demands innovative societal action.

The foregoing discussion indicates the falsity of claims that Arab culture and freedom are incompatible. Impediments to freedom do exist in the Arab reality and in the global and regional context, but these are not insurmountable.

We hope that the coming pages offer new beginnings for moving purposefully and peacefully in these directions.

Persisting tendencies in Arab social structures could well lead to spiralling social, economic and political crises.

This challenge concerns, first and foremost, the intellectual and political vanguards of the region.

Part II

Part II: Reinforcing Freedom and Establishing Good Governance

Section 2: The State of Freedom and Governance in Arab Countries

This section presents a brief assessment of the state of freedom and governance in the Arab countries at the beginning of the third millennium.

CHAPTER THREE

The State of Freedoms and Rights

Introduction

This chapter attempts a response to the question posed in Chapter One about how far the current Arab situation corresponds to the ideal of freedom and good governance. It provides a summary account of the violations of civil and political rights and freedoms in Arab countries at the beginning of the 21st century. The chapter next diagnoses the failure to realize social and economic rights in a human development perspective, in terms of the acquisition and employment of human capabilities. It concludes with the findings of the Freedom survey, which was an integral input in preparing this Report. The survey samples public opinion in five Arab countries on the components of people's concept of freedom and on how far those components of freedom were enjoyed by the public at the time of the survey. It also asked respondents to assess changes in the level of such enjoyment over the previous five years.

FREEDOMS AND HUMAN RIGHTS

While it is customary to classify human rights, including freedom, according to the categories set out in Chapter 1, they are complementary, interrelated, unlimited and mutually reinforcing, forming an indivisible whole.

When discussing freedom and human rights, or the self and society, the most widely used classification is that between individual and collective freedoms, i.e. private and public freedoms. Individual freedoms exercised in the private sphere include freedom of thought and belief among others. Individual and collective freedoms exercised in the public sphere include freedom of opinion and expression, freedom of peaceful assembly, freedom to form associations and parties, and freedom to

> BOX 3-1
>
> ### Ali Ibn Al Hussein: The Epistle on Rights
>
> Imam Ali Ibn Al Hussein, who died in the year 95 of the Hijra, wrote this letter in the early 8th century A.D., the last third of the first century of the Hijra. To our knowledge, it is the first epistle that sets out the main rights as perceived by the age and the first attempt that does not approach the concept of rights in its negative dimension. For the concept of a 'right', as we know, came into human cultures to confine entitlements to one race, or one group, or a circle of close family, or members of a given faith or a given nation. In this sense, it led to discrimination, for example, between men and women, kin and strangers, citizens and aliens, believers and atheists, etc. The prevailing view was that the positive concept of rights appeared with the European Age of Enlightenment and the rise of the concept of natural rights which gave back to all human beings incontrovertible rights which they are meant to enjoy as a gift of God or of Nature. Modern international studies however, indicate that the concept preceded European civilization and took several forms, some resulting from a direct conflict between presumptive knowledge and religious knowledge, others from attempts to reconcile the two.
>
> The epistle goes on to list these rights (50 of them) methodically. They are, in spirit, anchored to the early Islamic precepts.
>
> Source: Haytham Manna'a, based on Abu Muhammad al Hassan Ibn Ali Ibn al Hussein Ibn Shuba al-Harrani (al-Halabi), in Arabic, 4th century A.H., 184).

participate in the range of activities that make up the public sphere. Freedom is limited only in the framework of public order, which all citizens participate in shaping. Yet this classification is open to the criticism that it subdivides freedom, whereas it is of the nature of freedom that it cannot be divided. To restrict any part of it would be to negate its dynamic essence and its potential for development. Similarly, where even basic rights are not assured, such as the right to life and personal security, freedom is bound to remain theoretical.

Yet however we classify rights and freedoms, the level to which they are actually enjoyed in Arab countries remains poor, with some variations, as a result of complex defects, discussed briefly below.

Where basic rights are not assured, such as the right to life and personal security, freedom is bound to remain theoretical.

STRUCTURAL CONSTRAINTS ON FREEDOM

Flawed structure of Arab nation-states

Arab nation-states, particularly those of the Mashriq, took shape, in most cases, under the pressure of historical events on which the will of Arabs themselves had very little effect. The people were not the source of sovereignty. As the Ottoman Empire began to collapse, foreign economic interests were able, under the Sykes-Picot Agreement, to divide up the Arab region into states without taking the interests of the peoples of that region into account, and regardless of their relationship to the land in which they lived. This created pockets of tension within the borders of most Arab countries, especially in the Mashriq. Nor was the will of the people heeded in the establishment of political systems. The social contract was arbitrary and devoid of legitimacy. In Arab countries, the notion of a "contract" in the political sphere is not commonly found. The majority of the Arab people are persuaded that the political authority in place is their fate, is inevitable and that there is nothing to be done to restrain or change it. The modern Arab states as such suffer as a result of the way in which they came about. They did not emerge from the collective agency of the people, unlike nation-states in the West, which developed their own political and constitutional way of life.

The Arab-Islamic heritage is one that values consultation and justice, but to understand the nature of Arab political power, it is important to make a distinction between religion and faith on the one side, and history on the other. While religion undoubtedly prized these values, history shows that they were not sufficiently prevalent in society to foster a culture based on a political contract, and allow for the legitimacy of differences of opinion, dialogue and the transfer of power. It is significant that most Arab constitutions did not come about as a result of the kind of participatory process normally due. Most emerged either as a consequence of the individual ruler's wishes, inscribed in a document bestowed on the people, or through a popular "yes-no"

Citizen participation in government is weak.

The state based on the rule of law... has not come into being.

referendum (despite the obvious reservations as to the credibility of the results) drafted in such a way as to preclude any discussion. In any event, Arab states were often strangers to their environment from birth and, with a few exceptions, promulgated constitutions without extensive participation of the people concerned, even though most constitutions declare that the sovereignty of the state rests with the people or the nation.

As a consequence of the weak notion of political contract in Arab societies, the principle of constitutional legitimacy is similarly fragile, especially in all that relates to the requirement that laws, institutions and people must respect the constitution as a binding document, as well as the provisions it contains. Worse, citizen participation in government is weak. Feeble electoral mechanisms, and marginalized legislative assemblies, which tend to be tools of the executive power, as epitomised in the person of the Head of State, account for this low participation. Consequently, since the law does not represent the sovereignty and power of the community, it is ineffectual as an authority for structuring relations among people and between them and state power, and has not served as a tool for maintaining freedom. Moreover, state power, especially where it is corrupt, can manipulate the law to suit its interests, and through the means of coercion at its disposal, can efficiently create a situation in which it cannot be challenged or held to account. As a result, the state based on the rule of law, which guarantees human rights and freedom, has not come into being.

Political constraints on the authority of the human rights system

Acceptance of the legally valid nature of human rights, and enactment of human rights principles in the context of the nation-state by the nation-state, together determine whether a State can be said to show a minimum of respect for human freedom and human rights. Civil and political rights are the cornerstones of a system in which democracy and social justice, i.e. good governance in both its political and social aspects can be realized.

However, a number of serious obstacles prevent the Arab individual from benefiting from this human rights system. In the first place, the system presupposes that states enjoy sovereignty, and this is not the case with all Arab states, as some remain subject to foreign occupation. In states that do enjoy sovereignty, even if defective, the human rights system is confronted by undemocratic regimes, which block the adoption of human rights in order to preserve the privileges which they enjoy at the expense of their own peoples. Moreover, the system has had difficulty in accommodating an Arab cultural attribute of stasis under repressive political regimes, social forces that fear freedom, and entrenched traditions that preserve the tribal–based status quo and deny creativity.

Opportunities for the human rights system to achieve its noble goals are also not enhanced by the current state of global governance. The international order that allows a few countries to override the will of a majority of other nations and gives them the power to negate just resolutions that run counter to their interests, seriously undermines many of the principles on which international law is based.

All this has weakened the hope that people will be able to enjoy freedom, justice and peace. Nonetheless, the human rights system remains a starting-point and an authority. Despite the climate that limits its effectiveness, it nevertheless represents a gleam of hope.

The crisis of citizenship

What is the actual situation with respect to the civil and political freedoms of the ordinary Arab individual, caught between official declarations of principle that recognize some of them and practical restrictions on the exercise of most of them? Why does the ordinary good citizen not show more initiative?

Even disregarding the factor of foreign intervention, freedoms in Arab countries are threatened by two kinds of power: that of undemocratic regimes oblivious to the welfare of their peoples, and that of tradition and tribalism, sometimes under the cover of religion. These twin forces have combined to curtail freedoms and fundamental rights and have weakened the good citizen's strength and ability to advance. Freedom in the public sphere is, in the main, a prerogative of power, and the model citizen, in the view of the regime, is an unquestioning creature, not participating in political life and, in particular, not asking questions or holding his rulers accountable. Meanwhile, power in the domestic and private sphere is mostly a prerogative of the man, given the prevalence of paternalism, especially in the family, and the corresponding duty of obedience is incumbent upon women and children. This produces, as a result, the model citizen as the regime wants her or him to be.

In between these two spheres stand civil society institutions, which originate in the desire of citizens to express their views and their interests and activities freely. These institutions are the key to a free civil society that includes all citizens. A citizen is good insofar as (s)he participates in all situations, and insofar as (s)he asks questions and holds rulers accountable. Yet civil society institutions themselves are in conflict with the culture of violence and oppression that the regime exploits to crush every dynamic initiative, targeting in particular free individuals who are active in the human rights field.

Such challenges will be hard to overcome, partly because of the inhibiting effect of internalized constraints and partly because of national constraints that paralyse institutions or divert them from their proper ends, owing to the absence of an overarching regional structure. These constraints are exacerbated because of foreign occupation.

NATIONAL FREEDOM

The foreign occupation of Arab countries brings the pursuit of freedom back to the question of liberation from foreign domination, an issue that the world left behind decades ago with the end of colonialism. Today, that issue is almost entirely restricted to the Arab region to the exclusion of others.

Arab countries under foreign occupation endure serious violations of human rights: The Palestinian people are suffering under an Israeli occupation that seeks to displace them and deny their legitimate, inalienable rights that are recognized in international law, including resolutions on the right of return for refugees, and

Freedoms in Arab countries are threatened by two kinds of power: that of undemocratic regimes…and that of tradition and tribalism.

The foreign occupation of Arab countries brings the pursuit of freedom back to the question of liberation from foreign domination.

the right to freely establish their own political system. The occupation also systematically violates all civil and political freedoms and denies Palestinians the protection to which they are entitled under the Geneva Convention's provisions for the Protection of Civilian Persons in Time of War.

Meanwhile the US-led occupation of Iraq has created a tragic situation in Iraq, Part I.

BOX 3-2

Marwan al-Barghouti (from his prison cell): I will overcome the cell and the occupiers

He was arrested on charges of resisting the Israeli occupation in 1978 while in the 10th grade, but was determined to complete his studies in prison, and succeeded in obtaining his secondary school certificate. Leaving prison in 1983, he went to Bir Zeit University to study political science, and joined the student movement where he assumed a leading role in the youth and student movement affiliated to the Palestine National Liberation Movement (Fatah).

Al-Barghouti believed the Oslo Accords could lead to an end to occupation and the establishment of a Palestinian State within the 1967 borders. It was this that drove him to turn from the political struggle to work for the peace process. In 1996 he stood for the Palestinian legislative council elections and won the Ramallah seat, establishing himself as a member of the first elected Palestinian Parliament. He was among the most fervent opponents of corruption and supporters of human rights, and social and economic justice. The Palestinian women's movement considers him to be one of their closest allies in the struggle for equality.

Israel's continuing and relentless appropriation of more Palestinian territory and creation of more settlements in different areas following the Oslo Accords was the most decisive factor in al-Barghouti's change of view.

"We have lived through seven years of the intifada without negotiations, and then seven years of negotiations without the intifada. Perhaps the time has come to try them both at the same time."

Marwan al-Barghouti sums up Palestinians' demands in the following way: Israel must accept independence for the Palestinians. Negotiations between masters and slaves will lead nowhere without resistance and without expressing the Palestinian national will.

Al-Barghouti went on to become a charismatic spokesman and leader, calling for total resistance to occupation. With the new intifada he came to be known as its leader, not only as a leader and activist in the field but also in endeavouring to provide political direction and shape the intifada's goals.

Marwan al-Barghouti miraculously survived an assassination attempt by Israeli helicopter gun ships in August 2001, but he continued to call for the intifada, despite repeated calls for his assassination. After the Israeli incursion of Ramallah, al-Barghouti was at the top of the Israeli security forces' wanted list, and he was arrested on the afternoon of Monday, 15 April 2002.

In detention, al-Barghouti was subjected to both psychological and physical pressure. As a result of these conditions his health has deteriorated and he now suffers from chest pains and respiratory difficulties, in addition to back pains as a result of his cramped quarters (his cell, including the lavatory, is three square metres.) The Israeli occupation authorities have also prevented al-Barghouti from seeking hospital treatment, in contravention of the Geneva Conventions, particularly the Third and Fourth.

Even from his prison cell Marwan al-Barghouti still affirms that the Palestinian will for freedom will never be crushed, and that the only alternative is to end the 57 year-old occupation. Despite his fury at Israel's continuing tyranny and profound sorrow for the many Palestinian martyrs, Marwan al-Barghouti holds firm in his belief in the fundamental principle of securing a just peace through the establishment of two States for two peoples.

Excerpts from a letter to his wife: "I will overcome the cell and the occupiers...they will never break my will."

Source: Lead author, based on communications with Bargouthi's wife and lawyers.

CIVIL AND POLITICAL FREEDOMS IN ARAB STATES

The official positions of Arab states on civil and political freedoms vary depending on the democratic margins permitted. However, with some limited exceptions in some countries or some areas, the state of those freedoms ranges from deficient to seriously deficient.

Freedom of opinion, expression and creativity

An authoritarian regime fears, above all, that freedom of opinion and freedom of expression may give rise to alternative viewpoints or opposition. Accordingly, the regime frequently tightens its grip on publication and the media, and those working in these fields; it imposes censorship, and redoubles measures for intimidation. But the more ruthless censorship becomes, the more the people resist, especially journalists, media institutions and intellectuals, who stubbornly continue to exercise and defend their rights.

During the three-year period 2001-2003, journalists in Algeria, Egypt, Jordan, Morocco, the Sudan, Syria, Tunisia, Yemen and other Arab countries were repeatedly targeted for prosecution on the grounds of opinions they had expressed. Some of them were convicted and given harsh sentences, while in Jordan, Morocco, Tunisia and Yemen, journalists were assaulted or detained.

Many newspapers that were self-financing have come under pressure by the authorities, which have reduced their share of advertising and blocked distribution, even to subscribers. The head offices of newspapers have been subject to police raids in many Arab countries, and Arab television networks have been subjected to particularly heavy pressure. Arab satellite broadcasters have come under foreign pressure to change their reporting of events.

While many Arab states adopt a public discourse supporting press freedom and openness towards the privatisation of public space, in reality, the situation is only becoming worse. International organizations working for press freedom have published reports packed with references to violations. In its 2002 report, Reporters sans frontiers, for example, stated that the region was the second largest prison for journalists in the world.

A phenomenon unique to the Arab region consists of organized attempts that were successful until recently, to suppress the freedom of the media, and prevent it from harnessing the potential of linguistic and cultural unity to launch a media renaissance. Taking place in stages, these attempts started with rivalry between radical and traditional Arab regimes in the 1960s to influence the free Arab media in countries such as Lebanon. Following the Lebanese war, the action moved to Europe. Not only did the regimes lavish large sums of money on buying or neutralizing information media; some resorted to assassinating journalists and blowing up press offices (Abdelwahab el-Affendi, 1993). That stage ended with an almost total clampdown on media freedom in the Arab diaspora. The trend was reinforced by the increasing influence of oil countries and a rapprochement among Arab regimes after radical countries changed their position towards "moderation".

There was also the temporary setback with the invasion of Kuwait in 1990; but this stage ended in 1995 with the opening of Arab satellite stations offering programmes that were remarkable for their relative freedom and frankness. Criticism and dialogue started to revive in the Arab press.

With the information revolution and the expanded use of the Internet, the region entered a new era and it was no longer feasible to muzzle information as a tool for political control and manipulation. With the rising level of education among young people and increased access to world information sources, the Arab citizen is no longer convinced by old propaganda methods.

Nevertheless, early in 2003, Arab Ministers of Information and Ministers of the Interior agreed to an anti-terrorism strategy, leading to further restrictions on freedom of opinion and expression and indeed on other human rights, and to the potential expansion of provisions of the Arab Anti-Terrorism Agreement to cover the media. This would greatly increase the danger of continued misuse of the Agreement to punish individuals for non-violent activities since the terms "terrorism", "legitimate resistance to occupation", "violence", "terrorist purposes" and "terrorist attacks" still lack clear-cut and agreed upon technical definitions in law. The terminology of freedom of expression also remains vague, especially as regards the Internet.

Since the events of 11 September 2001, the Internet has been subjected to direct interference and censorship, disrupting the flow of information.

Since 2001, the penal codes of a number of Arab countries have been amended to provide for longer prison terms and heavier fines for publishing-related offences. This situation is reflected in greater pressure on journalists and a narrower margin of freedom of opinion and expression. Violations of freedom of opinion and freedom of expression have included attacks on political activists and human rights advocates who had expressed their views openly.

Curtailment of freedom of opinion and expression in the form of officially imposed censorship extends also to literary and artistic creativity, exacerbated in some countries by unofficial censorship by influential political or social forces of society. Some Arab states have gone to such extremes to monopolize "intellectual activity" that they have banned circulation of some of the most treasured works in the Arab literary heritage, such as The Prophet, by Gibran Kahlil Gibran, and A Thousand and One Nights. There has, however, been a noticeable increase in the number of books and publications appearing on the Internet, or published in the West, but which the Arab reader can only obtain as smuggled copies.

Stifling creativity

Freedom is an essential dimension of, and an incentive for creative work, whether in the domain of language in the form of essays, poetry, short stories, novels, drama and criticism, or in the plastic arts such as painting, photography and sculpture. Freedom is also a basic condition for intellectual creativity in works dealing with history, politics, society and beliefs.

While Arab poets, novelists and dramatists remain prolific, the "freedom" to write and freedom of expression have often been chal-

With the rising level of education among young people, and increased access to world information sources, the Arab citizen is no longer convinced by old propaganda methods.

Since the events of 11 September 2001, the Internet has been subjected to direct interference and censorship.

The suppression of creativity in the Arab world does not stem exclusively from the strict religious discourse. It also originates with political authorities.

lenged by political authority and by certain traditional interpretations of religion. Public reactions to this freedom range from violent criticism, to misdirection and misguidance, to the referral of writers and their works to the courts and the imposition on them of harsh sentences. Some writers have been victims of violence and even of assassination or execution.

For example, legal measures were taken against Taha Hussein for his book Fi al- Shi'r al-Jahili, 1926 (On Pre-Islamic Poetry), against Sadeq Jalal Al Azem for his Naqd Al Fikr Al Dini, 3rd edition, 1927 (A Critique of Religious Thought) and Nasr Hamed Abu Zeid for a number of his controversial writings. Naguib Mahfouz was the victim of an assault due to a misinterpretation of his novel Awlad Haritna (The People of our Alley). The Islamic thinker Sayyed Qotb was executed in 1966 for opinions expressed in Ma'alem fi-Tariq,

1964 (Landmarks Along the Road) and so was Mahmoud Mohammed Taha in the Sudan for expressing religious opinions to which the political regime objected. Farag Foda's writings, which were critical and somewhat sarcastic in their treatment of Islamists, led to his assassination. There are also contemporary cases of authors whose writings have provoked strong religious antagonism, which has landed them in court.

Certain ideological and cultural groups have also been responsible for censoring or curtailing creative work. These groups are usually dominated by party dogmatists seeking to impose a preconceived mode of expression, production and commitment on creative artists, which militates completely against the freedom required for creativity. In some instances, considerable tension exists between creative authors and the political parties to which they originally belonged, as was the case with Badr Shakir al-Sayyab.

The suppression of creativity in the Arab world does not stem exclusively from the strict religious discourse. It also originates with political authorities. Cartoons lampooning Arab rulers are frequently suppressed, and their artists persecuted. In the case of Palestine, the assassination of Naji al-Ali marks one of the most savage examples of the suppression of an opposition cartoonist's freedom of expression.

Cultural associations (associations of writers, artists and dramatists) have also suffered from the intervention of the state and its laws, or the party. They have been subjected to enquiries into their nature and purposes and to interference in their scope and freedom of expression and action. This is true of all Arab countries. Ibrahim Abdullah Ghaloum's study of laws governing cultural associations in his country may well serve as an example for any study of equivalent laws in other Arab countries. It testifies clearly to the disappearance of the legal personality of cultural associations and the suppression or curtailment of their freedoms. Such laws reflect the controlling spirit of state security laws, which, in the realm of culture, can only limit freedom and creativity (*ibid*, 313-341).

Freedom of association: civil society institutions

Arab authorities limit popular movements and expressions of popular sovereignty in the public sphere in order to prevent them from becoming sources of pressure. As far as possible, they try to keep them outside the political sphere. The regime can be assured of continuing to hold power only so long as it can keep the public space for itself, prevent democratic political forces from emerging, and weaken any institutions and mechanisms that might lead to political alternation.

Freedom to form political parties

Arab countries lack mechanisms for democratic participation. States either outlaw or marginalize political parties by encouraging traditional social structures, such as the clan, tribe or sect, which, with their pyramidal structures, are easier for the state to deal with.

In some Arab countries, legal reform has led to official recognition of multi-party politics. Even so, the freedom to form parties is subject to numerous legal restrictions that seriously impede its exercise. This has caused parties to adopt undemocratic practices, becoming authoritarian themselves, characterized by ideological, and, in some cases, religious fanaticism. In numerous parties, individual members are offered no role in developing party policy or manifestos. The parties rarely allow space for criticism, which could enrich diversity within their ranks.

Freedom to form associations and surveillance of their activities

In Arab countries, the freedom to form associations is restricted in varying degrees by law. Under the legislation of most Arab countries, associations are subject to various forms of oversight and surveillance. The most severe forms of state interference lie in the power to suspend associations or dissolve them by executive order. In some countries (for example Syria) any judicial review of such orders is prohibited. Offenders under these various laws are usually liable to imprisonment, although in some instances only monetary fines are imposed.

> BOX 3-4
> ### Khalida Said: Creativity - Between Consciousness and Dreams
>
> Creativity is a free action oriented towards freedom. It is a movement, in essence, between consciousness, in the sense of acquired knowledge and memory, and dream, in the sense of the aspiration, striving, discovery and endeavour that elevate knowledge to its utmost. It is a movement whose very nature is freedom both in its inception and its social destination, wherein those that it addresses are to be found. Creativity is an impulse that transcends its inner psychological level as an aspiration to seek embodiment or crystallization in some palpable form addressed to a receiver. This nexus of movement and freedom is an innate human characteristic, and a natural human right, it is the right declared by contemporary creators, one for which they claim the dual freedom to both send and receive.
> *(Khalida Said, background paper for this Report).*

The freedom to form associations has been violated by many marginally democratic governments, including those of Algeria, Egypt, Jordan, Mauritania and Tunisia. Would-be founders of organizations have been denied permission to proceed, and existing organizations have been dissolved. Most of these adverse measures have been directed against grassroots human rights organizations. Arab authorities have sought to drown the voices of voluntary civil society organizations by setting up what they claim to be non-governmental organizations, (NGOs.) These sham groups are in fact governmental entities (GNGOs) which work for, and are financed by the regime, whose discourse they echo and whose interests they pursue.

Since 2001, the global "war on terror" has seen a new development in the region: Arab governments have begun to monitor Islamic charitable organizations closely, sometimes cracking down on their activities on the basis of US lists, with their political bias.

Historically speaking, civil associations are progressive forces that prepare the way for civil society to emerge and help to create the kind of public sphere required for freedom (Chapter 1). It is thus of great concern that the many restrictions imposed on them may leave Arab citizens with only the traditional, narrower options of tribal or clan-based action, which in turn will strengthen the grip of "clannism" (al-'asabiya) on Arab society (Chapter 6).

Nonetheless, associations continue to spring up and pursue their activities, even without the blessing of the law, finding alternative legal formulae such as styling themselves

The freedom to form parties is subject to numerous legal restrictions that seriously impede its exercise.

The freedom to form associations has been violated by many marginally democratic governments.

as companies, which are lawful in most Arab states, to protect their members. Significantly, while poorly represented in political party activity, women are very much in evidence in civil and cooperative associations, holding leadership positions in some Arab countries.

Trade unions and professional associations

The status of Arab trade unions ranges considerably: they are numerous and enjoy varying degrees of freedom. In some countries, state interference in the essential and defining democratic processes of trade unions, has driven them into political activism and opposition, which has brought them harsher restrictions still.

Workers in countries that approve the plurality of unions, such as Morocco and Lebanon, are free to choose which body to join, in contrast to states where only one union is allowed. In general, workers in many sectors are still outside union bodies.

Experience in some Arab countries has shown that support for unionized labour usually leads to stronger and more effective unions, and that this, in turn, helps create a competitive democratic climate marked by activism, respect for human rights and a flourishing civil society.

In contrast, where there is no competition between unions, the regime can contain and control the single union, which becomes a tool for enforcing government policy. This is the case in most Arab countries, especially since the advent of economic liberalization, which has had the effect of weakening unions and, therefore, reducing public trust in them. Unions have thus become unable to protect their members or defend their interests. In response to this situation, new non-governmental organizations have begun to emerge to support workers. The Union and Labour Services House in Egypt, for example, was founded in 1990 as an independent organization for that purpose. It may be noted, however, that Arab, and more especially Asian, migrant workers enjoy very little protection in any Arab state, especially the Gulf States.

The right to participation:

Participation in elections, by running for office or by voting, is how citizens and groups express their political preferences and hold officials accountable for their performance. Participation is a step towards political alternation. Consequently, regimes take advantage of their position to nullify the outcome of voting through various legal mechanisms, or simply to disregard it, thereby keeping themselves in power.

While the Arab world has exhibited a broad array of electoral processes at all levels, the right to political participation has remained little more than a ritual representing a purely formal application of a constitutional entitlement. In most cases elections have resulted in misrepresenting the will of the electorate and in low levels of representation for the opposition and women.

With a few exceptions, some of which are purely cosmetic, presidential elections do not take place freely in Arab countries in the sense of involving more than one candidate competing in a general election. In only three Arab countries (Algeria, Sudan and Yemen), and in a fourth under occupation (palestine), are presidents elected through direct elections with more than one candidate and with presidential term limits. While direct presidential elections take place in Tunisia and Djibouti, no term limits are set. Syria and Egypt (and previously Iraq) depended on referendums where the president is nominated by the parliament, after which a national referendum is held. In presidential referenda the outcome varies between an absolutely majority and total unanimity.

Except in two countries - Saudi Arabia and United Arab Emirates – parliaments in the region are either totally or partially elected. However, parliamentary elections have not played their designated role in balancing power, or holding the government accountable or even in reflecting public opinion. These elections have generally reproduced the same ruling elites. Legislative elections routinely suffer low turnout rates. Opposition candidates have charged that electoral laws are rigged to suit the interests of the regime and that the alliances put together by the existing government

State interference in the essential and defining democratic processes of trade unions has driven them into political activism.

In most cases, elections have resulted in misrepresenting the will of the electorate and in low levels of representation for the opposition and women.

block all chances of winning. Consequently, they have frequently boycotted elections or denounced their outcomes as travesties of due process.

INDIVIDUAL FREEDOMS

Individual freedoms constitute the most cherished component of freedom, because they are closest to the individual and to her/his status as a unique human being. The legal regime governing freedoms applies with particular force to freedoms in this category. The function of law in the matter of the right to freedom is simply to acknowledge that right by creating a space in which the free individual can exercise choice; all that is required of the law is to ensure that this space is not violated by others. Such law is known as passive law. Within that space, freedom is entire, subject only to restrictions for the sake of public order. But the sphere of individual freedom affords only limited potential for affecting public order, and none at all in the case of private individual freedoms. Those freedoms serve as the framework within which the individual constructs a stable identity and consolidates the bases of personality and action, and they have a major impact in unleashing the dynamic potential of individual and collective freedoms alike.

Freedom of opinion and belief:

These are private individual freedoms that are inviolable and recognized as such by all the monotheistic religions. Perhaps the Qur'an sums up the matter most succinctly: "Whoever so wishes, let him believe, and whoever so wishes, let him prefer unbelief."

Freedom of opinion and belief are among the civil rights that are enshrined in the International Covenant on Civil and Political Rights (ICCPR), and in the constitutions of some Arab states. But Arab authorities, both civil and religious, usually join forces to curtail this right in law and in practice, speaking with one voice in terms reminiscent of a tribal social system. They uphold a uniform pattern of behaviour characterized by obedience and submission that makes any departure from that pattern unlawful or sinful so as to contain society by homogenising its constituent individuals. Arab

countries have witnessed several abuses of the freedom of social groups on religious, sectarian or ideological grounds.

Official models of belief that bolster tradition and traditional values and negate freedom of opinion, treat those who do not conform to them as enemies, as in the case of the conflicts between the Islamists and the various Sufi orders. Those who think are proscribed, even though they may be faithful believers. As a result, the polity breaks up into politico-religious factions that are more easily contained, and society loses its vitality.

Freedom of privacy and personal life:

Personal life constitutes a free zone for the individual to enjoy and which the state is not entitled to infringe or curtail. Yet in Arab countries political authorities at times appropriate this space, breaching the inviolability of the home at any hour of the day or night, monitoring private correspondence and tapping telephones; religious authorities or particular social groups similarly usurp the personal freedom of citizens.

Women suffer acutely in this respect, as they are also subject to surveillance by male members of their family, or even of the local community. A woman is at risk of violence, to the point of being killed in a so-called "crime of honour", which constitutes lawful grounds in some Arab countries and an extenuating circumstance in others. It is generally recognized, however, that in many cases "crimes of

Arab countries have witnessed several abuses of the freedom of social groups on religious, sectarian or ideological grounds.

Official models of belief that bolster tradition and traditional values and negate freedom of opinion, treat those who do not conform to them as enemies.

honour" are committed on nothing more than unfounded suspicion, or to cover up a situation where a girl has been raped by a member of her own family.

Female genital mutilation, despite its known harmful effects, continues to be practiced in some Arab countries, in some cases by traditional methods devoid of even the most rudimentary safety precautions, with the result that girls die from the operation.

DENIAL OF FUNDAMENTAL INDIVIDUAL FREEDOMS

Violation of basic rights

The human rights system is founded on a collection of rights at the very heart of the system, which are considered totally inviolable. Yet in Arab countries these sacred and basic rights are frequently violated.

The right to life

Violations of the right to life in Arab countries have taken multiple forms. The most conspicuous examples are Israel's military aggression against the Palestinian people, at the cost of civilian lives, in addition to the physical liquidation of leaders and cadres of the resistance. Tens are killed daily in Iraq by occupation forces or terrorist groups. Internal conflict continues to rage in the Sudan and Somalia, representing a further source of violation of this right, while the global anti-terrorism campaign has added a new dimension to the issue.

Capital punishment is an infringement of the right to life.[1] Yet certain Arab states remain untouched by the human rights system's position on the death penalty, which confines its use to the most serious crimes, imposes procedural and judicial safeguards, and prohibits its use in political cases. Capital punishment has been retained in all Arab countries, although in certain countries (such as Bahrain, Algeria, Lebanon[2], Morocco and Tunisia) it is rarely applied.

Some Arab governments also violate the right to life extra-legally and extra-judicially. Human rights organizations have observed that official reports on killings tend to be short on facts. In most Arab states the names of the victims are not mentioned, and no public investigation is conducted, giving rise to suspicions of the possibility of "liquidation" or extrajudicial execution of suspects. In most cases of disappearance or abduction in Arab countries it is feared that the victim has been executed outside the law. According to the files of the UN there were 11,000 cases of unknown disappearances in the Arab countries in 1993 (Arab Organization for Human Rights).

The right to life is often violated in cases when people are expelled or arrested, and in prisons, especially those run by security and intelligence services, where torture is used or health care neglected.

Extremist groups who perpetrate assassinations and bombings and espouse the use of violence also violate the right to life. Armed confrontations between security forces and armed groups may result in civilian casualties; in some instances, civilian victims have outnumbered victims in the ranks of the combatants.

Lastly, the repression of peaceful demonstrations by security forces in Arab countries has been yet another source of violation of the right to life.

The right to liberty and personal safety

This right is massively and consistently violated. Since the global "war on terror" campaign began, there have been unprecedented numbers of arrests. Legal safeguards have been violated, and people have been deprived of their liberty and, in many instances, tortured and ill-treated in prisons, camps and detention centres where their personal safety is uncertain. The disappearance of a family member in prison is a tragedy that often haunts Arab citizens. Following the disappearance of Kuwaiti prisoners in Iraq, it emerged that hundreds had disappeared in some Arab jails.

---

[1] This position has been emphasised in Resolution 2857 –XXVI, December 20, 1971 of the UN General Assembly and in two resolutions of the UN Economic and Social Council, on May 20, 1971 and May 9, 1971 respectively.

[2] It is important to note that the former Prime Minister of Lebanon adduced reasons of conscience for refusing to sign execution orders for those sentenced to death.

Certain Arab states remain untouched by the human rights system's position on the death penalty.

The disappearance of a family member in prison is a tragedy that often haunts Arab citizens.

Following the September 11 attacks, lists of suspects were circulated by the US security services, requesting their detention on sight, giving human rights organizations cause for concern.

The right to a fair and impartial trial

Most Arab regimes do not respect the principle of the separation of powers, with the result that the judiciary comes under political pressure, especially from the executive power, and loses credibility. The risk to the judiciary has recently grown as some of the finest judges have become exposed to violence and prosecution; indeed, judges have been murdered in their own courtrooms (in Sidon, Lebanon). Yet while the institutional structure of the judiciary has come under assault from politicians, it may still fairly be said that many judges in most Arab countries are reliable, learned and upright.

Safeguards surrounding the right to a fair trial are being eroded. This is happening mainly outside the regular judicial system. Contributing to this erosion are such practices as referring civilians for trial by military courts (as in Egypt, Jordan, Lebanon and Tunisia,) and the use of various exceptional procedures. The latter include emergency courts in Egypt and the Sudan, state security courts in Iraq (until the recent fall of the regime) Jordan and Syria, special courts in Iraq, Libya, and the Sudan, and martial law tribunals in Somalia. In Algeria, Mauritania and Tunisia, the regular courts have been little better, especially in security and political cases, and trials of civilians in cases of terrorism in the past two years have met with strong criticism.

Exclusion from citizenship

Deprivation of citizenship

The withdrawal of nationality from an Arab citizen, as permitted under certain legislation through an administrative decision by a government official of less than ministerial rank, is one the most extreme forms of exclusion from citizenship. This is closely followed by the deprivation of certain categories of citizens of their right to obtain nationality in their own country.

Abusing the rights of minority groups.

National legal systems do not protect members of groups outside the mainstream, which are often marginalized. For example, Article 27 of the ICCPR is still the mainstay of the protection of such persons, despite the 1992 Declaration on the Rights of Persons Belonging to National or Ethnic, Religious and Linguistic Minorities.

Individuals belonging to such groups are citizens as well and entitled, in principle, to enjoy all the rights of citizenship, yet those rights are frequently violated along with the rights of citizens in general. These individuals may also suffer additional violations at the hands of the law or the administration or as a result of entrenched social practices, simply because of their background.

Violations of human rights in Arab countries are more pronounced when cultural, religious or ethnic dimensions are present, particularly since marginalized groups have fewer opportunities to protest their rights. Repression directed specifically at such groups reflects an odious "minority mentality" in parts of society and in oppressive regimes alike.

In areas of protracted conflict in northern Iraq and the southern Sudan, some cultural, ethnic or tribal groups, especially the Kurds in Iraq, have suffered overt or covert persecution. Government policy has fluctuated between recognizing the principle of autonomy and responding to dissidence as insurrection. In both cases, however, the outcome has been a solution along federalist lines. The southern Sudan is unique in that an agreement was reached based on recognition of the right to self-determination following a specified period of time. However, a complete settlement has not yet been achieved in either case, and some local conflicts continue, as with the case of Arab and Turkmen citizens in northern Iraq, and in border regions of southern and western Sudan. Recently the Qamishli events in Syria have brought to light the suffering endured by Kurds seeking their most basic legitimate rights, namely the right to citizenship.

The Kabylie regions of Algeria have ex-

Most Arab regimes do not respect the principle of the separation of powers, with the result that the judiciary comes under political pressure.

Violations of human rights in Arab countries are more pronounced when cultural, religious or ethnic dimensions are present.

perienced many disturbances since 2001. Demonstrations in 2002 resulted in dozens of victims. Democratic developments in Algeria have helped to resolve Berber demands and the Amazigh language was recognized as a national language. The authorities subsequently moved towards making it an official language, after ending the debate on whether this would require a popular referendum.

Christians in some Arab countries also suffer from restrictions on their freedoms.

This kind of double subjugation affects a number of other social groups, notably bidun and naturalized citizens in Arab Gulf countries. The former are regarded as foreigners, while the latter, being stateless, have nowhere to go and are treated as second-class citizens; they are denied the right to stand for election to representative bodies or to vote. A similar prejudice affected Iraqi citizens whom the previous government designated "Iranian nationals"; their status as citizens of Iraq was not recognized, and some of them were expelled to Iran, while others remained as an under-class. "Card holders" in the border areas of Saudi Arabia, Kurds deprived of citizenship following the 1962 census in Syria, and akhdam in Yemen are in much the same boat.

Migrant workers in oil producing Arab states, including Arabs, suffer certain forms of discrimination according to international standards, the most notorious being the "guarantor system" and the abuse of domestic servants, chiefly women.

Socio-economic and military circumstances are creating bizarre situations in Mauritania and the Sudan. In the former, members of the group known as haratin (emancipated slaves) are hardly better off than when they were slaves. Since the legal abolition of slavery in 1980, the Government has been unable to provide them with sources of income, while social prejudices have prevented their integration into society. Consequently, many haratin have been compelled to return to the families for which they formerly worked, and their condition is similar to slavery. In the Sudan, different tribes involved in the military conflict have abducted one other's women and children; here again, the victims' condition is tantamount to slavery. This situation has given

rise to international accusations that the Sudan tolerates slavery, and those accusations have been enlarged by propaganda. Despite the Government's efforts to solve the problem, thousands of people are still in this wretched condition, and the Government of the Sudan continues to endure the odium of this charge. The affirmative action of allocating a "quota" in the parliament for Christians, and Chechans in Jordan is positively noted.

The Arab people cannot be satisfied as long as the dilemma of the Palestinian diaspora continues. Its members are deprived of their right to return, in addition to being denied many of their other fundamental rights – even in Arab countries. The Palestinians have been left alone to bear the consequences of expulsion by Israel, in which it enjoyed outside support, while those expelled suffered. This double injustice calls for the international community to come together to guarantee the right to return and, in the meantime, to secure the other basic human rights of Palestinians.

The legal rights of Arabs living in some industrialized countries have deteriorated lately following the "war on terror".

Women doubly excluded

Arab women find themselves in different situations, depending on their respective circumstances, and depending on the extent to which democracy is practiced both within their families and by the national system. But nowhere in the Arab world do women enjoy equality with men, even though equality is a fundamental human right. Women are subject to discrimination both at law and in practice, and as a result they tend not to participate very extensively in the public sphere, and relatively little in decision-making within the family.

To be sure, concern for the status of women has increased in recent years, as may be seen from various developments. Governmental structures have been established expressly to address women's issues, both at the regional level, with the establishment of the Arab Women's Organization, and at the national level, with the founding of national councils and commissions on the status of women in a number of Arab countries. Political discourse regularly addresses the issue of equality, and governments have adopted a number of programmes aimed at promoting it. There has been an exponential growth in NGOs concerned with women's rights. Despite all this, in most Arab countries women are still subject to numerous forms of discrimination. Perhaps education marks the sole exception to the rule, where girls comprise the majority at certain levels in some Arab countries, with an academic record superior to that of their male peers.

Statistics point to a generalized gender gap in various areas, including education, employment, property ownership, public office, decision-making posts, and leadership positions in political parties and trade unions. There have been laudable efforts to promote the status of women in some areas, but others have been largely neglected both by governments and by society in general. Little progress has been made regarding political participation by women, changes to personal status laws, integration of women in the development process, the right of a woman married to a foreign husband to transmit her citizenship to her children, and the inability of existing legislation to protect women from domestic violence or violence on the part of the state and society.

Discrimination is becoming more acute in the Gulf countries and, in particular, in Saudi Arabia. Violence against women is most prevalent in areas of armed conflict, notably in Sudan, Somalia and Iraq.

As regards women's rights, Kuwaiti society has been less progressive than some Arab governments. The National Assembly has more than once voted against an enlightened decree of the Emir that would have allowed women to participate in political life. In the more democratic Arab countries, where such participation is lawful, voters tend not to elect women candidates: there are legislatures that do not have a single woman member, while the legislatures of some other countries, such as Egypt and Yemen, have no more than token numbers of women members. However, a trend to introduce such quotas has developed in the past two years, as in Morocco, Jordan, Qatar and Oman.

It is important to stress here that positions on gender equality have emerged in a multi-layered and complex societal context which must be taken into careful consideration when examining both the issue of equality and the respective society's shaping of ways to achieve it. These issues will be fully discussed and analysed in the fourth AHDR on the "Rise of Women" in Arab countries.

As indicated in Annex 1 of AHDR 2, the World Values Survey found that the Arab people are reluctant to accept total equality between women and men (see also the results of the Freedom Survey in Annex 1 of this Report). While gender equality in education was almost universally supported, there was noticeably less support for equality in employment and politics, particularly in Jordan and Morocco (figure 3-1).

SOCIAL AND ECONOMIC RIGHTS

This section concludes with a review of economic and social rights, which, according to the definition of human development, are embodied within two fundamental human capabilities: leading a long and healthy life, and knowledge acquisition.

The first AHDR documented various ways

In most Arab countries, women are still subject to numerous forms of discrimination.

Figure 3-1

Percentage agreeing that women should have equal rights, five Arab countries, Freedom Survey, 2003

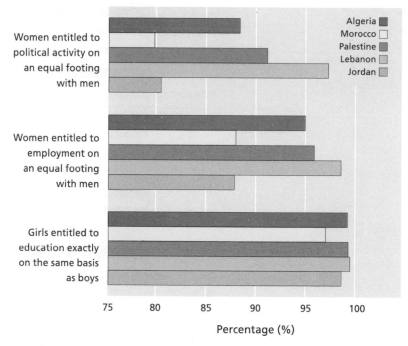

THE STATE OF FREEDOMS AND RIGHTS

93

in which, first, these two fundamental human capabilities are not realized in Arab countries, second, the weakest social groups, notably women and the destitute, are especially disadvantaged in that respect, and third, these capabilities are inappropriately or under-utilized in terms of activity within society. This unsatisfactory situation intersects with the issues of freedom and good governance on two levels. To begin with, the absence of freedom and good governance itself aggravates the impoverishment and under-utilization of human faculties, as under those conditions decision-making serves the interest of the ruling elite rather than the public interest in general. In addition, experts agree that a situation of subjugation produces adverse effects on health, including the individual's physical health. From that standpoint, the impoverishment and under-utilization of human capabilities are not only disabling for human development, they also reflect a disregard for economic and social rights that are recognized in international human rights law.

Moreover, the impoverishment and under-utilization of human capabilities in Arab countries amount to a basis for perpetuating the status quo. Such deprivation blunts the critical

sense and fosters passivity and inertia, thereby sapping the individual and societal vitality that is essential to any meaningful renaissance in Arab countries.

According to the Freedom Survey, Annex 1, interviewees were of the opinion that, at the beginning of the third millennium, more than 10% of Arabs still suffer from hunger, disease, ignorance or poverty, whether in terms of low income or deprivation of human capabilities. In one country covered by the survey interviewees estimated that almost 25% of the population suffered from low income, while in three of the five countries surveyed the level of poverty was estimated at around one quarter of the population, using the deprivation of human capabilities indicator, figure 3-2.

THE RIGHT TO LEAD A LONG, HEALTHY LIFE

The right to food and adequate nutrition:

Hunger is an outcome of inadequate food and micronutrient intake, and it can be measured in terms of arrested physical and mental growth, impaired health, early death, low life expectancy at birth, learning disabilities and ir-

Figure 3-2

Estimate of the extent of deprivation of human capabilities, five Arab countries, Freedom Survey, 2003

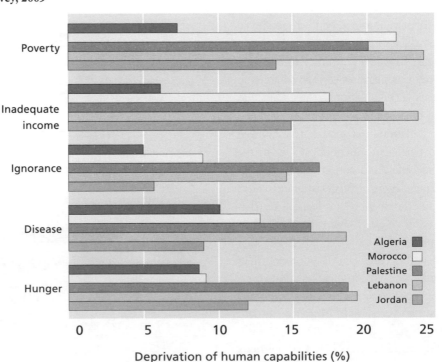

Deprivation of human capabilities (%)

regular school attendance. Hunger also weakens the immune system, and thus is reflected in epidemics, infection and HIV, and in low productivity at work and in social activity.

Children are among those most seriously affected by food insecurity, since malnutrition in early life has a serious, frequently irreversible impact, even when the immediate life environment of the person concerned subsequently improves. Malnutrition stunts the child's growth and affects her/his weight. It also has an adverse impact on physical and psychological performance, making the child dull and impairing her/his mental faculties if continued into adulthood.

Results of a study of 15 Arab countries found that 32 million people suffer from malnutrition. This figure represents nearly 12 per cent of the total population of the countries concerned. The same studies found that even in some of the wealthiest Arab states, such as Kuwait and the United Arab Emirates, certain population groups are not adequately nourished.

Between 1990-1992 and 1998-2000, i.e. in the first stages of the hunger eradication policy adopted at the Rome Conference, the absolute numbers of hungry people in the Arab world increased by more than six million. The worst results were observed in Iraq and Somalia (Rafia Ghobash, background paper for this Report).

The right to a healthy life

The World Health Organization defines health as "a state of complete physical, mental and social well-being."

Physical health

Arab countries have made great strides in reducing mortality rates, especially infant mortality rates, but the goal of health, in the comprehensive and positive sense of the above definition, has not yet been attained.

Progress in reducing mortality rates is generally reflected in improved life expectancy at birth. Over time this indicator has risen at varying rates in Arab countries and in some "wealthy" ones it has now reached a level approximating that in industrialised countries.

However, physical illness still takes years off the life of the ordinary Arab individual, as may be seen from a comparison of the standard formula used to estimate life expectancy at birth with a modified version of that formula developed by the World Health Organization. The latter is known as "HALE", for "health-adjusted life expectancy at birth", which excludes years of illness from the estimate. Applying the HALE formula in Arab countries for which data are available, we see that illness reduces average healthy life expectancy at birth by ten years or more. Noticeably, in all those countries, the reduction is greater for women than for men by a matter of two years or more. This shows that women suffer a relatively greater health deprivation. Clearly, according to available data, reductions in life expectancy at birth in Arab countries are higher than in all the comparator countries featured, particularly for women. The gap between men and women is larger in most Arab countries than in the majority of comparator countries, figure 3-3.

Between 1990-1992 and 1998-2000…the absolute numbers of hungry people in the Arab world increased by more than six million.

Figure 3-3

Years of life expectancy lost to disease, by gender, Arab countries and comparator countries, 2002

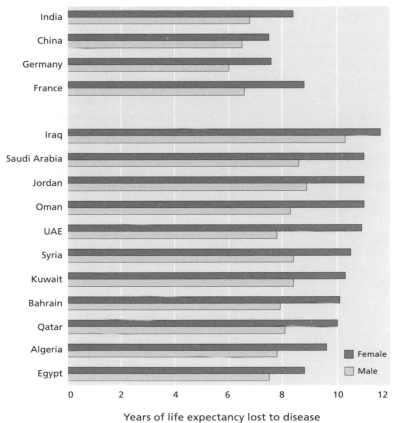

Years of life expectancy lost to disease

Source: The World Health Organization Report, 2003

The fact that years of life are lost to illness reflects relatively low levels of human development in Arab countries. A broad stratum of the population of any given Arab country lives in difficult socio-economic conditions with respect to employment, housing and living standards; people are under heavy pressure in economic terms. In social terms, the relationship of the individual to the state and the society to which he or she belongs is characterised by a feeling of lack of esteem, exclusion and marginalization, resulting in constant psychological pressure. Research has shown that psychological pressure of this kind, arising from social, economic and political factors, brings about biological changes, which in turn may cause physical and psychological infirmity. Studies have found that a person who lives under such circumstances is at risk of hormonal imbalance, nervous breakdown and even immune system failure.

Psychological health

Individuals who are continuously subjugated, insecure and marginalized bottle up various forms of violence. As authoritarian pressure grows, quietism and withdrawal become more pronounced, along with a sense of fatalism and submissiveness. Many studies in the field of psychology have found a growing incidence of anxiety and tension among Arab people, giving rise to unpredictable, despairing forms of behaviour as the individual involved attempts to relieve the tension, unaware that its causes are rooted in deprivation and the fact that his/her basic needs, most notably the need for security, are unsatisfied. There is undoubtedly a connection between fully achieving one's personal potential through participating in development on the one hand, and feeling secure on the other. Accordingly, the Arab individual's feeling of security may be expected to deteriorate in line with his/her increasingly acute awareness of deprivation at many levels, and this explains the prevalence of anxiety disorders, tension and inability to achieve self-fulfilment (Rafia Ghobash, background paper for this Report).

The right to acquire knowledge

A prerequisite for fulfilment of the right to acquire knowledge is an active, vital system for spreading knowledge through four social processes: upbringing, education, media and translation. The second AHDR documented various inadequacies in those processes in Arab countries and proposed ways of addressing the situation. Accordingly, we shall not go into the issue in detail here. In general, the profile of deprivation of the right to acquire knowledge in Arab countries is similar to that outlined above in the case of health. This, too, is a distinctive feature of the state of human development in Arab countries.

Consider education, for example. There has been appreciable quantitative progress in access to education in Arab countries, although the significance of that accomplishment is marred by the persistence of unacceptable levels of illiteracy (approximately one third of the men and half the women in 2002), and the fact that some Arab children, albeit only a small percentage, are still denied their fundamental right to basic education.

However, education in Arab countries is essentially flawed by its poor quality. People who have been to school often lack the cognitive skills of learning, criticism and analysis, while their creativity has not been encouraged. These are indispensable for the acquisition of knowledge, and even more indispensable for producing it. Moreover, little emphasis is placed on science and technology in curricula. Consequently, as with deprivation of the right to health (in the comprehensive sense), deprivation of the right to acquire knowledge, quantitatively and qualitatively, reflects a social profile that discriminates against the most disadvantaged social groups, especially women and the poor.

The quality of education and health services in Arab countries

According to the results of the Freedom Survey, Annex 1, education services were considered satisfactory to a large degree and public education services were adjudged of higher quality than the private counterpart, in Jordan, Morocco and Algeria. Nevertheless,

As authoritarian pressure grows, quietism and withdrawal become more pronounced, along with a sense of fatalism and submissiveness.

Education in Arab countries is essentially flawed by its poor quality.

the cost of private education was considered less satisfactory compared to public education (figure 3-4). The quality of health care services provided by the government was considered lower than that of private providers, with interviewees consistently complaining of rising costs of private health care. Thus the poorest and most vulnerable sectors of society, in addition to being financially disadvantaged, are further penalized in acquiring the two basic human capabilities, particularly health.

PERCEIVED ENJOYMENT OF FREEDOM IN CONTEMPORARY ARAB OPINION, FREEDOM SURVEY 2003

THE PERCEPTION OF FREEDOM AMONG CONTEMPORARY ARABS

This section utilizes the results of the Freedom Survey, Annex 1, to profile perceptions of freedom among contemporary Arabs. The survey questionnaire included a section where interviewees were asked whether any of a large number (35 elements) of components of freedom, derived from the concept presented in Chapter 1, formed part of their perception of freedom.

Figure 3-5 summarizes the results of this aspect of the Freedom Survey.[3]

Survey interviewees agreed that their concept of freedom incorporated the majority of these elements. In one case, interviewees favoured a majority of the elements by a very large margin (75% or more).

Interviewees perceived liberation from foreign occupation and the freedoms of opinion, expression and movement as the most important components of freedom. They gave least importance to the right of 'minorities' to self-rule. A lower level of importance was attached to having a significant political opposition able

Interviewees perceived liberation from foreign occupation and the freedoms of opinion, expression and movement as the most important components of freedom.

Figure 3-4

Extent of satisfaction with the level and cost of education and health services by sector (public/private), five Arab countries, Freedom Survey, 2003

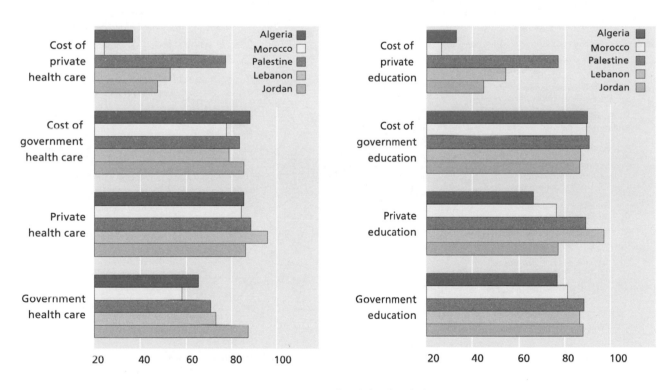

Extent of satisfaction (%)

[3] Ratios are calculated relative to the total number of interviewees (including missing observations), and arranged in figure 3-5b in descending order according to their relative importance in the Palestine survey.

Freedom Survey, Arab Human Development Report

In an effort to overcome the deficient measurement of freedom in Arab countries employed in AHDR 1 and 2, and to better serve the rich concept of freedom adopted in this report, the Report team, in collaboration with Arab institutions specializing in polls and surveys, designed a special field survey. It set out to gauge Arab attitudes towards freedom, and seek people's views on the extent to which various freedoms are enjoyed in their countries. The design called for polling nationally representative samples of Arab citizens, aged 18 years and older, selected to ensure proportional representation of both men and women.

While it was hoped to conduct the survey in a large number of Arab countries, this was likely unrealistic given the constraints facing field research in the region. Restrictions on freedom of research and knowledge acquisition on the one hand, and scarce data and information on human development on the other, remain real challenges in the region. Yet what information can be drawn from the survey still augments current knowledge.

Chastened by previous experience, the Survey team did not try to implement the survey in some Arab countries. At least one Arab country (Egypt) refused to grant a permit for the survey.

At the time of writing, survey results were available only for five Arab countries (Algeria, Jordan, Lebanon, Morocco, Palestine) comprising about one quarter of the Arab population, more than 70 million, in both the Arab East and West. Annex 1 contains details of the survey and its findings.

Undoubtedly, the scope of this survey falls short of a comprehensive representation of the Arab public. On a more positive note, its findings on perceptions of freedom among the sample countries are nonetheless instructive. Hopefully, the time will come when such studies are much easier to conduct, to the benefit of both knowledge and freedom.

Note: Ratios presented in the graphs derived from survey results are calculated relative to the total number of interviewees (including missing observations).

Figure 3-5a

Percentage of interviewees considering the elements of freedom part of their concept of freedom (%)
Average of five Arab countries (weighted by population), Freedom Survey, 2003

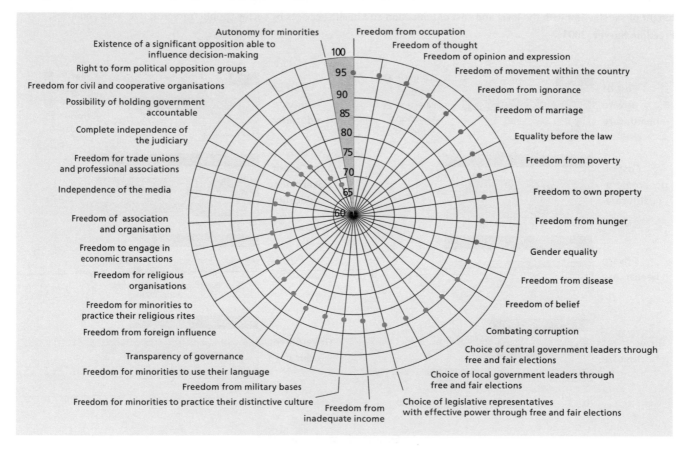

to influence decision-making; and to the right to form opposition groups. This may indicate rather conservative attitudes or frustration with the present political situation.

There were noticeable differences in the results obtained among the five countries, whether in the degree to which interviewees considered the elements of freedom as presented part of their concept of freedom, or in the relative preferences given to some elements over others. The Lebanese, followed by the Palestinians and then by the Algerians, were more strongly inclined to see almost all these elements as part of their own notion of freedom. One might therefore say that the concept of freedom in Lebanon, Palestine, and Algeria is broader and also more intensely in evidence than in Morocco and Jordan.

Citizens of the five countries were clearly of one mind regarding the priority they give to national liberation from occupation, military bases, and foreign influence; to freedom of thought, belief, opinion and expression; to freedom from hunger, poverty and ignorance; to equality before the law and between the sexes, and to combating corruption. They considered all these to be important elements in their concept of freedom.

Freedom and independence of the media and civil society organizations emerged as a priority in Algeria, Palestine and Lebanon.

All these are fundamental elements of the concept of freedom and good governance, as adopted by the AHDR.

There were noticeable differences in the results obtained among the five countries.

Figure 3-5b

Percentage of interviewees considering the elements of freedom constituents of their concept of freedom Five Arab countries, Freedom Survey, 2003

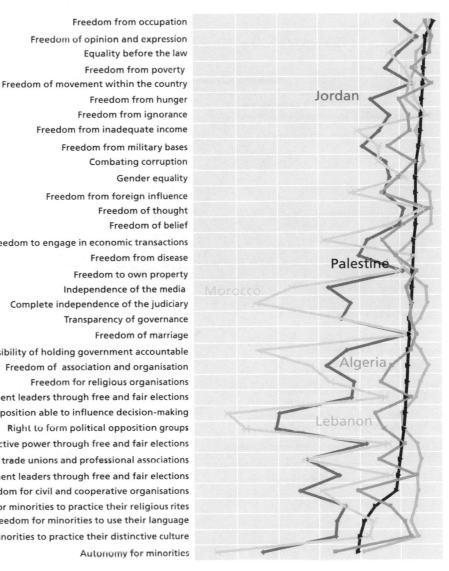

EXTENT OF ENJOYMENT OF FREEDOM AT THE TIME OF THE SURVEY (2003)

...the level of enjoyment of individual freedoms was comparatively high, whereas the enjoyment of 'public' freedoms was relatively low.

Interviewees in all five countries indicated that, in their view, the level of enjoyment of individual freedoms was comparatively high, whereas the enjoyment of 'public' freedoms was relatively low, especially as regards good governance.

Freedoms of movement, marriage and ownership of property, and the freedom of 'minorities' to practice their own culture headed the list of elements of freedom enjoyed in the five countries. The existence of effective opposition, the independence of the media and the judiciary, transparency and accountability of governance, and combating corruption were put at the low end of the scale of enjoyment.

These results can be viewed as constituting a set of priorities for the reform of freedom and governance in Arab countries.

Interviewees' opinions varied among the five countries, reflecting their respective characteristics and situations (figure 3-6b).

PERCEIVED CHANGE IN THE ENJOYMENT OF FREEDOM IN CONTEMPORARY ARAB OPINION

The Freedom Survey questionnaire, Annex 1, contains questions on the interviewees' perception of the extent of change (improvement or deterioration) in the enjoyment of the elements of freedom during the five years preceding the survey.

In the interviewees' estimation, the state of freedom in Arab countries has generally deteriorated during that period. They considered that enjoyment of most elements of freedom deteriorated in the five years preceding the survey with some improvements in individual

Figure 3-6a

Extent of enjoyment of the elements of freedom (%), average of five Arab countries (weighted by population), Freedom Survey, 2003

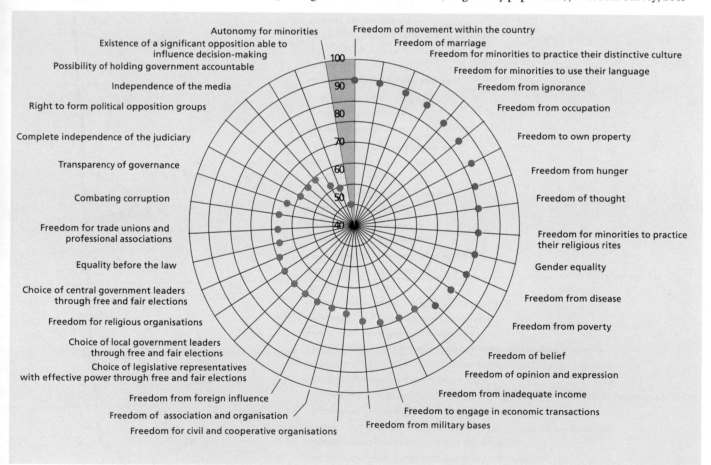

Figure 3-6b

Extent of enjoyment of the elements of freedom (%), average of five Arab countries, Freedom Survey, 2003

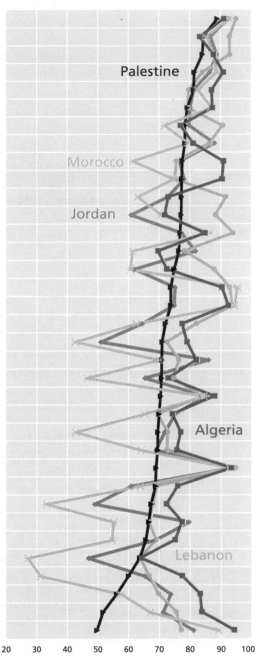

Freedom of marriage
Gender equality
Freedom to own property
Freedom from ignorance
Freedom from disease
Freedom from hunger
Freedom to engage in economic transactions
Freedom of belief
Freedom from inadequate income
Freedom from poverty
Freedom for religious organisations
Freedom for civil and cooperative organisations
Freedom for minorities to practice their religious rites
Equality before the law
Freedom for trade unions and professional associations
Freedom for minorities to use their language
Freedom for minorities to practice their distinctive culture
Freedom of association and organisation
Right to form political opposition groups
Freedom of opinion and expression
Independence of the media
Freedom of thought
Choice of legislative representatives with effective power through free and fair elections
Complete independence of the judiciary
Choice of local government leaders through free and fair elections
Freedom of movement within the country
Choice of central government leaders through free and fair elections
Existence of a significant opposition able to influence decision-making
Combating corruption
Transparency of governance
Autonomy for minorities
Possibility of holding government accountable
Freedom from foreign influence
Freedom from military bases
Freedom from occupation

Palestine Morocco Jordan Algeria Lebanon

20 30 40 50 60 70 80 90 100

freedoms. The results of this aspect of the study are given in figures 3-7a and 3.7b.[4]

Interviewees considered that the greatest improvement had been achieved in the enjoyment of individual freedoms regarding gender equality and marriage, freedom of thought, freedom from ignorance and disease, freedom of 'minorities' to practice own culture, and freedom of civil and co-operative organisations. However, interviewees perceived the

greatest deterioration in five areas reflecting bad governance -- corruption, lack of transparency and accountability in governance, lack of independence of the judiciary, inequality before the law and mounting poverty, figure 3-7a.

Some of the results reflect the distinctive characteristics of the various countries in which the survey was conducted (figure 3-7b). In general, the percentage of interviewees who

Some of the results reflect the distinctive characteristics of the various countries in which the survey was conducted .

[4] Ratios are calculated relative to the total number of interviewees (including missing observations), and arranged in figure 3-7b in descending order according to the relative importance in the Palestine survey.

considered that the enjoyment of freedom had deteriorated was greater than the percentage of those who considered that it had improved. This was especially marked among Palestinian interviewees, whose answers reflected the deterioration of their plight with respect to occupation and foreign influence and freedom of movement within their country. In contrast, most Lebanese interviewees indicated that in their view, there had been a relative improvement in their situation with respect to occupation and foreign influence, probably because of the Israeli withdrawal from southern Lebanon. Lebanese and Palestinian interviewees alike complained of deterioration in the components of good governance citing weaker opposition, less transparency, and little possibility of holding authorities accountable or of combating corruption.

Algerian interviewees, for their part, perceived some gains in the freedom of minorities to use their language, while Lebanese interviewees considered the situation had improved with respect to freedom of movement within the country, equality between men and women, and freedom of marriage. Moroccans alone considered that there had been some improvement in the effort to combat poverty. They also stated that in their view, gender equality had improved.

Figure 3-7a

Perceived change in the enjoyment of elements of freedom (net %) during the five years preceding the survey, average of five Arab countries (weighted by population), Freedom Survey, 2003

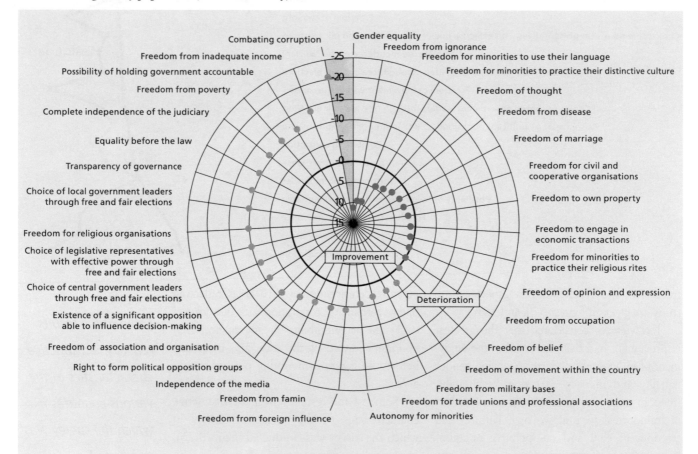

Figure 3-7b

Perceived change in the enjoyment of elements of freedom (net %) during the five years preceding the survey, average of five Arab countries, Freedom Survey, 2003

Freedom of marriage	
Freedom for minorities to practice their distinctive culture	
Freedom for civil and cooperative organisations	
Freedom for minorities to use their language	
Gender equality	Palestine
Freedom for minorities to practice their religious rites	
Freedom of belief	
Freedom from ignorance	
Freedom to own property	
Freedom for trade unions and professional associations	
Freedom of thought	
Freedom of opinion and expression	Lebanon
Freedom for religious organisations	
Autonomy for minorities	
Freedom of association and organisation	
Freedom from disease	Morocco
Independence of the media	
Right to form political opposition groups	
Freedom to engage in economic transactions	Algeria
Freedom from poverty	
Choice of central government leaders through free and fair elections	
Choice of local government leaders through free and fair elections	
Existence of a significant opposition able to influence decision-making	
Choice of legislative representatives with effective power through free and fair elections	
Equality before the law	
Complete independence of the judiciary	Jordan
Freedom from foreign influence	
Freedom from hunger	
Freedom from inadequate income	
Possibility of holding government accountable	
Combating corruption	
Transparency of governance	
Freedom from military bases	
Freedom of movement within the country	
Freedom from occupation	

60   40   20   0   20   40

deterioration ←   → improvment

Part II

Reinforcing Freedom and Establishing Good Governance

Section 3: The Societal Context of Freedom and Governance

This section aims at explaining the deficit in freedom and good governance in Arab countries at present through an analysis of the determinants of the state of freedom and governance covering the institutional (legal and political) structure and the societal context, including the external environment.

CHAPTER FOUR

The Legal Architecture

Introduction

Among the institutional prerequisites of freedom and good governance, respect for the fair enforcement of a legal structure that protects liberties takes decisive precedence. An analysis of the legal structure of freedom and governance is therefore key in explaining the current deterioration in the status of freedom and governance in Arab countries. Chapter Four traces and illustrates the origins of restrictions on freedom that are embedded in the legal provisions of constitutions, and which impact the autonomy of legal institutions.

This chapter explores two basic questions: What are the salient features of Arab legislation on public freedoms and human rights? What key variations exist between different legal standards?

The concept of freedoms and rights applied here is that of the various human rights instruments, including the UDHR, the ICCPR, the ICESCR and numerous conventions and declarations relating to different human rights. In discussing Arab legal systems, we shall examine different levels of legislation beginning with international rules by which the Arab states are bound, followed by the rules of constitutional law, ordinary legislation, regulatory rules and finally the practices of various State authorities, in particular the executive.

THE INSTITUTIONAL ARCHITECTURE OF FREEDOM AND GOVERNANCE

Two sets of discrepancies commonly mar Arab legislation concerned with different levels of freedom and human rights. The first set reflects a gap between international norms and national constitutions and one between those national constitutions and national laws. The second set reflects a breach between international norms, national constitutions and national laws on the one side, and actual practice on the other.

By no means all of the international human rights commitments of Arab states are incorporated in domestic legislation or applied in practice. Some Arab regimes seek to exonerate themselves on the international stage and to conceal violations of citizens' rights by embracing international human rights standards and signing the appropriate treaties. In addition, many Arab constitutions contain safeguards for citizens' freedoms and fundamental rights, which are rarely fully reflected in ordinary legislation. Finally, many safeguards prescribed by ordinary legislation may not be respected in practice and are violated in the absence of any legal sanction or effective monitoring mechanisms. This is discussed in detail below.

ARAB STATES AND INTERNATIONAL HUMAN RIGHTS STANDARDS

Arab states are bound by a number of the principal international human rights instruments, some having ratified or signed two such key instruments, namely the ICCPR and the ICESCR. The United Arab Emirates, Bahrain, Saudi Arabia, Oman and Qatar, however, have ratified neither, and the First Optional Protocol to the first Covenant[1], providing additional rights for individuals, has been signed only by Algeria, Djibouti, Somalia and Libya. The majority of Arab states have ratified the CAT, apart from the United Arab Emirates, Syria,

Some Arab regimes seek to exonerate themselves on the international stage and to conceal violations of citizens' rights by embracing international human rights standards.

---

[1] The Protocols to human rights treaties are important in that they provide effective mechanisms to monitor human rights violations within the State, enabling individual victims to submit complaints of violations committed by the State directly to the specialized Committee.

Most Arab states have shown no interest in acceding to international conventions relating to union rights and freedoms.

Iraq, Mauritania and the Sudan, which has, however, signed it. Neither the Sudan, Somalia, Oman nor Qatar has signed the CEDAW. No Arab State has signed its Optional Protocol. Only Jordan and Djibouti have ratified the Statute of the International Criminal Court, although nine states have signed it, table 4-1.

By and large, Arab states have paid scant regard to International Labour Organization (ILO) conventions relating to trade unions, the freedom of trade union organization and the protection of trade union rights, other than in a few cases, and then mostly in connection with a limited number of conventions. Arab states seem content to ratify certain international human rights treaties, but do not go so far as to recognize the role of international mechanisms in making human rights effective.

The proof lies in their position towards the rights enshrined in the ICCPR. While most have ratified the Covenant, they have not ratified its first Optional Protocol. This impedes the work of the Human Rights Committee established under the Covenant, as it is thus confined to considering the official reports of states on their implementation of the Covenant's provisions and has no opportunity to receive complaints of violations from citizens, whether directly or through non-governmental organizations (NGOs), when rights are violated by an Arab state which has not ratified the Protocol. Furthermore, most Arab states have shown no interest in acceding to the international conventions relating to union rights and freedoms.

TABLE 4-1

Status of Ratifications of the Principal International Human Rights Treaties, January 2005

Country	International Covenant on Economic, Social and Cultural Rights (CESCR)	International Covenant on Civil and Political Rights (CCPR)	Optional Protocol to the International Covenant on Civil and Political Rights (CCPR-OP1)	Second Optional Protocol to the International Covenant on Civil and Political Rights (CCPR-OP2)	International Convention on the Elimination of All Forms of Racial Discrimination (CERD)	Convention on the Elimination of All Forms of Discrimination against Women (CEDAW)	Optional Protocol to the Convention on the Elimination of All Forms of Discrimination against Women (CEDAW-OP)	Convention against Torture and Other Cruel, Inhuman or Degrading Treatment or Punishment (CAT)	Optional Protocol to the Convention against Torture and Other Cruel, Inhuman or Degrading Treatment or Punishment (CAT-OP)	Convention on the Rights of the Child (CRC)	Optional Protocol to the Convention on the Rights of the Child- the involvement of children in armed conflict (CRC-OP-AC)	Optional Protocol to the Convention on the Rights of the Child- the sale of children, child prostitution and child pornography (CRC-OP-SC)	International Convention on the Protection of the Rights of All Migrant Workers and Members of Their Families (MWC)
Algeria	12 Sep 89*	12 Sep 89	12 Sep 89*		14 Feb 72	22 May 96*		12 Sep 89		16 Apr 93			
Bahrain					27 Mar 90*	18 Jun 02*		06 Mar 98*		13 Feb 92*	21 Sep 04*	21 Sep 04*	
Comoros					27 Sep 04**	31 Oct 94*		22 Sep 00**		22 Jun 93			22 Sep 00**
Djibouti	05 Nov 02*	05 Nov 02*	05 Nov 02*	05 Nov 02*		02 Dec 98*		05 Nov 02*		06 Dec 90			
Egypt	14 Jan 82	14 Jan 82			01 May 67	18 Sep 81		25 Jun 86*		06 Jul 90		12 Jul 02*	19 Feb 93*
Iraq	25 Jan 71	25 Jan 71			14 Jan 70	13 Aug 86*				15 Jun 94			
Jordan	28 May 75	28 May 75			30 May 74	01 Jul 92		13 Nov 91*		24 May 91	06 Sep 00**	06 Sep 00**	
Kuwait	21 May 96*	21 May 96*			15 Oct 68*	02 Sep 94*		08 Mar 96*		21 Oct 91	26 Aug 04*	26 Aug 04*	
Lebanon	03 Nov 72*	03 Nov 72*			12 Nov 71*	21 Apr 97*		05 Oct 00*		14 May 91	11 Feb 02*	10 Oct 01	
Libya	15 May 70*	15 May 70*	16 May 89*		03 Jul 68*	16 May 89*	18 Jun 04*	16 May 89*		15 Apr 93*	29 Oct 04*	18 Jun 04*	18 Jun 04*
Mauritania	17 Nov 04*				13 Dec 88	10 May 01*		17 Nov 04*		16 May 91			
Morocco	03 May 79	03 May 79			18 Dec 70	21 Jun 93*		21 Jun 93		21 Jun 93	22 May 02	02 Oct 01	21 Jun 93
Oman					02 Jan 03*					09 Dec 96*	17 Sep 04*	17 Sep 04*	
Qatar					21 Aug 76a			10 Feb 00a		03 May 95	25 Aug 02a	18 Jan 02a	
Saudi Arabia					23 Sep 97*	07 Sep 00		22 May 02*		26 Jan 96*			
Somalia	24 Jan 90*	24 Jan 90*	24 Jan 90*		26 Aug 75			24 Jan 90*		09 May 02**			
Sudan	18 Mar 86*	18 Mar 76*			21 Mar 77*			04 Jun 86**		03 Aug 90	09 May 02*	02 Nov 04*	
Syria	21 Apr 69*	21 Apr 69*			21 Apr 69*	28 Mar 03*		19 Aug 04		15 Jul 93	17 Oct 03	15 May 03	
Tunisia	18 Mar 69	18 Mar 69			13 Jan 67	20 Sep 85		23 Sep 88		30 Jan 92	02 Jan 03	13 Sep 02	
UAE					20 Jun 74*	06 Oct 04*				03 Jan 97*			
Yemen	09 Feb 87*	09 Feb 87*			18 Oct 72*	30 May 84*		05 Nov 91*		01 May 91		15 Dec 04	

Notes:

The dates listed refer to the date of ratification, unless followed by: "*" signifies accession, "**" signifies signature only.

Source: (Office of the United Nations High Commissioner For Human Rights).

LEGISLATIVE REGULATION OF FREEDOMS IN ARAB CONSTITUTIONS

LAW AND JUSTICE, PUBLIC ORDER AND NATIONAL SECURITY AS EXCUSES TO LIMIT FREEDOM

People do not allow legislators to pass whatever laws they please, especially laws contradicting freedom, unless they live under a harsh or despotic governance regime. Indeed, justice, as a standard for evaluating legislation, occupies a clear and important place in public affairs and has been the subject of considerable philosophical, religious, moral and legal discussion down the ages.

The standards and instruments of justice and freedom, as enshrined in the international legal and human rights system, have evolved from the laborious endeavours of humanity to develop a normative framework that controls the national legislator. The latter is not at liberty to bend the law to serve autocrats and violate human rights and public freedoms. Right is always above the legislative authority.

Nevertheless, many national legal systems twist various concepts to circumvent freedom and justice. These systems often invoke higher national considerations, which are held up as sacrosanct even if they affect the rights and freedoms of the public and individuals. Both the concept of public order and that of national security lend themselves to abuse, if interpreted wilfully. Invoking public order, the State can limit civil and commercial freedoms. By citing national security, it can justify any action it wishes, even those that infringe individual freedoms.

OVERVIEW OF ARAB CONSTITUTIONS

The move to adopt constitutions as high-level legal instruments to which all state authorities are subject and by which state legislation is governed has extended to all Arab countries, though some such as Saudi Arabia (1992), and Oman (1996) were slower to do so. All provide for the protection of public freedoms and human rights. Measures taken to include certain rights and freedoms in constitutions and harmonize them with relevant international instruments are a welcome development, but more important is that they should be safeguarded in ordinary legislation, together with the conditions that secure them in actual practice.

Arab constitutions generally regard the people as the source and holder of sovereignty, apart from the Constitutions of Kuwait, Jordan and Morocco, which employ the term "nation", which requires extending the circle of participation and strengthening accountability and oversight. Popular sovereignty theoretically increases opportunities for the people to have a say in the management of public affairs.

Arab constitutions refer to the principle of equal rights and public duties before the law and to the protection and assurance of fundamental rights and freedoms. The substance of those rights, however, varies along with the scope of freedom and protection in accordance with each state's cultural and liberal heritage, the extent to which it adopts the principles of democracy and civil and political freedoms, and the overall religious or secular influence on the state's system of governance. The provision for freedoms in national constitutions is an essential stage in the ascent of freedom to the point where it is constitutionally regulated, the constitution being the primary legal instrument in the hierarchy of legal rules.

Arab constitutions commonly prioritize rights and freedoms, placing them after the preamble and the initial section on fundamental provisions and principles. Some countries, however, have gone further and, have explicitly declared their commitment to the rights contained in international instruments, as decreed in article 5 of the Constitution of Yemen and the preamble to the Constitution of Morocco.

FREEDOM OF OPINION AND EXPRESSION

Many Arab constitutions[2] include special provisions on freedom of thought, opinion and

Both the concept of public order and that of national security lend themselves to abuse, if interpreted wilfully.

Arab constitutions generally regard the people as the source and holder of sovereignty.

---

[2] The Constitutions of Tunisia (article 8), Algeria (article 30), Morocco (section 9), the Sudan (section 1), Jordan (article 15), Kuwait (article 36), Yemen (article 26), Mauritania (article 10), the United Arab Emirates (article 30), Egypt (article 47), Bahrain (article 23) and Lebanon (article 13).

belief, varying from concise to detailed references, according to the general style of the constitution itself. Few constitutions contain no reference to freedom of thought and opinion, although the Interim Constitution of Qatar, (article 13) simply states: "Freedom of publication and the press is guaranteed in accordance with the law." The Saudi Arabian Basic Law adopts an extremely conservative approach to freedom of opinion and expression, stipulating, in article 39, that the information and publishing media, as well as all other means of expression, shall employ courteous language and comply with state regulations.

FREEDOM TO FORM ASSOCIATIONS AND FREEDOM OF PEACEFUL ASSEMBLY

Arab constitutions contain special provisions on freedom of peaceful assembly, association and affiliation. The overall concept of association also includes political associations (parties) and professional associations (unions).

The right to form and join associations is essential to the exercise of freedom of opinion and expression, as well as to other freedoms and rights which people sharing the same opinions or interests cannot fully exercise without joint efforts. A study of the relevant Arab constitutional texts, however, reveals discrepancies between the provisions which encompass those rights; some constitutions provide for the right of association, without mentioning parties or trade unions, as in article 33 of the Constitution of the United Arab Emirates. Others elaborate in more detail on the freedom to form associations and unions but remain silent about the freedom to form political parties, as in article 27 of the Constitution of Bahrain.

Arab constitutions assign regulation of the right of association to ordinary legislation, which tends to restrict the right under the guise

of regulation.

The constitution may also stipulate numerous restrictions on the right of association in order to safeguard national security or national unity. The Egyptian Constitution thus recognizes citizens' right to form associations in the manner prescribed by law and prohibits the establishment of associations that are inimical to the order of society, secret or military in nature. The Tunisian Constitution guarantees the freedom to establish associations, provided it is exercised as regulated by law, and also recognizes trade union rights. The Syrian Constitution guarantees citizens' right of association and peaceful demonstration within the framework of its principles, provided that the exercise of that right is regulated by law. The Bahraini Constitution provides that: "The freedom to form associations and trade unions on national principles, for legitimate objectives and by peaceful means, is guaranteed in accordance with the terms and conditions prescribed by law, provided that the foundation of religion and public order is not undermined…" Other Arab constitutions, however, make no provision for the right to form associations (and trade unions), despite providing for most political freedoms, as in the Constitutions of Oman, Qatar and Saudi Arabia.

FREEDOM TO FORM POLITICAL PARTIES

The right to form political parties is permitted in 14 Arab countries. Libya and the member states of the Gulf Cooperation Council (Saudi Arabia, the United Arab Emirates, Qatar, Bahrain, Kuwait and Oman) prohibit the formation of political parties. Some states, which, for many decades, adhered to the one-party system have moved towards establishing the multiparty system in their constitutions. While this is an advance towards democracy and pluralism, it is hampered by lingering traces from the restrictive one-party phase, which detract from these constitutions.

Some regimes, forced to abandon the one-party system for pluralism at the end of the 1980s, also took care to place restrictions on the exercise of such freedoms, with the result that pluralism was in fact a continuation of the

---

BOX 4-1

The right to form political parties

Setting up a political party is not fundamentally contingent on a permit being issued by the [executive] authority when and as it wishes and withdrawing the permit when the party falls from favour. It is a fundamental right deriving directly from the Constitution and other legal texts defining the conditions. In this respect the law has no function other than to regulate the exercise of this right and to provide it with the necessary elements and conditions.

Extract from the Administrative Court judgement in Case no 115, judicial year 38, New Wafd Party v. the Government, Egypt.

one-party system, as in Tunisia after 7 November 1987. In some constitutions, moreover, the provisions relating to pluralism were ambiguous and open to interpretation, as in the Permanent Constitution of Egypt of 1971. Although amendments made in 1980 to article 5 stipulated that "the political system in the Arab Republic of Egypt shall be established on a multiparty basis", the Constitution continued to refer to the coalition of the people's work force, representing the theoretical basis of the sole political organization (the Arab Socialist Union). This type of constitutional ambiguity is clearly attributable to the changes that occurred in the political and economic spheres, but with no accompanying amendment of constitutional values to reflect those changes. Certain constitutional provisions therefore fail to reflect the current reality.

THE HUMAN RIGHT TO LITIGATION AND THE PRINCIPLE OF THE INDEPENDENCE OF THE JUDICIARY

The international perspective and the Arab constitutional reality

Heading the list of civil rights is the human right to litigation, together with the associated guarantee of the independence of the judiciary and assurance of the necessary procedural safeguards that secure the right to a fair trial, in accordance with articles 8 and 10 of the UDHR. (Annex 3)

Similarly, article 14 of the ICCPR sets out in some detail the elements of the human right to litigation and the safeguards of that right in terms of the principle of equality before courts and tribunals, the right to a public hearing, the impartiality and independence of the judiciary, the right of defence and legal assistance, presumption of innocence and other principles required to make the right to fair trial operative.

Fair trial safeguards can generally be divided into three closely related and interdependent categories: institutional safeguards embodied in the principle of the independence of the judiciary, procedural safeguards set down in a body of procedural principles essential to protect the rights of litigants and the fairness of

trial, and objective safeguards embodied in the requirement to respect a number of objective principles during trial.

Recognizing that the independence of the judiciary is an important institutional safeguard to protect freedom, the international community has devoted considerable attention to the principle. The 1983 World Conference on the Independence of Justice, in Montreal produced the Universal Declaration of the Independence of Justice, which sets out detailed requirements for the independence of the judiciary. The most important elements include that judges shall be free to decide matters impartially in accordance with their assessment of the facts and their understanding of the law without any restrictions, pressures, threats or interference, direct or indirect, from any quarter; and the judiciary shall be independent of the executive and the legislature.

The Seventh United Nations Congress on the Prevention of Crime and the Treatment of Offenders (Milan, 1985) also adopted the Basic Principles on the Independence of the Judiciary and called for them to be implemented at the national and regional levels. These Principles are similar to those of the Montreal Declaration, most importantly the principle that the judiciary shall have exclusive authority to decide whether a case submitted for its decision is within its jurisdiction as defined by law. The fifth principle also provides that everyone shall have the right to be tried by ordinary courts or tribunals using fair legal procedures and that no tribunals shall be created that do not apply the duly established procedures of the legal process. The seventh principle calls for the provision of adequate resources to enable the judiciary to properly perform its functions.

Principles guaranteeing the independence of the judiciary can generally be divided into those relating to the independence of the judicial authority and those relating to judges as individuals. As an independent authority, the judiciary's affairs are managed by a supreme council composed of judges, which has exclusive authority over all matters relating to the budget, determining judges' remuneration, the appointment, discipline and transfer of judges, allocation of work and all other matters relating to the administration of justice, without

The independence of the judiciary is an important institutional safeguard to protect freedom.

Judges shall be free to decide matters impartially…without any restrictions, pressures, threats or interference, direct or indirect, from any quarter.

interference from the executive. The judicial authority is embodied in the natural judiciary, which alone has jurisdiction to examine lawsuits. Consequently, no form of exceptional judiciary that displaces the jurisdiction belonging to the judiciary can be created.

Judges as individuals are independent in discharging their duties, which may under no circumstances be subject to any form of interference or influence. They may not be intimidated by punishment or induced by reward to settle disputes in a certain manner. Consequently, judicial office may not be combined with any executive and political office, to ensure that judges are removed from any context of partiality and bias. Judges cannot be dismissed for reasons other than disciplinary; additional safeguards are as indicated above.

The independence of the judiciary should not be seen as an end in itself. It is a prerequisite for ensuring the right to fair trial, a right that obtains in no other way, even if other conditions for a fair trial are satisfied.

Procedural safeguards for the right to fair trial can be summed up in a number of principles: there shall be no criminal punishment unless a final judgement is rendered by a properly constituted judicial court; crime and punishment are personal; trials shall be conducted without undue delay; no one may be tried or punished twice for the same act; trials shall be heard in public; the principle of oral proceedings and the right of litigants to attend trial proceedings (the principle of appearing in person); trial proceedings shall be recorded; and shall be restricted by the boundaries of the case, whether in terms of the persons concerned or its subject matter; the right to appeal against judgements before a higher court; and the principle that the appellant shall not be prejudiced by her/his appeal.

The most important objective principles guaranteeing the right to a fair trial, include: presumption of innocence, or, in other words, innocence as the rule; there shall be no crime and no punishment other than in accordance with a pre-existing law (nullum crimen, nulla

poena sine lege) that clearly and unquestionably covers the conduct which is the subject of the criminal offence; penal law shall be non-retroactive; the right of the accused to application of the most appropriate law; freedom of defence and the guaranteed right to defence; punishment shall fit the crime; and the operation of all such principles within the overall framework of human rights principles, in particular equality and the sovereignty of the law.

On paper, Arab constitutions encompass most of these principles and rules, following a consistent line on the independence and inviolability of the judiciary, that judges are independent and, in their administration of justice, subject to no authority other than the law. Some constitutions even elaborate at length, highlighting the status of judges, the importance of their independence and the rights of litigants, as in the Egyptian Constitution, which devotes the whole of chapter IV, consisting of nine articles (articles 64-72), to the subject. Article 147 of the Yemeni Constitution provides for the independence of both the judiciary as an authority and judges as individuals, stipulating that: "The judiciary is an independent judicial, financial and administrative authority and the Office of the Public Prosecutor is one of its organs. The courts shall assume responsibility for the settlement of all disputes and offences and judges shall be independent and subject to no authority other than the law in their administration of justice. No party may in any way interfere in lawsuits or in any affair of justice. Such interference shall be regarded as an offence punishable by law and legal proceedings relating to such offences shall not lapse by statute of limitation."

It is interesting to note that while a number of Arab constitutions refer to the independence of judges and not to the independence of the judiciary, others[3] do refer to the independence of the judiciary. Such variations are, however, of little significance, since all Arab judicial systems have lost their independence to some degree or other by virtue of the executive's historical domination over Arab society

---

[3] The Yemeni Constitution, the Saudi Arabian Basic Law and the Syrian Constitution, do refer to the independence of the judiciary (compare, for example, article 97 of the Jordanian Constitution, article 96 of the Tunisian Constitution, article 82 of the Moroccan Constitution, article 94 of the Constitution of the United Arab Emirates and article 104 of the Constitution of Bahrain, which refer to the independence of judges or the judiciary, with article 46 of the Saudi Arabian Basic Law, which provides that the judiciary is an independent authority and that judges shall be subject to no authority in their administration of justice other than that of Islamic law (Shari'a), article 165 of the Egyptian Constitution, which provides that the judiciary is independent, and article 131 of the Syrian Constitution, which also provides that the judiciary is independent and that this is guaranteed by the President of the Republic).

and its sway over both the legislature and the judiciary.

While they may contain significant provisions establishing the principle of the independence of judges, Arab constitutions nevertheless maintain the executive presence within the judiciary and its institutions. Hence, not only are judgements delivered and enforced in the name of the head of state (of whatever designation or title), but also the head of state is additionally vested with the right to preside over the constitutional bodies that oversee the judiciary. Morocco is an instance: article 86 of the Constitution (1996) provides that: "The King shall preside over the Supreme Council of the Judiciary…". The King also appoints judges by royal decree at the proposal of the Supreme Council of the Judiciary (article 84). Meanwhile, article 173 of the Egyptian Constitution provides that the President of the Republic shall preside over the Supreme Council of Judicial Organs. Article 100 of the Sudanese Constitution also provides that the judiciary is responsible for its actions before the President of the Republic and article 132 of the Syrian Constitution provides that the President of the Republic shall preside over the Supreme Council of the Judiciary. Other examples of the unbalanced relationship favouring the executive over the judiciary will be discussed when we examine legislative violations and the social reality of the independence of the judiciary.

Many Arab constitutions also stipulate safeguards for fair trial, such as the principles of criminal legitimacy in particular and the fairness of trial in general. In the absence of either, a trial is rendered unlawful and unfair, in addition to which any completed trial proceedings are invalid and both procedures and any judgements handed down are void. They are also rendered ineffective, if delivered pursuant to procedures incompatible with the principles of the rights system stipulated in the constitution, and they are regarded as a violation of human rights before the judiciary.

The legal profession and public freedoms

Independent, proficient lawyers give substance to the legal profession's obvious concern with protection of public freedoms, human rights and guarantees for the rights of defence. The independence of the legal profession and the freedom of lawyers has been a subject of significant interest to the international community; as early as 1955, the International Commission of Jurists organized a conference in Athens to address key issues on the rule of law, and which issued a declaration that: "Lawyers of the world should preserve the independence of their profession, assert the rights of the individual under the Rule of Law…". In Oslo, the Congress of the Union Internationale des Avocats adopted a resolution introduced by the Arab Lawyers' Union, urging international organizations to launch a wide-ranging campaign to defend the independence of the legal profession and the freedom of lawyers. The Universal Declaration on the Independence of Judges (Montreal, 1983), the third section of which is devoted to principles guaranteeing the independence of the legal profession and the freedom, safeguards and rights of lawyers was a major international achievement for the legal profession.

The Seventh United Nations Congress on the Prevention of Crime and the Treatment of Offenders (Milan, 1985) produced recommendations relating to the legal profession that called for lawyers' protection from restrictions and controls that could influence their defence of their clients. They also called for greater attention to lawyers' training and strengthening professional skills.

Independence of the legal profession is generally understood to include independence of the professional institution and lawyers as professional practitioners of the right of defence. The independence of the professional institution guarantees lawyers the right to form an independent professional union free from State interference. The independence of the lawyer in exercising her/his profession requires a body of legal safeguards to enable her/him to fulfil the duty of defence.

Some Arab states still do not permit lawyers' unions or associations to be set up. Historically, certain Arab regimes were hostile to lawyers' unions, a position not unrelated to their hostility towards freedoms in general. One example is the Egyptian Government's intervention in the 1980s to dissolve the Bar

Arab constitutions nevertheless maintain the executive's presence within the judiciary and its institutions.

Historically, certain Arab regimes were hostile to lawyers' unions, a position not unrelated to their hostility towards freedoms in general.

Council of the Egyptian Bar Association and form a council to manage the Union's affairs (under Act No. 125 of 1981). Libya had already abolished the legal profession as such, eliminating the Bar Association under Act No. 3 of 1981, while the Syrian authorities had promulgated Legislative Decree No. 39 of 21 August 1981 regulating the legal profession so as to place it under excessive constraints.

In Arab legislation the presence of a lawyer at the preliminary investigation is not considered mandatory, other than for a number of major criminal offences (felonies). The different forms of exceptional judiciary impose restrictions on lawyers' exercise of the right to defence as well as on the right of appeal.

Some Arab legal and judicial systems suffer structural defects, with poor standards of education in law faculties given the massive increase in the number of students, so that many who join the legal profession lack proficiency. Other defects include corruption in the administrative apparatus supporting the courts, all of which contributes to denying the Arab citizen's right to litigation and appropriate legal advice to permit the full exercise of the right of defence.

Most Arab states have no effective systems of legal aid for the needy, even if guaranteed under constitutional or legislative provisions. In reality, the least financially able are also the least able to enjoy the right of defence or benefit from appropriate legal advice.

RIGHT OF NATIONALITY

Nationality is one of the more complex areas of civil rights. It gives a person the legal status that confers rights and duties and helps her/him to acquire full citizenship. International instruments therefore prescribe that: "everyone has the right to a nationality" and that "no one shall be arbitrarily deprived of his nationality nor denied the right to change his nationality." There is a noticeable difference between the status of this right and the situation of those who benefit from it in Arab countries; some constitutions remain silent on the subject, while others refer the matter of its regulation to the law, as in Egypt (article 6), Lebanon (article 6), Jordan (article 5), Saudi Arabia (article 35)

and Algeria (article 30). In addition, some constitutions allow for its forfeiture and provide the conditions required, as in Qatar (article 4), Oman (article 15), the United Arab Emirates (article 8) and Kuwait (article 27).

It is generally recognized that standards for conferring the original nationality vary between the right based on blood relations (i.e. with either parent holding the nationality of the state) or on the basis of the actual place of birth. A new trend is emerging in some Arab countries of granting original nationality to the children of a mother bearing the nationality of the state. This is commendable as it recognizes the principle of equality between mother and father in securing the nationality of their children and ends the misery that arises from the state denying nationality to the children, where the mother is married to a foreign national.

PERSONAL RIGHTS

Civil rights also include those affecting the person, private life and dignity of the individual. International standards emphasize respect for these rights, as in article 17 of the ICCPR, which states that: "No one shall be subjected to arbitrary or unlawful interference with his privacy, family, home or correspondence, nor to unlawful attacks on his honour and reputation."

Arab constitutions variously address these rights in brief or in detail. All agree on the need to safeguard the inviolability of the home and the freedom of different types of correspondence, but matters other than honour are not encompassed within their protection. Some, like the Egyptian Constitution (articles 41-45) and, to a lesser degree, those of Algeria and Somalia, contain more detailed safeguards, providing that homes shall not be searched other than with the occupants' consent or in cases of utmost necessity as designated by law or with a written warrant by the competent judicial authority. They also contain special provisions on freedom of movement and choice of place of residence, although most invest the legislator with considerable authority to restrict the exercise of such freedom by means of the law. In rare exceptions, the judiciary is empowered to consider and rule on the lawfulness of the authorized grounds for restriction.

Other rights, no less important, include the right to establish a family: the right of men and women to marry without discrimination, to enjoy the entitlements of marriage and to own and inherit property. A number of Arab constitutions accord the family a distinct status, regarding it as the basis of society, and emphasize the duty to ensure its preservation, safeguard it from disintegration and breakdown, secure the conditions for its survival and for its harmony with public order and the system of civilized and moral values.

CONSTITUTIONAL VIOLATIONS OF HUMAN RIGHTS

A number of Arab constitutions contain provisions that conflict with international human rights principles by assuming an ideological or religious character that removes public rights and freedoms or permits their removal. The amendments to the Yemeni Constitution of 1994 illustrate this. They strike at the very core of the principle of the legality of crimes and punishments and the right to fair trial. As an example Article 46 was introduced to replace article 31, which originally provided that "there shall be no crime and no punishment other than as stipulated by law", the new provision stipulates that "there shall be no crime and no punishment other than on the basis of a provision of religious law (Shari'a) or law."

There is no objection here to the principle that provisions of Shari'a should be a source of legislation prescribing crime and punishment, but rather that the discourse is directed to the judge, instead of the legislator. Investing discretionary powers in the judge to interpret the Shari'a text and choose among the multiple opinions of jurisprudence, entails a lack of legal precision. It is imperative, therefore, that the constitution of those states which adopt the Shari'a, stipulate the principle that there is no crime or punishment other than prescribed by law. Thus the legal text will be in harmony with the Shari'a, given that the constitution has provided that Shari'a is a source of legislation.

Furthermore, article 33 of the Yemeni constitution, which originally provided that "repugnant and inhuman methods of enforcing punishments shall not be permitted, nor

shall the enactment of laws which so permit", was replaced with article 49 which provides that "punishments may not be enforced by unlawful means and the matter shall be regulated by law." This essentially undermines the principles of the legality of crime and punishment, and equality before the law, since criminalization and punishment become dependent on subjective interpretations of Shari'a.

A further example is provided by article 26 of the Saudi Arabian Constitution (Basic Law), which provides that the state protects human rights in accordance with religious law (Shari'a), without specifying what is meant by religious law. Does this mean those Islamic schools of law that promote justice, equality, reason and respect for human dignity? Or does it refer to the doctrines of Islamic jurisprudence, which may be understood only within their cultural and historical context and which give rise to various forms of conflict between them and present-day human rights principles?

The above observation on the amendment to the Yemeni Constitution applies equally to article 38 of the Saudi Arabian Basic Law, which provides that there shall be no crime and no punishment other than in accordance with a provision of religious law (Shari'a) or statutory law, without specifying what is meant by a provision of religious law.

The confusion between religion and state is nowhere more clearly demonstrated than in articles 4 and 18 of the Sudanese Constitution of 1998. Article 4 provides that God, the Creator of humankind, holds supremacy over the State, without specifying the meaning of supremacy. Governance practice apparently sanctioned by God is likely to be immune to criticism and opposition (Box 4-2).

A number of Arab constitutions contain provisions that conflict with international human rights principles.

The confusion between religion and state is nowhere more clearly demonstrated than in articles 4 and 18 of the Sudanese Constitution of 1998.

BOX 4-2

Constitutional restrictions on rights

The citizen pledges his allegiance to the King on the Book of God Almighty and the Custom of His Prophet, to obey his least command in destitution and in prosperity and under any adverse circumstances.

(Article 6 of the Basic Law of Saudi Arabia)

Workers for the State and in public life shall observe at all times the subservience of the latter to the worship of God, Muslims adhering in this regard to the Book [of God] and the Custom [of the Prophet], and all workers preserving an intention for godliness and maintaining this spirit in their conduct of plans, laws, policies, and official business. This is applicable to the political, economic, social, and cultural spheres.

(Article 18 of the Sudanese Constitution)

Where certain Arab states consider Shari'a as a source of legislation, this does not constitute in itself a violation of human rights principles, provided that those principles, intentions and interpretations of the Shari'a that favour freedom and equality (of which there are many), are those employed. Oppressive rulers should be prevented from making use of the Shari'a as a pretext to conceal their tyranny, as various other pretexts have been exploited in different historical contexts. According to contemporary scholarship (ijtihad) on this issue there is no contradiction between Shari'a and human rights, as the intentions of the Shari'a are in harmony with international human rights law.

The constitutional violation of human rights may assume a confessional shape, as illustrated by article 24 of the Lebanese law, which provides that parliamentary seats in the Council of Deputies shall be divided on a religious and confessional basis. Article 95 of the Constitution adopts the same criterion dealing with the highest positions (among citizens) of the State This situation arises from the legacy of historical and political circumstances experienced by the Lebanese legislator and the various sectors of the people of Lebanon at a particular stage in their history. With the Constitution of 1990 the legislator took the commendable course, with the intent of putting an end to sectarianism.

Constitutional violations of human rights can also take the form of an ideological bias, which excludes differing opinions or political affiliations. For example, article 8 of the Syrian Constitution, affirms the Ba'th party as the leadership of society and the state, meaning that the multiparty system has no constitutional legality. The same applies to those constitutions where freedom of expression and criticism, contingent on criticism being constructive and that it guarantees the integrity of the national and pan-Arab structure and promotes the socialist system.

Constitutional provisions for the creation of exceptional courts further illustrate the constitutional violation of liberties and human rights. Examples include article 171 of the Egyptian Constitution, which provides for state security courts, article 179, on the Socialist Public Prosecutor, and article 183, on military courts, referring their regulation and the definition of its jurisdiction to the law, without stipulating further details. This contrasts with the Constitution of Bahrain, Article 105b, which states that the jurisdiction of the military courts is limited to military crimes committed by members of the Defence Force, the National Guard, and the Public Security forces and does not extend to others except on the declaration of martial law. Article 122/3 of the Sudanese Constitution is similar to the Egyptian Constitution.

LEGISLATIVE RESTRICTIONS ON HUMAN RIGHTS IN ARAB LEGISLATION

Clearly, Arab constitutional provisions for rights and freedoms do not reflect the same comprehensive and effective level typical of international instruments. The Arab constitutional legislator is always careful to leave a loophole by referring regulation of rights and freedoms to ordinary legislation so that the national legislator may violate these same rights and public freedoms. In fact the legislative text frequently goes far beyond regulating rights and freedoms to the extent of restricting them, if not removing them altogether. Where the constitutional text therefore provides rights and freedoms - notwithstanding that they may at times be inadequate – it simultaneously deprives them of much of their worth, turning them into a mere facade before the international community in a display that is empty of any real substance. In other words, the constitution becomes a front for the legislative violation of freedoms and human rights.

LEGISLATIVE RESTRICTIONS ON THE RIGHT OF PEACEFUL ASSEMBLY

Arab countries provide many examples of legislative violations of human rights, some of which are reviewed here.

Examples include provisions which prohibit or restrict exercise of the right to strike, demonstrate, hold mass gatherings or assemble peacefully and which clearly show that Arab authorities live in fear of the Arab street. In Egypt, the Assembly Act No. 10 of 1914 penalizes gatherings of five or more persons (Box 4-3).

The Meetings and Demonstrations Act No. 14 of 1923 requires advance notification to the police of any meeting. The police are empowered to ban a meeting from taking place and always have the right to be present at a meeting, choose the venue and disperse a meeting. Electoral meetings are confined by law to a brief period extending from the day when voters are called to the day of election, thus diminishing the importance of such meetings. The police also have the right to ban an electoral meeting from taking place and to disperse it if it is convened. In Jordan, the Interim Public Meetings Act No. 45 of 2001 regulates public meetings and marches, for which prior authorization is required from the competent administrative governor, whose decision on the matter is not subject to any judicial authority. The police also have the right to be present at and disperse meetings, as well as break up marches. The Jordanian Penal Code similarly provides for the offence of assembly (articles 164 and 165). Other Arab legislation is similar, with varying details regarding bans on public meetings, requirements of prior authorization for public meetings and demonstrations and the powers of the executive to disperse such events and impose penalties for violations (see Royal Decree No. 377 of 1958 in Morocco, Act No. 18 of 1973 in Bahrain, Act No. 65 of 1979 in Kuwait, section 13 of the Qatari Penal Code, Act No. 29 of 2003 in Yemen and article 335 of the Syrian Penal Code, pursuant to which any meeting of a non-private nature is deemed by law to be a form of stirring up unrest).

LEGISLATIVE RESTRICTIONS ON THE RIGHT OF POLITICAL ORGANIZATION

In addition to those constitutions which ban or place restrictions on the right to form political parties, as illustrated above, we find legislative restrictions limiting this right even in countries whose constitutions prescribe the multiparty system. In Egypt, the law requires prior authorization from the Party Affairs Committee,

BOX 4-3
Restrictions on the rights to assembly and association

Anyone who is present in a gathering on the public highway consisting of at least five persons shall be punished, even if no crime is committed, if a representative of the Public Authority believes that public peace may as a result be endangered and if he orders the members of the gathering to disperse and they do not comply.

(Article 2, Public Assembly Law No. 10, 1914, Egypt).

The holding or organization of a public meeting is not permitted without previously obtaining a permit for that purpose from the Governor in whose area of authority the meeting will take place, and all public meetings that are held without a permit will be prevented and dispersed.

(Article 4, Decree Law concerning the holding of public meetings and assemblies, Kuwait)

predominantly governmental in its composition, before any party can be established. The committee's decisions may be appealed before the Supreme Administrative Court, which, exceptionally, consists of both judicial and non-judicial members, and its rulings final and not subject to any appeal.

To establish a political party in Jordan the law requires prior authorization from the Interior Minister, who has the right to refuse, and party founders have the right of judicial appeal against such refusal. The party may not publicly declare itself or pursue its activities until either the Minister has approved it or the court has ruled to revoke the Minister's refusal. In Yemen, prior authorization must be obtained from the Committee on Party Affairs and Political Organizations, largely an administrative body, which may oppose the establishment of the party. In such case the party founders are entitled to appeal by all legal means. The Moroccan legislator adopts a more liberal approach: part IV, sections 15-20, of the law in question regulates political parties and politically oriented associations, requiring only notification of a political party being established (section 15).

In Syria, maximum restrictions apply, with no recognition of party pluralism. Act No. 53 of 1979 regulates the protection of the Arab Socialist Ba'th Party, the only political party for which the Constitution makes provision. The Arab Socialist Ba'th Party is the leading party for society and State (Article 1). Any party member who belongs to another political organization is punished by imprisonment of five to ten years (Article 5/a). Any person who infiltrates the party ranks with intent to work

Arab authorities live in fear of the Arab street.

The police have the right to be present at and disperse meetings, as well as break up marches.

for the benefit of any other political or party organ receives the same punishment (article 5/b). Under Law No. 49 of 8 July 1980, any person belonging to the Muslim Brotherhood is a criminal and punished by the death penalty. Act No. 263 of 19 July 1960, disbands Baha'i assemblies and Legislative Decree No. 47 of 9 May 1967 disbands the Association of Islamic Guidance.

Political parties in Tunisia are regulated by Basic Law No. 32 of 1988, which requires prior authorization by the Interior Minister, who is entitled to object (Article 8). Appeals against a refusal are permissible before a special division of the administrative court, composed of judicial and non-judicial members, whose decisions are final and not liable to any form of appeal (Article 10).

There is no legal regulation of the freedom to form political parties in Arab Gulf states, since parties are illegal. In most Arab states, the law imposes restrictions on political party financing, either proscribing or setting heavy restrictions and controls over acceptance of donations from any foreign person or public bodies corporate, (Egypt, Jordan, Morocco, Tunisia and Yemen). Other laws contain vaguely worded conditions concerning party activity, permitting the state to exercise its power to dissolve a party whenever it considers the conditions have been breached. (Yemeni law, for example, stipulates that parties must not undermine the people's Islamic faith or engage in any activity opposed to the aims of the Yemeni revolution). Most legislation contains provisions empowering the executive to seek the dissolution of a party through a court ruling.

Given that most courts considering party affairs can hardly be said to be independent, it is safe to say that the power to dissolve a party rests with the executive.

LEGISLATIVE RESTRICTIONS ON FREEDOM TO FORM ASSOCIATIONS

In imposing restrictions on the freedom to form and establish associations, Arab legislation makes a distinction between charitable associations and other associations. All Arab legislation requires advance notice of public benefit associations and that they be licensed. All Arab legislation, apart from Moroccan and Lebanese, requires private associations to have a prior licence with many imposing stiff penalties on those carrying out activities without licence. Restrictions are imposed on associations' right to receive donations, particularly from foreign entities, where prior approval from the executive is mandatory. Affiliation with foreign associations is also forbidden without executive approval. In most Arab countries, associations are subject to daily monitoring of their activities, and in some cases the executive can object to decisions taken by associations. Most legislation permits the administrative dissolution of associations or management structures or provides for a temporary board of management to be imposed, while in other cases the judiciary may dissolve an association at the executive's request. Clearly then, both the establishment of civil associations and their activities are heavily circumscribed and subject to rigorous control in Arab countries, with few exceptions, such as Morocco and Lebanon.

RESTRICTIONS ON FREEDOM OF OPINION, EXPRESSION AND THE PRESS IN ARAB LEGISLATION

Press freedom is blocked or curtailed in Arab countries under the guise of regulating laws that permit prior or other newspaper censorship. Laws impose restrictions on the right to publish newspapers by requiring a licence whose withdrawal or threat of withdrawal is used by the executive to deter newspapers from crossing the set boundaries of freedom of expression (articles 24 and 32 of the relevant legislation in the United Arab Emirates, article 13 of the legislation in Kuwait, article 44 of the legislation in Bahrain; similar provisions are contained in other Arab legislation). Not a single Arab regime can be said to have a liberal approach towards newspaper publication: in 15 Arab states the law requires prior licence or authorization and also restricts the freedom to publish newspapers. The following observations concern laws regulating freedom of expression, publication and the press in Arab countries:

There is no legal regulation of the freedom to form parties in Arab Gulf states since parties are illegal.

Both the establishment of civil associations and their activities are heavily circumscribed and subject to rigorous control in Arab countries.

Pre-censorship and suspension by administrative decision

The Arab legislator believes that media of expression and information transfer can be substantially controlled by public authority agencies and has yet to grasp that, thanks to modern technology, the potential to control freedom of opinion and expression is steadily diminishing. A survey of legislation in 19 Arab states reveals that pre-censorship of newspapers is imposed in 11 cases (Algeria, Bahrain, Iraq, Kuwait, Libya, Oman, Qatar, Saudi Arabia, Syria, Tunisia, and the United Arab Emirates). It finds its actual implementation through the legislation giving the executive the authority to control national newspapers and impose administrative bans on them.

The study showed that all Arab legislation concerning the media with the exception of Jordan (subsequent to amendments by Act No. 30 of 1999), empower the executive, whether the Ministry of Information, the Interior Ministry or the Council of Ministers, to ban the circulation of newspapers, and exercise administrative impoundment. In Kuwait, Morocco, Oman, Qatar, Saudi Arabia and the United Arab Emirates, the executive can suspend newspapers by administrative decision. All states adopting the system of licence or prior authorization also provide for newspapers' suspension by administrative decision if they publish without licence or authorization. Arab legislation is therefore consistent in broadening executive powers to exercise administrative control, including suspension, over newspapers. In most cases the executive is similarly empowered to abolish a newspaper administratively providing legislative conditions are met. The study of 19 Arab states plainly shows that, of these, 10 give the executive free rein to revoke a licence with no judicial oversight. There is a striking similarity among the legislative provisions in this respect.

Curtailment of freedom on the pretext of security

When regulating freedom of opinion and expression, including the media and mass communications, the Arab legislator prioritizes what s/he perceives as security and public in-

terest considerations above freedom, diversity and respect for human rights. The result is that Arab legislation is full of provisions which regard newspaper publication, audio-visual broadcasting and the free exercise of expression in general as highly dangerous activities warranting a panoply of bans, restrictions and deterrent sanctions, all to preserve what the legislator believes to be in the public interest, for national security, doctrinal purity or the ideological or sacrosanct constants of the nation.

In Arab legislation, the fine balance between freedom and security/order is clearly weighted in the latter's favour. According to the study of legislation, the Arab legislator has enormous leeway to criminalize media activities given the broad scope for prohibiting media content. We shall therefore present here only the most salient features of this policy. The most obvious are the infringement of the principles that punishment is personal and the presumption of innocence. Given that the legislator has a free hand in providing for ambiguously worded offences, the principle of rule of law has become meaningless. Scrutiny of the body of Arab laws concerning freedom of opinion, expression and the press reveals that it is virtually identical, particularly regarding criminalization and prohibition. It would seem that the Arab legislator surpassed himself by copying the most draconian provisions enforced by despotic regimes around the world in specific historical circumstances, which, elsewhere, were eliminated with the passage of time. In the Arab world, however, they were to remain and even proliferate as part of the permanent legal system. The Arab legislator is clearly not inspired by the vision of democracy as, when it comes to setting down laws relating to opinion, s/he is at pains to seek out and apply any measures to the individual that involve tightening up, clampdown and excess.

Denying the right to obtain information

The principle of free circulation of information and the rights of journalists and citizens in general to obtain information are viewed with extreme scepticism by the Arab legislator. The overriding principles here seem to be prohibition and restriction rather than permission and

A survey of legislation in 19 Arab states reveals that pre-censorship of newspapers is imposed in 11 cases.

In Arab legislation, the fine balance between freedom and security/order is clearly weighted in the latter's favour.

opportunity. Journalists' right to obtain information and news is assured in law in only five Arab states: Algeria, Egypt, Jordan, the Sudan and Yemen. Circulation of information however, is heavily circumscribed under all Arab legislation. For instance, imported foreign newspapers and magazines are subject to censorship, control, and confiscation. Some Arab countries even forbid Internet access to shut out the electronic press, and even when permitted, access may be under surveillance.

Harsher conditions for newspaper publication

Arab legislation consistently applies stringent restrictions on newspaper publication and ownership and facilitates arbitrary clampdowns. A total of 17 Arab states prohibit newspaper publication without licence or prior authorization and in some states the licence is conditional upon payment of a large deposit and sometimes a minimum level of capital.

While many Arab states have a system of public or mixed ownership of newspapers, all prohibit foreign ownership and any form of foreign involvement.

During states of emergency and other exceptional situations the clampdown on newspapers is even more acute.

LEGAL RESTRICTIONS ON PUBLIC FREEDOMS DURING A STATE OF EMERGENCY

One of the most serious legislative violations of human rights in the Arab world is where the Arab legislator permits the executive to declare a state of emergency and abuse all safeguards for individual rights and liberties. The state of emergency is a legislative weapon prescribed by constitutions and laws alike that enables the executive to confront unforeseen emergencies that endanger the homeland and threaten its integrity. In some Arab countries, however, the state of emergency has exceeded these boundaries to become permanent and ongoing, with none of the dangers to warrant it. What was the exception has now become the rule (e.g. in Egypt, Syria and Sudan).

Article 4 of the ICCPR states explicitly: "In time of public emergency which threatens the life of the nation and the existence of which is officially proclaimed, the States Parties to the present Covenant may take measures to the extent strictly required by the exigencies of the situation, provided that such measures are not inconsistent with their other obligations under international law and do not involve discrimination solely on the ground of race, colour, sex, language, religion or social origin."

Most Arab constitutions lay down rules for declaring a state of emergency, though in some states it is no longer regarded as such, having acquired semi-permanent status. Human rights and freedoms are commonly violated under a state of emergency (or rules of martial law), as it strips the citizen of many constitutional rights, such as inviolability of the home, personal liberty, freedom of opinion, expression and the press, confidentiality of correspondence, rights of movement and assembly. It removes certain legislative powers from the elected parliament and transfers them to the executive or military governor (emergency authority); and it bars the natural judge from impartially and independently exercising her/his full authority, where judicial entities lacking independence are appointed to the judiciary, who are more concerned with giving a ruling than with neutrality, independence and the right to fair trial. Despite the adverse effects on public rights and freedoms, politicians and jurists loyal to the regimes vigorously defend the state of emergency on a number of pretexts. In this regard, perhaps the most commonly repeated argument is the need to fight terrorism, meaning that the state is in no position to combat terrorism by individuals unless it engages in intimidation through measures authorized under emergency measures.

Yet repugnant terrorist crimes have occurred in a number of Arab states during a declared state of emergency. The usual scenario is that the executive is swift to declare and extend a state of emergency, even without the backing of parliament, which is usually merely a pawn in the hands of the executive to carry out its orders. So it is that the executive can cement its control over legislative, executive and judicial matters and sweep aside the safeguards for individual rights, unfettered by the procedural and objective rule of law.

Arab legislation consistently applies stringent restrictions on newspaper publication and ownership.

One of the most serious legislative violations of human rights...is where the Arab legislator permits the executive to declare a state of emergency and abuse all safeguards for individual rights and liberties.

LEGISLATIVE REGULATION OF THE ROLE OF THE JUDICIARY IN PROTECTING HUMAN RIGHTS AND FREEDOMS

The justice system, with its two branches of an independent judiciary and a free legal profession, represents an institutional safeguard that is indispensable to human rights protection in a free democratic society. International instruments recognize this and set down elaborate criteria and prerequisites to ensure such independence.

Independence of the judiciary (legislative regulation and practice)

Our earlier discussion of this topic considered the international perspective and various provisions in Arab constitutions. International literature considers the independence of the judiciary to apply to both the institutional authority and the individual judge.

However, independence of the judiciary is assured not merely through constitutional and legislative guarantees and a body of related safeguards, nor does it come about only through the institutions with oversight of judicial affairs. Independence of the judiciary relates to more universal and profound considerations; for instance, the extent to which the political system embraces democracy as a value and respect for the law as a framework governing the whole of society. Accordingly, in an undemocratic society, neither the judiciary nor judges enjoy independence, regardless of constitutional and legislative guarantees. It relates also to the judge as individual, the level of training, the nature of her/his education and qualifications, and the value system governing her/his conduct, or, professional ethics in general.

While the independence of the judiciary is a prerequisite for justice, it does not guarantee a credible justice that wins trust and enjoys the respect of litigants unless the conditions to promote it are in place. Hence, for the individual judge, independence demands moral and intellectual probity on her/his part, since the judge's role does not acquire the profound connotations desired unless the judge is neutral, impartial and upright, both morally and

intellectually. Essentially, this calls for a system to be set up to monitor professional ethics and conduct to ensure that the independence of the judiciary remains intact, while also guaranteeing judges their right to progress by increment and benefit, as they are entitled to, and so maintain their distance from enticements by the state or society. Credible justice also calls for judicial and procedural regulation to make it effective, since judicial rulings are not the work of the judge alone, but are the outcome of concerted efforts by lawyers, experts, judicial assistants and others. Just as the system must be rigorous on judges' neutrality, in accordance with professional ethics, the law must similarly guarantee an effective system that ensures the right of defence, lawyers' rights and duties, and the availability of highly skilled experts and judicial assistants. Without this the ills afflicting the legal profession or the performance of judicial assistants are bound to undermine credible justice in society.

Arab constitutions refer regulation of the judiciary to ordinary legislation. However, when the Arab legislator steps outside that framework and imposes restrictions on freedoms and human rights in breach of international standards and national constitutional provisions, s/he is inhibiting the human right to litigation and invalidates the principle of the independence of the judiciary, turning constitutional texts into facades to conceal flaws in substance.

Despite constitutional and legislative guarantees for the independence of the judiciary and fair trial safeguards, scholars and human rights activists note a disparity between the texts and reality. Legal experts, for instance, hold that constitutional and legislative provisions on the independence of the judiciary and the right to fair trial are not applied in their countries, for mainly political reasons, while others point to the traditional kinship structure in certain countries, which also makes it difficult to apply such legal provisions.

Where there is conflict between a political regime unfettered by legal controls and the judiciary, whose independence is upheld in the constitution and law, the Arab regime swiftly sweeps aside the independence of the judiciary without any hesitation (Source: Ahmad Makki,

In an undemocratic society, neither the judiciary nor judges enjoy independence, regardless of constitutional and legislative guarantees.

Where there is conflict between a political regime unfettered by legal controls and the judiciary…the Arab regime swiftly sweeps aside the independence of the judiciary.

1990), as numerous historical examples in Arab countries show.

Independence of the judiciary as an institution and of judges as individuals is jeopardized on two counts in the Arab world. First, ideological and autocratic regimes frequently interfere, using the pretext of "protecting the ideological foundations" of their authoritarian regimes. Second, the decline in living standards among those of fixed income, including judges, opens the profession to corrupting enticements from certain sectors of the nouveau riche.

As regards the separation and balance of powers, the authority accorded to justice ministries to inspect courts and control the judiciary's budget clearly constitute a restriction on the independence of the judiciary as an institution. This situation, in which the executive controls their finances and intervenes in the appointment, transfer and dismissal of judges, means that, in practice, judges in many Arab countries are not independent. Indeed, many are sometimes fearful in delivering their judgements, particularly when the State has a direct or indirect interest in the case in question.

In some Arab countries, judges are tempted with material and moral inducements to make them pliable instruments in the hands of the executive particular in cases where the executive has a special interest, This may take the form of a part-time appointment to conduct legal business for the executive for additional remuneration, and/or appointment to high executive and political office on leaving the judiciary. These are all too persuasive and can cause judges to discharge their functions less than impartially in return for short or longer-term reward.

The vast increase in the number of cases brought to court in some Arab countries obstructs the administration of justice and exercise of the human right to litigation to a considerable degree. Inevitably, in Arab countries where there are millions of lawsuits and no more than several thousand sitting judges, court cases are delayed for years before they are settled. Meanwhile litigants' rights are set aside, particularly the rights of defence and to prompt and consummate justice. This slow pace of litigation harms both the economy and society; in such an environment rights are delivered only with the greatest difficulty, with the judicial system seen as an obstacle to the growth of national and foreign investment. The absence of an authority capable of enforcing the law, and within a reasonable time, can encourage recourse to violence and individual reprisals, and make people less willing to go to court to seek a solution (figure 4-1).

According to the Freedom Survey, Annex 1, willingness to go to court to settle disputes barely exceeded 50%. This percentage showed a relative decrease in cases related to freedoms, and in Palestine and Morocco in general

Corruption within the auxiliary apparatus of the judiciary, including secretaries, clerks and experts, has an adverse impact on the justice system in a number of Arab societies. Civil servants who eke out a living by breaching the law and justice every day are scarcely fitted to help apply them. Ultimately, the situation resembles a farce in which justice is trampled underfoot and rights degraded, with little standing in the way.

Various forms of exceptional courts undermine the jurisdiction of the natural judiciary, primarily State security courts and military tribunals, which diminish fair trial safeguards, as demonstrated below.

Inevitably, in Arab countries where there are millions of lawsuits and no more than several thousand sitting judges, court cases are delayed for years.

Figure 4-1

Extent of willingness to go to court, Five Arab countries, Freedom Survey, 2003

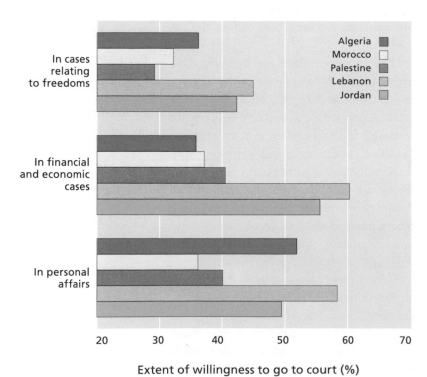

Extent of willingness to go to court (%)

Exceptional courts

The Arab legislator has learned through experience that direct clashes with judges and the judiciary may bring public odium, with judges portrayed as martyrs of freedom in an autocratic regime. Many Arab regimes therefore prefer other methods of dealing with the judiciary that cause less public outcry and also more effectively strip the judiciary of its independence and ensure it complies with the regime's wishes. The regime's first method is to create an exceptional judiciary under the executive's direct influence, to which it refers politically sensitive cases and major security cases. This tradition descends from the time of foreign occupation when the British and French occupying powers created emergency courts to try their opponents.

In the Arab world, the exceptional judiciary that is most threatening for human rights is the military. The military judicial system exists in a number of states, including democratic ones. Its existence alone does not breach public freedoms or human rights, provided that stringent controls are in place to safeguard against the military judiciary aiding the ruling authority to encroach on liberties, human rights and safeguards. The first control is that judges in military tribunals must be legally qualified. Secondly, the tribunals' rulings must be subject to appeal before the ordinary judiciary. Thirdly, their jurisdiction should be confined to military offences committed by individual members of the military in the course of duty within their military units. Fourthly, legal guarantees for the neutrality and impartiality of military judges must be effective.

Most of these guarantees are lacking in Arab military tribunals. The most blatant example is provided by Egypt's Act No. 25 of 1966, where article 6 greatly expands the jurisdiction of the military judiciary, particularly during a state of emergency, when it may consider any offence in the Penal Code and referred to it by the President of the Republic. Cases in which Islamic movements are accused of violence are commonly referred to military courts. In fact recourse to the military judiciary (even though properly a type of professional judiciary with a narrowly defined jurisdiction)

is encouraged by Arab constitutions which make explicit provisions for it, (article 183 of the Egyptian Constitution, for example). Other forms of exceptional judiciary lacking fair trial safeguards include state security courts, courts of values, revolutionary courts, people's courts and tribunals dealing with economic and judicial matters, such as revolutionary committees and so on, that are run by popular communities loyal to the regimes. State security courts exist in several Arab countries in the Near East and North Africa. In Egypt, for example, the State security court provided for under emergency law continues to exercise jurisdiction even after the permanent state security courts have been abolished. State security courts were established in Jordan pursuant to Act No. 17 of 1959, as amended, which can consider offences relating to internal and external State security and drug offences. Article 7 (a) of the Syrian State Security Court Act states: "The State security courts shall not be bound by the usual procedures stipulated in the legislation in force during any of the stages or procedures of prosecution, investigation and trial." Their sessions are held in camera and their rulings are not subject to appeal.

Another model exists in Arab countries with a traditional liberal heritage influenced by practices and methods of foreign occupation. One example is the Justice Council in Lebanon, which, although composed of ordinary judges, lacks independence and does not offer litigants recognized guarantees for fair trial, since its decisions may not be reviewed or appealed before a higher court. More importantly, its jurisdiction to examine cases is determined by political decision of the Cabinet. This Council was set up during the French mandate pursuant to Decree No. 1905 of 12 May 1923, which has been amended several times, and it now considers offences against external state security.

THE IMPACT OF AUTHORITARIAN POWER RELATIONS ON FREEDOM AND HUMAN RIGHTS

One of the principal reasons that violations of freedoms and human rights, both in law and practice, are widespread in the Arab region

The Arab legislator has learned through experience that direct clashes with judges and the judiciary may bring public odium...

In the Arab world, the exceptional judiciary that is most threatening for human rights is the military.

lies in the nature of the political authority and its relationship with society. Consequently, the way to approach the question of legislation that violates freedom is to deal with the issue of power in the Arab world. Distribution of power should be based on genuine respect for the principle of separation of powers; the principle of political alternation should be set down and this, together with ending the monopoly of power, should be assigned to the ballot box alone for decision. Sound laws that are supportive of freedom can only come about where the Arab political regime as a whole is supportive of the values of democracy and people's right to participate in political life.

The monopoly of power, which renders the regime untouchable in terms of accountability, is at the heart of the deteriorating state of freedom and human rights in the Arab world.

CHAPTER FIVE

The Political Architecture

Introduction

Chapter Five looks at another pivotal area that explains the current and critical deterioration in the state of freedom in Arab countries, namely in the political structure of governance. The crisis of the current political structure is manifested most clearly in the generally authoritarian nature of the executive, often reduced to the person of the head of state, and in the role played by the security forces of the state. It is also reflected in the severe restriction of freedom, particularly freedom of expression and association in civil and political societies. The chapter considers the features of corruption drawn from the Freedom Survey and highlights the state of Arab corporate governance. It concludes with an evaluation of the relative situation in the Arab region in comparison to other world regions, with respect to a number of governance indicators derived from the World Bank's database on this subject.

THE CRISIS OF GOVERNANCE IN ARAB COUNTRIES

There is near consensus in the Arab world today concerning the serious flaws in the state of Arab affairs; it is a rare consensus among rulers and ruled in which class distinctions disappear and regional, sectarian and even ethnic differences fade. There is also consensus, as demonstrated by the agreement at the May 2004 Arab summit meeting in Tunis which focused on political reform, that the heart of the failing lies in the political sphere, specifically the architecture of the Arab State, and that reform must begin there. Agreement, however, stops here, as differences emerge, particularly over where the malaise starts and which is the most appropriate prescription for cure.

This consensus is the result of living together with the widespread crisis which overshadows the Arab world and points to a collective failure among Arab states to address major issues, such as the Palestinian question, Arab cooperation, foreign interference, and human development. It also points to the failure to provide citizens with a decent life, whether in terms of the basic requisites of daily life, or human rights or both, which has created an atmosphere of oppression, suffering and instability. This sentiment intensified with the occurrence of major disasters such as the invasion of Kuwait in 1990 and the consequent foreign intervention and Arab disintegration. More recently, the foreign invasion of Iraq and the escalating conflict in Palestine have similarly affected Arab public opinion, particularly since, as a result of the information revolution, the Arab citizen lives these tragedies by the moment and feels tormented by helplessness.

The information revolution and globalization, accompanied by the fall of ideologies and rise of awareness and education in the Arab world, also intensified the crisis of legitimacy of Arab regimes, whether they were based on tradition (religious/tribal), revolution (national/liberationist) or patriarchy. This in turn deepened feelings of crisis and created a vicious circle of frustration, grass-roots disenchantment and a general lack of confidence in governments, which in turn saw the need for further repression and the consolidation of barriers between them and the people.

CHARACTERISTICS OF AUTHORITARIAN GOVERNANCE

The modern-day Arab state monopolizes the public space, insisting on controlling all things, from personal religious belief to international

There is near consensus in the Arab world today concerning the serious flaws in the state of Arab affairs; it is a rare consensus among rulers and ruled.

The modern-day Arab state monopolizes the public space.

relations, and allowing little leeway for initiatives from outside its space or without its blessing. At first glance, it may seem difficult to talk about the common features of governance in the Arab world owing to the wide diversity of its regimes, ranging from absolute monarchies to revolutionary republics and radical Islamic states. Closer scrutiny, however, reveals an interesting affinity in the architecture and methods of Arab systems of governance and brings out features of an interwoven regional architecture comprising an Arab "integral whole" in which the systems are mutually reinforcing. It is therefore possible to speak of an "Arab model" of governance with specific traits common to most systems and in turn based on an Arab regional system that constitutes its political infrastructure.

THE "BLACK-HOLE" STATE

The general features of this Arab model, which some have named the "authoritarian state" (Khaldoun Hassan al-Naqib, in Arabic, 1996) and which has been described at length in a number of studies (Ghassan Salameh, in Arabic, 1995; Ghassan Salameh et al, in Arabic, 1989, 28-40, 89; Hopkins and Ibrahim, 1997, 24; Roger Owen, 1992), are captured in the recent comments of an Arab journalist and activist. The latter describes governance in his country as a system in which there are no free and transparent parliamentary elections, resulting in a "monochrome" parliament. Under that particular system, press freedom is also restricted, as is political and human rights activity, the judiciary is used to make an example of opponents and the constitution establishes a regime that is "unlimited by time and not subject to the control of parliament or the judiciary." In such a regime, even the ruling party becomes a mere piece of administrative apparatus run by "civil servants with neither enterprise nor efficiency" (Rashid Khashana, in Arabic, 2003).

We can call this the model of the "black-hole State", likening it to the astronomical phenomenon of extinguished stars which gather into a ball and are converted into giant magnetic fields from which even light cannot escape. The modern Arab state, in the political

sense, runs close to this model, the executive apparatus resembling a "black hole" which converts its surrounding social environment into a setting in which nothing moves and from which nothing escapes. Like the astronomical black hole, this apparatus in turn forms into a tight ball around which the space is so constricted as to paralyze all movement.

This increasing centralization of the executive is guaranteed in the constitutional texts of certain states, which enshrine the right of the king, the president or the emir (or the Revolutionary Command Council) to legislate and vest wide powers in the head of state. The latter becomes the supreme leader of the executive, the council of ministers, the armed forces, the judiciary and public services, for it is he who appoints and has the power to dismiss ministers, members of the judiciary, senior officials and officers, and it is he who convenes and has the authority to dissolve parliament (where one exists). The laws also prescribe the central control of local authorities, since the ruler appoints governors and prefects, who are responsible to him and not to citizens (Ayoubi, 1995, 322-323).

The centralization of the executive also shows in bureaucratic expansion, greater state interference in the economy and higher government spending of national resources, particularly on security and military organs. This trend is evident, both in radical states with planned economies and in conservative states which, from the outset, declared their adherence to the market economy (Khaldoun Hassan al-Naqib, in Arabic, 1996, 181-207; Ayoubi, 1995, Chapter 9).

Many governments are nevertheless not content with these wide constitutional and administrative powers. They thus turn to emergency laws, which, in some countries, have remained in force for over 40 years. When other countries, which have been governed without a constitution since their establishment, decided to enact basic laws, they not only laid down the absolute powers enjoyed by the ruler in the absence of the rule of law but also vested him with powers previously unavailable to him, such as the power to choose and remove his successor. The ruler did not uniquely enjoy such powers before.

We can call this Arab system of governance the model of the "black-hole State".

This increasing centralization of the executive is guaranteed in the constitutional texts of certain states.

EXTRA-JUDICIAL CONTROLS

In addition to the absolute central powers in the hands of the executive (and, in practice, in the hands of the president, king or ruler), which are not subject to normal legal restraints, there are, for instance, additional mechanisms that increase the centralization of power in the executive. For example, the so-called ruling parties (where they exist) are, in reality, simply institutions attached to the executive, since party officials (or electoral candidates) are designated by the president, who is also regarded as the party leader (Ibrahim, in Arabic, 1996, 194-195). In practice, this means that parliament is a bureaucratic adjunct of the executive that does not represent the people whose mistrust in it continues to grow. The World Values Survey shows that confidence in the legislative assembly (theoretically elected) is less than 50% when averaged over four Arab countries (figure 5-2).

Furthermore, the executive uses the ordinary and exceptional judiciary to eliminate and tame opponents, rivals and even supporters who step out of line. This is linked with what is known as "unspoken corruption" or corruption which is hushed up (Ayoubi, 1996, 321), where close supporters are allowed to exploit their positions for unlawful gain, while "enforcement of the law" against them remains a weapon to ensure that their total loyalty will continue.

The key support buttressing the power of the executive is the intelligence apparatus; each Arab state has multiple intelligence agencies that differ from their counterparts in democratic countries insofar as they enjoy powers over and above their authority to gather intelligence information. Nor are they responsible to the legislature or to public opinion. The intelligence services are regarded as the essence of the ruling apparatus in almost all Arab states. They are directly under the control of the president or king and possess powers greater than those of any other organ. The security apparatus has enormous resources and intervenes in all the powers of the executive, particularly in regard to appointment decisions and the legal regulation of associations, to the point where the modern-day Arab state is frequently dubbed "the intelligence state" (cf. Ayoubi,

1995, 449; Khaldoun Hassan al-Naqib, in Arabic, 1996, 185).

Arab states vary in their embodiment of these general traits, particularly in the margin of freedom permitted without being regarded as a threat. However, what they have in common is that power is concentrated at the tip of the executive pyramid and that the margin of freedom permitted (which can swiftly be reduced as required) has no effect on the state's firm and absolute grip on power. The margins of freedom are relatively wide in countries like Jordan and Morocco, where there is greater freedom to form political parties and freedom of political participation than in the other Arab states. Three Arab republics, namely Lebanon, the Sudan and Yemen, are in a special position in that the central state finds it difficult to impose unilateral centralization owing to its religious and ethnic diversity and the strength of the solidarity and loyalty that characterise such groups. As a result, a margin of freedom exists by default.

For some states, the situation looks promising: Algeria, for example, has moved towards greater political openness and national reconciliation, with competitive elections having recently taken place, to the satisfaction of broad sectors of the populace, despite some flaws. In the Sudan too, there has been a step forward following the conclusion of a Framework Agreement in May 2004 between the Government of Sudan and the Sudan People's Liberation Movement/Army (SPLM/A). Nevertheless, the overall picture in the Arab world indicates a similarity in the architecture of regimes, which "indeed makes it possible to speak about a single unified, integrated Arab system for tyranny and control" (Burhan Ghalioun, in Arabic, 2001). These are systems based on maximizing the focus of power at the top of the executive, so that the license of a certain margin of freedom is part of the strategy of consolidating power rather than reducing it.

It is therefore not surprising that around a quarter of the respondents to the Freedom Survey, Annex 1, said there was a lack of freedom of opinion and expression in their countries, with a higher ratio saying there was no way to hold the government accountable (figure 5-1).

The key support buttressing the power of the executive is the intelligence apparatus.

Arab states vary in their embodiment of these general traits... what they have in common is that power is concentrated at the tip of the executive pyramid.

Figure 5-1

Perceived absence of government accountability and lack of freedom of opinion and expression, five Arab countries, Freedom Survey, 2003

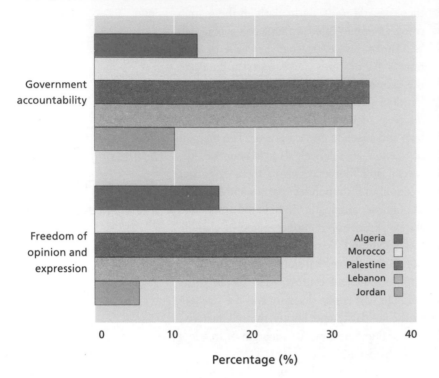

In the same context, the results of certain international studies (World Values Survey, 2004) indicated a strong preference in the Arab countries covered for democratic governance, and against authoritarian rule. They also stated a preference for a government of experts, and objected to rule by the army.

"The real flaw causing the delay of democracy in the region is not cultural, but lies in the convergence of political, social and cultural structures that have suppressed or eliminated organized social and political forces."

TRACING THE FLAW

Analysts look for common structural factors to explain why, politically speaking, the Arab states have contracted while the rest of the world has moved towards democratic openness. Some point at the cultural heritage, particularly its religious dimension, arguing that Islam and democracy do not go together (Chapter 2). Others see the problem as the tribal and patriarchal nature of Arab society (Sharabi, 1990), or the absence of a tradition of social contracts recognizing freedom, individualism and civil society (Gilner, 1994; Ayoubi, 1995: 398). Still others fault the economic structure of Arab societies, specifically their rentier basis, which characterizes most Arab countries (Chapter 6). Islamic movements are sometimes cited as a major emerging

factor insofar as some of them have adopted an anti-democratic discourse, creating deep cleavages among forces opposed to the despotic State and giving regimes additional excuses to disrupt democratic transformation (Ghalioun, 2001; Al-Afendi et al, 2002).

No doubt, these factors have all contributed, in varying degrees, to shaping the current political environment in Arab countries yet they do not sufficiently explain the concentration of power at the top of the authoritarian pyramid. For example, there is evidence that it is the central state that reinforces tribal and clan formations, rather than the other way around (Ibrahim, in Arabic, 1996, 294-296).

Political factors may ultimately be more important. It may be argued that "the real flaw causing the delay of democracy in the region is not cultural, but lies in the convergence of political, social and cultural structures that have suppressed or eliminated organized social and political forces capable of turning the crisis of authoritarian and totalitarian regimes to their advantage. The elimination of such forces has led to the of loss any real forward momentum" (Ghalioun, in Arabic, 2001).

We can conclude that at the root of the problem lies the political architecture and the "strategic marginalization" by the state of all institutions and social forces, including state institutions, together with the all-pervading reality of state appropriation. In other words, while preventing most social forces from having any effective influence over it, the state intervenes in all matters and permits no independent social initiative to threaten its monopoly of power. Because the state controls the economy and intimidates those who might otherwise use their economic clout against it, the ruler is not obliged to bargain with the bourgeoisie or others in order to sustain his rule, particularly since the bourgeoisie is usually a dependent client of the state (Hopkins and Ibrahim, 1997, 382-384). As regards the élites, the state proffers the choice between being loyal and hence richly rewarded and being a dissenter and hence suppressed. In such circumstances the position of the majority is easily understood.

THE CRISIS OF LEGITIMACY

The current situation of Arab governance, with its associated weakness in terms of effective representation of societal forces means that Arab states are facing a chronic crisis of legitimacy, often relying on inducement and intimidation in dealing with their citizens.

When the Arab states were newly independent, their regimes depended on traditional forms of legitimacy (religious-tribal), or won legitimacy through fighting for independence or building the State. But traditional regimes were soon challenged by a revolutionary élite espousing Arab nationalist or leftwing ideologies, and regimes bolstering their legitimacy by mobilizing the people around calls for unity, liberation, justice and development. These also relied on their leaders' charismatic popular appeal. Several regimes developed the concept of "the eternal mission" (unity, liberation, modernization, Islamization, development, socialist transformation, etc.) to justify a legitimacy built on the custodianship of the people and not its representation (Waterbury, 1995, 81).

The successive setbacks encountered by the new so-called revolutionary regimes (defeats by Israel, the failure of development projects, unity and modernization, the failure in combating corruption) played to the interest of traditional regimes boosting their legitimacy centred on religion and Islamic traditions. However, these regimes, which acquired and strengthened their regional influence on the back of the oil boom and the subsequent economic successes, today find themselves challenged by new representatives of the Islamic movement and the fresh ambitions of rising generations, who are no longer persuaded of their developmental achievements (cf. Ibrahim, in Arabic, 1996, 330-332; Luciani, in Arabic, 1995).

Most Arab states have now turned away from the populist course that characterized the revolutionary regimes of the past; instead, they have chosen to promote the ruler's person who, more often than not, lacks charisma, unlike some of the leaders of the revolutionary-populist era. To a certain extent, most regimes also avoid demagoguery, unless they are caught in an 'impasse', as was the former Iraqi regime

after the war with Iran. In addressing the mass of people, they concentrate on the legitimacy of their achievements (or promises thereof) in specific areas such as the economy, peace, prosperity, stability, or safeguarding values and traditions. Sometimes the mere preservation of the state entity in the face of external threats is considered an achievement sufficient to confer legitimacy. Perhaps paradoxically, some regimes have recently resorted to the discourse of democratic legitimacy and the language of civil society and human rights. According to one Arab thinker, democratic discourse has become a new "salvation myth" (Tarabishi, in Arabic, 1999, 71) though the deeds do not yet match the words.

Most regimes, nowadays, bolster their legitimacy by adopting a simplified and efficient formula to justify their continuation in power. They style themselves as the lesser of two evils, or the last line of defence against fundamentalist tyranny or, even more dramatically, against chaos and the collapse of the state. This formula is what Ibrahim and his colleagues have dubbed "the legitimacy of blackmail" (Ibrahim, in Arabic, 1996, 324-325). To a certain extent, it can be considered an implicit admission of the bankruptcy of the claims of positive legitimacy on which official propaganda still insists, with growing despair. Sometimes this political blackmail is pitched in idealistic terms as in claims that modernization stands up to fundamentalism or terrorism, or that a strong state counters a passive course of drift and resignation. The predominant approach can be described as pragmatic, characterized by its flexibility in selecting bases of legitimacy that fit the moment. Many a regime has converted from socialism to capitalism, or from secularism to Islamic discourse and vice-versa, whenever such a move seemed likely to protect its survival. Some regimes, such as the "reformist" monarchies, may rely on mixed alliances, based on their traditional influence (in alliance with the rural and traditional forces of society) on the one hand, and on an almost radical modernization programme developed through close ties with the new élite, the local bourgeoisie and some global forces, on the other.

The "legitimacy of blackmail" has been

Arab states are facing a chronic crisis of legitimacy.

Most regimes, nowadays, bolster their legitimacy by adopting a simplified and efficient formula...dubbed the "legitimacy of blackmail".

eroded by the growing realization that the absence of any effective alternative in itself is one of the outcomes of the policies of regimes that block all avenues for political and civil activity, and so prevent any other alternatives from materializing. Even so, the survival of "the black-hole State" depends essentially on control and propaganda; on marginalizing the elites through scare-and-promise tactics; on striking bargains with dominant global or regional powers; and on mutually supportive regional blocs to reinforce one another against emerging forces.

BOX 5-1

Muhammad Al-Charfi: Arab democracy - form without substance

Since the beginning of the Arab renaissance, élites have demanded an end to the system of absolute rule and its replacement with the rule of law and institutions that respect the individual and collective freedoms of citizens, uphold the separation of powers and use elected structures as their basis. These demands were so enthusiastically supported by the popular masses that rulers had no choice but to display a response to such aspirations. In so doing, however, they laid down conditions on the pretext of following a policy of achieving social and political development in gradual stages. In practice, these conditions produced results that clearly conflicted with the official message and of which examples abound.

• Arab countries are run largely on the basis of the republican system or the system of the constitutional monarchy.

• In the constitutional monarchy, however, the monarch retains such wide-ranging powers that he effectively has the final say on major issues and the full freedom to choose ministers and those who oversee the administration.

• Hitherto, the republican systems have all consisted of officially declared presidencies for life or automatic re-election on the strength of improbable percentages that are frequently as high as 99 %. Worse still, in some cases the presidency is now hereditary, meaning that the republic is devoid of any substance.

• The Arab state works on the principle of the separation of powers in that the state president retains the executive power, the parliament exercises the legislative power and the courts exercise the judicial power. The actual state of affairs, however, differs radically from this model.

• The party of the president holds all the seats in parliament or at least controls the parliament by a wide majority. The president himself or one of his delegates appoints candidates from his party to elect the members

of parliament in what is usually a sham, given the bias of the administration, the excesses of the police and the falsification of the election results. It is thus clear that the state president can adopt such laws as he pleases. The true legislative authority therefore rests with him.

• In the days of absolute rule, the state president would place his signature to a new law on the day on which he decreed its adoption. The only change has been to introduce a procedural stage in which the president is required to propose the bill to parliament and wait a few days until it has been discussed and ratified.

• As regards the judiciary, despite its independence as prescribed in the constitution, it hands down only those judgements which meet with the approval of the state president; given that he is the person responsible for the independence of the judiciary, he has the upper hand in the appointment, promotion and, where necessary, disciplining of judges. A judge may take the heroic route and pass sentence following his conscience, regardless of what the Government expects of him. In so doing, however, he jeopardizes his future, notwithstanding that he is a citizen like any other and is entitled not to forget about his own livelihood and fate as well as that of his family. A judge is guaranteed genuine independence when he is able to pass fair sentence without the need for heroics.

• The change which has taken place is that, previously, an absolute ruler would order the punishment of one of his subjects and his order would be immediately enforced, without further procedure; now, the order is similarly enforceable - in other words, instantly – by way of a trial that follows specific procedures, including a preliminary judgement against which an appeal may then be lodged and also including open sessions during which the public prosecution and defence are heard. A judgement satisfactory to the Government then follows. Each party performs the assigned role and the outcome

is known in advance, just as when an audience reads the novel before seeing the play. Legislative and presidential elections follow the same script.

Freedom of the press and publication is guaranteed, as provided for by the constitution or law. Although censorship is outlawed, publishers must provide pre-distribution copies of any newspaper or book so that the administration is informed of its content and can apply to the court for an order of seizure if it finds that a work violates public order or offends decency. In essence, this is the democratic system at work. The administration, however, refrains from giving the required receipt for copies provided whenever it is unhappy with a text to be published. Freedom of the press and publication therefore lacks any substance.

• The right to demonstrate and organize public meetings is subject to administrative practices of the same nature, as is the right to establish political parties and civil and humanitarian associations. The guarantee of such rights by constitutions and laws is therefore merely ink on paper.

• A citizen no longer has any guaranteed right unless s/he wishes to cheer the ruler, voice gratitude for his accomplishments and extol his qualities and wisdom.

Over time, as such practices recurred, the mask has slipped and no longer is anyone deceived; citizens and foreign observers alike are aware that the current form of democracy is nothing more than a cumbersome and tedious piece of theatre.

There are statesmen who contend that they resort to such practices in order to stem the tide of religious fanaticism. The fact is that the popular masses never applauded such fanaticism; if a move back to fundamentalism shows signs of emerging, it is more the result of disillusionment after a deceiving experiment in modernism and with a formal democracy without substance.

REPRESSION AND POLITICAL IMPOVERISHMENT

WEAKENING OF POLITICAL PARTIES

The current crisis came about with the collapse of the Arab liberal experiment. This was an ideological, political reformist movement that emerged towards the end of the 19th and in the early 20th century, which led to the appearance of populist parties and independence movements, and parliamentary systems in such countries as Syria, Iraq, Egypt, Morocco and the Sudan. But these movements encountered difficulties: internal tensions within society, an unsettled regional climate, and internal/external challenges, in addition to foreign intervention (Youssef al-Shuweiri, in Arabic, 2003, 87-114).

As a result, Arab "political society" suffered a major setback, reflected in the fragmentation of popular liberal parties, and the failure of governments to rise to the new challenges of development, modernization and independence. The political arena was invaded by ideologies and parties that deprecated democracy either believing that Arab societies were backward and did not know what was for their own good, or that they were not sufficiently Islamic or revolutionary. With time, however, radical governments became "conservative" governments and revolutionary parties became ruling or dominant parties. The ban on free party activity was nevertheless maintained on the pretext that societies had become too Islamic or too radical.

The Arab political scene today is quite varied. Some states categorically prohibit any political organization. Other states allow conditional political pluralism and, as a rule, ban the strongest and most important opposition party, while favouring the party of the ruling authority. States which allow party activity nonetheless try to trip up the opposition parties, by depriving them of resources and media exposure, controlling nomination and election procedures, using the judiciary, the army and security services to curtail their activities, hounding their leaders and activists while tampering with election polls.

Some States have witnessed a massive rise in the number of political parties (27 in Algeria, 26 in Morocco, 31 in Jordan and 22 in Yemen). Some see this as a reflection of the divisions among political and cultural élites, or of the ruling regime's manœuvres to divide the opposition, rather than a sign of democratic vitality. Fragmented as they are, these parties are incapable of rallying popular support to achieve the objectives for which they were created. Indeed, this proliferation has engendered an aversion to political activity among citizens, a fact evident in their obvious reluctance to take part in the electoral process. On the other side, Governments deliberately freeze and ban parties that rally popular support: in Egypt 7 out of 17 licensed parties have been frozen, in Mauritania 6 out of 17 and in Tunisia 3 out of 11.

In addition to official repression, opposition parties suffer from internal problems that are no less serious. Despite theoretical references to democracy in their charters, their practice shows that the influential political élite holds sway in most of these parties, resulting in immovable leaderships who, with rare exceptions, only leave their posts when they die, casting doubt on their claims to modernity and democracy. To a great extent, official policy contributes to the situation, since the laws authorizing parties turn them into monopolies, or "franchises", given to certain persons in particular, while those who disagree with the 'leader' are not allowed to form another party. Yet if a 'leader' crosses the line, the judiciary is used so as to transfer the party authorization to another person more inclined to respect the rules of the game.

Beyond all that, there is the acute "sectarian split" in the political community between the Islamic parties on the one hand and the liberal and nationalist secular parties on the other (not to mention other sectarian divisions along doctrinal, ethnic, tribal and regional lines). As a result of this sectarian fragmentation some parties and political forces have preferred to co-operate with undemocratic governments rather than work with their rivals to lay the groundwork for a democratic rule open to all.

Such constriction, in addition to hobbling

The current crisis came about with the collapse of the Arab liberal experiment.

The laws authorizing parties turn them into monopolies or "franchises".

The closure of the political sphere has convinced activists and scholars to turn to civil society organizations.

opposition, has led to the marginalization of some parties and hastened their demise. Restrictions on opposition parties have made it impossible for them to accede to power and form governments through elections. Citizens, perceiving such parties to be ineffectual, choose either not to support them or to work through clandestine political activities. Constraints on political space have led some activists and scholars to rely on civil society organizations, especially trade unions and professional organizations, on the grounds that they are better equipped than Arab political parties to lead Arab society towards development and democracy (Saadeddin Ibrahim, in Arabic, 1991, 18).

According to the World Values Survey, political parties rated the lowest among societal institutions enjoying people's confidence in all five countries covered (figure 5-2).

THE MARGINALIZATION OF CIVIL SOCIETY

The closure of the political sphere has convinced activists and scholars to turn to civil society organizations, especially trade unions and professional associations, as actors more capable of leading Arab society towards development and democracy than Arab political parties (Ibrahim, 1991, 18).

There is consensus around a definition of civil society as "a realm of life institutionally separated from the territorial state institutions", one that "describes and envisages a complex and dynamic ensemble of legally protected non-governmental institutions that tend to be non-violent, self-organizing [and] self-reflexive" (Keane, 1998, 6).

Many hopes were pinned on civil society and its role in helping "to endow republican regimes with the true meaning of republicanism by liberating them from their autocratic content, their oligarchic form and their absolute monarchic streaks, thus rendering them genuinely republican regimes." It was also hoped that civil society would help "to transform absolute monarchies into constitutional monarchies, liberate princedoms from their closed family contexts by exposing them to social and economic dynamism and free military republican regimes from dictatorial militarism." (Belqazir, 2001, 144-145).

The status of Arab civil society

As detailed in Part 1, civil society organizations (CSOs) have intensified their change and reform initiatives despite the many obstacles they face, These include, on the one hand, state constraints on civic activities and, on the other, the dependence of many CSOs on political parties that use them as fronts through which to expand their political influence at the popular level - which limits their initiative and independence of action. As a result they lose their capacity for initiative and self-moti-

Figure 5-2

Extent of confidence in political institutions, five Arab countries

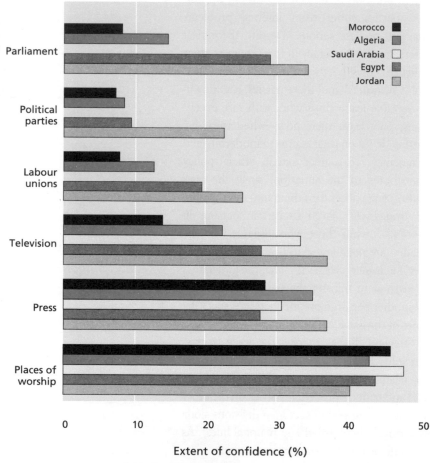

Extent of confidence (%)

Percentage of missing observations
Egypt 3.03%, Jordan 11.80%, Saudi Arabia 5.75%, Algeria 8.53%, Morocco 17.57%.
Note:
- No results were available for the questions concerning the extent of confidence in labour unions, the political parties and the parliament in Saudi Arabia.
Source: World Values Survey, Annex 1

vation, which robs them of their most distinctive feature, independence and non-political action. Civil society organizations lose their core function when they become mere fronts for political parties; they lose their usefulness if they become part of the government apparatus. To give but one example, some civil, trade union or human rights associations controlled by the Islamists do not devote as much effort to defending non-Islamist victims of oppression. Conversely, organizations controlled by secularists do not recognize organizations of an Islamic nature as part of civil society and agree with the repressive state on the need to ban them and contain their activists.

In addition, civil society faces the same problems as the political community vis-à-vis those authorities who seek to control civil organizations, directly or indirectly, by using a dual strategy of containment and repression. On the one hand, such authorities interfere with the establishment, financing and focus of the organizations; some even speak the language of civil society as a strategy to attack their rivals, particularly if they belong to the Islamic opposition; they then resort to establishing semi-official organizations to undertake functions that stay in line with, and defend the authorities' positions. On the other hand, the authorities constrain the work of these organizations, denying them the right to legal existence and financing, in addition to pursuing and repressing those who are actively involved in them.

Consequently, civil society organizations have not been significant actors in resolving the existing political crisis, as they, too, have been caught up in its vortex. Although there are tens of thousands of civil society organizations in Arab states (the estimated number in 2003 was more than 130,000), their impact remains very limited. They tend to be concentrated in certain countries (18,000 in Egypt, 25,000 in Algeria, 7,000 in Tunisia). Some states limit the presence of civil society organizations to almost insignificant levels; there are no more than one hundred non-governmental organizations in Kuwait and almost the same number in the Emirates. There is more scope for civil activity in countries such as Bahrain (400 associations), Jordan (1,500), and Lebanon (4,600).

The solidarity and democratic potential of civil society thus depend on active consensus among all its actors, starting with agreement on a non-exclusionist definition of their membership and beneficiaries, away from ineffectual definitions that link the concept to a Western, liberal definition and ending with a minimum agreement among all parties to respect one another's freedoms.

THE STATE OF CORPORATE GOVERNANCE IN THE ARAB WORLD

Some governments in the Arab region have shown gross disregard for Article 17 of the UDHR which clearly states that: (1) Everyone has the right to own property alone as well as in association with others; (2) No one shall be arbitrarily deprived of his property. In addition, the body of laws adopted by governments of the region has not effectively defined titles to property. These historic limitations and the lack of enforcement of individual property rights protection have significantly stalled the development of the region by restricting the efficient interchange of titles between the public and private sector and among individuals.

TRANSPARENCY

Lack of transparency in Arab markets is severely hindering economic prospects. Not only are transparency and disclosure keys to the efficient operation of the market, enabling traders and economic agents to make informed decisions, but they are also important in terms of attracting foreign investment. Closed, opaque systems do not instil confidence in the economic and investment environment and this reduces the attractiveness of doing business in such markets.

Yet some positive steps aimed at improving transparency and disclosure have been taken in many Arab countries. For instance, the scope of information and data disclosed has widened and disclosure has become mandatory. Moreover, most Arab markets have signed agreements with world class companies specialized in automated instant reporting on trading, including Reuters and Bloomberg.

Civil society organizations have not been significant actors in resolving the existing political crisis as they, too, have been caught up in its vortex.

Lack of transparency in Arab markets is severely hindering economic prospects.

However, the quality of disclosure remains sub-standard because the information provided is incomplete and/or not timely. One of the consequences of insufficient disclosure and lack of transparency is inadequate risk assessment, since it follows that if the financial information available is incomplete, the financial analysis based on that information will be inaccurate and ineffective.

ACCOUNTABILITY

The accountability of private sector enterprises in the Arab region is constrained. Arab securities markets for instance used to be either regulated by a committee constituted from the board of the exchange or not regulated at all. So for the most part, the exchanges controlled both the regulatory functions and the operational functions. However, in the 80's Arab markets experienced transformations in their governance, and reforms took the form of separation of regulatory functions from the exchanges and establishing governmental authorities or securities commissions to regulate and monitor the markets.

Among factors that hinder enforcement of rules and regulations are overlapping regulatory functions among authorities that monitor listed companies (for example in Egypt and Jordan), which hinders their effectiveness. Also, where transgressions are discovered, the high costs of seeking legal recourse and lengthy court procedures place major barriers before shareholders. Add to that the lack of skilled judges knowledgeable about financial market issues, and there are evidently some real problems in the enforcement of laws relating to securities markets and companies.

INCLUSIVENESS

Most of the rules and regulations in the Arab world that preserve shareholder rights are stated clearly in the laws and by-laws of securities markets and companies' laws. However, as is the case in many world markets, there is a gap between laws and regulations and the effectiveness of enforcement and implementation. The size of this gap varies across the region. The rules and regulations in Arab markets have clearly identified shareholders' rights, yet there is a gap between the letter of the law and practice. Morocco, Egypt, Jordan and Lebanon's Company and Securities Laws have provisions that specifically address the issue of minority shareholder protection. Within these economies, it is the job of the security market's regulating agencies to enforce these laws.

Much of the recent corporate governance debate has focused on the "principal-agent" problem between shareholders (principals) and managers (agents) owing to the separation of ownership and management in companies with widely dispersed "public" ownership of shares. It is argued that the purpose of corporate governance is to protect the interests of shareholders, because the interests of other investors can be protected through contractual relations with the company.

What prevails in Arab economies is the corporation with concentrated ownership i.e. dominant shareholders who directly control managers. Hence, the key conflict of interest tends to arise not between managers and shareholders, but between controlling shareholders on one hand and minority shareholders and other investors, on the other. This conflict of interest is referred to as the expropriation problem, because of the tendency for dominant owner-managers to take advantage of their effective control over corporate resources to expropriate/divert resources from their corporation in ways that deprive minority shareholders and other investors.

Unfortunately governance systems within the Arab region are mostly insider systems characterized by concentrated ownership by interested parties. Controlling shareholders' interests may conflict with those of minority shareholders, such as when controlling shareholders abuse the firm's resources for personal gain. The dilution of major shareholders' voting rights has been recommended to the extent that it provides room for other stakeholders' rights. Complete separation of ownership and control may not be realistic given the prevalence of family firms and because that might hinder the business environment.

Furthermore, the lack of a strong shareholder culture and ignorance as to the rights of

The accountability of private sector enterprises in the Arab region is constrained .

(Corporate) governance institutions within the Arab region are mostly insider systems characterized by concentrated ownership by interested parties.

investors has meant that shareholders' participation in corporate decision-making has been rather limited. Encouraging proxy voting by approving the concept of registered and beneficial ownership (as in Jordan and Egypt) could promote further participation. However, technological differences between markets have meant that this is not a viable means for voting in all markets – electronic voting is either not practiced or not permitted.

Corporate governance and Arab stock markets

Particular focus needs to be paid to corporate governance within stock markets given the crucial role the latter play in mobilizing resources and attracting foreign direct investment in Arab countries. The Arab region compares very poorly with other regions in terms of its ability to attract capital flows, which goes some way towards explaining its weak growth performance.

There are several reasons for the sluggish performance of stock markets in the Arab world. For one thing, the supply of equities is limited because public enterprises continue to dominate a broad range of economic activities (although privatization efforts have improved in the region over the last decade). Moreover, poor corporate governance standards (such as inadequate accounting standards, insufficient transparency and a poor regulatory environment) have discouraged capital movement to the Arab countries and have resulted in a lack of inclusiveness in the regional market. In addition, the family-owned structures of most firms constrain the demand and supply of equities.

Some countries in the region have taken several steps to increase their markets' depth and liquidity, as well as to limit transaction costs and technical risks. Specific measures have also been adopted which target the stock markets in particular.

THE VICIOUS CIRCLE OF REPRESSION AND CORRUPTION

Government measures to curtail the development of political and civil society by applying a battery of laws (some dating back to the beginning of the last century), in turn require

---

BOX 5-2

Capital market legal reforms

With the increased realization that higher standards of development may be achieved through efficient financial markets, many Arab countries have passed new legislative reforms:
- In Jordan, laws and regulations governing the securities markets and joint stock companies' activities have undergone a series of improvements and amendments since their issuance in 1997.
- In 2000, the United Arab Emirates issued a Federal Securities Law regulating the securities markets for the first time since the 1970's.
- In 2003, by Royal Decree a law in Saudi Arabia was passed that, by separating regulatory activities from operational activities, resulted in major changes in the architecture of the market.

- The Egyptian and Kuwaiti securities markets have been regulated for over a decade. In Kuwait, an Amiri decree had been issued in 1983 to regulate the Kuwaiti securities market as a response to the collapse of the unofficial Kuwaiti market, Suq Al-Manakh, in 1982.
- In mid-2002 Oman was the first in the region to issue the "Code of Corporate Governance of Muscat Securities Market listed companies".
- By end-2002, supervisory and executive roles were separated in the following seven Arab capital markets: Jordan, Egypt, Oman, Tunisia, Morocco, the United Arab Emirates and Algeria. The two roles remained combined in the hands of the capital market itself in the rest of the Arab countries.

---

complex bureaucratic structures to perform the tasks of prohibition and curtailment.

In addition to the police and the Ministries of Interior and Justice (and paradoxically some new government structures created especially to monitor non-governmental activity), the security apparatus spearheads the control strategy of some contemporary Arab states.

With control as an end in itself and the law as its tool, the prevailing trend is to turn legislation into support for the trusted arm of the executive apparatus, i.e. the security branches. With the authority of the law weakened, security and enforcement agencies are free to disregard or manipulate the most stringent laws, as happens when emergency laws are used to set aside all other law, or to fabricate criminal charges against members of the opposition and civil society activists. In this environment political prisoners may be rearrested on the day they are due for release, sometimes even before leaving prison, while others can be re-arrested on trumped-up charges such as refusal to comply with arbitrary orders like reporting daily to a police station.

Manipulation of the law also opens the way for economic corruption, the natural result of political corruption. Those who falsify election results and tamper with the law acquire tempting tools for forgery and their own personal gain.

With the authority of the law weakened, security and enforcement agencies are free to disregard or manipulate even the most stringent laws.

International scales for a "common perception of corruption" in business are available from surveys carried out by Transparency International, whose 2003 survey included 133 countries of the world, 18 of them Arab (figure 5-3).

The Arab countries span a wide range in terms of the 'spread of corruption' with no Arab country exhibiting a total absence of corruption (grade 10 on the score).

International criteria, however, may not fully account for the specific nature of the Arab situation. The politico-legal structure of some Arab states makes it difficult to differentiate between corruption in its conventional form (abuse of public office for personal gain), and an inherent failing (rigged rules) in the system itself. For example, in some states both law and custom decree that the land and its natural resources belong to the ruler, and fail to distinguish at this level between the private and public life of the ruler, while the private property of the ordinary citizen becomes a grant from the ruler. In such a situation, it is difficult to talk of corruption in governance, for whatever the ruler does, he is disposing of his own property. Some regimes set up economic institutions attached to their military or security apparatus, to finance their activities. Here again matters become confused; it becomes difficult to draw the line between the exercise of an official function (since individual corruption may be but a reflection of the corruption of the whole situation) and what can be described as personal corruption. In addition, there are ways to manipulate laws that, in many Arab countries, do not allow senior officials to carry out private business while they occupy an official post. Many officials circumvent the law by allowing members of their families to set up companies and enterprises that often benefit from the official's position and relations.

There does appear to be a real need to re-examine the question of corruption and its relationship to the political set-up. Corruption exists, the governments themselves admit as much, by periodically launching their anti-corruption campaigns.

Aspects of corruption are also clearly visible to citizens, particularly those in the business sector who complain that the people in power monopolize the main areas of the economy, either directly or as "partners" of successful businessmen. Moreover, persons in power and their close circle receive huge commissions for contracts concluded between the state and international or local companies, including armament contracts (Ayoubi, 1995, 227-243; Ibrahim, in Arabic, 1996, 283-286).

It is, nevertheless, necessary to differentiate between corruption as part of a systematic state policy and corruption as indicative of the failure of the state; a distinction should also be drawn between different levels of corruption. Corruption may not be widely spread among the lower ranks in oil states where employees are well paid. Yet even in these countries many such practices (such as obtaining commissions for government deals) are frequently carried out with the knowledge and blessing of the highest échelons of power.

This type of corruption may be termed "structural corruption", since personal abuse of public office and misuse of public finances are considered normal according to prevailing custom, or even necessary for the regime to endure. It is distinct from conventional corruption where the perpetrator acts behind the

Figure 5-3
Corruption Perception Index, World and Arab Countries, 2003

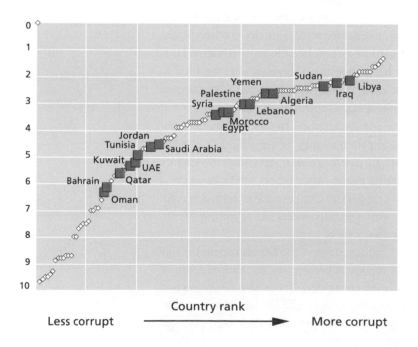

Source: Transparency International, 2003

back of officialdom, in fear of the law.

If ending corruption entails, among other measures, deep economic reform, active laws and mechanisms of accountability, and transparent governance, "structural corruption" can be overcome only by radical reform of the political architecture. "Structural corruption" is one of the biggest obstacles to reform since it is systematically used to sabotage political and civil activity through its containment of the élites and by creating classes with vested interests in the status quo who are ready to defend it at all costs.

CONTOURS OF CORRUPTION IN ARAB COUNTRIES

The Freedom Survey, Annex 1, incorporates detailed measures of corruption in five Arab countries, which were used in carrying out a field survey on the subject. Some of the results are given below.

The perceived spread of corruption (the ratio of participants in the survey who believe that corruption is pervasive) exceeded 90% in the five participating Arab countries. It is not expected to be less widespread in those countries that were not part of the survey.

Respondents believed that corruption is more pervasive in politics. Corruption is considered prevalent in the economy and social relations. Neither parliaments nor the judiciary escaped the perception of corruption (Figure 5-4).

In general politicians, businessmen and high-ranking officials head the list in the spread of corruption in the surveyed countries. The comparative rank of each country varies. In some countries, respondents complained more about corruption at the lower levels of the civil service (Figure 5-5).

PETTY CORRUPTION

Petty corruption refers to situations where Arab citizens have to rely on personal contacts (wasta) or pay a bribe to obtain services that are legitimate and to which they are entitled, or to avert a punishment by the authorities. The majority of respondents said that they were aware of a bribe paid or favours rendered

Figure 5-4

Areas in which corruption is perceived to be widespread, five Arab countries, Freedom Survey, 2003

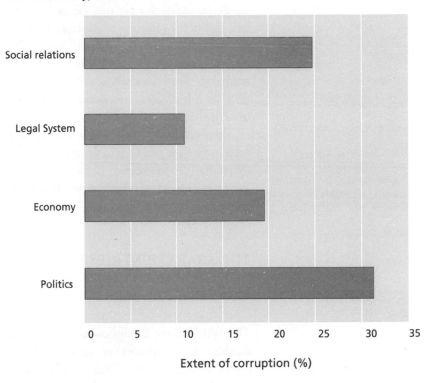

Extent of corruption (%)

Figure 5-5

Extent to which different societal groups are believed to be involved in the spread of corruption, five Arab countries, Freedom Survey, 2003

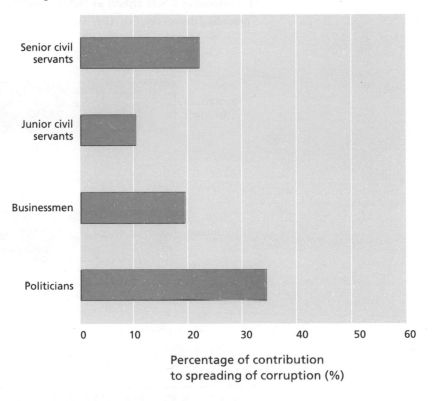

Percentage of contribution to spreading of corruption (%)

through personal contacts during the year preceding the survey. Of the two, wasta is the more widespread occurrence (Figure 5-6).

Respondents thought that the most important reason for resorting to wasta and bribery was to obtain a service. This underscores that often it is not possible to obtain a satisfactory service in these countries without such practices. In a few cases, wasta and bribery were used to escape a punishment (Figure 5-7).

Respondents thought that it was less useful to take their cases up in the media or with the authorities in order to obtain a service or avert punishment and that the two most effective resorts remained paying a bribe or wasta (Figure 5-8).

THE ARAB COUNTRIES IN THE GLOBAL CONTEXT OF GOVERNANCE, 2002

The World Bank publishes an international database on indicators of governance and corruption[1] (Kaufmann, Kraay and Mastruzzi, 2003). In this section, we utilize this database to indicate the position of the Arab region relative to other country groupings, on five major groups of indicators:

• *Voice and accountability*: a cluster of indicators measuring various aspects of civil and political rights and the political process;

• *Political stability and absence of violence*: the indicators cover the likelihood of the government being destabilized or overthrown via unconstitutional or violent means, including terrorism;

• *Government effectiveness*: this describes the quality of services provided by the public sector; efficiency of the civil service and the extent to which it is independent and free of political pressure; and the credibility of government policies;

• *Rule of Law*: this measures the extent to which legal provisions enjoy confidence and are adhered to, particularly as regards the extent to which crime is widespread; efficiency of the judiciary, and the fulfilment of contractual obligations;

• *Control of Corruption*: this indicator measures the extent to which corruption is perceived to be widespread, bearing in mind that this is "an abuse of public power for private benefit."

Figure 5-6

Knowledge of acts of bribery or "favouritism" (wasta*) during the 12 months preceding the survey, five Arab countries, Freedom Survey, 2003

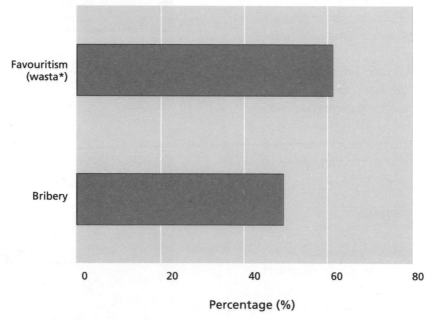

Percentage (%)

* Use of personal influence or connections.

[1] Based on a few hundred variables measuring perceptions of governance derived from 25 sources provided by 18 different organizations.

Figure 5-7

Reason for paying a bribe or using wasta during the 12 months preceding the survey, five Arab countries, Freedom Survey, 2003

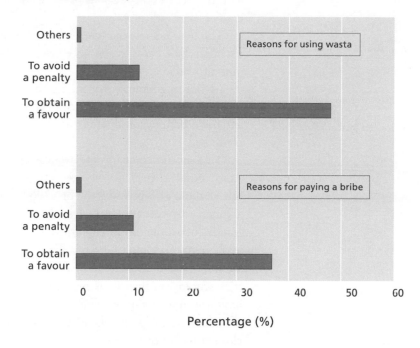

Figure 5-8

The best way to obtain a favour or to avoid a penalty, five Arab countries, Freedom Survey, 2003

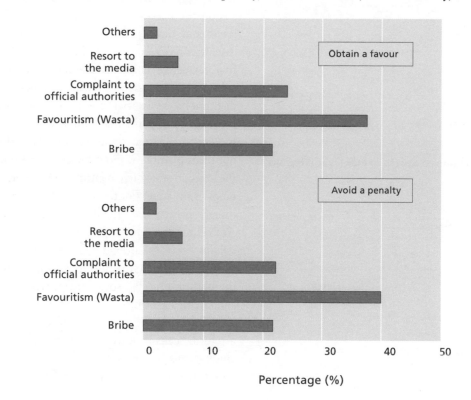

Voice and accountability, the Arab region compared to other world regions, 2002

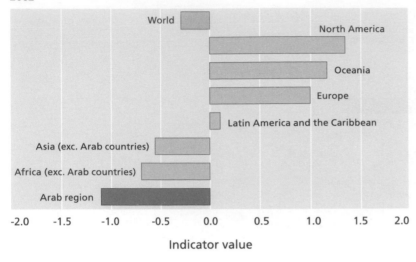

Indicator value

Figure 5-10

Political stability, the Arab region compared to other world regions, 2002

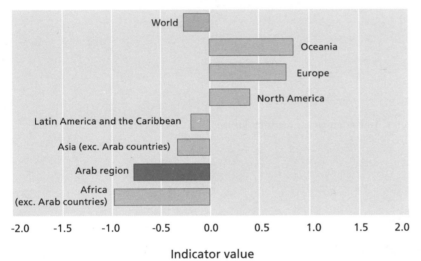

Indicator value

Figure 5-11

Government effectiveness, the Arab region compared to other world regions, 2002

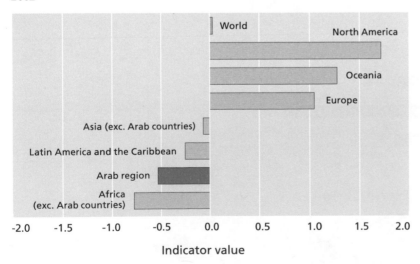

Indicator value

Figures 5-9 - 5-13 contain graphical representations of the position of the Arab region with respect to other regions of the world on each of these indicators.

The figures show that the average of Arab countries falls close to the lower end of the indicator value.

In this quantitative perspective then, the features of poor governance in Arab countries and the need for radical reform are once again confirmed.

This section compares the average among Arab countries (which vary from one to another): table a1-8 provides the breakdown on a country by country basis. A study of these results shows that Arab countries rate worst in the cluster of indicators relating to representation and accountability. All Arab countries scored less than 0, as measured by this indicator. Arab countries exhibit a wider range of ratings on the scale where other indicator clusters are concerned.

THE DEBATE ON HOW TO REFORM

In view of the Arab and international consensus on the need to reform the Arab political scene and build good governance, there are essential requirements to be fulfilled. The first challenge is to reduce the centralized role of the executive in favour of other state institutions, civil society and local government in order to expand freedoms and guarantee fundamental human rights. However, this does not seem possible without the co-operation of the executive, which controls the underpinnings of the state. For this reason there is acute disagreement and even polarization among the Arab élites about the right way to reform. The debate revolves around whether to reform from the top-down (from the state), or from the bottom-up (civil society); whether change should spring from inside or through outside assistance and, ultimately, what values such a reform seeks to instil: traditional values, including religious ones, or modern, democratic and secular values along Western lines.

Change from the top or at grass-roots?

Advocates of Arab political reform, backed by international organizations and donor states, tend to opt for gradual reform from the "bottom-up", through civil society activity. This position has several justifications, among them the deep-seated belief that Arab societies are not yet sufficiently mature for democracy and that the Arab political community is not ready to assume the responsibilities of change. In this view, civil society can bridge the gap on the one hand, and pave the way for change on the other, through education and culture-building for democracy. There is also a belief that the regimes may be more inclined to accept civil activity, which poses no direct challenge to their authority, than direct political activity.

By contrast, there are those who believe in the priority of political reform, particularly because civil society cannot exist without a state respectful of a minimum of freedoms; this makes the situation more of a vicious circle. It is their view that direct pressure should be exerted on governments to make them accept reform. Undoubtedly, voluntary reform by regimes that have come to realize that reform is inevitable, either under foreign pressure or owing to a rift in the ruling élite, would, if genuine, be the shortest route to good governance and the least costly; that all remains, nevertheless, in the realm of promises. Regimes apparently want to apply a policy of "escaping forward" and manœuvering, making changes that are mere formalities and do not represent any true reform. Those effected and even those proposed remain limited. Some observers believe that Arab regimes have developed a unique model of "liberalized autocracy", one that the limited powers of civil society cannot gradually change in the absence of an effective political community (Brumberg, 2003, 43).

These two perspectives can be reconciled if we bear in mind that these reforms, however limited their impact, have created space for movement in both the social and political arenas that can be exploited to change and develop the political situation, as we shall see below.

Figure 5-12

The rule of law, the Arab region compared to other world regions, 2002

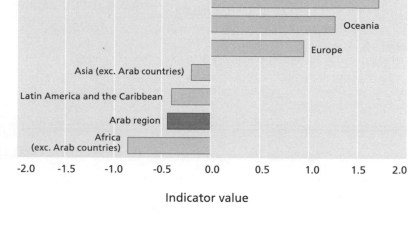

Figure 5-13

Control of corruption, the Arab region compared to other world regions, 2002

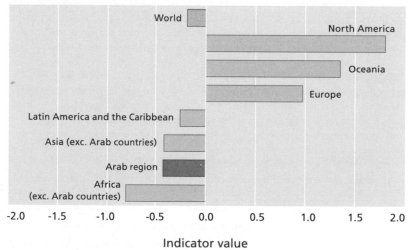

External versus internal

The critical Arab political situation has led some to pin their hopes on foreign action. To them this seems, practically speaking, the only available solution to bring about change, either by using the military to bring the regime to an end as in Iraq, or by exerting pressure on the regime while offering compromise solutions as in the Sudan. This situation has led to a heated debate in Arab élite circles about the usefulness of associating external factors with change. Many object on principle, while others

Voluntary reform by regimes…would, if genuine, be the shortest route to good governance and the least costly.

BOX 5-3

Moncef Al-Marzouqi: Giving democracy every chance

The idea of democracy has penetrated minds among the élites, politicians and ever widening groups of society following a slow evolution begun by the few "reconnaissance units" which, at the beginning of the last century, took it upon themselves to start considering democracy as a possible alternative and begin thinking about its adaptation and Arabization. This small band of intellectuals and politicians was fiercely opposed by the autocratic system in intellectual and political battles over contrived problems, such as the priority of economic progress over freedoms, cultural specificity, the suitability or otherwise of democracy for Arabs and the need for a slow transition to democracy so as not to make it indigestible.

The collapse of such ideas, however, does not mean that the Arabs collectively have come close to harvesting this crop or that they can plant it in a wasteland which still requires a lot of preparation. They have taken only their first steps along the road, and few can say where that road is truly heading. Even the "forward reconnaissance units" of political pioneers have difficulty picturing the phases of transition from their former political system to democracy. Will it happen gradually, peacefully or violently, with or against the West? With the Islamists, or on condition of their elimination? To this I would add that few are interested in examining the actual mechanisms of democracy with a critical eye. The common denominator among advocates of democracy is their blind faith in it as the ideal prescription for curing the ills of the political system with a magic wand. Let us not forget that we once believed in "the homeland" and in socialism and unity; in embracing democracy, we are today adopting the same uncritical mental attitude we had then. It is crucial that we should listen carefully to its enemies, since:

He who is content is blind to every flaw
He who is discontent sees nought but failings

If, in the 1930s, the communists had listened to the enemies of communism and understood that discontent is like a magnifier that enlarges any intrinsic flaws, and if they had promptly addressed these flaws, history might have taken a different course.

This passing observation underscores that the corrosive flaws which ate into nationalism, pan-Arabism and socialism were present in the mechanisms, institutions, ideas and values on which they were based and that they simply surfaced when they were able to do so. This is a general rule and we believe democracy to be no exception. We should therefore ask ourselves about the negative aspects of democracy to which we are blind and which may render all our sacrifices in vain, as occurred with many of the aspirations nurtured by socialists, whose socialism betrayed them before the world did.

We should be extremely wary of any democracy that manifests any or all of the following characteristics in which:

- It is unaware that its essential function is to expand economic and social rights;
- It fails to remember that its development and even its survival are dependent on the expansion of citizenship through the genuine participation of each person at her/his own level;
- It focuses narrowly on representation (bearing in mind that the word must also be understood in its theatrical sense), meaning that its mechanisms are built on electoral rites dominated and exploited by hidden aristocracies using private finance, their virtual monopoly of the media which they own, and elected officials with neither power nor strength that ultimately resign in frustration and angrily exit the stage in search of another solution to their problems;
- It puts the reins of power in the hands of campaigners carrying out programmes marketed through publicity methods designed to ensure that politics and politicians have the lowest status among the people, as is often the case in liberal countries.

As advocates of democracy, we therefore demand a three-pronged campaign to break down the defences of the autocratic system; drive the democratic venture forward into people's hearts and minds, and deep into the political arena; and generate serious thinking about alternatives that use the experience of different peoples to advantage, without applying ready-made prescriptions, particularly at the institutional level. The aim of this war is to avoid making rash ideological statements along the lines of "democracy is the solution". Such slogans might one day bring us to grieve over its remains, repeating meaningless phrases such as "democracy is so very attractive and its advocates are so very repellent."

Certain groups hold that the ideal form of foreign intervention to promote democracy would be to stop supporting dictatorial regimes in the Arab world.

justify it as a necessity and others still warn that foreign intervention will become inevitable if those concerned do not hasten to take the initiative from inside (Dorgham, in Arabic, 2003, Ibrahim, in Arabic, 2003, al Zayyat, in Arabic, 2003).

By way of contrast, certain groups hold that the ideal form of foreign intervention to promote democracy would be to stop supporting dictatorial regimes in the Arab world (Sadiqi, 2004, 320).

The Optimum Choice

This brings us to the alternative possibility, that of change stemming from within and led by dynamic social forces with a clear stake in such change. Past experience in Eastern Europe and Latin America (and in some Arab states like the Sudan) point to the importance of a move that can come from civil society organizations, trade unions, voluntary associations and religious movements, a move to end the state's monopoly over political activity; a move to strengthen society's ability to resist the mechanisms of systematic repression used by the State to immobilize social forces.

Methods of repression and state terrorism are for tyrannical regimes "like bank reserves", to quote Waterbury "effective only if the clients do not rush in droves to withdraw their money. If most citizens defy the regime, the latter fails to find enough terror, jails and savage cruelty to meet the requirements of domination" (Waterbury 1995, 82).

The next step, namely transition to direct political action, requires a consensus among the élites. After all, one of the main reasons why current circumstances do not change is that the regime has succeeded in dividing society's vanguards, even convincing some that it is in their interest to resist democratic change while also encouraging sectarian, tribal and other divisive trends. Such a consensus is of great importance, first because it represents the very essence of the democratic process and what distinguishes it from popularism, which is, basically, the outcome of negotiations among parties to an as-yet-unresolved conflict (Przeworski, 1988; Waterbury, 1995, 91-102). Secondly, because the expected popular uprisings against the state of affairs will, in the absence of such consensus, inevitably turn into civil wars, as in Algeria and Somalia.

Bridging the gap between political forces

If consensus among the political forces is a prerequisite for positive transformation of the political arena, formulas for its achievement are needed. There are, in the Arab world, several splits dividing the political forces into sectarian, racial, regional and tribal groups.

The biggest divide, however, is that separating the Islamists on one side and the secularists, liberals and nationalists, on the other. In fact, this rift has come to replace the traditionalist/radical one which dominated the political arena in past years. To bring about a consensus among all these forces undoubtedly requires creative thinking out of the box. We would add that the matter must go beyond tactical and phased agreements (without underestimating their importance, since democracy is the outcome of a series of successful bargains and agreements). Rather, it must result in intellectual and methodological reconsideration by the parties concerned. Some reviews have already begun and these should be encouraged and built upon. They should include a re-examination by the Islamists of their views on democracy, human rights and the question of citizenship. Other movements should review their exclusionist and dictatorial tendencies, their condemnation of past mistakes and re-

pressive actions. For all, the goal is to develop a new way of thinking, more in keeping with the requirements of democracy and peaceful co-existence with competing movements.

"If most citizens defy the regime, the latter fails to find enough terror, jails and savage cruelty to meet the requirements of domination."

CHAPTER SIX

Arab Societal Structures and the Regional and International Environments

Introduction

The societal context in Arab countries is the third key factor in explaining the currently deteriorating state of freedom and governance in the region. This chapter looks at both the internal and external dimensions of that context. The first dimension includes the characteristics of societal structures in Arab countries and of the dominant (rentier) mode of production. The second dimension relates to the impacts of the regional and global environments surrounding the Arab world, which have recently had a stronger influence in detracting from freedom in Arab countries, particularly in terms of national liberation.

SOCIETAL STRUCTURES

THE CHAIN THAT STIFLES INDIVIDUAL FREEDOM

A number of interrelated factors constricting freedom are embedded in Arab societal structures. Despite their diversity and complexity,[1] each of these factors is a link in an interconnected chain. Starting with the child's upbringing within the family, passing through educational institutions, the world of work, and societal formation, and ending with politics - both internal and external - each link in the chain takes its portion of freedom from the individual and delivers her or him to the next, which, in turn, steals a further share. These links reinforce one another in a highly efficient coercive system.

Clannism (al-'asabiya) in Arab Society—the Authoritarian Paternalist System and the Family

Clannism, in all its forms, (tribal, clan-based, communal, and ethnic) (Mohammad Abed al-Jabiri, in Arabic, 1995) tightly shackles its followers through the power of the authoritarian patriarchal system. This phenomenon, amply discussed in the literature (Hisham Sharabi, in Arabic, 1990), represents a two-way street in which obedience and loyalty are offered in return for protection, sponsorship, and a share of the spoils.

Clannism implants submission, parasitic dependence and compliance in return for protection and benefits. More damagingly still, clannism is the enemy of personal independence, intellectual daring, and the flowering of a unique and authentic human entity. It blocks the energies that lead to growth and a mature, self-reliant intellect. It must do this to ensure its own smooth functioning and to guarantee its sway. The reproduction of this phenomenon across society turns it into an array of suffocating institutions that reward loyalty and discount performance. One is good so long as one's loyalty is guaranteed; it does not matter, naturally, if one's performance is poor; and woe betide clan members whose loyalty falters, however good their performance.

The worst effect of clannism is that it eats into the cohesive force of citizenship and its institutional manifestations. Yet clannism is not an unalloyed evil.[2] Its positive aspects include a sense of belonging to a community and the desire to put its interests first. This can amount to a total dedication, or self-abnegation, for

Each link in the chain takes its portion of freedom from the individual and delivers her or him to the next, which, in turn, steals a further share.

Clannism implants submission, parasitic dependence and compliance in return for protection and benefits.

---

[1] A sustained and careful research effort is called for in order to deconstruct the Arab societal order, especially in terms of its relation to freedom and good governance.

[2] It has been handed down that the Prophet said that "A man's love for his people" is not clannism, but "it is clannism when a man supports his people in injustice" (Farid Abdel Khaliq, in Arabic, 1998, 213)

Clannism flourishes,
and its negative
impact on freedom
and society becomes
stronger, wherever
civil or political
institutions are weak
or absent.

Contributing
powerfully to the
erosion of clannism in
Arab households is the
rise of women within
the family, sometimes
at its head.

the sake of the community that bespeaks an impressive sense of common purpose, one often stronger than that found in some modern forms of societal organization.

The problem with clannism in Arab countries is that it produces types of societal organisation that are modern in form but objectively backward. Class structure is an example. In East Asia, for instance, traditional family capitalism is responsible for important modern achievements, but in the Arab environment it is associated with a rent-based economic model, with all that that suggests by way of exalting the values of obligation, favouritism, and inefficiency. Consequently, family capitalism in the Arab world has failed to realize the advances of "the Asian miracle."

A creative – and difficult – challenge for the future is to find ways to blend such positive aspects of clannism with the concept of citizenship in order to develop a basis for freedom and good governance.

Clannism pervades a large number of Arab societal structures, which it transforms into centres of influence. There are political, military, regional, and administrative allegiances, and Arab citizens cannot avoid becoming ensnared in their nets if they wish to preserve their status in society, their livelihoods, and their personal security.

Clannism flourishes, and its negative impact on freedom and society becomes stronger, wherever civil or political institutions that protect rights and freedoms are weak or absent. Without institutional supports, individuals are driven to seek refuge in narrowly based loyalties that provide security and protection, thus further aggravating the phenomenon. Partisan allegiances also develop when the judiciary is ineffective or the executive authority is reluctant to implement its rulings, circumstances that make citizens unsure of their ability to realize their rights without the allegiances of the clan.

In varying degrees, the family, the primary unit of Arab society, is based on clannism. The dosage is larger in clan-based societal groups and lower in modern urban families, especially affluent ones.

The Arab family started as an extended (tribal or clan-based) unit and has ended up as a nuclear one. It has however retained at its heart a power structure in which a "pure form" of authority remains. This consists of a father (or other male in the absence of the natural father) who often tends to be authoritarian, bestowing and withholding favours; a mother, usually tender-hearted, submissive, and resigned, who has no say in important matters except behind the scenes; and children who are the objects of the father's instructions and the mother's tenderness. These children are referred to in everyday language as "ignorant kids" and "scroungers" and are barred from any say in their dealings with adults, or any confrontation with them, whatever the Convention on the Rights of the Child may provide for on that score.

Obviously, in such male-oriented structures girls are subject to a double dose of freedom-denying authority.

Yet this traditional picture of the authoritarian Arab family is starting to break up as a result of the increased pace of social change, the influence of modernity, including information and communication technologies, and changes of a political nature.

Contributing powerfully to the erosion of clannism in Arab households is the rise of women within the family, sometimes at its head. There are several reasons for this: increased education for girls and their aptitude for, and excellence in educational achievement; women's increasing contributions to family earnings as a result of their growing participation in the labour market, -especially amid economic slumps and rising poverty- and particularly in the informal sector, where working conditions are both flexible and difficult. Another factor is that more families are breaking up through increasing marital separation of various kinds, arrangements that often lead to the woman's shouldering of responsibility for the children. Women in the occupied Arab territories and those in theatres of war have also come to shoulder increased familial responsibilities because men are frequently disabled, lost or detained as a result of the conflict.

Another force eroding clannism is the rise of a younger generation inclined, for various reasons, to rebel against the clannish practices of its forebears.

Education

The second AHDR (2003) analysed the status of knowledge acquisition and diffusion in the Arab world and identified a growing knowledge gap. It underlined that the largest challenge facing Arab education was its declining quality. In Arab educational institutions, curricula, teaching and evaluation methods tend to rely on dictation and instil submissiveness. They do not permit free dialogue and active, exploratory learning and consequently do not open the doors to freedom of thought and criticism. On the contrary, they weaken the capacity to hold opposing viewpoints and to think outside the box. Their societal role focuses on the reproduction of control in Arab societies.

However, the educational system is not uniform in Arab countries. In addition to the predominant government-provided education sector, there are at least two other sectors that are at odds with public education from one or more perspectives. The first is private education mainly serving the affluent, a sector that is expanding exponentially as a result of the deterioration of public education. Privately educated students may gain a better level of knowledge and skills and may perhaps preserve a greater measure of freedom. This is so, however, mostly in an individual sense. Education in this sector is often tied to foreign curricula or to foreign educational institutions and lessons are taught in a foreign language. This type of education is thus faulted at times for instilling in its students a measure of detachment from their own societies, and especially from their culture, since they are acquiring a different culture - manifested in their curricula as well as in the language and style of their education. In many cases, their detachment can prevent students from communicating effectively with their societies and from transferring to it whatever knowledge and skills they may acquire.

The second sector is the religious education system found in some Arab countries, which attracts those who do not find a place in either public or private education. Teaching in these places is more restrictive of freedom and more reinforcing of traditional loyalties than in either of the two alternatives.

The subdivision of the educational system into three mutually exclusive sectors leads to the weakening of the social fabric and the narrowing of opportunities for the growth of a shared space whose common denominator is citizenship.

The suppression of freedom in the educational system is not reserved for students but rather encompasses the totality of the system. Thus teachers, "oppressors" of their pupils, are in turn subject to oppression by the educational administration whether at the teacher-training institute, or local, or central levels. And this is to say nothing of the oppression of

The subdivision of the educational system into three mutually exclusive sectors leads to the weakening of the social fabric.

*More recent
generations of Arabs
may well be more
strongly influenced
by the media than
by educational
institutions.*

*The way the concept
of freedom figures in
schoolbooks confirms
a deficiency, not only
in relation to the
concept itself, but also
to values related to
human rights.*

teachers as a group within society as a whole, a trend that reflects the decline in the material and moral status of the majority of teachers.

What of those who never attend school or do not go on to complete its upper stages, most of whom are the children of the weaker social strata? Usually, this group joins the labour market early, and so receives training via the apprenticeship system, which imparts useful practical skills, at least in terms of those required by the labour market. To that extent, the labour market may substitute for the lack of education, even if only in part.[3] This group may, then, be more fortunate in acquiring skills that translate into a higher level of earnings, as studies in certain Arab countries have shown (Nader Fergany, 1998). From a freedom perspective, early school-leavers escape the loss of freedom that the educational system exacts but often do not preserve their freedom in full, since the apprenticeship system, especially in the manual and technical professions, is itself a rigid and authoritarian pyramid.

For all its deficiencies and flaws, education, particularly at the higher levels, remains a vital source of knowledge, enlightenment and leavening for the forces of change. Perhaps the most eloquent and dynamic expression of that vitality is the vigour of university students' protests, despite the political intimidation characteristic of Arab societies.

Included in the educational apparatus in its broad sense are the media, which are characterised by one-sided views and a tendency to puff imagined achievements and glorify "the one leader". Many also serve up forms of cheap entertainment aimed at gratifying the senses rather than edifying the mind.[4] As a result, the public mind is not opened to opportunities for self-development, knowledge acquisition or new thinking, let alone to criticism of contemporary events and to creative ways of changing it. More recent generations of Arabs may well be more strongly influenced by the media than by educational institutions.

Not all media channels are mediocre. For those able to access them, the "new wave"

media, such as the Arab satellite television stations and some newspapers and their web sites, have started to provide avenues for knowledge acquisition and for freedom of expression and opinion that were previously unattainable.

Freedom in the content of education in three Maghreb countries

A study carried out in three Maghreb countries — Morocco, Algeria, and Tunisia — focusing on curricula for the subjects Arabic Language and Civic Education at the preparatory or intermediate level, reached the following conclusions (Lemrini and Marwazi, background paper for this Report):

The way the concept of freedom figures in schoolbooks confirms a deficiency, not only in relation to the concept itself, but also to values related to human rights as a whole. Omitting freedom, which is one of the fundamental principles and values on which other values rest, can only lead to omissions in the concepts of personal dignity, equality, justice, and associated civil, political, economic, social, and cultural rights.

- Given how thin Arab freedom is in reality, references to it in these texts relate to a freedom indistinguishable from homeland and religion. The source from which freedom is said to derive its authority fluctuates between these two. In practical terms, this influences the choice of texts, which, for the most part, are set either in the recent past (the colonial and/or independence period) or the distant past (the initial stages of Islam). This invites the learner to live in the past more than the present, and this basic feature of the texts determines the development of knowledge and personality in the following ways:

- A disjunction between text and reality.

- Double standards in the way things are viewed ("our actual situation is poor and its parameters are set by defeat on a number of levels, but we are the best of nations in existence").

- The propagation of illusion ("regardless of the givens of our current situation, we shall be

---

[3] The other side to the equation is of course that the education system's poor outcome in terms of skills valued by the labour market is one aspect of the deteriorating quality of education.

[4] Recently many have contrasted the surfeit of short video clips in the Arab media, which are aimed at sensual arousal, with the paucity of nourishing intellectual content.

victorious, if only because we were victorious in the past." What is not specified is that victory here refers to the current battles against poverty, ignorance, or despotism... Thus the point of departure is religion and the point of arrival is the homeland, which supports the point of departure while failing to evoke the present reality by examining society).

Taking the past as the starting point introduces a self-justifying logic into the lesson, because the present, which does not bear out the opinion proffered, is not allowed to challenge it. Hence the lesson becomes mere pretence, divorced from reality.

• The existence of individual and collective freedoms is acknowledged in Civic/National Education classes dealing with citizenship, but the appearance of the same freedoms varies from rare to nil in Arabic Language classes. The fact that individual and collective freedoms are interrelated and mutually reinforcing and that both rest on such freedoms as the law may guarantee (e.g. freedom of opinion) is relevant for students; but this point is not addressed at the level of the Arabic Language texts. Instead, these texts analyse particular freedoms via narratives relying on suggestion, explicit direction, and manipulation of the language. What does the guarantee of the individual's right to own property, cited in the Civic Education books, mean to a citizen who is unemployed and thus unable to exercise that right in the simplest of the forms described in the books used in the Arabic Language class? And what do guarantees of freedom of opinion and expression (mentioned in the same books) mean when people's thinking is restricted to one school of religious law or the ideology of one ruling party? What, above all, does freedom of choice mean when the Arabic Language texts deal with everything connected with marriage and the family in the language of command, prohibition, submission, tutelage, and obedience?

• The reality of the freedoms depicted in school-books (the Arabic Language texts, for example) is the reality of their absence. They are not available and cannot be enjoyed. They are present only to the extent that prohibitions and restrictions, which negatively imply that they exist, abound and because many are deprived of them.

• Given the distinguished status of training as a basic pillar in the process of qualification, its evaluation provides a mirror that reflects the defining vision and background of the authors of schoolbooks. If these books themselves show scant regard for the concept of freedom and its associated principles, values and human rights (Arabic Language texts) or for its legal basis (Civic Education), the questions and activities in the accompanying exercises reveal much about the trends that determine the pedagogical imagination. Whenever the texts incline, in context or meaning, to overlook rights and freedoms, it should be insistently required that training correct this deficiency by deconstructing those values that are not compatible with rights and freedoms and by introducing the values that would reinforce them. Thus the texts that touch on slavery could serve a beneficial purpose if the exercises provided an affirmation of equality, the right to life, freedom, and personal dignity. Texts themselves could build a framework and opportunity for reviewing and enacting outcomes of Civic Education at this level.

• The standardized nature of exercise questions does not allow the learner to discover, absorb, or assimilate the values that reinforce freedoms and human rights. On the contrary, learners are limited to a few set illustrations that are maintained rigidly through an interpretation that is linked to the text, memorization and the language. As a result, the material becomes a mere vehicle for itself (language), disassociated from its subject (values).

• The different levels of exercises not only fail to provide the learner with information related to freedom; they also fail to make him or her aware of its value. Discussion, opinion, expression, and understanding are all circumscribed by the text and are converted through it into mere footnotes or marginalia that take a proper understanding of the text for granted. Learning comes to be governed by dictation, without the learner being educated in, or practicing, freedom.

The World of Work

After completing their higher education, children of the middle class usually seek a job of

What does freedom of choice mean when the Arabic Language texts deal with everything connected with marriage and the family in the language of command, prohibition, submission, tutelage and obedience?

Learning comes to be governed by dictation without the learner being educated in, or practicing, freedom.

some note (according to prevailing criteria). This generally comes after a period of unemployment whose length depends, in the absence of efficient labour market mechanisms, on the capacity of the family to mobilize whatever money and power they may be blessed with. While awaiting their release, the graduates return to the bosoms of their families, where their dependence on patriarchal bounty increases in proportion to their expanding needs as they get older and in the absence of the independent resources that would enable them to act freely.

When fate or chance ends the period of unemployment, the graduate steps onto the lowest rung of a rigid, restrictive hierarchy, especially if the job is with the civil service. The graduate's lowly status in this hierarchy is compounded by the poor work skills he or she has acquired, as a result of the declining quality of education. Only a small minority of young people, usually the children of the influential few with money or political authority, emerges from the attrition of the work world with a portion of individual and personal freedom intact.

The Arab public space is small and constricted.

The Political Realm

For those that are impelled to take an active interest in current affairs and political trends and to express that interest publicly, or that try and organize to achieve some social goal, society has several risks in store. Such people meet, at the hands of the authorities and their instruments, enough troubles to guarantee that, in most cases, their appetite for social action will be short-lived. At this point, the grip of the social chain on freedom in Arab countries becomes intense.

The Arab public space is small and constricted. Its limited dimensions do not enable civil society institutions to provide effective group protection to citizens who are vulnerable to oppression as individuals. This weakness increases the oppressive impact of politics on the individual in Arab countries and allows overt and covert powers to curtail the fragile freedoms of society's atomised members. As discussed in the second section of this chapter, violations from the outside world compound this situation.

Poverty and the Class Structure

Poverty is the antithesis of human development, depriving people of the opportunity to acquire capabilities and to utilise them efficiently to achieve a decent life. Poverty also prevents people from participating effectively, as families and individuals, in civil and political society. It thus robs the public sphere of its vitality and contributes to the impoverishment of politics.

Thus, champions of freedom and good governance tend to emerge more strongly higher up the social structure, to the extent that the upper echelons are sympathetic to the cause of freedom and support the organizations of civil and political society. Nonetheless, an aversion to involvement in public life, and especially in political activity, continues among those in the better-off social groups who are concerned with protecting their possessions and special social status. Eliminating poverty in coercive societies where citizens are striving for freedom is especially important because poverty tends to force people to focus on meeting their basic needs and thus prevents them from contributing to the public space, more so than in other types of societies.

There is a perception that poverty in Arab countries is higher than levels indicated in international databases. Insofar as inequalities in income and wealth distribution are increasing, the numbers of the weaker social groups are growing. It is feared that the class structure in Arab countries does not support a free and well-governed society. Indeed, it may impede the societal transformation required to bring that about.

Is This Stranglehold Eternal?

As they tighten and grow, the constrictions of the chain on freedom become internal constraints on the self. Suppression leads individuals to become their own censors and to contain every urge to speak or act. Deprivation succeeds most when people feel hostility towards themselves and rein in normal human aspirations and rebellions. At that point, the individual is transformed into a complaisant subject "more royalist than the king".

This complicated structure has led Arab citizens, including some among the intelligentsia, to a state of submission fed by fear and marked by denial of their subjugation. This state is manifested in acts of self-censorship and in an evident retreat from public engagement that sometimes amounts to "resigning from politics", a pattern that is reaffirmed among younger generations (for example: Nader Fergany, 1995). Yet there are signs, even among segments traditionally considered pillars of the establishment, that this state of affairs cannot continue and that the natural urge of human beings to claim their freedom will re-surface.

The stifling of freedom also pushes Arab individuals to retreat into a preoccupation with the basic needs of security and livelihood, for they are neither master of their own persons nor master in their own countries. Their citizenship becomes a kind of gift conceded to them on condition that they remain docile. The very fabric of a free and open society is thus eroded. As the individual enters into a state of learned impotence (Westin, 1999) and society lapses into a state of historical stagnation, custom and repetition become the desiderata rather than change, transformation, and growth (Mustafa

Hijazi, in Arabic, 2001).

Yet beneath the layers of submission and stagnation there remains a frustration that could explode in ways seriously detrimental to human development if ever the container grows weak. This kind of violent outcome would be destructive of both people and civilisation and the antithesis of those vital energies that drive a purposeful being and existence. Such frustration, however, could be channelled in a positive developmental direction if appropriate civil and political frameworks were in place.

Such a transformation would spearhead a transition from oppression and waste to revitalised human capacity by nurturing total competence in the individual and creating capacity and competence in institutions. These are the components of psychological and institutional health that guarantee growth and strength in society. It would be a transition from a morbid state of chronically weakened human and institutional resources and flagging societal resilience, to one of social efficacy that would be capable of creating a role for Arab society and raising its status. Strengthening any one of these three dimensions (of psychological, institutional, and societal health) will trigger growth and a new dynamic with a mutually reinforcing effect on the other dimensions. It is this that will bring about a change of orientation from silence and historical stagnation or retreat to development and progress (Mustafa Hijazi, in Arabic, background paper for this Report).

A MODE OF PRODUCTION THAT REINFORCES AUTHORITARIANISM

A society's mode of production is the method by which its economic surplus is derived, distributed and invested, particularly in developing and improving the productive system itself through investment in human and physical assets. The mode of production, however, produces a mixture of societal arrangements, notably in the form of political structures and a societal system of incentives that preserve and reproduce the main characteristics of the mode.

Chapter 7 of the second AHDR discussed how the Arab countries' prevailing rentier

Suppression leads individuals to become their own censors and to contain every urge to speak or act.

Yet beneath the layers of submission and stagnation there remains a frustration that could explode.

mode of production weakens incentives for knowledge acquisition. Here we discuss the consequences of this mode of production for freedom and governance.

In essence, the rentier mode of production provides an economic foundation supportive of authoritarian governance or at least fails to provide the foundation of good governance, particularly with regard to representation and accountability (George Abed, 2004).

The basic source of rent in Arab countries comes from the extraction of mostly unprocessed natural resources, primarily crude oil. The direct benefit of oil rents is not confined to Arab Gulf countries; in an increasing number of other Arab countries, oil is also the main source of public revenue. Oil rents flow into non-oil Arab countries by way of financial remittances, whether official or sent by their citizens working in the oil countries.

Arab states also receive other rents, some of which are derived from geographical location such as the income of the Suez Canal. A small number of Arab states that are positioned for an influential role obtain rent on the strategic position of the region and the challenges which that position brings. They receive such inflows principally in the form of aid.

As many studies have indicated, the rentier mode of production opens cracks in the fundamental relationship between citizens as a source of public tax revenue and government. Where a government relies on financing from the tax base represented by its citizens, it is subject to questioning about how it allocates state resources. In a rentier mode of production, however, the government can act as a generous provider that demands no taxes or duties in return. This hand that gives can also take away, and the government is therefore entitled to require loyalty from its citizens invoking the mentality of the clan. In Arab oil countries, such generosity has taken the form of the "welfare State" particularly in times of affluence. This form of governance has been distinguished by the absence of taxation.

In the rentier State, therefore, government is absolved of any periodic accountability, not to mention representation. As long as the rent continues to flow, there is no need for citizens to finance government and thus expect it to

be accountable to them. On the contrary, when the flow of rent depends on the good will of influential outside forces, as in the case of some Arab countries, the right of accountability passes to those who control the flow of rent, instead of remaining with citizens, who are turned into subjects.

By contrast, in countries where there is representation and concomitant accountability government revenue comes from taxes paid by citizens. The latter therefore have the right to hold the ruling bodies accountable about what is being done with funds that they provide for the public good and which they authorise the government to manage on their behalf. Representative institutions play a pivotal role in this regard. A social mentality is firmly established and patterns of behaviour are generally consistent with the social contract that goes with this political economy model.

In the Arab countries, taxes account for only a small percentage of public revenue, (Figure 6-1), with an even smaller percentage than the average in Arab oil countries. In 2002 taxes in non-oil Arab countries accounted for 17% of GDP, and for around just 5% in Arab oil countries (Arab Joint Economic Report, in Arabic, 2003). This can be compared, for example, to around 23% in Germany, 24% in Italy, and 28% in UK. Thus taxes in themselves provide no major stimulus for Arab citizens to call the government to account for what it does with their money.

This type of tax structure also minimizes the opportunity for citizens to protest against their government. Direct taxes, in particular income tax, are viewed as the category of tax that gives citizens most proof that they are contributing to the public purse. In Arab countries, the majority of tax receipts are derived from indirect sales and customs taxes hidden in the price. In addition to falling more heavily on the most vulnerable groups in society, these types of tax typically conceal the direct link between tax payments and funding of the public purse, thus weakening public pressure for accountability. At the same time, income tax revenue is negligible and tax evasion is on the rise, particularly among influential social groups, which, in principle, should shoulder the greatest burden in funding the public

In the rentier state, government is absolved of any periodic accountability, not to mention representation.

Taxes in themselves provide no major stimulus for Arab citizens to call the government to account for what it does with their money.

purse, if only as fair return for their greater share of power and wealth.

Moreover, in Arab countries, the share of direct taxes appears to have dropped over time, as a result of increasing resort to indirect taxes (Figure 6-1).

In addition, this rentier mode of production gives rise to specific arrangements for reinforcing authoritarian rule through the generous financing of agencies of organized repression and the mass media, invariably owned or monopolized by the regime. Such financing can even be extended to the judiciary and representative councils. As a result, the dominant few can utilize these channels to sustain their rule and facilitate and ensure the effective exercise of oppression, especially by restricting civil and political society (Chapter 5).

THE LONGING FOR FREEDOM AND JUSTICE IN POPULAR CULTURE

Despite the repressive chain that stifles freedom in Arab societies and the negative effect of the rentier state on political participation, there remains a longing for freedom in the Arab world expressed in popular culture. No discussion of freedom in Arab culture would be complete if it confined itself to formal culture, or the culture of the "elite". In fact, the horizons of popular or folk culture are often broader than those of thinkers, philosophers, intellectuals and scientists, notwithstanding the latter's great impact on the life and destiny of peoples. In its own way, the "collective consciousness", with its mythological, symbolic heritage, its folklore, tales, oral tradition, scientific knowledge or "pre-scientific" knowledge, folk poetry and epics, national songs and so on – also shapes the history of peoples.

In Arab cultural history, folk culture may, at first glance, seem out of sorts with freedom. It is a culture characterized by images, beliefs and legends that came from a distant past steeped in magic, and in fables and tales that defy imagination. Such beliefs have remained alive since pre-Islamic times, into the Islamic age and up to the modern day. They reached their peak at the time of Ibn Khaldoun, considered the symbol of the age of "magic, of talismans, of Zodiac signs and of astrology".

Figure 6-1

The share of taxes in public revenues and the share of income taxes in total tax revenues (%), Arab countries, 1992-2002

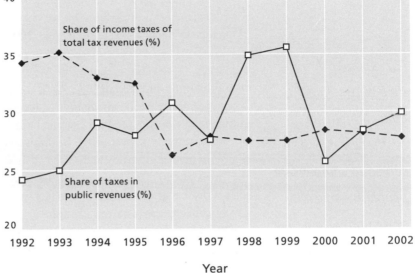

Source: Data from the Joint Arab Economic Report for 1998-2003, in Arabic.

It is well known that Ibn Khaldoun's project, in one of its original multiple facets, was "the positive, realistic opposite" of the spirit of that age, the mists of which he aimed to dispel. Yet that heritage of the "absurd" "with its belief in magic, astrology, genies, spirits, divination, the miracles and powers of holy men, dreams, fables devils, ghosts, winds, etc. (Muhammad al-Gohary, in Arabic, 1981, 2: 163-233, 411-440; Shawqi Abdel Hakim, in Arabic, 1994, 1, 87-120), has not disappeared from the Arab individual and collective memory. It only began to ebb slowly in "the age of Arab enlightenment" in the mid-nineteenth century. It is no secret that this folk heritage, where people relinquish their will and determination to act in the real world, submitting instead to the magic forces of the unknown, is a superstitious state contrary to freedom.

Such categories of folk culture are only a limited part of the Arab folk heritage and oral tradition. The greatest literary manifestations of that tradition – folk epics and *siras* (life stories) – are glowing examples of the elevation of the "dream of freedom". They confirm that this heritage venerated nationalist and social causes and aspired to social and national liberation. When those epics and life stories were being created, such aspirations belonged to the category of "what remained unsaid", and they expressed a popular desire

There remains a longing for freedom in the Arab world, expressed in popular culture.

for freedom in the face of internal tyranny, oppression and external dangers. Apart from their entertainment, educational and aesthetic value, they also served to compensate people for adversity and provoke a desire for change (Mohammad Rajab al-Najjar, in Arabic, 1995, 1, 226-243). The *Lives* of Antara, of Hamza of the Arabs, of Seif Ibn thi Yazan, of Al Amira that al- Himma, of Bani Hilal and of Al Zaher Bibars are not what the champions of formal culture made them out to be: i.e. adulterations of Arab history or fabrications to be dismissed as tales of myth and magic. (Some even advised the "men of the hisba" to prohibit the copying and exchange of such works). In fact, such works were creative historical literature inspiring "the spirit of struggle and resistance against the enemies of creed and religion". As such, they played a social and nationalist role which was not limited to confronting the armies of the Crusaders and Abyssinians, but continued into the modern age to help encourage the nationalist spirit of resistance to British, French and Italian occupation in Egypt and, in the Maghreb, the Algerian struggle, beginning with the uprising of Abdel Qader and extending to the armed liberation revolution (*Ibid*, 228-229).

Their compensatory function resided in their epic significance which, for ordinary people in the Arab dark ages of disintegration and weakness, profoundly expressed popular anger against injustice, oppression and tyranny. In calling for unity and liberation of the land, in voicing the dream of a better world, in nourishing the popular spirit by creating popular or epic heroes capable of overcoming adversity, they lifted people's souls and minds above the trials of their time (*Ibid*. 233). The aspiration for freedom is clear in those epics. In *The Life of Antara*, the central issue is the emancipation of the individual self from class injustice and of the public self at the social level. In *Hamza of the Arabs*, the anonymous narrator considers true national liberation to be not only a political but a "social liberation first and foremost, particularly during periods of historical transition in the life of peoples – transition from a nomadic tribal society to an urban national one". In *The Life of Seif Ibn thi Yazan*, the popular narrator raises an issue

aimed at emancipating popular culture, from the circle of magic, idolatry and other inherited myths. In *Al Amira that Al Himma* ("The Story of Palestinian Genealogies") which covers almost five thousand pages, some of the main events revolve around a central social issue, "the emancipation of Arab women" in a backward time when a relapse into Jahiliyya was under way. The epic narrator exposes the society of traditions and the harem. He then replaces it with "a society of free women", making an epic heroine of its central figure of Palestinian descent (That Al Himma) who becomes a national heroine, the equal of men in the making of history and life, despite what befalls her at the end because of the 'caliph's politics". These are all social issues symbolizing freedom, emancipation and national liberation (*Ibid*., 261-282; Shawqi Abdel Hakim, in Arabic, 1994, different passages).

Contemporary Arab popular culture continues to draw upon the sources of this freedom-affirming heritage. This culture too, under the pressure of its own present realities, is full of different popular aspirations for freedom, particularly the myriad folk songs and poetry about Arab struggles in Morocco, Algeria and Egypt on the eve of independence or revolution. Freedom is also very much present in the revolutionary popular Palestinian poetry of today. Arab popular culture, despite some freedom-inhibiting aspects, represents for the most part, a living treasury of freedom's symbols and one of its rich and boundless spaces.

THE GLOBAL AND REGIONAL CONTEXT

It is not possible to understand the problem of freedom in Arab society without also considering the effects of regional factors and of influences coming from outside the region, particularly those related to globalization and global governance.

GLOBALIZATION AND FREEDOM

Globalization has the potential to buttress the freedom of the individual as a result of minimising the State's capacity to repress people, particularly their ideas and aspirations. Also,

---

(Epics), apart from their entertainment, educational and aesthetic value, also served to compensate people for adversity and to provoke a desire for change.

It is not possible to understand the problem of freedom in Arab society without also considering the effects of regional factors and influences coming from outside the region.

globalization can expand people's opportunities to acquire knowledge and broaden their horizons by facilitating communication and the circulation of ideas. Indeed, some argue that globalization constitutes an extension of the concept of freedom, and "a chance to renew the fundamental rights of the individual," after the 20th century witnessed further expansion of the State's powers over the individual (Micklethwait and Wooldridge, 2003).

In particular, globalization can support freedom by strengthening civil society through wider networking among its actors, using modern information and communication technology. This is of particular importance in Arab countries. The task of building regional civil society networks and establishing links between them and civil society institutions outside the Arab world remains essential.

There has been direct and important interaction at the international level, particularly between industrialized and developing countries, in the areas of freedom and good governance. Historically, relations with democratic countries in the West played an important role in spurring democratic transition in regions that were struggling to be free. One thinks specifically here of Eastern Europe as the former Soviet Union was breaking up.

Yet globalization also entails the selective restriction of certain liberties worldwide when it comes to the free flow of knowledge. Useful knowledge is not easily accessible – even on the Internet - under the rigid, often one-sided intellectual property protection regimes favoured by the industrialized nations. The negative impacts of this "selective" restriction of knowledge flows are evident in areas vital to developing countries. An example is the restricted flow of cheap medicine, particularly in the case of deadly and widespread diseases from which large numbers of poor people in the world suffer.

Restrictions on freedoms, also apply to the free movement of people. The industrialized nations do not usually permit entry to individuals unless this serves those nations' interests; yet, at the same time, they call for the removal of barriers to the movement of goods and capital globally. This selective freedom, enforced by developed countries, has favoured the highly qualified in patterns of migration from less developed countries. In the case of the Arab world, the resulting drain of talents and capabilities severely limits opportunities to acquire knowledge in the region, one of the most important cornerstones of human development.

At a time when good governance—in the sense of rational public administration—is considered important to attract foreign investment, experience with global capital shows that investors might not be concerned about establishing good governance except as it pertains to guaranteeing capital, transferring profits, and settling labour disputes. Sometimes it is feared that the overseas investor might well prefer societies and governments that neglect certain freedoms, especially those concerning workers' rights to strike or institute work stoppages, for instance. Thus, while foreign investment is beneficial for development, it does not necessarily advance good governance.

The influence of the global environment on developing countries in knowledge, economics and politics, is growing both negatively and positively. Yet Arab countries, like other developing countries, have little or no control of that environment. This underscores the importance of working to reform global governance in order to serve the goals of security, peace, and human development throughout the world.

GOVERNANCE AT THE GLOBAL LEVEL

After the collapse of the Soviet Union and the end of the Cold War; and as economic globalization accelerated, bringing worldwide social and political change in its train, governance throughout the world underwent pivotal changes. Arab countries, in particular, have been affected by the global environment, which has had important effects on freedom and governance in the region.

In particular, globalization led to deep changes in the role and functions of the State, which lost part of its sovereignty to international actors, such as trans-national corporations and international organizations, notably in the areas of economic activity and media. Consequently, the destinies of states and their

Some argue that globalization constitutes an extension of the concept of freedom.

Yet globalization also entails the selective restriction of certain liberties worldwide.

citizens are now influenced more closely than ever before by the nature of governance at the global level. As states have given up a portion of their sovereignty, it has become essential to strengthen global governance, as embodied in the United Nations, by transferring some of the powers relinquished by states to a global body committed to the values of justice, freedom and equality. However, this has yet to come about. The end of the equilibrium between the two great powers and the advent of a uni-polar world has resulted at times in the weakening and marginalization of the world organization (Ghalioun, in Arabic, 2003, b, 68-69).

BOX 6-4

Counsellor Yahya al-Rifai: Justice Above Might

Different points of view, incompatible interests, even human conflict are part of God's way with His creation. The Qur'an says, "They continue in their disagreement... It was for that that He created them." The Qur'an also says, "Had God not set mankind against one another, the earth would have gone to rack and ruin."

There are two, and only two, ways of settling disputes: with the bludgeon of force or the justice of law, there is no third possibility. With force, a person's life, honour and property are never safe; he lives like a wild animal, hunting his prey without ever being sure that he will be able to keep any of it, never planting a crop because the harvest will go to the strongest, never building a house because there is no certainty that he will be able to live in it, and, indeed, afraid to settle anywhere.

On the day when God guided mankind to law, by His permission, the first time that two antagonists decided not to fight, but instead to seek the arbitration of a third party, not deeming it unbecoming to submit to his judgement, despite their strength—on that day the first step on the road to civilization was taken. Man realized that he had rights that were protected by the law, and consequently he could be assured of being able to enjoy the fruits of his labour. He learned to keep livestock, to cultivate the land, and to build.

Protected by the principle of arbitration, the law grew and developed, serving to safeguard individuals' lives, property and honour. The State grew and devel-

oped to secure their right to litigate. That right was entrusted to a particular group of their number, namely their arbitrators, not so that the latter could use force as they saw fit for their own ends, but rather so that they could use it to safeguard the community as a whole. It was a weapon that they wielded on behalf of all members of the community to safeguard the rule of the community's law, under the community's supervision.

Litigation enables an individual to go to a judge—who is an individual like the litigant—and ask for redress in an abuse of power, or initiate a prosecution or seek restoration of a right that has been denied. In the courtroom, the litigant and adversary stand on a footing of equality, out of the reach of all manifestations of power, whether in the form of money, weapons or the pressure of public opinion, and the judge can harness the power of the State to protect the law.

On this basis, all humanity adopts a charter proclaiming the principles of human rights, inspired from the concepts of natural law and the principles of justice, give that charter pre-eminence over national constitutions, and seek periodically to broaden its scope. The only way to make it effective will be to establish international courts in which individuals can bring suit against their own States and all their institutions, constitutions and laws. It has consistently been the hope of humankind that the competence of these courts will extend to all individuals and all States, so that all will be subject to law and enjoy peace, which can only be based on justice.

Source: Ahmed Makki, in Arabic, 1990

This has limited the effectiveness of the Security Council in establishing peace in the region. Such marginalization has been among factors contributing to continued or increased human suffering and to the creation of new facts on the ground, which militate against a just and lasting peace in Palestine. The US' use, or threat of veto has made it possible for Israel to establish new settlements in the Occupied Territories, and to start construction of the separation wall that incorporates additional Palestinian land. Silence regarding Israel's defiance of international legitimacy has undoubtedly pushed many people in the region to lose hope of obtaining justice from global governance and may have exacerbated extremism.

As many in the Arab world have had their confidence in the impartiality of the US as an honest broker weakened, reformers have found themselves lacking what they had hoped would be a critical ally (Barry, 2002).

It is thus essential that international law is upheld, and that international collective action and UN reform are implemented in that context. International public opinion ought to be encouraged to provide checks and balances in international behaviour, to help minimize the negative impacts of globalization and influence Israeli-American relations for the sake of a just peace. This should be complemented by the creation of a regional system that is able to interact with global changes, deal appropriately with aspects of globalization and inspire Arab citizens with confidence in its identity.

THE IMPACT OF THE "WAR ON TERROR" ON FREEDOM

The events of September 11, 2001 in the United States led to a substantial measure of international consensus around the proposition that terrorism has become one of the greatest perils of the age. That is why the entire world demonstrated solidarity with the United States after the attacks, and then again with countries from Turkey to Morocco to Spain to Saudi Arabia that have suffered their own terrorist attacks in recent years. In this context, nobody disputes the right and responsibility of Governments to take strong actions to ensure the security of their citizens. In practice, however, some aspects of the way in which the "war on terror" has been conducted, have come to pose real threats to civil liberties and reform in the Arab region and beyond.

While Western leaders have strongly asserted their support for freedom and democracy as the best long-term solution to terrorism, in practice many have also understandably sought to tighten their own security legislation, providing new power to monitor and detain terror suspects at home and abroad. While some successes have been achieved, an unfortunate by-product in some countries has been that Arabs are increasingly the victims of stereotyping, and disproportionately harassed or detained without cause under new restrictions. At the same time, in the Arab world, several Governments have cited fear of terrorism as justification for steps to impose even tighter restrictions on their citizens.

It is essential to rebuild a new climate of understanding, confidence and trust that rejects the indiscriminate grouping of all violent actions as "terror" and breaks the unfair and deeply damaging association of terrorism with Arabs and Muslims, or indeed any group or faith. Such an approach also needs to include a clearer definition of terrorism that distinguishes between terrorist organizations and acts of legitimate resistance, including the fight "against colonial domination and alien occupation and against racist regimes", which is protected by Protocol I Additional to the Geneva Conventions relating to the Protection of Victims of International Armed Conflicts.

For their part, Arabs need to resist strongly any temptation to surrender to the very real frustration and anger felt by many at the damaging impact of the "war on terror" on their own aspirations for reform and freedom. On the contrary, terrorism and war crimes, whoever commits them, should be resolutely condemned. Instead, Arabs everywhere should make a renewed commitment to make the Arab world a place where all citizens are fully secure from state-sponsored and other forms of violence.

The only lasting way to achieve that goal and uproot terrorism is to pursue equitable development and to establish systems of good governance, both in Arab countries and on the global level, under which injustices can be confronted through channels that are both peaceful and effective. In a word, the ultimate antidote to terrorism is freedom, based on respect for international human rights law and respect for the rights and dignity of individuals. Such a political environment, underpinned by a genuine regard for cultural diversity both in Arab countries and Western countries in which Arabs and Muslims live, will, in the long run, dry up the wellsprings of terrorism.

GOVERNANCE AT THE REGIONAL LEVEL

A good governance system at the regional level could potentially have a positive impact on freedoms and good governance at the national level. Regional governance institutions – as supra-national bodies - would provide norms and points of reference for national systems of good governance. An example of this would

It is essential to rebuild a new climate of understanding, confidence and trust that rejects the indiscriminate grouping of all violent actions as "terror" and breaks the unfair and deeply damaging association of terrorism with Arabs and Muslims, or indeed any group or faith.

BOX 6-5

The UN Special Rapporteur on Terrorism and Human Rights: The Root Causes of Terrorism

Addressing the root causes of terrorism has now become a rather highly contentious area, with a number of States and scholars insisting that, as there is no justification whatever for terrorism, there should be no effort made to try to understand its root causes. Instead, they argue, there should be ever more militant action against terrorists and terrorist groups, with the goal of wiping them out. This position is met with dismay by the majority, who insist that it is foolhardy to ignore review of root causes, which are, in some situations, directly or indirectly related to the non-realisation of human rights. The Special Rapporteur sides with those who support study of root causes in order to fashion more rational means of eliminating terrorism.

Some of the actions undertaken in the cause of the global war against terrorism have been the cause of consternation also for the highest officials in the UN system. For instance, the UN Secretary-General has pleaded on a number of occasions for States to uphold all human rights, stressing that greater respect for human rights, not their curtailment, is the best means of preventing terrorism. Addressing recently the Commission on Human Rights, he stated, "Let us ensure that our security measures are firmly founded in law. In defending the rule of law, we must ourselves be bound by law"[a]. He has also pointed out that the Council and the Counter-Terrorism Committee "must… be sensitive to human rights as they pursue their work."[b]

Attention has already been drawn to the concerns of the UN High Commissioner for Human Rights, also expressed in a number of statements and comments throughout the period. The UN High Commissioner for Refugees also has repeatedly voiced his own consternation about some measures, which, even though adopted in good faith, have victimized people in need of international protection[c].

Source: Commission on Human Rights, Sub-Commission on the Promotion and Protection of Human Rights, 2002, Terrorism and Human Rights, second progress report prepared by Ms. Kalliopi K. Koufa, Special Rapporteur.

(a) See SG/SM/8196-HR/CN/989 of 12 April 2002.
(b) *Ibid.*
(c) See, for instance, statement by Ruud Lubbers, UN High Commissioner for Refugees, to the Third Committee of the General Assembly, New York, 19 November 2001; UN News Centre, 20 February 2002.

be the establishment of an Arab human rights court for delivering justice to all Arab citizens and for counteracting any government's infringement of its citizens' rights and freedoms.

A stronger and more effective Arab regional system would enhance freedom in Arab countries in at least two important ways: first, it would reverse the deterioration of the pan-Arab liberation movement brought about by its division and weakness, and by some of its members' vulnerability to external pressures. Second, it would help seize the opportunity currently being missed to establish the knowledge society in the Arab countries. This requires close and effective inter-Arab co-ordination the elements of which are present except for the political will and commitment.

What can be said about regional co-ordination and the knowledge society in Arab countries can be said about most human development issues in the region. Acquiring and using human capabilities at the national levels is enhanced through regional complementarity. For example, the challenge of unemployment facing Arab countries could be dealt with more effectively with a freer regional labour market responding to supply and demand across countries, promoting the full use of human capabilities and ensuring the rights of workers. Such a regional market by itself would push the economic growth wheel in most Arab countries. In economic terms, some important

aspects of freedom in the Arab world are first class "regional public goods".

Unfortunately, repression at the national level and distractions created by animosity among ruling regimes has led to squandering the possibilities of Arab complementarity in securing freedom in the Arab states.

Despite various attempts at Arab unity, at least in the economic sphere, the chief pattern, ever since the founding of the League of Arab States (LAS) in 1945, has been the loose arrangement for co-operation that leaves matters in the hands of national governments with equal voting rights. Regional decisions are reached by consensus. The regional co-ordination structure is multifaceted, with several specialized organs. There is the Council, which convenes at the level of Foreign Ministers and, more recently, once a year at the level of Heads of State. There is also an Economic and Social Council that addresses matters determined by the governments of member states. Essentially this is an economic council that was established pursuant to article 7 of the Common Defence Pact, which called for economic cooperation without further clarification.

This superficial, non-binding formula has been useful in fostering participation by all Arab states, despite differences in their socio-economic systems. At the same time, however, it has led to a weakening of the regional structure and a decline in its credibility (figure 6-2).

This superficial, non-binding formula...has led to a weakening of the regional structure and a decline in its credibility.

Figure 6-2

Credibility of the Arab League and the United Nations
Estimates by five Arab states and comparator countries

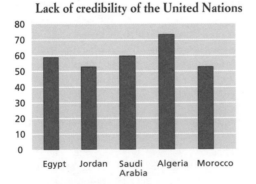

Lack of credibility of the United Nations

Percentage of missing observations:
Egypt 4.10%, Jordan 13.79%, Saudi Arabia 12.05%, Algeria 12.71%, Morocco 40.77%, comparator countries 21.76%.

Source: World Values Survey, Annex 1.

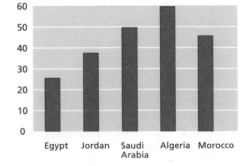

Lack of credibility of the Arab League

Comparator countries:
Simple arithmetic average of the results of South Africa, Argentina, South Korea, Brazil, Nigeria, Pakistan, Turkey, Bangladesh and Indonesia.

Percentage of missing observations:
Egypt 4.60%, Jordan 17.04%, Saudi Arabia 10.99%, Algeria 14.04%, Morocco 39.88%, comparator countries 11.34%.

The credibility of the League of Arab States is quite low, especially in Algeria, with relatively higher credibility in Egypt and Jordan. The credibility of the UN is also low, especially in Algeria and Saudi Arabia.

The second LAS Summit in Alexandria in 1964 resolved that an Arab Court of Justice should be established. Today, forty years later, the Court has still not seen the light of day. There have been repeated calls for an Arab Parliament, but owing to differences in parliamentary representation among the respective Arab states, that institution has not been established either.

There are a number of institutions that work at the regional level outside the official framework. These include various professional groups, among them parliamentarians, workers, lawyers, economists, businessmen, investors, contractors, farmers and academics. Many of them have campaigned effectively on behalf of popular demands for freedom, good governance and development.

Within the official regional framework, agreements have been reached that could have advanced freedoms and people's rights at the regional level. However, these agreements have not been implemented as foreseen because national governments have insisted on retaining their right to approve or refuse to approve regional decisions, with the result that all agreements must be ratified in accordance with the constitutional procedures in force in the various states. For example, a number of agreements in the field of labour were reached in the 1960s. The Arab Agreement on Labour Standards was designed to raise standards and improve working conditions in the Arab world. The Arab Regional Labour Force Mobility Agreement was designed to facilitate the flow of Arab workers and ensure that they enjoyed hiring preference and obtained the same rights and benefits as nationals of the country in which they were employed. The Agreement on Basic Social Insurance Levels allowed workers to retain entitlements earned in one country when they took jobs in another country; while under the Reciprocity Agreement on Social Insurance Plans workers could accumulate insurance periods entitling them to benefits in accordance with the legislation in force in the contracting states. In the main, however, countries that were suppliers of labour ratified those agreements, but not countries that employed labour from abroad. As a result the agreements have remained largely ineffective.

Despite large-scale labour force migration within the Arab region, workers are generally denied many of their rights when they migrate, and in addition they are likely to find themselves excluded when a political crisis results in strained relations between their host country and their home country. Under the terms of the Economic Unity Agreement, individuals are supposed to enjoy freedom of movement between Arab states, but efforts to develop a unified identity card have ended in failure, and the process of abolishing entry visas is subject to the vagaries of political relations. On the other hand, the Agreements on Arab Capital Investment in Arab States are designed to protect investors from nationalization or confiscation, and to ensure their right to repatriate their capital and profits from their investments. Those agreements also give investors the right to travel to, and reside in countries in which they have invested. The Unified Agreement on Investment (1980) makes provision for an Arab Investment Court, pending the establishment of an Arab Court of Justice. Lastly, with a view to stimulating economic activity in Arab states, CAEU has approved an agreement aimed at avoiding double taxation and preventing income and capital tax evasion between states that are members of the Council. This agreement has recently been amended.

In sum, current institutional arrangements for regional co-ordination have failed to give substantive support to Arab development, to maintain security and peace in the Arab world and to end occupation. Inter-Arab cooperation has not contributed to enhancing freedom and good governance. Symbolizing this failure, the best example of successful cooperation remains the Council of Arab Ministers of Interior.

Unsurprisingly, people in the Arab region feel that co-operation at the pan-Arab level is poor (figure 6-3).

According to the Freedom Survey, Annex 1, the vast majority of respondents said they were dissatisfied with the level of Arab cooperation.

The credibility of the League of Arab States is quite low…the credibility of the UN is also low.

Current institutional arrangements for regional coordination have failed to give substantive support to Arab development, to maintain security and peace in the Arab world and to end occupation.

Figure 6-3

Extent of satisfaction with the current level of Arab cooperation, five Arab countries, Freedom Survey, 2003

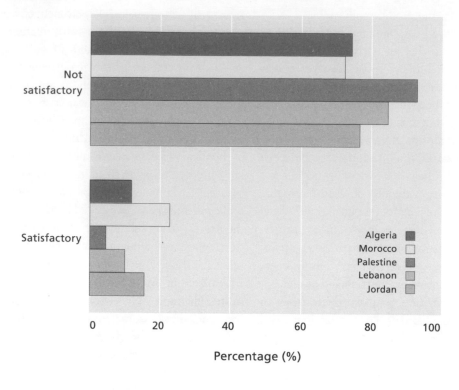

Percentage (%)

Part II

Reinforcing Freedom and Establishing Good Governance

Section 4: Towards Reinforcing Freedom and Establishing Good Governance in the Arab Countries

Our assessment of the state of freedom and governance, coupled with the advanced explanation of the deficit in freedom and good governance (chapters 3-6) enable us to attempt answering the historic question raised at the end of chapter1: could the future bear out a trajectory that would lead Arab societies to enjoy freedom and good governance traversing the required process of historical struggle.

CHAPTER SEVEN

A Strategic Vision of Freedom and Governance in Arab Countries – Alternative Futures

Introduction

This chapter offers a general view of the substance of societal and institutional reform needed to establish a society of freedom and good governance in the Arab region. It starts by underlining the need for the periodic alternation of power in Arab countries. It next discusses three alternative futures that could define the course of freedom and governance in the Arab world: the first is to be avoided; the second would be ideal, but may be difficult to attain quickly; and the third may be more realistic and could potentially contribute to the preferred alternative, if properly managed. The chapter and the Report conclude by highlighting the main features of the preferred alternative future. This scenario is named the "izdihar[1] alternative", using the Arabic word that denotes the full flourishing of individuals and societies.

As in previous Reports, recommendations made in this chapter are presented as broad guidelines. They are offered to all dynamic forces of Arab society, regardless of their position within the prevailing power structure, for consideration in defining their own path towards a society of freedom and good governance. Such recommendations may also be helpful to those outsiders who are genuinely interested in supporting an Arab renaissance.

GROUNDS FOR PEACEFUL AND DEEP POLITICAL ALTERNATION, ALTERNATIVE FUTURES

REASONS FOR CHANGE

Modernization in Arab countries has yielded notable achievements, especially in combating morbidity and mortality - particularly among children – in building infrastructure, in the quantitative expansion of education, particularly among females, and in increasing the integration of women in society. Yet by 21st century standards, Arab countries have not met the Arab people's aspirations for development, security and liberation despite variations between one country and another in this regard.

As the AHDRs of 2002 and 2003 showed, the vast majority of the Arab people do not enjoy the higher forms of human development, notably in relation to knowledge, freedom and good governance, and women's empowerment.

"Bread before freedom" is a common dictum in the Arab region. Yet putting the satisfaction of basic human needs before people's essential liberty has in practice meant that most Arabs[2] have risked losing out on both.

The previous chapters of this Report has provided a detailed analysis of the freedom and governance problem in the Arab world. Central to that problem is the fact that at the political level, decision-making has remained in the hands of a minority that monopolises the two spheres of power - financial resources and political authority - and has hence focused on

By 21st century standards, Arab countries have not met the Arab people's aspirations for development, security and liberation.

Putting the satisfaction of basic human needs before people's essential liberty has in practice meant that most Arab have lost out on both.

---

[1] Individual and collective flourishing. English borrows from French the term 'épanouissement' to fill a lexical gap in denoting this phenomenon. However, the Arabic word "izdihar" captures the intended sense closely. Thus, rather than use a French term, which has to be explained in English, to describe something which most people in the region will recognize from the Arabic, we have opted for the Arabic word, with this explanation for non-Arab readers.

[2] Idiomatically, the word "Arab" is used to denote all citizens of Arab countries, inclusively

serving its own interests. The vast majority of people are excluded, and thus left to impoverishment and marginalization. The results of the World Values Survey (annex 1) indicate that nearly 70% of the public in five Arab countries believe that " the country is run for the benefit of the influential few".

Nor have Arab regimes been able to protect Arab interests in the international arena. Arab lands remain occupied, with the occupation of Iraq having recently been added to that of Palestine. About 10 per cent of Arabs now live under occupation and, after several decades, foreign military forces have reappeared in the region. This provokes an extremely high level of discontent in the region, as indicated in the Freedom Survey (Annex 1 and figure 7.1)

Finally, present-day regimes have not achieved fundamental reform from within which would correct their course and enhance hopes for a better future.

ALTERNATIVE ARAB FUTURES

Given current trends, and looking into the future, several scenarios can be envisioned. We focus here on the three most relevant to the subject of this report.

The Impending Disaster Scenario: Maintaining the 'Status Quo'

If the situation in Arab countries today continues, intensified societal conflict is likely to follow.

Under the skewed distribution of power in its two spheres - wealth and political authority – and escalating foreign encroachment, Arabs suffer multiple injustices and see little hope for a better future. Anger combined with despair is an explosive mixture that pushes some towards violence, with undesirable consequences that threaten social cohesion and debilitate national structures and institutions.

Simply branding violent protesters as "terrorists" or further tightening the security restrictions already in place will not provide an answer. The way of strict security alone is ultimately ineffective, even if it buys a brief respite.

Contemporary history shows that continuation of the status quo might lead to destructive upheavals that could force a transfer of power in Arab countries. However, such a transfer could well involve armed violence and human losses that would be unacceptable however small. Nor would this transfer of power through violence guarantee that successor governance regimes would be any more desirable.

If this should materialize, the future for Arab countries holds more failures in the arena of human development. We label this prospect the "impending disaster" scenario.

The Ideal Scenario: The "Izdihar" Alternative

Disaster can be averted. The alternative is to pursue an historic, peaceful and deep process of negotiated political alternation adopted by all pro-reform segments of Arab society, whether they are in power or not, on all fronts and by all democratic means, to guarantee rights and freedoms. A process of peaceful negotiation on the redistribution of power in Arab countries represents the optimum approach for a transitional phase towards good governance. The desired outcome is a redistribution of power

Figure 7-1

Extent of dissatisfaction over the presence of foreign military bases, five Arab countries, Freedom Survey, 2003

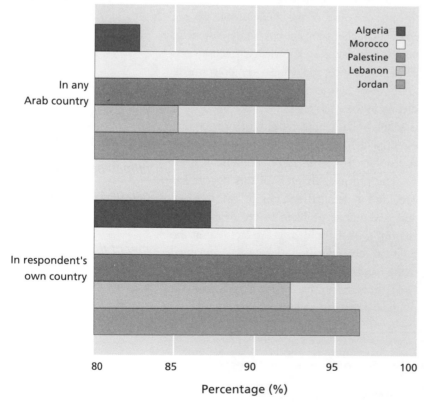

Percentage (%)

within Arab societies, restoring power to its rightful owners, the vast majority of people in the Arab world. The process would also establish good governance as a solid foundation for a human renaissance. We call this alternative the "izdihar" scenario.

Unlike a continuation of the status quo, good governance will help to address social injustice properly, by means that are both peaceful and effective, thus removing the sources of disaster.

The "Half Way House" Scenario: the Accommodation of External Reform

A third alternative is gathering momentum within the region and across the globe: a Western-supported project of gradual and moderate reform aiming at liberalization in Arab countries but falling short of real democratization. An example of this project of cautious reform is the "Broader Middle East Initiative", adopted by the G8 summit (see Part I). This and similar plans might well lead to a series of internal reforms in Arab countries. Arab regimes are, in general, susceptible to foreign pressure and will try to respond positively to some external demands for reform. At the same time, most of these regimes will try to contain the impact of reform measures and stop short of the desired political reform and the equitable redistribution of power, which constitute the core of the "izdihar"" alternative.

This third or "half way" alternative, falls short of the "ideal" scenario in two crucial respects. First, measures imposed from outside according to the vision of foreign powers are not fully consistent with the concepts of freedom and good governance advocated by successive AHDRs, especially in relation to liberation and independence. Second, such reforms will not benefit from the dynamics of change driven from within. Indeed, they maintain the tradition of accepting that the destinies of Arab states have to be shaped from outside.

Despite the serious shortcomings of this alternative, it has to be acknowledged that although the historical project of renewal of the Arab region started two centuries ago, it has not succeeded yet in fulfilling Arab aspirations for freedom and dignity; and that this less-than-perfect "half-way house" alternative

does contain at least some elements of the preferred option.

The challenge facing the advocates of renaissance in the Arab world is how to manage this alternative – which is expected to grow in significance - and maximize its contribution to advancing the "izdihar" alternative. This would allow those outside initiatives for reform adopted by Arab regimes to be led from the inside and would minimize the impact of their most critical defects.

Dealing with this challenge successfully will be an important milestone for renaissance advocates and will test their ability to shape the future of the Arab region from the perspective of human development.

HOW TO DEAL WITH REFORM INITIATIVES FROM OUTSIDE?

Arab countries cannot ignore the fact that the world, especially the powerful players in the global arena, will continue actively to safeguard their interests in the region. Their call for reform in Arab countries falls within this context. But external pressures cannot be disregarded, no matter why they are applied. Arabs cannot afford the luxury of isolation from developments in the outside world. The extent of interconnection between those external forces and Arab governing and social structures is strong enough to warrant a positive approach towards external reform initiatives, but strictly from the perspective of building societies of freedom and good governance in the Arab world.

In addition, there are active international NGOs that can provide significant support to the forces of reform in the Arab world if the latter were willing to work with them.

Co-operation with external forces can be rewarding if all parties respect the following principles:

• Freedom for all and complete respect for international human rights law, in particular the right to national liberation. Furthermore, deeds must be consistent with words in order to end the double standards that have characterized some Western policies towards the Arab region. Also, the violation of human rights must be proscribed, and no impunity permitted, irrespective of the perpetrator.

Arab regimes are, in general, susceptible to foreign pressure and will try to respond positively to some external demands for reform.

Co-operation with external forces can be rewarding if all parties respect principles (of good governance).

• Absolute respect for the tenet that Arabs should find their own way to freedom and good governance through innovation by Arab social forces, without pressure to adopt ready-made models, as the firm guarantee of a successful and sustainable historic transformation.

• Inclusion of all societal forces in Arab countries in a system of good governance to ensure popular representation instead of the trend towards exclusion that has marred the Arab political landscape, sometimes prompted by external forces. All societal forces must have the right to organize and be active in both civil and political society as long as they abide by democratic principles and respect the rights of others. This includes:

• Full respect for the outcomes freely chosen by the people through a good governance regime. The free will of the people, and not foreign interests or designs, should be the ultimate arbiter in determining the Arab future.

• Dealing with the Arab people through a partnership of equals anchored in mutual respect and deep understanding, rather than patronage.

UNIVERSAL FEATURES AND AIMS OF THE DESIRED SYSTEM OF GOVERNANCE

The political alternation desired in the Arab world should lead to establishing good governance based on the following principles:

• Preservation of freedom in order to expand people's choices; i.e. protect the essence of human development.

This good governance regime should guarantee the rights of citizenship, in full, to all citizens.

• Effective popular participation, with universal popular representation of all the people.

• Efficient, transparent and accountable institutions as counterweights to the monopoly of power by individuals. These institutions work among themselves under the separation and balance of powers, and are accountable to each other and the people directly through free and fair choice exercised periodically.

• The rule of law, as the protector of freedom, applied fairly to all people.

• Laws administered by an efficient, impartial and completely independent judiciary, whose judgments are upheld and applied by the Executive Authority.

This good governance regime should guarantee the rights of citizenship, in full, to all citizens, and unequivocally end all forms of exclusion outside of the frame of "citizenship", regardless of all pretexts or justification.

This governance system should balance freedom with correct mechanisms of good governance. In particular, through free and credible elections, such a system should guarantee peaceful political alternation in the future.

REFORMING ARAB SOCIETAL STRUCTURES TO GUARANTEE FREEDOM

No matter which reform scenario unfolds in the coming years, or whether Arab reformers seek to take advantage of external pressure to advance their cause, freedom and good governance will not materialize fully until three sets of problems are addressed: the domestic problem of governance; the regional crisis that affects all Arab countries, including the problem of occupation; and the problems of governance that affect the entire international system, putting Arab countries at a serious disadvantage.

THE INTERNAL CHALLENGE

Enhancing the Legal and Institutional Foundations that Underpin Freedom

There is an urgent and compelling need to modernize Arab legal systems, to make them compatible with international human rights standards and effective in protecting human

BOX 7-1

Mahdi Bunduq, Post-Bourgeois Society

"As Tragedy announces the demise of one world (and thus implicitly the birth of a new one), the seed of post-bourgeois society should be thought of as being formed (in the womb of time) from the elements and structures of civil society: parties without tutelage, a press beyond the reach of confiscation, unions independent of government authority, clubs and cultural associations practicing the free study of all intellectual, artistic and literary schools and movements without criminalization or moral terrorism, and a cinema and theatre answering to the moral needs of the people without patriarchal censorship from anyone. All this would come under the framework of a constitution whose articles do not conflict with human rights and under the aegis of a modern State that does not discriminate between one school of thought and another, between one idea and another, between a man and a woman; a modern State that makes a distinction between itself and religion (as a practice of authority) but makes no such distinction between religion and society, as one of its heartbeats or spiritual aspirations."

Source: Mahdi Bunduq, in Arabic, 2003, 114

rights and freedoms in practice.

To that end, intensive efforts are called for to develop sound legislation and competent institutions to better safeguard, protect and support freedoms and human rights in the Arab world.

Adherence to International Human Rights Law

Arab states must take steps to ratify the component elements of international human rights law to include all major human rights treaties, particularly the ICCPR, the ICESCR, CAT, CEDAW and the CRC. These are considered the minimum requirements in terms of Arab ratification. Ideally, states should go considerably beyond this to embrace all elements of international human rights law, including the Optional Protocols.

Arab legislatures ought to take steps to revise legislation currently in force to bring it into conformity with international human rights standards and constitutional provisions that safeguard these rights.

Binding the Ruling Authority to the Rule of Law

The reform of Arab constitutions is essential to achieve the following four goals: a) Political power should be subject to a defined, reasonable time frame, ending permanency of power. b) Political power should not be absolute. The ruling authority should be responsible for its actions before the judiciary and elected representational bodies. c) Political pluralism should be guaranteed by an effective system based on the principle of equality in law and practice, with equal access to rights and opportunities and equal responsibilities. d) Arab citizens must be able to exercise their right to political participation in the fullest sense and to enjoy their fundamental rights.

The ruling authority in Arab countries, should be defined and bound by the law, and hence the law should be above all and not subject to the will of individuals. This is the case with the system of constitutional monarchy where the king or queen rules but does not govern. Under the republican system, which is parliamentary-based, it can be achieved through a clearly defined separation of powers

and where the free will of the electorate is the sole arbiter in determining the choice of parliament and government. In all cases, authority and responsibility stay with an elected individual in free and fair elections.

Guaranteeing freedoms and rights at the heart of the constitution

Arab constitutions must guarantee fundamental rights and freedoms. The constitution should clearly provide that it is unlawful to enact any legislation that restricts rights and freedoms. All Arab constitutions should provide that international human rights treaties by which they are legally bound take precedence over ordinary law. These measures all serve to expand the legal framework to protect freedoms and human rights in the Arab world, which would be strengthened further by setting up a constitutional judicial body to monitor the constitutionality of legislation, and prevent the passage of legislation which infringes the freedoms or rights prescribed under the constitution or international treaties. World experience has highlighted the importance of a constitutional judicial body to establish general principles in law, making freedom, justice and fair treatment governing principles for ordinary legislation, even when they are not stated explicitly in the constitution. This would undoubtedly help to free Arab legislation from arbitrary control by the executive.

The ruling authority in Arab countries should be defined and bound by the law.

All Arab constitutions should provide that international human rights treaties by which they are legally bound take precedence over ordinary law.

BOX 7-2
Perpetuating power in the name of democracy and the people

1- The Tunisian Constitution formerly stated that the President of the Republic is elected for a five-year term, and that an incumbent cannot hold office for more than three consecutive terms. But on March 18, 1975, the National Assembly elected President Bourquiba as President-for-Life and, by a unanimous vote, amended Article 40 of the Constitution to provide for this.
2- Article 77 of the Egyptian Constitution of 1971 confines the maximum term in office of the President of the Republic to two consecutive terms, stating that "The term of office for the presidency is six years, from the date on which the referendum results are declared. The President of the Republic may be re-elected for an additional consecutive term."

As the end of President Sadat's second term of office approached, the constitutional provision was amended, on 30 April 1980, to permit the President of the Republic to be re-elected for further terms of office (with no upper limit prescribed). The reasons for seeking this constitutional amendment were explained as follows:

"President Sadat's term of office began before the Constitution was promulgated, and in accordance with article 190 and article 77, his term of office concludes in November 1983. This outcome, resulting from the application of this provision, is not consistent with the democratic principles which our society safeguards and seeks to further entrench …more importantly, this result is one which the steadfast people of Egypt rejects with their hearts, minds and souls…"

> *The Supreme Constitutional Court in Egypt has had an extremely positive impact in supporting freedoms and human rights.*

Ten Principles for a Constitution of Freedom and Good Governance

1. Freedom from any ideological stamp; political orientations are decided at the ballot box that represents the will of the people.

2. Adoption of the multi-party system, so that political parties may be established by mere notification, within the limits of public order, and the affirmation of the principle of equality among political parties in terms of benefiting from State services. The Constitution should stipulate a separation between the ruling party and the State.

3. Adoption of the principle of binding power with responsibility, and separating the symbol of sovereignty from the authority of government. Sovereignty belongs to the nation or the people, as symbolized by the king or president, while government (i.e., the tasks undertaken by the executive authority) is carried out by a cabinet formed by the party with the parliamentary majority or a coalition of constituent parties in a legislative assembly that represents the majority. Accordingly, the king or the president is not responsible before parliament except in specified situations, while the cabinet bears joint responsibility before parliament since it practices authority. There should be no authority without responsibility and no responsibility without authority.

4. Adoption of the principle of the non-permanence of the elected authority. Limiting the mandate of the head of State and to four years, for example, and under no circumstances beyond two terms, would achieve this. The principle of direct election of the head of State from among multiple candidates should be adopted.

5. Formation of a neutral, independent body to supervise all elections, this body to be in charge of all procedures relating to, and supplementing the electoral process.

6. Prohibition of declarations of a state of emergency other than in accordance with the strictest limits, with severe constraints and for a set period, with majority agreement, especially in the legislative assembly. Creation of a system of judicial oversight, to review the legality of the declaration of emergency as well as of decrees issued by the emergency authority.

7. Establishment of a Supreme Constitutional Court responsible for overseeing the constitutionality of laws and for facilitating procedures to allow individuals to bring their grievances before it, especially cases related to legislative abuses of human rights. The Supreme Judicial Council of the Court alone should appoint Judges of the Court.

8. Explicit stipulation of the principle of the independence of the judicial authority and the judges in content and guarantees, so that the judiciary is a completely independent authority from the other two. Judges should be immune from any influence on them in their work. The regular judiciary should look into all disputes. No-one may be tried before any but the regular judiciary. Special or exceptional courts should be prohibited as should the trial of civilians before military courts. All matters relating to the appointment, promotion and disciplining of judges should fall within the competence of the Supreme Judicial Council, composed of judges, with a senior judge presiding. The text should stipulate immunity of judges. Members of the Public Prosecutor's Office should enjoy the same guarantees and immunity as judges.

9. Stipulation of all civil, political, economic, social, and cultural rights and liberties, with explicit prohibition of the restriction of these rights by any lower legislative instrument. The text should state unequivocally that freedoms of opinion, expression and association must be fully respected, with explicit reference to the media, which should be free from restrictions or censorship, or any form of interference with its activity or ownership. There must be no punishment of imprisonment in relation to publication or the expression of opinions.

10. Affirmation of the principle of the individual's right to compensation for damages done to her/him as a result of being deprived of their liberty through imprisonment or preventive detention, having been charged with offences of which they have been proven innocent.

Strengthening Civil and Political Rights in Law

Arab legislation in most urgent need of a thorough review includes laws regulating the exercise of political rights, the legislature and its electoral processes, the right to set up civil society organizations, including political parties, and their activities, and laws on the judicial authority.

Laws regulating political rights should elaborate on the principle of gender equality

The Supreme Constitutional Court in Egypt

The Supreme Constitutional Court in Egypt has had an extremely positive impact in supporting freedoms and human rights vigorously, playing a vital role in removing provisions from the statute books that conflicted with them. While the law establishing the Court came under criticism because of restrictions imposed on the right to bring individual grievances related to the Constitution before the Court, it has succeeded nonetheless in playing an influential role in support of democracy and freedom.

to ensure that it is applied in practice. They should also ensure that the principles of citizenship and equality apply to all constituent elements of national society.

Legislation should introduce effective mechanisms to ensure fair elections. Legal provisions must assure total impartiality for the body charged with election oversight and guard against the state or its apparatus resorting to any form of electoral malpractice. Total neutrality of the official media should also be assured. Election-related offences should be addressed seriously and effectively. Electoral rolls should be updated to ensure they correspond with those entitled to vote, together with a fair delineation of constituencies.

Legislation must guarantee that citizens are free to set up their parties without requiring the executive's authorization and with no supervision other than that required to protect the values of freedom and good governance. The law should proscribe racist parties or military organizations, for example, but this should not lead to the imposition of increased restrictions. Freedom to form political parties should be assured under conditions of political pluralism. It should protect the right of parties to carry out peaceful political activities, publicize their programmes, and mobilise their members by all available means, without restriction other than that required to maintain public order in a democratic state. There should be a clear distinction in both law and practice between the state apparatus and the party in power, so that the party concerned does not enjoy the prerogative of using state services to strengthen its presence, in breach of the principle of equality before the law.

Legislation regulating civil society organizations should also be revised to embody the following principles: freedom to set up civil society organizations, removing the requirement for state or other official forms of authorization where the simple notification of the legal existence of the organization should suffice; the activities of civil society organizations should not be subject to restrictions, surveillance or administrative control and the freedom and independence of these organizations should be guaranteed; no organization should be dissolved as a result of an administrative decision,

and such measures should apply only after a court ruling that all necessary conditions are satisfied.

Guaranteeing the Independence of the Judiciary

An independent judiciary is a basic pre-requisite for any society if individuals are to enjoy their rights and freedoms. However, the synergy between the independence of the judiciary and a free political environment is a matter for some consideration. However exemplary the laws regulating the judiciary may be, the judiciary will never play an effective role in an environment where rights and freedoms are suppressed and where the law and its institutions are sidelined. Similarly, a state system that makes no provision for an effective judicial system is inherently weak. Progress towards good governance, on the one hand, and towards guaranteeing the independence of the judiciary and the efficient and equitable discharge of its duties, on the other, must be made side-by-side. International standards that provide for the independence of the judiciary as an institution (independence of the judicial authority) as well as the independence of judges as individuals should be adopted.

Abolishing the State of Emergency.

Special attention should be given to abolishing the state of emergency in Arab countries where the conditions defined by international standards and the constitution for declaring a state of emergency are not met. Combating "terrorism" should not be used as a pretext to maintain a state of emergency, given that terrorism thrives whenever freedoms are quashed, and never more so than under a state of emergency.

In particular Arab states must desist from abusing the declaration of a state of emergency and the disastrous effect this has on freedoms and human rights.

Guarantees for Personal Freedom

Arab legislation must be amended urgently to guarantee the individual's protection from attacks on personal freedom, such as unlawful arrest, torture, administrative detention, enforced disappearance, and to provide in law for deter-

Freedom to form political parties should be assured under conditions of political pluralism.

Combating "terrorism" should not be used as a pretext to maintain a state of emergency.

rent penalties for public servants responsible. Effective mechanisms should be established to end these practices and provide victims with avenues to obtain fair compensation.

Ending discrimination against societal groups

The second AHDR emphasized that the facilitation, encouragement and celebration of cultural diversity in every Arab country was an important factor in establishing the knowledge society. To that, we may now add freedom in the Arab world as well.

That the extension of citizenship rights to all citizens of Arab countries inclusively necessarily involves ending all forms of discrimination against any societal group is beyond dispute. In a society of freedom and good governance, no group remains deprived of citizenship rights. To emphasize this spirit of inclusiveness, we stress here again that the word 'Arab' is used in this Report, for brevity, to denote all citizens of Arab countries.

But even before attaining that ideal, there are no grounds for maintaining any form of discrimination against various societal groups in Arab countries. Administrative decrees, which can readily be issued and swiftly implemented, can speedily resolve persistent issues of citizenship among unjustly treated groups. Such action would repair the national fabric, which has been torn by arbitrary measures in the past. The first step in this direction is to repeal all executive orders turning citizens into 'minorities' whose rights are violated.

THE POLITICAL ARCHITECTURE

Problematic issues in guaranteeing sound democratic arrangements

For the most part, political institutions in the Arab world, even those that are superficially democratic, such as elected parliaments, in reality do little to further the cause of freedom in the region because they lack substance, as argued in Chapter 2. As a result, the political architecture of Arab countries needs much restructuring.

We referred earlier to the necessity of having an extensive public sphere in place, one independent of the current ruling power, even in the event that it represents the popular majority. This public sphere would enable individuals to form their opinions and express them freely as well as work for their implementation.

It would also help to impose constitutional regulations on majority decisions in order to prevent legislation or policies that could restrict freedoms; and to delegate to the judiciary, and ombudsmen, the power to review decisions of the legislative body and, if necessary, correct them (Chapter 1).

It is crucial to ensure that the ruling authorities are appointed as a result of direct popular choice, and that good governance practices are implemented down to the lowest levels of local governance. This not only extends and reinforces good governance throughout the country, but is also important given that future leaders of central government start out and hone their experience in local government.

The way to achieve good governance in the Arab region is thus through fundamental reform of its architecture. This means, in particular, ending the executive's monopoly of power, and marginalization of other state organs, which obstructs the free and healthy development of society's capabilities and potential. This task is however made difficult by the fact that the very structural factors that concentrate power at the top of the executive branch also prevent civil society from advancing political reform.

This can, however, lead indirectly to conditions that are conducive to reform, since excessive concentration of power at the apex of society isolates an authoritarian regime from people and unifies political and social opposition groups behind a common goal.

At this stage of transition needs differ from one country to another. The various achievements made to date need to be defended, alliances set up, and appropriate demands articulated. It follows then that the nature of working for governance reform will vary according to the issues and means appropriate to each case.

In effecting the transformation, perhaps the heaviest responsibility lies with the élites: intellectuals and political and civil society

In a society of freedom and good governance, no group remains deprived of citizenship rights.

Excessive concentration of power at the apex of society isolates an authoritarian regime from people and unifies political and social opposition groups behind a common goal.

activists who will need to forge a middle way for themselves and the Arab world, neither bowing to the influence of the powerful and wealthy, nor following the route to despair and violence to which many angry young people, whose peaceful and effective avenues for action have been blocked, are drawn. This calls for considerable wisdom, genuine solidarity across national borders, and many sacrifices.

The role of the élites is thus crucial in securing an Arab renaissance, but which élites?

These are all groups supportive of freedom and good governance inside and outside the existing power structure, whose members are committed to a renaissance and will work assiduously to bring it about.

CODE OF CONDUCT FOR SOCIETAL FORCES ON THE PATH TO REFORM

Reform confers duties and responsibilities on the state and all societal forces, starting with committed elites. It falls to the latter to set an example through their own ethical and fair conduct, by acting in ways beyond reproach and avoiding the traps of corruption, enticement or manipulation by ambitious foreign powers. The duties that are required to effect genuine reform might be seen as follows:

Obligations of the State:

1. Allowing freedom of expression and organization as a first step towards agreement with political forces on reforms of the electoral and legal systems and guaranteeing the fairness and independence of the judiciary.
2. Starting a direct and immediate dialogue with all active forces in the society, whether they are opposition political movements or active civil society institutions. Dialogue must be serious and produce concrete results.
3. Assuring institutional stability without encouraging stagnation.
4. Safeguarding the independence and integrity of governance institutions so that they fulfil their role at the service of the people in the best possible way.
5. Carrying out comprehensive structural and functional reform of the security services.

All service branches must obey the law, and should be at the service of the people and the nation, and not the ruler, party, sect or tribe.

Obligations of the Political Élites:

1. The élites of political society, leaders and activists need to develop a constructive discourse and reject policies of exclusion. They must also strive to find common ground among all political forces and create a new mould for the political scene, clearly distinct from past trends of polarization and fragmentation which could seriously hamper genuine democratic transformation in the Arab region.
2. The political élites must demonstrate adherence to their principles, seeking democratic solutions to settle differences, rejecting any form of compromise which could make them tools of authoritarian regimes and articulating clearly the demands for freedom for all. They must never associate themselves with repression or seek ways to justify its use.
3. Political forces should strive to build democratic alliances, and openly demonstrate solidarity in the face of despotism, repression, corruption and election-rigging.

Obligations of Civil Society:

1. Developing appropriate methodologies and conceptual frameworks to adapt civil and human rights work to the local Arab environment, involving the widest possible spectrum of different sectors of society at large.
2. Securing internal resources to support and finance voluntary and civil work
3. Seeking to safeguard the independence of civil society organizations both from the State and from competing political associations. This does not imply that the organizations have no political role to play, since their role is clearly set within the political space, particularly when it comes to defending freedoms, human rights and the disadvantaged.
4. Setting up networks of associations and organizations with similar goals, or broader-based networks to strengthen solidarity and consolidate the capabilities of the forces of civil society.
5. Expanding Arab networks and initiatives.
6. Exploiting to the full attained rights and

The role of the élites is crucial in securing an Arab renaissance, but which élites?

It falls to the élites to set an example through their own ethical and fair conduct.

freedoms and insisting that they are enjoyed in their most complete sense; optimizing all opportunities for action, all available space for freedom, including opportunities provided by information and communication technology.

Parliamentary representation:

With roles assigned respectively to the state and the political and civil society élites, there remains a crucial need to reform parliamentary representation in Arab countries. Good governance is unattainable without free and fair parliamentary representation, which is both independent and effective, particularly in giving voice to matters of public interest. Public representation should afford effective scrutiny of the executive and hold it to account. Improving parliamentary representation should not prove too great a challenge given the current lamentable state of affairs. In addition, in the transitional phase towards the society of freedom and good governance, improved parliamentary representation helps both to facilitate the process itself and to root out the various forms of corruption in Arab countries.

To ensure effective and fair parliamentary representation, it is essential to:
1. Establish the principle of total equality among citizens, especially as regards expression and association, voting and standing for election, and related procedures; provide safeguards against disqualifying from parliamentary representation on the basis of gender, social status, culture, religion or other discriminatory feature.
2. Adopt the principle of consensual democracy as a basis for forming the government, so that other parties participate in addition to the party that wins the elections, under a formula and standards to be agreed on. This principle is particularly important in states with subgroups, as it avoids ethnic or sectarian divisions between government and opposition. This also provides opportunities for smaller opposition parties, which would not otherwise have the means to access power.
3. Adopt policies based on affirmative action, at least in the initial transitional stages, which will lead to more democratic conditions. This can take various forms, such as allocating a quota of posts in government and the

legislature, but still maintaining the principle of competition within quotas. Within the legislature this would be a matter for the parties themselves to agree upon, such as setting a specific quota or a minimum ratio of candidates representing these groups.
4. Where a bi-cameral system is in place, authorize the lower, elected assembly to monitor government performance and hold it to account.
5. Establish ethics committees for fairness in parliaments to prevent the deputies from using their political influence for private interests and to call deputies to account for their unfair conduct.

REFORMING ARAB INSTITUTIONAL PERFORMANCE

The institutions of the three sectors of society (the state comprising the government, legislature and judiciary; civil society; and the private sector) should be reformed through applying the principles of rational public administration. Reform would be based on the restriction of authority – public or private - by law and on efficiency, transparency, disclosure, and accountability (in the case of the state, to other institutions and to civil society including the media; and, in the case of government institutions and the legislature, to the general public).

From the perspective of building and utilizing human capabilities, it is evident that institutions providing public services, particularly in education and health care, should function well. Applying the principles of rational public administration in the context of legal reform, as just described, should serve to root out administrative and financial corruption.

The most important reforms for guaranteeing freedom need to be implemented in the educational institutions. A mix of measures relating to administration, curricula, pedagogy and student evaluation methods is required to open the door to freedom, as an ultimate value in itself, and as a means to knowledge acquisition leading to the attainment of human dignity. These reforms should work together to create a mentality of freedom and respect for human rights, and implant the values and tools of good governance in the minds of learners.

Good governance is unattainable without free and fair parliamentary representation, which is both independent and effective.

The most important reforms for guaranteeing freedom need to be implemented in the educational institutions.

The family can make concerted efforts to nurture freedom and encourage enlightened education; and thus prevent any subsequent stages of social development from impairing individual freedoms established at the family levels and enhanced by the school (Chapter 6).

Reform of these two fundamental institutions of society should be complemented by the creation of a social structure supportive of freedom and good governance. First: by combating poverty, the antithesis of human development, by ending the poor acquisition and under-utilization of human capabilities; and second: through the redistribution of income and wealth on a more equitable basis through taxation. These steps would clearly require deep changes in the path of development in the Arab countries.

CORRECTING THE ARAB DEVELOPMENT TRAJECTORY

In Arab countries, especially the wealthier states, the concept of development may be associated with a high standard of living and consumer prosperity, rather than with the establishment of a strong, advanced production system capable of steady growth that provides individuals and society with income, security, vitality and the strength to face the challenges of the time and the world.

The metamorphosis to freedom and good governance in Arab countries requires a qualitative change in development thinking and its dynamics, to secure an economic basis for the progress society desires. It also calls for structural institutional transformation to good governance, which is the safeguard of a rational economic system.

Mobilizing resources, providing incentives for productive investment in human and physical assets, especially those that support knowledge-based production (the second AHDR) and steadily increasing productivity can bring about such a change. Creating a vigorous economic system calls for the acquisition of fundamental human capabilities, the institution of lifelong learning, societal incentives and models that value knowledge and other social changes aimed at rewarding productive work, rather than relying on rents or access to influential groups. It also entails changes to enhance competitiveness and efficiency in Arab economies, and implies an obligation on Arab states to work for distributive justice.

THE REFORM OF CORPORATE GOVERNANCE

The challenge is how to move successfully from institutions of corporate governance that tend to be centralized and heavily relationship-based to those that are more effectively rule-based.

Sound corporate governance also requires the establishment of appropriate laws to protect property rights, enable competitive market forces, foster entrepreneurship and provide an efficient market infrastructure that ensures transparency and accountability. This includes transparency of public tenders, efficient third-party auditing, anti-trust legislation, strict anti-corruption legislation, and eliminating all forms of extra-legal transactions. The development of the region will be hobbled if free enterprise and efficient competition are withheld by a limited or weak legislative structure.

As noted in Chapter 5, three major principles of corporate governance are vital: transparency, accountability, and inclusiveness, which are mutually reinforcing and need to be upheld together.

Transparency is not only an earnest of corporate probity. It also ensures the disclosure of financial information on which corporate accountability to stakeholders rests.

Decision-makers in the private sector need to be held accountable to the public as well as to institutional stakeholders. Accountability is an important deterrent against legal and ethical transgressions, and it is only through swiftly redressing such misdeeds that confidence can be built within a market. Effective supervisory and regulatory boards are one of the means by which firms may be held accountable.

Inclusiveness is one of the core values of good governance everywhere. Inclusiveness means ensuring the equal participation and equal treatment of anyone who has a stake in the governance process and wants to participate in that process. Individuals' basic rights must be defined and protected by creating

The metamorphosis to freedom and good governance in Arab countries requires a qualitative change in development thinking and its dynamics, to secure an economic basis for the progress society desires.

The challenge is how to move successfully from institutions of corporate governance that tend to be centralized and heavily relationship-based to those that are more effectively rule-based.

governance mechanisms for that purpose in addition to providing remedies and recourse guaranteed by rule of law. Within the corporate sector, an area where inclusiveness needs substantial strengthening pertains to the rights of shareholders.

AT THE PAN-ARAB LEVEL

Establishing good governance at the pan-Arab level means replacing the fragmented and change-resistant regional set-up of the present day (Chapter 6) with structural arrangements aiming at integration and based on a new level of political will and commitment. Regional integration would bring its constituent members together in an economic, and possibly also political, union. This would call for more consistency and common standards in social and economic systems as well as the enhancement of general awareness, solidarity and collective thinking among citizens themselves.

The results of the Freedom Survey, (see Figure 7-2), demonstrate the Arab people's aspirations for stronger Arab cooperation, including support for the "Arab Free Citizenship Area" as called for in the AHDRs, and even "complete political unity".

The leading model of this kind is the EU, which recently became an economic and mon-

etary union and is making moves in the political and defence spheres. This experience is distinguished as it has enhanced the effectiveness of the regional organization in two ways: first by giving the regional structure precedence over national structures, empowering it to take decisions which are binding on member states; and second, by providing a broader space for citizens and the social sectors to participate in decision-making processes and scrutiny of its performance. This presupposes that: citizens are entitled to participate in government at the national level; representational bodies are already equipped with extensive legislative powers; there is a partnership between the government, civil society organizations and market institutions; while the judiciary protects the rights of all parties.

The binding nature of decisions taken by the regional organization leads to the adoption of the founding agreement, with the force of law. On this foundation, the regional judicial institution bases its interpretation and rulings on disputes over implementation, whether between citizens and their governments or agencies of the regional body on matters within their competence. The regional body must work transparently. It should publish its decisions in the media and engage citizens in dialogue using information and communica-

Figure 7-2

Preferred forms of stronger Arab cooperation, five Arab countries, Freedom Survey, 2003

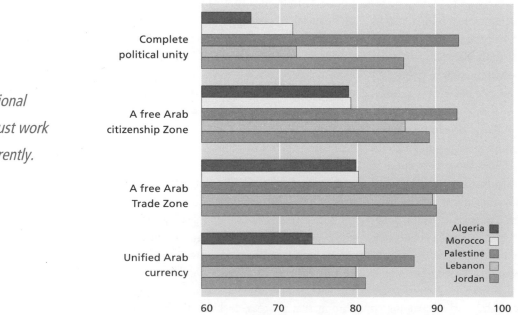

tion technology. It can set up advisory bodies to include representatives of special interest groups and involve parliamentary assemblies in decision-making where the regional authority is involved in implementing the decision. It can also address the people directly through the Internet to create greater awareness and invite their views on regional issues.

As at the international level, regional mechanisms are set up to settle disputes or support preventive diplomacy between states and prepare draft regional agreements for state ratification, which are then integrated by states' into their respective national laws. Treaties may deal, for example, with human rights in general, or matters relating to specific disadvantaged social sectors, such as women, children or people with special needs. The regional body also sets up multi-faceted partnerships with regional civil and economic institutions as well as networks that link national and local institutions and individual citizens directly with regional activities. Networking of this kind is among the most effective tools that information and communications technology can provide to increase participation. Given the significant variations in standards of living both within countries and between states, committees and funds should to be set up to help raise the standard of living of, and enhance the community spirit for the less fortunate social sectors and regions. Finally, the regional organization offers opportunities for treaties or joint measures on common defence and security issues, as well as the potential to negotiate collectively with international bodies and in international forums, which reinforces the capabilities of individual member states.

In particular, it has become necessary for Arab countries to conclude a new Arab Human Rights Convention, fully conforming to the human rights system as a whole as represented by all the components of international human rights law. This treaty should start where other protected rights conventions end and add to, rather than diminish them. The new convention should provide all necessary mechanisms to stop violations at the country and pan-Arab levels. Perhaps the most important of these mechanisms would be an Arab Council of Human Rights and an Arab Court of Human

Rights, which would allow individuals to bring action directly against governments if the national system failed to give them justice. These bodies should be empowered to adopt mandatory resolutions.

The European example however leaves room for innovation in creating an Arab model with broader scope for integration. While the Europeans have succeeded in achieving unity among diverse nationalities, the Arabs have the opportunity to explore the horizons of a single nation, which is still in disarray despite sharing a common culture, language, history and future.

LIBERATION FROM OCCUPATION

Governance reform at the national and pan-Arab levels would guarantee policy consistency

It has become necessary for Arab countries to conclude a new Arab Human Rights Convention.

Figure 7-3

Perception of just solutions to the Palestinian question, five Arab countries, Freedom Survey, 2003

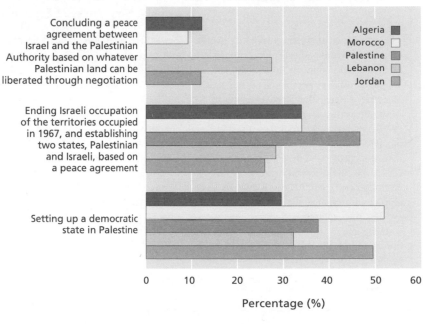

between the aspirations of the Arab people for liberation from occupation, particularly Palestine, figure 7-3, on the one hand, and the objectives and actions of the Arab good governance regime, at the national, pan-Arab and global levels on the other. A good regional governance order would also enhance the prospects of liberation from occupation. This could take the form of support for resistance to occupation or collective bargaining to restore and safeguard Arab rights in international arenas and to act towards their realization. Undoubtedly, the prospect of protecting the legitimate rights of the Arabs improves with the reform of governance at the global level.

As such, governance reform at all three levels: the national, pan-Arab and global, is of crucial importance. Even more important perhaps is that synergy in good governance at all three levels could shield Arabs from the painful experience of occupation in the future.

According to the results of the Freedom Survey, Annex 1, interviewees, particularly those in Palestine, do not expect the current state of affairs to result in a just solution to the Palestinian question. The just solution is represented either by setting up a Palestinian State on the 1967 borders, the preferred option of Palestinians in particular, or by "setting up a democratic State in Palestine".

GOVERNANCE AT THE GLOBAL LEVEL

The Arab region continues to be labelled as volatile and to suffer occupation by outside forces and internal and cross-border conflicts that deprive people of their basic, inalienable rights and impede human development in affected areas. While much of the responsibility for ending such conflicts lies with the parties themselves, the failure of global governance to address and help resolve such conflicts cannot be ignored. This system will need to be reformed to provide effective and peaceful channels for settling disputes and a framework of fair rules that are subscribed to, and implemented by all. The system has to uphold the rule of law on the weak and the strong alike.

The first priority must be reform within the UN to make it the model for good governance at the global level and an effective instrument for protecting peace, security and prosperity throughout the world. This is the faithful translation of the society of freedom and good governance at the global level.

Many ideas have been advanced in this respect, ranging from changing the composition of the United Nations Security Council and limiting the dominance of certain members, to expanding the enforcement authority of General Assembly resolutions.

BOX 7-6:
Excerpts from the Address by the UN Secretary General, Kofi Annan, at the Opening Session of the General Assembly, New York, 21 September 2004.

The prevalence of suffering faced by people around the world and acts of violence reflect our collective failure to uphold the rule of law, and instill respect for it in our fellow men and women. We all have a duty to do whatever we can to restore that respect. To do so, we must start from the principle that no one is above the law, and no one should be denied its protection. Every nation that proclaims the rule of law at home must respect it abroad; and every nation that insists on it abroad must enforce it at home.

At the international level, all states – strong and weak, big and small – need a framework of fair rules, which each can be confident that others will obey. Fortunately, such a framework exists... And yet this framework is riddled with gaps and weaknesses. Too often it is applied selectively, and enforced arbitrarily. It lacks the teeth that turn a body of laws into an effective legal system...Those who seek to bestow legitimacy must themselves embody it; and those who invoke international law must themselves submit to it. Just as, within a country, respect for the law depends on the sense that all have a say in making and implementing it, so it is in our global community. No nation must feel excluded. All must feel that international law belongs to them, and protects their legitimate interests.

Rule of law as a mere concept is not enough. Laws must be put into practice, and permeate the fabric of our lives... It is by reintroducing the rule of law, and confidence in its impartial application, that we can hope to resuscitate societies shattered by conflict...And it is by rigorously upholding international law that we can, and must, fulfill our responsibility to protect innocent civilians from genocide, crimes against humanity and war crimes. As I warned this Assembly five years ago, history will judge us very harshly if we let ourselves be deflected from this task, or think we are excused from it, by invocations of national sovereignty.

I believe we can restore and extend the rule of law throughout the world. But ultimately, that will depend on the hold that the law has on our consciences... Each generation has its part to play in the age-old struggle to strengthen the rule of law for all – which alone can guarantee freedom for all. Let our generation not be found wanting.

What concerns us from the perspective of Arab human development is the establishment of an impartial and effective international authority, which guarantees humanity security, peace and prosperity on a solid basis of human rights and justice for all. The transitional target towards that can be the achievement of "the Millennium Development Goals", which were adopted by an extraordinary international consensus.

A ROLE FOR THE UN AND OTHER INTERNATIONAL AGENCIES

The UN enjoys widespread credibility, particularly among the people, a credential not associated with any other international presence, although this standing fluctuates in some political situations. This credibility can be expected to increase as good governance at the global level advances in the directions mentioned above.

The UN's credibility centres on its fair, constructive and positive role, which is widely accepted, to help peoples and States overcome difficult periods in their history especially in the context of political reform. The UN can play a crucial role in the process of transformation towards good governance and freedom in Arab countries. It can help assure the completion of initial legal reforms guaranteeing civil society organizations the freedom to exist and carry out their activities; it can guarantee that conditions are met for holding free and fair elections and it can provide observers to monitor elections during transitional periods when the electoral system first becomes operational.

This role for the UN should be complemented by stronger co-operative links among global civil society groups, in particular those working for human rights worldwide.

ACHIEVING PEACEFUL POLITICAL ALTERNATION IN ARAB COUNTRIES IN ORDER TO BUILD FREEDOM AND GOOD GOVERNANCE: THE 'IZDIHAR' SCENARIO.

As has become the tradition with the Arab Human Development Reports, what we present here are only the broad outlines of our preferred scenario: first, for Arab society to discuss them, second, to place them within their respective context, and third, to work for them after they are adopted.

In Max Weber's terminology, what is proposed here is a "pure" or ideal type for desired change. If adopted, such a type would most certainly be adapted and modified by each Arab country to reflect its respective characteristics and capabilities.

We formulate here one of the possible trajectories for attaining the "izdihar" scenario. Societal innovation could generate many more, around a sequence of acts leading towards a society of freedom and good governance in Arab countries. In our scenario, the completion of each act leads to the emergence of the next. The sequence of events leading to this historic metamorphosis in the Arab world, according to this one possible trajectory passes through two major stages. The first is total respect for the key freedoms of opinion, expression and association. The second is a historic and peaceful process of negotiation among all dynamic societal forces in Arab countries, including authorities currently in power, aimed at redistributing power in favour of the people at large and establishing the institutional structures of good governance.

Vision dims the further one peers into the future, and prospects for alternatives multiply. We therefore focus on the first opening act of this sequence, it being the closest to us, and the most accessible to reflection. Since this opening act initiates the historic leap towards freedom and good governance in the region, it merits close attention. Indeed, in this light, this first act is so crucial that it represents, in our view, the yardstick by which to judge the seriousness of governance reform in Arab countries.

The opening act is then presented in enough detail to appreciate its dimensions and how it subsequently leads to a sequence of acts representing variations on the trajectory sufficient to launch the region towards freedom and good governance. The formulation of possible sequences of acts, leading to the society of freedom and good governance, is left to the creativity of reform forces in Arab societies, each acting within their own circumstances.

The UN's credibility centres on its fair, constructive and positive role.

This first act is so crucial that it represents, in our view, the yardstick by which to judge the seriousness of governance reform in Arab countries.

ACT 1: LIBERATION OF CIVIL SOCIETY, LAYING THE FOUNDATION FOR COMPREHENSIVE LEGAL AND POLITICAL REFORM

Present-day civil society has its own flaws, brought on by a climate of corruption and restricted freedom.

The curtain rises, so to speak, on a historic process of transformation towards freedom and good governance in the Arab countries through the unleashing of societal forces in order to ensure the emergence of a societal movement for change in service to an Arab renaissance.

The theatrical analogy implies that this historic transformation can only start with such an opening act and will unfold only on its completion. That ending will be marked by the total respect of the key freedoms of opinion, expression and association in Arab countries[3]. These key freedoms must coexist, because freedom of expression, for example, is ineffective if not complemented by freedom of association in both civil and political society, and other rights and freedoms usually follow thereon.

In this opening act, civil society institutions, in particular, acquire autonomy. Their situation changes from one where the executive branch of government licenses them to exist, subject to supervision, intervention and control, to one of absolute freedom to organize and operate under the protection of the rule of law and an independent judiciary.

Present-day civil society has its own flaws, brought on by a climate of corruption and restricted freedom. Legal and organizational reform in this act will therefore incorporate measures to guarantee good governance in those institutions themselves, notably to eliminate financial and administrative corruption and safeguard the public interest.

Initial conditions for this first act to materialize include, in addition to the above, the elimination of all types of marginalization and discrimination against societal groups and an end to all types of exceptional legal arrangements such as emergency laws and exceptional courts. Foundations also need to be set down for the principles of transparency and disclosure in all organizations throughout Arab societies.

As such, this act requires an initial far-reaching legal and organizational reform the crux of which is the guarantee of key freedoms and independence of the judiciary and changes that limit the role of security forces to their original mandate in protecting the security of citizens and the nation.

In this sense, this initial reform is the indispensable prerequisite for the historic process of change, aiming at ensuring freedom and "izdihar" in Arab societies.

The successful enactment of this stage is assured by the development of a public attitude supportive of change and progress; and by the emergence of a societal movement that includes all societal forces that support freedom and good governance. Participants in this movement come from both within and outside the government and particularly from civil society institutions, and are eligible to lead the struggle for freedom and good governance. The realization of this opening act will significantly contribute to the achievement of these two goals.

The successful emergence of this opening act in political alternation is assisted by and guaranteed – particularly in preparation for subsequent acts - by the formation of dynamic pan-Arab networks, with active country-level nodes. These networks would agree on the minimum level of social reconstruction in Arab countries required to ensure an Arab consensus on the previously described historic negotiation and on renaissance objectives, and they would call for it in an effective manner. This would require the mobilization of popular forces and the creation of a climate of change towards the society of freedom and good governance. This in turn would set the stage for

---

BOX 7-7

Guaranteeing freedom for civil society

Current status:
Civil society organizations must be authorized and supervised, with executive authority intervention in their activities.

Desired status:
The law, upheld fairly by an independent judiciary, guarantees freedom of organization and expression for all.

---

[3] We recall that this was the first pillar of the strategic vision for building the knowledge society in Arab countries, AHDR2.

subsequent acts of the "izdihar" scenario to unfold. The chances of the first act succeeding would be enhanced if an "Arab renaissance network" established its own media outlets that would call for these goals, independently of both ruling governments and the profit-seeking sector.

This first act depends as well on an enabling regional and global environment amid the plethora of initiatives and plans competing to influence the Arab future. Perhaps the potential partnership between internally generated and externally motivated reform initiatives, currently under exploration, could foster such a climate.

At the pan-Arab level, a solid Arab consensus on the required legal and institutional reforms would widen the path forward through the first act. This consensus can take the form of an Arab version of the Helsinki Accords.[4] It would centre on a convention to be concluded among Arabs in an Arab city (so to become for example the "Fez Accords" or the "Dubai Accords") that officially opens up the public sphere in Arab countries.

The climate of freedom created by unleashing the key freedoms can be expected to secure the remaining conditions for systemic change: high quality institutions within civil and political societies at the national and regional levels; and to prepare for subsequent acts in the "izdihar" scenario.

EPILOGUE: THE FURTHEST LOTUS TREE[5]

The foregoing pages have made it clear that formidable obstacles stand in the way of a society of freedom and good governance in Arab countries.

But hopefully, they also show that, at the end of this difficult journey, there lies a noble goal, worthy of the hardships endured by those who seek it. That goal is nothing less than a society of freedom. In that place, human dignity is respected and people's basic needs - material, emotional and spiritual - are met.

A society that is always open to the potentials of human progress through the acquisition and effective use of capabilities in the various spheres of human activity, with none subject to unjust force or coercion; a society in which an individual is secure against all adversities. That society is the outcome of human development, the goal which this series of Reports is dedicated to achieving in the Arab world in honour of its entire peoples.

There is a not inconsiderable distance between the present point of departure in Arab countries and this noble destination; and pitfalls and obstacles at the national, regional and global level line the way forward. Perhaps we Arabs have long been reluctant to engage in the social struggle that offers freedom and establishes the society of good governance. It may be that we have been too lenient and that this has invited usurpation by those greedy for what our region has to offer. The cost of our reluctance and passivity is the burdensome legacy that we are left with.

The time has come to make up for the missed opportunities of the past. It is to be hoped that the Arab people will not again fail to take the historic road leading it to its appropriate place in a better, fairer and freer world, one that it will have contributed to bring into being, and in whose benefits it will share.

The Arab world is at a decisive point that does not admit compromise or complacency. Let each rise to the challenge.

This (regional) consensus can take the form of an Arab version of the Helsinki accords.

The time has come to make up for the missed opportunities of the past.

---

[4] In 1975 representatives of 35 States met in Helsinki, capital of Finland, at a conference on security and cooperation in Europe. Negotiations led to the "Helsinki Accords" guaranteeing the principles for freedom and human rights. Participating states undertook to respect human rights for all, without discrimination. They also undertook to encourage and support the effective exercise of civil, political, economic, social and cultural freedoms and rights inherent in the dignity of the human person and necessary at the same time to attain her/his enjoyment of freedom.

[5] A tree in Paradise

References

In English and French

Abed, G.T., 2004
Personal communication with N Fergany

Ahram Hebdo, 2003.
"Réforme ou réformette", Ahram Hebdo, 3-9 décembre 2003.

Al-Ash'al, Abdallah, 2001.
"La mise en oeuvre des mesures coercitives prises par le Conseil de sécurité dans le droit international et le droit interne", Thèse, Paris II, Assas, Paris.

Amnesty International, 2004
International Secretariat, London, website: www.amnesty.org

Ayoubi, Nazih N., 1995.
"Overstating the Arab State: Politics and Society in the Middle East", I.B. Tauris, London.

Barry, Robin, 2002.
"The real roots of Arab anti-Americanism," Foreign Affairs, November-December 2002.

Berlin, Isaiah, 1969.
Four essays on liberty, Oxford University Press, New York.

Brumberg, Daniel, 2003.
"The Trap of Liberalized Autocracy," in: Diamond, Larry et. al., eds., Islam and Democracy in the Middle East, The Johns Hopkins University Press, Baltimore, 2003, pp. 35-47.

Dahl, R. A., 1971.
Polyarchy, Participation and Opposition, Yale University Press, New Haven.

Department of State-Office of Research, 2003
"Iraqi public has wide ranging preferences for a future political system", Washington Document, 21 October 2003.

El-Affendi, Abdelwahab, 1993.
"The Eclipse of Reason: The Media in the Muslim World," Journal of International Affairs, vol. 46, no. 2, Winter 1993.

Fergany, Nader, 1998
Human capital and economic preference in Egypt, Almishkat, Cairo, August 1998.
------------------, 1994
Urban women, work and poverty alleviation in Egypt, Almishkat, Cairo, February 1994

Fuller, G. E., 2004
Islamists in the Arab World, the Dance around Democracy, Carnegie Endowment for International Peace, Washington DC, September 2004.

Gellner, Ernest, 1994.
Conditions of Liberty, Civil Society and its Rivals, Hamish Hamilton, London.

Hayek. F. A., 1978.
The Constitution of Liberty, the University of Chicago Press, Chicago.

Health, Development, Information and Policy Institute, 2004.
"Health and Segregation"

Hook Sidney, 1987.
Paradoxes of Freedom, Prometheus Books, Buffalo, New York.

Hopkins, Nicholas S. and Sadd Eddin Ibrahim, eds., 1997.
Arab Society: Class, Gender, Power and

Development, American University Press, Cairo.

Human Rights Watch, 2003.
"Iraq; Civilians Deaths Needs US Investigation", Human Rights Watch, New York, 21 October 2003 (http://hrw.org/press/2003/10/Iraq102103.htm).

Huntington, Samuel P., 1996
The Clash of Civilisations and the Remaking of the Modern World. Simon & Schuster, New York.

Inglehart, R. (Ed.), 2003
"Human values and social change, findings from the world values surveys". International studies in Sociology and Social Anthropology, Brill, Leiden. Boston.

Kaufmann, Daniel, Aart Kraay and Massimo Mastruzzi, 2003
"Governance Matters III: Governance Indicators for 1996-2002."
The World Bank Policy Research Department Working Papers, First Draft, World Bank, Washington, 30 June 2003; Revised Version, 5 April 2004.

Keane, John, 1998.
Civil Society: Old Challenges, New Visions, Polity Press, Cambridge.

----------------, 1988.
Civil Society and the State: New European Perspectives, Verso, London.

Keddie, Nikki R, and Sayyid Jamal ad-Din, 1972. Sayyid Jamal ad-Din "Al-Afghani": A Political Biography, University of California Press, Berkeley, California.

Kennedy, M. D. and B. Porter, 2000
Negotiating Radical Change, Understanding and extending the lessons of the Polish Round Table Talks, U-M Center for Russian and Eastern European Studies, Ann Arbor, Michigan.

Khalidi, Rashid, 2004,
Resurrecting Empire, Beacon Press, Boston, Massachusetts.

Linz, J. J. and A. Stepan, 1996.
Problems of Democratic Transition and Consolidation: Southern Europe, South America and Post-communist Europe, Johns Hopkins University Press, Baltimore.

Lubbers, Ruud, 2002.
"Statement by Ruud Lubbers- United Nations High Commissioner for Refugees", the Third Committee of the General Assembly, New York, 19 November 2001; UN News Center, 20 February 2002:

Marcuse, Herbert, 1969.
An Essay on Liberation, a Pelican book, Penguin, London.

MEDACT, 2003.
"Continuing collateral damage: the health and environmental costs of war of Iraq", MEDACT, London, November 2003.

Micklethwait, J. and A. Wooldridge, 2003.
A Future Perfect, The Challenge and Promise of Globalization, Random House Trade Paperbacks, New York.

Mill, John Stuart, 1978.
On Liberty, edited with an Introduction by Elizabeth Rapaport, Hackett Publishing Company, Inc., Indianapolis/Cambridge (Originally published in 1859).

Oman, C., 2001
"Corporate Governance and National Development". OECD Development Centre, Technical papers No. 180, September 2001.

Owen, 1992.

Przeworski, Adam, 1988.
"Democracy as a Contingent Outcome of Conflicts," in: Jon Elster and Rune Slagstad (eds.) Constitutionalism and Democracy, Cambridge University Press, Cambridge,

Sadiqi, Larbi, 2004
The Search for Arab Democracy: Discourses and Counter-Discourses. Hurst & Company, London.

Sen, Amartya, 2002.
Rationality and Freedom, The Belknap Press of Harvard University Press, Harvard, Massachusetts.

----------------, 1999.
Development as Freedom, Anchor Books, A Division of Random House, Inc., New York.

----------------, 1988.
On Ethics and Economics, Blackwell publishers, Malden, Massachusetts.

Stepan, Alfred, 2001.
In Arguing Comparative Politics, Oxford University Press.

Transparency International, 2003.
Transparency International Corruption Perceptions Index 2003, Transparency International Website (www.transparency. org).

UN Department of Economic and Social Affairs, 2000.
Building Partnerships for Good Governance: The Spirit and the Reality of South-South Cooperation, United Nations, New York, ST/ESA/PAD/SER. E/6.

UNDP, 1990.
'1990 Human Development Report', Oxford University Press, New York.

Waltz, Susan, 2004
Muslim States' Contributions to International Human Rights Instruments, in Human Rights Quarterly, Vol. 26, Johns Hopkins University Press, Baltimore, November 2004

Waterbury, 1995.

Wiston, 1999.

World Bank, 2003.
Better Governance for Development in the Middle East and North Africa: Enhancing Inclusiveness and Accountability, The World Bank, Washington DC.,

----------------, 2004.
West Bank and Gaza Update, March 2004.

World Health Organization, 2003.
The World Health Report, 2003, WHO, Geneva.

World Values Survey Association, 2004.
World Values Survey, 1995-2001, World Values Survey Association (WVSA), Stockholm. website: www.worldvaluessurvey. org.

Zakaria, F., 2003.
The Future of Freedom, Illiberal Democracy at Home and Abroad, Norton, New York.

Zogby J.J., 2002
What Arabs Think: Values, Beliefs and Concerns, Zogby International/the Arab Thought Foundation. September 2002.

Palestinian Red Crescent Society website, www.palestinercs.org, September 2004.

B'Tselem website, www.btselem.org, September 2004.

Office for the Coordination of Humanitarian affairs. occupied Palestinian territory. Humanitarian Information Fact Sheet January 2005. www.Humanitarianinfo.org/opt/OCHA

UNICEF, At a glance: occupied Palestinian territory.www.unicef.org/infobycountry/opt_1535.html.

UNDP: Millennium Development Goals Report - Palestine,2002.

In Arabic

'Abd al-Khaliq, Farid, 1998/1319.
Mabadi' Dusturiyya fi al-Fiqh al-Islamiyya [Constitutional Principles in Islamic Jurisprudence]. Dar al-Shuruq, 1st ed.,Cairo.

'Abd al-Latif, Kamal, 1999.
Fi Tashrih Usul al-Istibdad: Qira'a fi Nizam al-Adab al-Sultaniyya [On Dissecting the Origins of Despotism: A Reading in the System of Sultanic Letters]. Dar al-Tabi'a, Beirut.
--------------------------, 1992.
Harakat al-Taharrur al-'Arabi: al-Mafhum wal-Ahdaf al-Mumkina [The Arab Liberation Movement: Concept and Achievable Goals].

Abd al-Hakim, Shawqi, 1994.
Turath Sha'bi [Popular Cultural Heritage]. Part 1, Al-Hay'a al-Misriyya al-'Amma lil-Kitab, Cairo.

Al Najjar, Muhammad Rajab, 1995.
Al-Turath al-Qisasi fi al-Adab al-'Arabi [The Narrative Heritage in Arab Literature]. Vol. 1, Dar Al-Salasil, Kuwait.

Al-'Aqqad, 'Abbas Mahmud, 2002
'Abqariyyat 'Umar [The Genius of 'Umar]. Dar Nahdat Misr lil-Tiba'a wal-Nashr, Cairo, February 2002.

Al-'Arawy, Abdallah, 1993.
Mafhum al-Hurriyya [The Concept of Freedom]. Arab Cultural Center, 5th edition, Beirut.

--------------------------, 1988.
Mafhum al-Dawla [The Concept of the State]. Al-Markaz al-Thaqafi al-'Arabi, Beirut.

--------------------------, 1981.
Mafhum al-Hurriyya [The Concept of Freedom]. Arab Cultural Center, 1st edition, Casablanca.

Al-'Awwa, Muhammad Salim, 1998.
Al-Fiqh al-Islami fi Tariq al-Tajdid [Islamic Jurisprudence on the Road to Renewal]. Al-Maktab al-Islami, 2nd ed.

--------------------------------------, 1989.
Fi al-Nizam al-Siyasi lil-Dawla al-Islamiyya [The Political System in the Islamic State]. Dar Al-Shuruq, Cairo.

Al-Afandi, 'Abd al-Wahhab and others, 2002.

Al-Haraka al-Islamiyya wa-Atharuha 'ala al-Istiqrar al-Siyasi fi al-'Alam al-'Arabi [The Islamic Movement and Its Impact on Political Stability in the Arab World]. Markaz al-Imarat lil-Dirasat al-Istiratijiyya, Abu Dhabi.

Al-Ansari, Muhammad Jabir, 1994.
Takwin al-'Arab al-Siyasi wa-Maghza al-Dawla al-Qutriyya [Arab Political Formation and the National State]. Center for Arab Unity Studies, Beirut.

Al-Dajani, Ahmad Sidqi, 1988.
Madrasa 'Arabiyya fi 'Ilm al-Siyasa, [An Arab School of Political Science]. 1st ed., Dar al-Mustaqbal al-'Arabi, Cairo.

Al-Fasi, 'Allal, 1977.
Al- Hurriyya [Freedom]. Matba'at al-Risala, Rabat.

-----------------, 1963/1382.
Maqasidal-Shari'aal-Islamiyyawa-Makarimuha [Islamic Law: Intentions and Qualities]. Maktabat al-Wahda al-'Arabiyya, Casablanca.

Al-Ghanushi, Rashid, 1993.
Al-Hurriyat al-'Amma fi al-Dawla al-Islamiyya [Public Freedoms in the Islamic State]. Center for Arab Unity Studies, Beirut.

Al-Habbabi, Muhammad Aziz, 1972.
Min al-Hurriyyat ila Al-Taharrur [From Freedoms to Emancipation]. Dar al- Ma'arif, Cairo.

Al-Harrani (al-Halabi), Abu Muhammad Al-Hasan ibn 'Ali ibn al-Husayn ibn Shu'ba (4th cent. AH).
Tuhaf al-'Uqul 'an Al ar-Rasul [The Gems of the Minds Concerning the Clan of the Prophet].

Al-Jabiri, Muhammad 'Abid, 1993.
"Ishkaliyyat al-Dimuqratiyya wal-Mujtama'
al-Madani fi al-Watan al-'Arabi" [The
Problematics of Democracy and Civil Society
in the Arab Homeland] in Al-Mustaqbal al-
'Arabi, Issue 167, 1993.

------------------------------, 1992.
Fikr Ibn Khaldon: al-'Asabia wa al-Dawla
[Ibn Khaldoun's Thought: Clannism and the
State] Center for Arab Unity Studies, Beirut.

Al-Jawhary, Muhammad, 1981.
'Ilm Al-Fulklur [The Science of Folklore]. Part
2, Dar Al-Ma'rifa al-Jami'iyya, Alexandria.

Al-Kandahlawi, Muhammad Yusuf, 1997.
Hayat al-Sahaba [The Life of the Companions].
Ed. By, Muhammad al-Tahir Abd al-Bari and
Ahmad Abd al-Fattah Tammam. Vol. 2, Dar
al-Salam lil-Tiba'a wal-Nashr, 1st edition,
Cairo.

Al-Kawakibi, Abd al-Rahman, 1984.
Taba'i' al-Istibdad wa-Masari' al-Istibdad
[The Characteristics of Tyranny and the
Killing Grounds of Enslavement]. Dar Al-
Nafa'is, Beirut.

------------------------------ ("Rahhala K"), n.d.
Taba'i' al-Istibdad wa-Masari' al-Istibdad
[The Characteristics of Tyranny and the
Killing Grounds of Enslavement]. Matba'at
al-Jamaliyya, Cairo.

Al-Ma'afiri, Abu Muhammad 'Abd al-Malik
ibn Hisham, 1418 AH/1998 AD
Sirat Ibn Hisham [Ibn Hisham's Life of the
Prophet], edited and annotated by 'Adil
Ahmad 'Abd al-Mawjud and 'Ali Muhammad
Mu'awwad in Al-Sira al-Nabawiyya [The Life
of the Prophet], Vol.2, Maktabat al-'Abikan,
1st ed., Riyadh.

Al-Manfaluti, Mustafa Lutfi, 1984.
Mu'allafat Mustafa Lutfi al-Manfaluti al-
Kamila Al-Juz' al-Awwal [The Complete
Works of Mustafa Lutfi al-Manfaluti. Part I].
2 vols.. Darf al-Jil, Beirut.

Al-Mawardi, 'Ali ibn Muhammad Habib al-
Basri, 1983/1404.
Al-Ahkam al-Sultaniyya [The Rules of
Government]. Dar al-Fikr lil-Tiba'a wal-
Nashr, Cairo.

Al-Na'ini, al-Muhaqqiq, 1909.
Tanbih al-Umam wa-Tanzih al-Milla [Alerting
the Nation and Exoneration of the Sect].

Al-Naqib, Khaldun Hasan, 1996.
Al-Dawla al-Tasallutiyya fi al-Mashriq al-
'Arabi [The Autocratic State in the Arab
East]. Center for Arab Unity Studies, 2nd edi-
tion, Beirut.

Al-Nasiri, Ahmad ibn Khalid, 1956.
Al-Istiqsa' li-Akhbar Duwal al-Maghrib al-
Aqsa, [Exploring the News of the Maghrib].
Dar al-Kitab, Casablanca.

Al-Qaradawi, Yusuf, 1977a.
Al-Hulul al-Mustawrada wa-Kayf Janat 'ala
Ummatina – Hatmiyyat al-Hall al-Islami
[Imported Solutions and Their Impact on
Our Community: the Dire Need for an Islamic
Solution]. Maktabat Wahba, 3rd ed., Cairo.

------------------------, 1977b.
Al-Khasa'is al-'Amma lil-Islam [The General
Characteristics of Islam]. Dar Ghurayyib lil-
Tiba'a, Cairo.

Al-Razzaz, Munif, 1985.
Al-A'mal al-Fikriyya al-Kamila [Complete
Philosophical Works]. Dar al-Mutawassit,
Munif al-Razzaz Foundation for National
Studies, 1st edition.
Al-Sayyid, Ahmad Lutfi, 1963.
Mabadi' fi al-Siyasa wal-Adab wal-Ijtima'
[Principles of Politics, Literature and
Sociology]. Dar al-Hilal, Cairo.

Al-Sayyid, Radwan, 2002.
Mas'alit Huquq al-Insan fi al-Fikr al-Islami
al-Mu'asir [Human Rights in Contemporary
Islamic Thinking] in Huquq al Insan fi al-Fikr
al-'Arabi – Dirasat fi al-Nusus [Human Rights
in Arab Thinking, Study of the Texts]. Ed. by
Salma al-Khadra' al-Juyusi, Center for Arab
Unity Studies, Beirut.

Al-Shuwayri, Yusuf, 2003.
"Al-Shura wal-Libiraliyya wal-Dimuqratiyya fi al-Watan al-'Arabi: Aliyyat al-Intiqal" in Al-Mustaqbal al-'Arabi, Issue 286, Beirut, March 2003.

Al-Suyuti, al-Hafiz Jalal al-Din,
Tarikh al-Khulafa' [The History of the Caliphs]. Dar al-Kutub al-'Ilmiyya, ?.

Al-Tahtawi, Rifa'a, 1872.
Al-Murshid al-Amin lil-Banat wal-Banin [The Honest Guide for Girls and Boys]. Cairo (also the Complete Works, edited by Muhammad 'Imara, Arab Foundation for Studies and Publication, Beirut, 1973).

----------------------, 1840.
Takhlis al-Ibriz fi Talkhis Bariz [The Golden Summary of Paris]. 2nd edition, Cairo (also the Complete Works, ed. Muhammad 'Imara, The Arab Foundation for Studies and Publication, Beirut, 1973).
Al-Turabi, Hassan, 2003.
Al-Siyasa wal-Hukm [Politics and Governance]. Dar Al Saqi, Beirut-London.

Al-Zayyat, Muntasir, 2003.
"Al-Taghyir bi-Yadina wa-Lan Naqbilhu Abadan min al-Kharij" [Change is in Our Own Hands and We Shall Never Accept Change Imposed from Outside] in Al-Hayat, 28 August 2003.

Arab Institute for Human Rights, 2001.
Dawr al-Tarbiya wal-Ta'lim fi Ta'ziz Huquq al-Insan fi al-'Alam al-Arabi [The Role of Upbringing and Education in Strengthening Human Rights in the Arab World]. Tunis.

Basyuni, Mahmud Sharif, Muhammad Sa'id al-Daqqaq and 'Abd al-'Azim Wazir, 1989.
Huquq al-Insan [Human Rights]. Dar al-'Ilm lil-Malayin, Beirut.

Bishara, 'Azmi, 1998.
Al-Mujtama' al-Madani: Dirasat Naqdiyya [Civil Society: Critical Studies]. Center for Arab Unity Studies, Beirut.

Bunduq, Mahdi, 2003.
Tafkik al-Thaqafa al-'Arabiyya [The Disintegration of Arab Culture]. Supreme Council for Culture, Cairo.
Dirgham, Raghida, 2003.
Al-Taghyirat Ta'ti min Al-Kharij Idha Lam Tanbathiq min Hayawiyya fi al-Dakhil [Changes Come from the Outside If They Do Not Emerge from Internal Dynamism] in Al-Hayat, 1 August 2003.

Fekri, Fathi, 2000
Al-Qanoon Al-Destouri, Al-Ketab Al-Thani, Al- Nezam Al-Hezbi- Solotat Al-Hokm Fi Destour 1971 [Constitutional Law, Book Two, Party System- Governance Authoroties in the 1971 Constitution]. Dar Al-Nahda Al-'Arabia, Cairo.

Fergany, Nader, 1995.
Al-Misriyyun wal-Siyasa [Egyptians and Politics]. Almishkat and Dar al-Mustaqbal al-'Arabi, Cairo.

-------------------, 1992.
'An Naw'iyyat al-Hayat fi al-Watan al-'Arabi [On the Quality of Life in the Arab Homeland]. Center for Arab Unity Studies, Beirut.

General Secretariat, League of Arab States/ Office of the High Commissioner for Human Rights, 2003.
Mashru' Tahdith al-Mithaq al-'Arabi li-Huqouq al-Insan [Updating the Arab Human Rights Charter, a report prepared by the team of Arab expert members of UN human rights bodies charged with revising the draft Arab Human Rights Charter]. December 2003.

Ghalyun, Burhan, 2003a.
Al-Dimuqratiyya al-Mafruda wal-Dimuqratiyya al-Mukhtara: al-Khiyarat al-'Arabiyya al-Rahina fi al-Intiqal ila al-Dimuqratiyya ["Imposed Democracy and Voluntary Democracy: Current Arab Options in the Shift to Democracy"] in Al-Mustaqbal al-'Arabi, no.286, Beirut, March 2003.

----------------, 2003b.
Al-'Arab wa-Tahawwulat al-'Alam, Min Suqut Jidar Birlin ila Suqut Baghdad [The Arabs and World Change, from the fall of the Berlin Wall to the fall of Baghdad]. Al-Markaz al-Thaqafi al-'Arabi, Casablanca.

----------------, 2002.
Huquq al-Insan fi al-Fikr al-Arabi al-Mu'asir [Human Rights in Contemporary Arab Thought] in Huquq al-Insan fi al-Fikr al-'Arabi-Dirasat fi al-Nusus [Human Rights in Arab Thought, Studies of Texts]. Ed. by Salma al-Khadra' al-Juyusi, Centre for Arab Unity Studies, Beirut.

----------------, 2001.
Mu'awwaqat al-Dimuqratiyya fi al-Watan al-'Arabi. Al Jazeera website.

----------------, 1994.
Al-Dimuqratiyya al-'Arabiyya – Judhur al-Azma wa-Afaq al-Numuww [Arab Democracy – The Roots of the Crisis and Horizons for Development] in Burhan Ghalyun, 'Azmi Bishara, Gurj Jaqman, Sa'id Zaydan, Musa al-Budayri: Hawla al-Khiyar Al-Dimuqrati – Dirasat Naqdiyya [The Democratic Option - Critical Studies], 1st edition, Beirut.

Ghulum, Ibrahim Abdallah, 2002
Al-Thaqafa wa-Intaj al-Dimuqratiyya, [Culture and the Production of Democracy]. Arab Foundation for Studies and Publishing, Beirut.

Hanafi, Mustafa, 2002.
"Al-Fikr al-Falsafi fi al-Maghrib: Su'al al-Hurriyya fi Kitabat 'Alal Al-Fasi Al- Falsafiyya" [Philosophical Thought in Morocco: The Question of Freedom in the Writings of 'Allal al-Fasi] in Al-Falsafa fi al-Watan al-'Arabi fi Mi'at 'Amm [A Hundred Years of Philosophy in the Arab Homeland]. Center for Arab Unity Studies, Beirut.

Hananda, Mahir, 2002.
Mafhum al-Hurriyya fi al-Fikr al-Falsafi al-'Arabi al-Mu'asir [The Concept of Freedom in Contemporary Arab Philosophical Thought]. Al-Mustaqbal al-'Arabi, October 2002.

Hijazi, Mustafa, 2001.
Al-Takhalluf al-Ijtima'i: Madkhal ila Sikulujiyyat al-Insan al-Maqhur [Social Backwardness: Point of Entry to the Psychology of the Oppressed Person]. Al-Markaz al-Thaqafi al-'Arabi, 8th ed.

Husayn, Taha, 1996.
Mustaqbal al-Thaqafa fi Misr [The Future of Culture in Egypt]. Dar al-Ma'arif, 2nd edition, Cairo.

Ibrahim, Sa'd al-Din, 2003.
"Na'm bi Yad 'Amr...In Lam Tusari' Aydina ila al-Taghyir" [Yes to the Hand of the Other...As Long As Our Hands Do Not Hasten to Change] in Al-Hayat, 13 August 2003.

------------------ (ed.), 1996.
Al-Mujtama' wal-Dawla fi al-Watan al-'Arabi [Society and State in the Arab Homeland]. Center for Arab Unity Studies, 2nd edition, Beirut.

------------------, 1991.
Al-Mujtama' al-Madani wal-Tahawwul al-Dimuqrati fi al-Watan al-'Arabi [Civil Society and Democratic Transformation in the Arab Homeland]. Matabi' al-Ahram al-Tijariyya, Qalyoub.

Ibrahim, Zakariyya, 1957.
Mushkilat al-Hurriyya [The Problem of Freedom]. Maktabat Misr, 3rd edition.

Jid'an, Fahmi, 2002.
"Al-Ta'a wal-Ikhtilaf fi Daw' Huquq al-Insan fi al-Islam" [Obedience and Disagreement in the Light of Human Rights in Islam] in Huquq al-Insan fi al-Fikr al-'Arabi – Dirasat Al-Nusus [Human Rights in Arab Thought] ed. Salma al-Khadra' al-Juyusi, Center for Arab Unity Studies, Beirut.

------------------, 1988.
Usus al-Taqaddum 'ind Mufakkiri al-Islam fi al-'Alam al-'Arabi al-Hadith [The Foundations of Progress according to Islamic Thinkers in the Contemporary Arab World]. Dar Al-Shuruq, 3rd edition, Amman.

Kawtharani, Wajih, 2002.
Min al-Tanzimat ila al-Dustur – Huquq al-Insan fi Nusus Kuttab al-Nahda, [From the Tanzimat to the Constitution: Human Rights in the Writers of the Renaissance] in Huquq al-Insan fi al-Fikr al-'Arabi [Human Rights in Arab Thought]. Ed. by Salma al-Khadra' al-Juyusi, Center for Arab Unity Studies, Beirut.

Khashana, Rashid, 2003.
Tunis ba'd 16 'Amm [Tunisia after 16 years] in Al-Hayat, 3 November 2003

Khayr al-Din (al-Tunusi), 1972.
Aqwam al-Masalik fi Ma'rifat Ahwal al-Mamalik [The Straightest Path to Knowledge of the Conditons of Nations]. Matba'at al-Dawla, 1st ed., Tunis, 1284 A.H. (also: Al-Dar al-Tunusiyya, ed. by Monsif al-Shinufi, 1972).

League of Arab States, Arab Fund for Economic and Social Development, The Arab Monetary Fund, The Organization of Arab Petroleum Exporting Countries, various dates.
Al-Taqrir al-Iqtisadi al-'Arabi al-Muwahhad [The Consolidated Arab Economic Report] 1998-2003. www.amf.ae.org.

Luciani, Giacomo, 1995.
"Al-Ri' al-Nafti wal-Azma al-Maliyya lil-Dawla wal-Taharrauk nahwa al-Dimuqratiyya" [Oil Revenue, the Financial Crisis of the State and the Move Towards Democracy] in Salama, Ghassan Dimuqratiyya bi-dun Dimuqratiyyin [Democracy without Democrats]. Center for Arab Unity Studies, Beirut, p 175-206.

Majalli, Fu'ad, 2002.
"Huquq al-Insan fi al-Maqala al-Ibda'iyya al-'Arabiyya hatta 'Am 1950" [Human Rights in Creative Writings in Arabic to 1950] in Huquq al-Insan fi al-Fikr al-'Arabi – Dirasat Al-Nusus [Human Rights in Arab Thought]. Ed. Salma al-Khadra' al-Juyusi, Center for Arab Unity Studies, Beirut.

Makki, Ahmad, 1990.
Al-Dimuqratiyya, Tatabiq al-Tawari' wa-Ifsad al-Taba'i': Ru'ya Tarikhiyya li-Haqq al-Tafawud wa-'Ilaqatihi bil-Tawari' [Democracry, the Application of Emergencies and the Corrupting of Characters: A Historical View of the Right to Negotiation and Its Relationship to Emergencies].

Murqus, Ilyas, 1997.
Naqd al-'Aqlaniyya al-'Arabiyya [A Critique of Arab Rationalism]. Dar al-Hisad, Damascus.

Nassar, Nasif, 2004.
Bab al-Hurriyya, Inbithaq al-Wujud bil-Fi'l [Gateway to Freedom, the Eruption of Existence Through Action]. Dar Al-Tali'a, Beirut.

----------------, 2000.
"Al-Nahda al-'Arabiyya al-Thaniya wa-Tahaddi al-Hurriyya" [The Second Arab Renaissance and the Challenge of Freedom] in Al-Nahda al-'Arabiyya al- Thaniya [The Second Arab Renaissance]. Edited and introduced by Ghassan Abd al-Khaliq, Abd al-Hamid Shuman Foundation, Al-Mu'assasa al-'Arabiyya lil-Dirasat wal-Nashr, Amman-Beirut.

Nusayba, Sari, 1995.
Al-Hurriya bayn al-Hadd wal-Mutlaq [Freedom, Limited or Absolute?]. Dar al-Saqi, Beirut–London.

Palestinian submission to the International Court of Justice, 88-89, in Arabic.

Sa'b, Hasan, 1981.
Al-Islam wal-Insan [Islam and Mankind]. Dar al-'Ilm lil-Malayin, Beirut.

--------------, 1975.
Islam al-Hurriyya La Islam al-'Ubudiyya [Islam as Freedom Not as Slavery]. Dar al-'Ilm lil-Malayin, Beirut.

Salama, Ghassan (ed.), 1995.
Dimuqratiyya bi-dun Dimuqratiyyin [Democracy without Democrats]. Center for Arab Unity Studies, Beirut.

Salama, Ghassan et al. (ed.s), 1989.
Al-Umma wal-Dawla wal-Indimaj fi al-Watan

al-'Arabi [The Community, The State and Integration in the Arab Homeland]. Center for Arab Unity Studies, Beirut.

Salama, Yusuf, 2002.
"Ishkaliyyat al-Hurriyya wa-Huquq al-Insan fi al-Fikr al-'Arabi al-Islami al-Hadith" [The Problematic of Freedom and Human Rights in Modern Islamic Arab Thought] in Huquq al-Insan fi al-Fikr al-'Arabi [Human Rights in Arab Thought]. Ed. by Salma al-Khadra' al-Juyusi, Center for Arab Unity Studies, Beirut.

Salim, Abd al-Rahman, 1999/1420.
Al-Rasul: Hayatuh wa-Tatawwur al-Da'wa al-Islamiyya fi 'Asrih [The Prophet: His Life and the Development of Islamic Propaganda in His Epoch]. Dar al-Fikr al-'Arabi, 1st ed., Cairo.

Sha'ban, Abd al-Husayn, 2004.
Mu'anat al-Mujtama' al-Madani al-'Iraqi min al-Istibdad al-Muzmin ila Fawda al-Ihtilal [The Sufferings of Iraqi Civil Society: from Chronic Tyranny to the Chaos of Occupation]. International and Regional Conference on Democracy and Human Rights, Sanaa, January 2004.

Shams al-Din, Muhammad Mahdi, n.d.
Nizam al-Hukm wal-Idara fi al-Islam [The System of Governance and Administration in Islam].

Sharabi, Hisham, 1992.
Al-Mujtama' al-Abawi wa-Ishkaliyyat Takhalluf al-Mujtama' al-'Arabi [Patriarchal Society and the Problematic of the Backwardness of Arab Society]. Center for Arab Unity Studies, Beirut.

-------------------, 1990.
"Al-Naqd al-Hadari lil-Mugtama' al-'Arabi fi al-Qarn al-'eshreen" [Cultural Critique of Arab Society in the Twentiteh Century] Center for Arab Unity Studies, Beirut.

Tarabishi, George, 2004.
"Limadha Inhasar al-'Unf fi al-Mujtama'at al-Dimuqratiyya wa-fi ma baynaha?" [Why Has Violence Been Contained Within and Among Democratic Societies?] in Al-Hayat, 30 May, 2004.

-------------------, 1999.
"Al-Idiyulujiyya al-Thawriyya wa-Istihalat al-Dimuqratiyya" [Revolutionary Ideology and the Impossibility of Democracy] in Al-Dimuqratiyya wal-Ahzab fi al-Buldan al-'Arabiyya: al-Mawaqif wal-Makhawif al-Mutabadila [Democracy and Parties in Arab Countries: stands and mutual fears]. Ed. by 'Ali Khalifa al-Kawwari, Center for Arab Unity Studies, Beirut.

United Nations High Commission for Human Rights, 2002.
"Huquq al-Insan: Majmu'at Sukuk Duwaliyya" [Human Rights: a Collection of International Legal Instruments] in Sukuk 'Alamiyya [Global Legal Instruments] Vol.I, Part I, New York, Summer 2002.

Waqidi, Muhammad, 1990.
Bina' al-Nazariyya al-Falsafiyya – Dirasat fi al-Falsafa al-'Arabiyya al- Mu'asira [Constructing Philosophical Theory – Studies in Contemporary Arab Philosophy]. Dar Al-Tali'a, Beirut.

Zurayq, Kustantin, 1981.
Fi Ma'rakat al-Hadara [On the Battle for Civilization]. Dar al-'Ilm lil- Malayin, 4th ed., Beirut.

ANNEX I. MEASUREMENT OF FREEDOM IN ARAB COUNTRIES

INTRODUCTION

In general, the measurement of freedom and governance in Arab countries suffers from weak databases, subjectivity in the identification of indicators, and a scarcity of indicators derived from solid empirical field studies that capture a representative range of popular opinions.

Starting from the planning stage, the AHDR team aimed to address these measurement problems by adopting two approaches. The first was to conduct a secondary analysis of the results of the World Values Survey 2003 (WVS). This extensive international study, which includes 96 countries throughout the world, provides an opportunity to compare Arab and other countries in the world with respect to elements of freedom and governance. The AHDR team's secondary analysis focused on comparing the Arab countries included in this large international study (five at the time of writing) with a number of non-Arab countries, all enjoying acceptable levels of democratic governance but varying in location. Results of this approach are relayed throughout this Report.

This analysis was based on field surveys carried out in a number of countries including five Arab (Algeria, Egypt, Jordan, Morocco, and Saudi Arabia[1]) comprising more than half of the Arab population. For comparison purposes, indicators on the Arab countries are contrasted with those on nine non-Arab countries from Latin America, Africa and Asia that are considered to enjoy acceptable levels of democracy (Argentina, Bangladesh, Brazil, Indonesia, Nigeria, Pakistan, South Korea, South Africa and Turkey).[2]

It is important to note that the perspective from which the WVS was designed differs from that of this report and its concepts. In addition, its field studies have some data limitations when it comes to Arab countries for essentially the same reasons that constrain other surveys in the Arab region.

The second approach consisted of striving to enrich knowledge on the measurement of freedom and governance in Arab countries through conducting controlled field surveys on opinions relating to the concept of freedom, the level of enjoyment of freedom and change therein over time, and means of expanding freedom.

FREEDOM SURVEY, ARAB HUMAN DEVELOPMENT REPORT

To overcome the deficient measurement of freedom used in the previous AHDRs to raise the issue of freedom in Arab countries, and to better serve the rich concept of freedom adopted in the present Report (chapter one), the Report team, in collaboration with reputable survey firms in Arab countries, designed a field survey to gauge the opinion of Arab populations with regard to the definition of freedom and the extent of enjoyment of freedom in their respective countries. The design called for polling weighted representative samples of Arab citizens, 18 years of age and above, selected to ensure gender balance.

The original hope was that the survey could be conducted in a large number of Arab countries. This hope, however, was frustrated by the general constraints faced by empirical research in Arab countries. It reflects restrictions on freedom of research and on the generation of knowledge in the region. The problem was compounded, no doubt, by the sensitive nature

---

[1] Differences among Arab States in terms of elements of the questionnaire are to be noted.

[2] Presented results in the graphs included in the Report represent simple arithmetic averages of these nine countries.

of the subject of this report. These constraints compound the paucity of data and information in these areas compared to other developmental spheres in Arab countries.

Based on previous experience, the field survey team did not entertain the possibility of implementing the survey in some Arab countries where the conduct of field surveys was clearly not possible. Among those countries approached, at least one Arab country (Egypt) refused to grant the permit required to conduct a field survey. In another country (Morocco), questionnaire items relating to corruption in the police and the army were excluded from the survey.

At the time of preparing this analysis, survey results were available for only five Arab countries (Algeria, Jordan, Lebanon, Morocco and Palestine), comprising about one quarter of the Arab population (more than 70 million people), located in both eastern and western Arab countries.

In terms of coverage, the survey sample is below the ambition of representing the totality of Arab peoples. However, and despite restriction on freedom and scientific research and lack of knowledge about measurements of freedom in the Arab countries, one is comforted that information made available by the limited sample is still a useful contribution. We hope that a day will come when such a research is easily conducted towards enriching freedom and knowledge alike.

MAJOR CHARACTERISTICS OF THE SURVEY SAMPLES

The survey included at least 1,000 cases providing a representative sample of the population in each of the five Arab countries (table AI.3).

According to the original design, survey samples were divided equally between women and men and provided for strong representation (no fewer than 250 respondents) of two generations, the older and the younger, with a gap of 35 years (figure AI.1).

The distribution of the survey samples by residence (rural/urban) and educational level as well as by age and gender is shown in table AI.3.

QUALITY INDICATORS OF SURVEY RESULTS

Percentage of Missing Observations

In less developed countries, opinion surveys face considerable problems that are exacerbated when the topic is thorny from one perspective or another. In these countries, such surveys are hampered by the fact that respondents might lack the knowledge or intellectual ability to comprehend the issues raised and form an opinion about them. This is normally reflected in a "do not know" response. When the respondent does have these two elements, knowledge and ability, and formulates an opinion, s/he might lack the courage to express it to avert a real or perceived punishment. This is reflected in survey results in the form of responses such as "no opinion" or "refused to answer".

Procedurally, "do not know" and "no opinion" and "refused to reply" responses are considered as missing observations. The effective impact of missing observations is that it reduces the sample size proportionally in relation to each of the survey items with variations from one item to the other. The impact of this loss is minimized when the sample size is initially large, as in our case, since the number of responses remains reasonably high despite the missing data. Conceptually, the high rate of missing observations indicates the sensitivity of the relevant survey elements. Technically

Figure AI.1

Freedom Survery, 2003 Sample distribution, by age and gender in Arab countries (%)

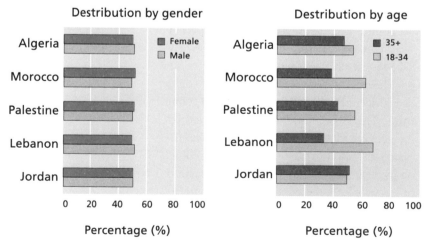

speaking, a large proportion of missing observations, especially with respect to non-controversial issues, indicates the low quality of a field survey and its conduct.

The average share of missing observations in the results of the Freedom Survey in the five countries about 15 per cent. If we take into consideration the rather high percentage of missing observations for some of the more sensitive items of the questionnaire in the Arab context, the percentage of missing observations declines to levels that are generally acceptable in opinion surveys.

It is to be noted that the survey results presented in the report refer to the responses of the total number of those interviewed during the survey, including the missing observations.

There are a number of the "opinion exploring" elements in the freedom survey in which missing observations rose to a great extent. This reflects, in our opinion, the extreme sensitivity of the issues raised in the Arab context or in specific Arab countries. These issues include:

• liberation from occupation, foreign military bases and foreign influence; particularly in Jordan, Morocco, and Algeria.

• minority freedoms, especially in Algeria, Jordan and Morocco;

• prevalence of corruption in the judiciary, police and army, especially in Morocco (where all observations were lost) and Algeria.

Strangely, however, this sensitivity extended to issues that are relatively non-controversial such as:

• freedom of thought and belief, especially in Algeria and Jordan;

• freedom of opinion, expression, association, and organization especially in Jordan;

• freedom of property, movement, marriage and economic activity, especially in Jordan and Morocco.

These results could mean that these freedoms are rather fragile in the countries concerned, or that the sensitivity of the controversial issues extended to responses to other elements.

SIGNIFICANCE OF THE AVAILABLE RESULTS

The results of the AHDR Freedom Survey

BOX AI-1

Description of survey samples

Jordan
Sampling areas: All governorates were covered. The country was divided into strata based on the results of the census of population and housing that was conducted by the Department of Statistics in 1994. The rural and urban segments of each governorate and each of the five main cities (Amman, Ar-Rossifa, Irbid, Wadi Sir and Zarqa) were considered a separate sector.
Sample selection method
Multistage stratified cluster sampling: Sectors were divided into clusters, each containing about a number of households (about 80 households on average in each cluster). Samples were drawn from clusters in each sector, proportionate to size, within each stratum. Finally, systematic sampling was adopted to select 10 households from each cluster.

Lebanon
Sampling areas: Administrative Beirut, Mount Lebanon, North, Beqaa, and the South.
Sampling units selection criteria: Residence (urban/rural), gender (male/female) and social status (household: rich, middle class, and poor).
Sampling selection method: Cluster sampling.

Weighting: Self-weighted.
Morocco
Sampling areas: Casablanca, Fez, Kenitra, Meknes, Marrakesh, Rabat and Settat.
Sampling units selection criteria: Region, residence (urban/ rural) and socio-economic status.
Sampling selection method: Quota sampling with reference to a predetermined itinerary.
Weighting: Self-weighted.

Palestine
Sampling areas: West Bank and Gaza; cities, villages and refugee camps.
Sampling units selection criteria: Residence (urban/ rural/ camps) and gender.
Sampling selection method: Probability sampling with reference to a predetermined itinerary.
Weighting: Self-weighted sample.

Algeria
Sampling units selection criteria: Region, residence (urban/ rural) and socio-economic status.
Sampling selection method: Quota sampling with reference to a predetermined itinerary.
Weighting: Self-weighted.

---

are quite strongly consistent with known and expected information on freedom and governance in Arab countries, as shown by the evidence presented throughout the present Report. They also reflect some of the known characteristics of the five countries/territory covered. These factors raise the level of confidence in the results of the surveys. Needless to say, as Arab countries embark on the historic transformation towards a society of freedom and good governance, the day will come in which such surveys can be conducted freely and regularly. Such a development would in itself surely accelerate the pace of the progress towards freedom and good governance.

The results of the surveys did not differ significantly by gender or generation, especially with respect to the three major dimensions: definition of freedom, extent of enjoyment thereof and change therein during the five years preceding the survey. This can be taken as an indication of a broad societal consensus on the main results of the AHDR 2004 Freedom Survey.

OPINION POLL QUESTIONNAIRE

The questionnaire used in the opinion poll for the survey follows.

Confidential Data

QUESTIONNAIRE

Public Opinion Poll
(November) 2003

Country of Study		
Jordan	1	
Egypt	2	I_I
Lebanon	3	
Palestine	4	

Questionnaire No.	5
Questionnaire Number	6

Introductory Data

1. Governorate: _____   I__II__I

2. District: _____   I__I

3. Sub-District: _____   I__I

4. Township : _____   I__I

5. Community: _____   I__II__I

6. Block No.: _____   I__II__II__II__II__I

7. Cluster No: _____   I__II__II__II__I

8. Bldg. No.: _____   I__II__II__I

9. House No.: _____   I__II__II__I

10. Household Serial No.: _____   I__II__II__I

11. Number of Household Members:_____   I__II__I

Household Visit Result	First Visit	Household Visit Result	First Visit
Occupied	1	Interview completed	1
Permanently closed	2	Required person is out	2
Empty	3	No qualified person	3
Used for non residence purposes	4	Travelling away	4
No longer exists	5	Sick / invalid / elderly	5
Refused interview	6	Refused interview	6
Other (Specify): _____	7	Other (Specify): _____	7

	Original	1
Interview completed	Substitute	2

Work Progress

Interviewer	Supervisor	Coder	Data Entry Operator
Name:	Name:	Name:	Name:
Date: / / 2003	Date: / /2003	Date: / /2003	Date: / / 2003

Introduction

Good morning/ Good evening. I am -------------- from --------------------, an independent organization specialized in the field of studies carried out by talking to people and obtaining their opinions on specific issues.
The organization is now conducting a survey on the issue of freedoms, and I would like you to give me some of your time to answer some questions. I assure you that the information will remain confidential and will be used only for professional research purposes.
(If the respondent is not a national of the survey country and has been living there for less than five years, end the interview).

Use the second column in the table below to record the ages of all family members who are 18 years old and above, starting with the eldest, and specify the sex in the table).
The intersection of the number of the youngest family member with the serial number of the household visit in the block specifies the person eligible for the interview.

Please tell me about the family members (males/ females) who are 18 years old and above.

Respondent's Selection Table

Sex:		1 - Male			2 - Female					|_|				

Household member number	Household members 18 years old and above, starting with the eldest	Serial Number of the Household														
		1	2	3	4	5	6	7	8	9	10	11	12	13	14	15
1		1	1	1	1	1	1	1	1	1	1	1	1	1	1	1
2		2	1	2	1	2	1	2	1	2	1	1	1	2	1	2
3		3	2	1	3	2	1	3	2	1	3	2	1	3	2	1
4		4	3	2	1	4	3	2	1	4	3	2	1	4	3	2
5		5	4	3	2	1	5	4	3	2	1	5	4	5	2	1
6		6	5	4	3	2	1	6	5	4	3	2	1	6	5	4

Note to the interviewer: Please circle ◯ the corresponding response.

100	Are you willing to take part in this poll?

Yes	1	
No	2 End interview	|_|

SECTION ONE

(Interviewer: Ask questions 104/105/106 for each of the items listed in the table below.)

101 To what extent do you think that (freedom from occupation) relates to your total concept of freedom? Does it relate to a large extent, a moderate extent, a small extent or not at all?

102 To what extent do you think that (freedom from occupation) is secured in -------------- (state the name of the survey country)? (Interviewer: If the answer was "to a large extent", move to second item in the table below.)

103 Do you think that (freedom from occupation) in ------------- (state the name of the survey country) has improved, has stayed at the same level or has deteriorated over the last five years?

	Question 101 Extent to which it is related to the concept of total freedom:							Question 102 Freedom from ------- secured to this extent:							Question 103 State of freedom from (------) over the last five years:					
	Large	Moderate	Small	Not related at all	Don't know	Refused to answer		Large	Moderate	Small	Not related at all	Don't know	Refused to answer		Improved	Stayed at same level	Deteriorated	Don't know	Refused to answer	
1. Freedom from occupation	1	2	3	4	8	9	|_|	1	2	3	4	8	9	|_|	1	2	3	8	9	|_|
2. Freedom from military bases	1	2	3	4	8	9	|_|	1	2	3	4	8	9	|_|	1	2	3	8	9	|_|
3. Freedom from foreign influence	1	2	3	4	8	9	|_|	1	2	3	4	8	9	|_|	1	2	3	8	9	|_|
4. Freedom from hunger	1	2	3	4	8	9	|_|	1	2	3	4	8	9	|_|	1	2	3	8	9	|_|
5. Freedom from sickness	1	2	3	4	8	9	|_|	1	2	3	4	8	9	|_|	1	2	3	8	9	|_|
6. Freedom from ignorance	1	2	3	4	8	9	|_|	1	2	3	4	8	9	|_|	1	2	3	8	9	|_|
7. Freedom from lack of income	1	2	3	4	8	9	|_|	1	2	3	4	8	9	|_|	1	2	3	8	9	|_|
8. Freedom from poverty (lack of basic human capabilities: health, education, social and political participation)	1	2	3	4	8	9	|_|	1	2	3	4	8	9	|_|	1	2	3	8	9	|_|

(Interviewer: Ask questions 104/105/106 for each of the items listed in the table below.)

104   To what extent do you think that (freedom of thought) relates to your total concept of freedom? Does it relate to a large extent, a moderate extent, a small extent or not at all?

105   To what extent do you think that (freedom of thought) is secured in -------------- (state the name of the survey country) without considerable obstacles?
(Interviewer: If the answer was "to a large extent", move to second item in the table below).

106   Do you think that (freedom of thought) in ------------- (state the name of the survey country) has improved, has stayed at the same level or has deteriorated over the last five years?

	Question 104 — Extent to which it is related to the concept of total freedom:							Question 105 — (Freedom of thought) secured without considerable obstacles to this extent in ------- (survey country):							Question 106 — State of freedom of (-----) over the last five years:					
	Large	Moderate	Small	Not related at all	Don't know	Refused to answer		Large	Moderate	Small	Not related at all	Don't know	Refused to answer		Improved	Stayed at same level	Deteriorated	Don't know	Refused to answer	
1. Freedom of thought	1	2	3	4	8	9	l_l	1	2	3	4	8	9	l_l	1	2	3	8	9	l_l
2. Freedom of faith	1	2	3	4	8	9	l_l	1	2	3	4	8	9	l_l	1	2	3	8	9	l_l
3. Freedom of opinion and expression	1	2	3	4	8	9	l_l	1	2	3	4	8	9	l_l	1	2	3	8	9	l_l
4. Freedom of gathering and organization	1	2	3	4	8	9	l_l	1	2	3	4	8	9	l_l	1	2	3	8	9	l_l
5. Independence of the media (from authority and money)	1	2	3	4	8	9	l_l	1	2	3	4	8	9	l_l	1	2	3	8	9	l_l
6. Freedom of union and professional organizations	1	2	3	4	8	9	l_l	1	2	3	4	8	9	l_l	1	2	3	8	9	l_l
7. Freedom of civil and cooperative associations	1	2	3	4	8	9	l_l	1	2	3	4	8	9	l_l	1	2	3	8	9	l_l
8. Freedom of religious organizations	1	2	3	4	8	9	l_l	1	2	3	4	8	9	l_l	1	2	3	8	9	l_l
9. Freedom of property	1	2	3	4	8	9	l_l	1	2	3	4	8	9	l_l	1	2	3	8	9	l_l
10. Freedom of movement within the country	1	2	3	4	8	9	l_l	1	2	3	4	8	9	l_l	1	2	3	8	9	l_l
11. Freedom of marriage	1	2	3	4	8	9	l_l	1	2	3	4	8	9	l_l	1	2	3	8	9	l_l
12. Freedom of economic transactions	1	2	3	4	8	9	l_l	1	2	3	4	8	9	l_l	1	2	3	8	9	l_l
13. Equality before the law	1	2	3	4	8	9	l_l	1	2	3	4	8	9	l_l	1	2	3	8	9	l_l
14. Gender equality	1	2	3	4	8	9	l_l	1	2	3	4	8	9	l_l	1	2	3	8	9	l_l
15. Freedom of minorities – if available – to use their language	1	2	3	4	8	9	l_l	1	2	3	4	8	9	l_l	1	2	3	8	9	l_l
16. Freedom of minori-ties – if available – to practise their own culture	1	2	3	4	8	9	l_l	1	2	3	4	8	9	l_l	1	2	3	8	9	l_l
17. Freedom of minorities – if available – to practise their own religious rites	1	2	3	4	8	9	l_l	1	2	3	4	8	9	l_l	1	2	3	8	9	l_l
18. Right to organize opposing political communities	1	2	3	4	8	9	l_l	1	2	3	4	8	9	l_l	1	2	3	8	9	l_l
19. Presence of significant opposition that has the opportunity to influence decisions	1	2	3	4	8	9	l_l	1	2	3	4	8	9	l_l	1	2	3	8	9	l_l
20. Complete indepen-dence of the courts	1	2	3	4	8	9	l_l	1	2	3	4	8	9	l_l	1	2	3	8	9	l_l
21. Fighting corruption	1	2	3	4	8	9	l_l	1	2	3	4	8	9	l_l	1	2	3	8	9	l_l
22. Transparent government	1	2	3	4	8	9	l_l	1	2	3	4	8	9	l_l	1	2	3	8	9	l_l
23. Government accountability	1	2	3	4	8	9	l_l	1	2	3	4	8	9	l_l	1	2	3	8	9	l_l
24. Freedom of minorities – if available – to self-govern	1	2	3	4	8	9	l_l	1	2	3	4	8	9	l_l	1	2	3	8	9	l_l
25. Electing leaders of central government through free and honest elections	1	2	3	4	8	9	l_l	1	2	3	4	8	9	l_l	1	2	3	8	9	l_l
26. Electing leaders of local government through free and honest elections	1	2	3	4	8	9	l_l	1	2	3	4	8	9	l_l	1	2	3	8	9	l_l
27. Electing powerful representatives to the legislative through free and honest elections	1	2	3	4	8	9	l_l	1	2	3	4	8	9	l_l	1	2	3	8	9	l_l

Section Two

A. Women and Society

I will read to you a number of statements. Please tell me the extent to which you agree or disagree with

201   To what extent do you agree that (girls have the same right to education as boys)? (Interviewer: Ask about all the items in the table below.)

	I agree to this extent :						
	Large	Moderate	Small	I don't agree	I don't know	Refused to answer	
1. Girls have the same right to education as boys.	1	2	3	4	8	9	I__I
2. Women have the same right to work as men.	1	2	3	4	8	9	I__I
3. Women have the same right to political action as men.	1	2	3	4	8	9	I__I
4. A woman's children have the right to acquire her nationality the same as a man's children have the right to acquire his nationality.	1	2	3	4	8	9	I__I
5. A woman has the right to assume a judiciary position.	1	2	3	4	8	9	I__I
6. A woman has the right to assume the position of Minister.	1	2	3	4	8	9	I__I
7. A woman has the right to assume the position of Prime Minister.	1	2	3	4	8	9	I__I
8. A woman has the right to assume the position of Head of State.	1	2	3	4	8	9	I__I

B. Activities of the Council of Deputies/ Parliament

202   To what extent do you think that the parliament (performs its legislative role effectively)? (Interviewer: Ask about all the items in the table below.)

	Parliament performs its legislative role to this extent:			Does not perform this role at all	I don't know	Refused to answer	
	Large	Moderate	Small				
1. Performs its legislative role effectively	1	2	3	4	8	9	I__I
2. Controls the Government's work effectively	1	2	3	4	8	9	I__I
3. Holds the Government accountable effectively	1	2	3	4	8	9	I__I

C. Courts

203   Do you have confidence in going to the courts (read):

	Constantly	Occasionally	Rarely	I don't know	Refused to answer	
1. In civil disputes	1	2	3	8	9	I__I
2. In financial and economic disputes	1	2	3	8	9	I__I
3. In disputes relating to freedoms	1	2	3	8	9	I__I

D. The media

I will read to you a number of statements. Please tell me the extent to which you agree or disagree with

204   To what extent do you think that the (government) media in ------------- are (Interviewer: State the name of survey country, then read and describe the extent.):

	Extent			Not / does not (-----) at all	I don't know	Refused to answer	
	Large	Moderate	Small				
1. Honest	1	2	3	4	8	9	I__I
2. Presents the opinion and the other opinion	1	2	3	4	8	9	I__I
3. Contributes to the acquisition of knowledge	1	2	3	4	8	9	I__I

205 To what extent do you think that the (non-government) media in ------------- are (Interviewer: State the name of survey country, then read and describe the extent):

	Extent			Not/ does not (-----) at all	I don't know	Refused to answer	
	Large	Moderate	Small				
1. Honest	1	2	3	4	8	9	I_I
2. Presents the opinion and the other opinion	1	2	3	4	8	9	I_I
3. Contributes to the acquisition of knowledge	1	2	3	4	8	9	I_I

E. Corruption

206 To what extent do you think that (corruption) in ------------ (Interviewer: State the name of survey country.) is common (read):

Common to a large extent	1
Common to a moderate extent	2
Common to a small extent	3
Not common at all	4
I don't know	8
Refused to answer	9

I_I

} move to Q 211

207 In which of the following areas do you think that corruption is the most common in ----------- (State name of survey country) (read):
(Interviewer: Only one response)

Politics	1
Economy	2
Courts	3
Social relations	4
I don't know	8
Refused to answer	9

I_I

208 To what extent do you think that corruption is common in the (Courts/ Judiciary) (read):
(Interviewer: Ask about all the items in the table below.)

	Corruption is common to this extent:			Not common at all	Don't know	Refused to answer	
	Large	Moderate	Small				
1. Courts/ Judiciary	1	2	3	4	8	9	I_I
2. Army/ Armed Forces	1	2	3	4	8	9	I_I
3. Police/ Security Forces	1	2	3	4	8	9	I_I
4. Traffic police	1	2	3	4	8	9	I_I
5. Education	1	2	3	4	8	9	I_I
6. Customs	1	2	3	4	8	9	I_I
7. Tax	1	2	3	4	8	9	I_I
8. Business community	1	2	3	4	8	9	I_I
9. Central government departments	1	2	3	4	8	9	I_I
10. Local government departments	1	2	3	4	8	9	I_I
11. Parliament	1	2	3	4	8	9	I_I

209   Which of the following groups contributes the most to the spread of corruption (read):
(Interviewer: Only one response)

Politicians	1	
Businessmen	2	
Low-ranking employees	3	|_|
High-ranking employees	4	
Don't know	8	
Refused to answer	9	

210   To which of the following reasons do you attribute the spread of corruption -------- (State the name of study country)
(read): (Interviewer: Only one response)

Poverty	1	
Lack of the rule of law	2	
Weak government transparency	3	|_|
Lack of effective government accountability	4	
Weak court system and inadequate law enforcement	5	
Don't know	8	} move to Q 213
Refused to answer	9	

211   Do you know of anyone who has paid a bribe to facilitate business over the last twelve months?

Yes	1	
No	2	
Don't know	8	|_|
Refused to answer	9	

212   Was this bribe offered (read):

To secure a service or benefit	1	
To avoid punishment	2	|_|
Other (specify): -----------------------------	3	
Don't know	8	
Refused to answer	9	

213   Do you know of anyone who has used favouritism (mediation/ special connection) to expedite a certain business or transaction over the last twelve months?

Yes	1	
No	2	|_|
Don't know	8	} move to Q 215
Refused to answer	9	

214   Was this wasta used (read):

To secure a service or benefit	1	
To avoid punishment	2	|_|
Other (specify): ------------------------------	3	
Don't know	8	
Refused to answer	9	

215   In your view, what is the best way to obtain a service (benefit)? (read):
       (Interviewer: One response only)

Bribe	1
Favouritism	2
Complaint to official authorities	3	|_|
Resort to the media	4
Other (specify): --------------------------------	5
Don't know	8
Refused to answer	9

216   In your view, what is the most successful way to avoid punishment? (read):
       (Interviewer: One response only)

Bribe	1
Favouritism	2
Complaint to official authorities	3	|_|
Resort to the media	4
Other (specify): --------------------------------	5
Don't know	8
Refused to answer	9

217   To what extent do you think that (establishing institutional governance system /the rule of law) contributes to fighting
       corruption? Would establishing the rule of institutional governance system contributes to fight corruption to a large,
       moderate, or small extent, or does it not fight corruption at all? (Interviewer: Ask about all the items in the table below.)

	Large	Moderate	Small	Does not fight at all	Don't know	Refused to answer	
1. Establishing the institutional governance system/ rule of law	1	2	3	4	8	9	|_|
2. Strengthening government transparency	1	2	3	4	8	9	|_|
3. Enforcing effective government accountability	1	2	3	4	8	9	|_|
4. Elimination of poverty	1	2	3	4	8	9	|_|
5. Ensuring the independence of the courts	1	2	3	4	8	9	|_|
6. Strengthening and rigorous enforcement of the sanctions against corrupt people	1	2	3	4	8	9	|_|

(Interviewer: Ask questions 218/ 219 for each of the items in the table below.)

F. Efficiency of Public Services

218   To what extent do you think that (government health services) are satisfactory in ------------- (State the name of the survey
       country)? Are they satisfactory to a large, moderate or small extent or are they unsatisfactory?

219   To what extent do you think that the cost of (government health services) is satisfactory in ------------- (State the name of
       the survey country)? Is it satisfactory to a large, moderate or small extent or is it unsatisfactory?

	Question 218 To what extent do you think that government health services are satisfactory:							Question 219 To what extent do you think that the cost of government health services is satisfactory:						
	Large	Moderate	Small	Unsatisfactory	Don't know	Refused to answer		Large	Moderate	Small	Unsatisfactory	Don't know	Refused to answer	
1. Government health services	1	2	3	4	8	9	|_|	1	2	3	4	8	9	|_|
2. Private health services	1	2	3	4	8	9	|_|	1	2	3	4	8	9	|_|
3. Government education	1	2	3	4	8	9	|_|	1	2	3	4	8	9	|_|
4. Private education	1	2	3	4	8	9	|_|	1	2	3	4	8	9	|_|

Section Three

301   Do you approve of/ accept (read):

	Yes	No	Don't know	Refused to answer	
1. Foreign military bases in your country	1	2	8	9	I__I
2. Foreign military bases in an Arab country	1	2	8	9	I__I

302   What, in your opinion, represents a just solution to the Palestinian problem? (read):
(Interviewer: One response only)

Setting up a democratic State in Palestine	1	
Ending the Israeli occupation of the Palestinian territories occupied in 1967 and establishing two States, Palestinian and Israeli, based on a peace agreement between them	2	
		I__I
Concluding a peace agreement between Israel and the Palestinian authority, based on whatever Palestinian land can be liberated through negotiation	3	
Don't know	8	
Refused to answer	9	

303   Are you generally satisfied with the current level of Arab cooperation?

Yes	1	
No	2	
Don't know	8	I__I
Refused to answer	9	

304   To what extent do you think that introducing a (unified Arab currency) will reflect your ambition for a better level of Arab cooperation? (Interviewer: Ask about all the items in the table below.)

	Reflects to this degree:			Does not reflect at all	Don't know	Refused to answer	
	Large	Moderate	Small				
1. Unified Arab currency	1	2	3	4	8	9	I__I
2. An Arab free trade zone (movement of goods between Arab States without customs limitations)	1	2	3	4	8	9	I__I
3. An Arab free citizenship area (free mobility of individuals, ideas, commodities and capital among all Arab countries)	1	2	3	4	8	9	I__I
4. Complete political unity	1	2	3	4	8	9	I__I

305   In your opinion, what are the three most important methods that, if implemented, may result in enhancing the scope of freedoms in ---------------- (State the name of the survey country)?

1. _____	I__II__I
2. _____	I__II__I
3. _____	I__II__I

Section Four

401   Living Area:

Urban	1	
		|_|
Rural	2	

402   Age:

_____	|_||_|

403   Sex:

Male	1	|_|
Female	2	

404   Nationality :

Jordanian	1
Egyptian	2
Palestinian	3
Lebanese	4
Other (specify) _____	5

(|_||_|)

405   Educational level (highest level successfully completed):

	(A.Respondent)	(B.Father)	(C.Mother)
No education (illiterate/ reads and writes)	1	1	1
Primary (6 years)	2	2	2
Basic (10 years)	3	3	3
Secondary (12 years)	4 |_|	4 |_|	4 |_|
College or university student	5	5	5
Completed first university degree	6	6	6
Higher studies (post-graduate)	7	7	7

406   Occupation:

A. Respondent's work		
Not working	1	|_|
Working (specify) _____	2	
B. Father's work		
Not working	1	|_|
Working (specify) _____	2	
C. Mother's work		
Not working	1	|_|
Working (specify) _____	2	

407   Household members

_____ Persons	|_||_|

408   Number of rooms in the house:

_____ Rooms	|_||_|

409   Does the family have one car or more?

One	1	
More	2	|_|
Does not haveð End interview	3	

410   What type is the most expensive car you have Ê

_____	|_||_|

Interviewer:
Thank the respondents and tell them that you might visit them again.

Table A-1 Average percentage of "do not know", "refused to answer" and "missing observation" responses, five Arab countries/, Freedom Survey, 2003

	Jordan	Lebanon	Palestine	Morocco	Algeria	Total
Average percentage of "do not know"	14.68	1.73	4.08	10.74	7.01	7.68
Average percentage of "refused to answer"	0.30	0.54	1.00	2.38	2.34	1.32
Average percentage of "missing observations"	11.01	5.46	3.65	11.39	7.15	7.74
Average percentage of total missing observations	26.18	7.73	8.72	24.50	16.49	16.74

Table A-2 Percentage of "missing observations", by question, five Arab countries/, Freedom Survey, 2003

Question	Jordan	Lebanon	Palestine	Morocco	Algeria	Total
Q 101 related to the comprehensive concept of freedom						
Freedom from occupation	6.90	0.00	0.40	1.48	1.61	2.07
Freedom from military bases	11.90	0.70	3.68	12.11	5.76	6.83
Freedom from foreign influence	9.80	0.30	3.08	14.37	6.89	6.91
Freedom from hunger	6.50	0.50	0.70	2.07	2.46	2.44
Freedom from sickness	6.60	0.60	1.49	2.07	2.27	2.60
Freedom from ignorance	6.20	0.30	1.09	0.69	3.49	2.36
Freedom from lack of income	7.10	0.40	1.69	14.17	2.36	5.14
Freedom from poverty	7.00	0.70	1.99	0.89	1.04	2.30
Q 102 Elements of freedom secured						
Freedom from occupation	13.10	1.30	1.59	5.71	1.61	4.63
Freedom from military bases	21.30	1.90	5.17	18.90	7.18	10.87
Freedom from foreign influence	16.10	2.60	6.87	17.52	7.84	10.18
Freedom from hunger	8.10	1.40	2.29	4.03	3.97	3.96
Freedom from sickness	9.50	1.70	2.69	4.82	2.83	4.29
Freedom from ignorance	8.00	1.30	1.89	2.56	4.15	3.58
Freedom from lack of income	8.70	1.00	1.59	21.36	3.02	7.13
Freedom from poverty	8.40	1.10	2.79	3.54	2.36	3.62
Q 103 State of enjoying freedom over the last five years						
Freedom from occupation	60.90	18.30	11.24	74.80	59.68	45.22
Freedom from military bases	62.70	20.00	18.11	69.39	71.77	48.7
Freedom from foreign influence	57.50	17.20	19.11	45.18	55.34	39.06
Freedom from hunger	38.30	11.20	9.75	52.46	45.23	31.00
Freedom from sickness	40.70	12.70	12.64	35.53	40.51	28.56
Freedom from ignorance	49.50	22.50	17.81	36.91	49.67	35.43
Freedom from lack of income	32.30	9.70	10.75	33.96	42.30	26.00
Freedom from poverty	33.20	12.00	13.040	24.61	39.66	24.67
Q 104 Elements of freedom as constituents of respondents' concept of freedom						
Freedom of thought	7.90	0.20	1.89	3.44	1.51	2.97
Freedom of faith	6.80	0.60	1.89	8.86	3.49	4.33
Freedom of opinion and expression	5.50	0.30	0.80	4.04	1.51	2.42
Freedom of gathering and organization	24.40	0.70	4.08	24.61	6.89	12.11
Independence of the media	23.20	0.50	3.28	29.04	6.14	12.4
Freedom of unions and professional organizations	28.90	1.60	4.88	27.46	10.67	14.69
Freedom of civil and cooperative associations	30.60	2.30	6.27	23.03	13.98	15.24

Question	Jordan	Lebanon	Palestine	Morocco	Algeria	Total
Q 104 Elements of freedom as constituents of respondents' concept of freedom						
Freedom of religious organizations	19.6	0.80	3.78	16.14	7.37	9.53
Freedom of property	7.00	1.50	3.08	6.50	3.68	4.35
Freedom of movement within the country	5.60	0.70	2.29	5.31	1.04	2.97
Freedom of marriage	5.10	0.60	1.99	1.58	2.17	2.28
Freedom of economic transactions	16.2	0.90	2.99	22.04	10.10	10.47
Equality before the law	8.30	0.50	1.49	9.45	1.61	4.25
Gender equality	7.00	0.70	1.49	4.33	1.89	3.07
Freedom of minorities – if available – to use their language	19.50	1.20	10.05	3.64	2.55	7.32
Freedom of minorities – if available– to practise their own culture	20.90	0.80	10.45	4.23	1.79	7.56
Freedom of minorities – if available – to practise their own religious rites	19.80	0.80	7.96	9.35	4.06	8.35
Right to organize opposing political communities	32.80	2.70	3.88	40.85	8.50	17.7
Presence of significant opposition that has the opportunity to influence decisions	31.80	2.40	5.37	44.00	10.39	18.76
Complete independence of the courts	19.00	1.00	3.68	31.89	4.91	12.07
Fighting corruption	10.00	0.70	2.59	5.91	2.27	4.27
Transparent government	21.30	1.30	3.88	20.96	4.25	10.3
Government accountability	21.40	1.10	4.18	36.71	4.91	13.62
Freedom of minorities – if available – to self-govern	33.20	3.00	10.25	31.10	14.16	18.33
Electing leaders of central government through free and honest elections	19.80	2.20	5.97	8.86	5.19	8.37
Electing leaders of local government through free and honest elections	18.50	2.40	4.58	8.76	6.52	8.13
Electing powerful representatives to the legislative through free and honest elections	15.90	2.00	4.98	9.06	6.89	7.76
Q 105 Elements of freedom secured						
Freedom of thought	11.10	0.40	2.29	5.51	1.32	4.09
Freedom of faith	8.90	0.80	2.09	10.93	6.04	5.77
Freedom of opinion and expression	9.10	0.50	2.19	6.79	2.36	4.17
Freedom of gathering and organization	27.00	1.60	4.58	28.05	9.44	14.11
Independence of the media	26.60	0.50	3.38	34.15	7.55	14.41
Freedom of union and professional organizations	32.60	1.60	6.67	33.17	15.96	18.01
Freedom of civil and cooperative associations	35.00	2.50	6.47	25.49	20.02	17.93
Freedom of religious organizations	21.80	1.10	3.88	19.78	11.24	11.57
Freedom of property	7.90	1.00	3.58	8.07	6.04	5.33
Freedom of movement within the country	6.00	0.50	1.49	5.70	1.79	3.09
Freedom of marriage	5.90	0.60	1.69	3.05	3.12	2.87
Freedom of economic transactions	18.60	1.40	2.89	25.00	16.71	12.99
Equality before the law	9.70	0.70	3.18	12.01	3.97	5.91
Gender equality	7.20	0.50	3.38	5.42	3.49	4.00
Freedom of minorities – if available – to use their language	23.40	3.20	13.43	3.84	2.74	9.23
Freedom of minorities – if available – to practise their own culture	24.20	3.10	13.23	4.72	2.55	9.47
Freedom of minorities – if available – to practise their own religious rites	22.80	2.50	10.65	10.73	6.89	10.67
Right to organize opposing political communities	38.10	4.60	5.97	43.50	10.86	20.55

Question	Jordan	Lebanon	Palestine	Morocco	Algeria	Total
105 Elements of freedom secured						
Presence of significant opposition that has the opportunity to influence decisions	38.50	4.30	6.37	47.24	13.98	22.05
Complete independence of the courts	23.0?	1.80	3.98	35.43	8.22	14.47
Fighting corruption	11.80	1.30	2.49	9.94	5.95	6.30
Transparent government	24.30	2.50	4.68	23.43	9.16	12.80
Government accountability	24.70	1.20	6.07	38.29	9.63	15.96
Freedom of minorities – if available – to self-govern	41.00	5.90	14.63	32.97	18.41	22.56
Electing leaders of central government through free and honest elections	23.70	4.00	7.56	12.40	9.63	11.44
Electing leaders of local government through free and honest elections	21.40	3.90	6.27	12.50	10.48	10.91
Electing powerful representatives to the legislative through free and honest elections	18.70	3.50	5.57	11.52	11.71	10.22
Q (106) State of elements of freedom over the last five years						
Freedom of thought	51.00	31.90	15.42	64.47	47.78	42.22
Freedom of faith	71.20	38.90	28.76	65.85	48.44	50.63
Freedom of opinion and expression	46.60	25.20	9.95	45.18	28.42	31.06
Freedom of gathering and organization	55.20	23.80	11.64	61.32	33.90	37.19
Independence of the media	51.90	14.70	10.05	48.33	26.25	30.24
Freedom of union and professional organizations	61.10	29.50	17.51	61.71	39.75	41.93
Freedom of civil and cooperative associations	63.70	33.60	19.30	71.56	51.46	48.01
Freedom of religious organizations	62.90	43.20	19.20	53.05	37.96	43.21
Freedom of property	77.00	45.80	29.15	74.02	50.05	55.18
Freedom of movement within the country	83.30	45.20	14.13	83.76	53.45	55.98
Freedom of marriage	80.80	46.70	33.33	73.13	56.28	58.05
Freedom of economic transactions	67.70	36.30	17.41	69.88	47.69	47.83
Equality before the law	54.90	17.10	10.85	37.70	19.26	27.87
Gender equality	58.80	26.00	16.22	48.62	35.98	37.13
Freedom of minorities- if available - to use their language	79.50	60.70	35.92	87.50	53.45	63.35
Freedom of minorities - if available - to practise their own culture	79.10	61.90	35.02	85.53	63.64	65.06
Freedom of minorities - if available - to practise their own religious rites	80.50	61.50	37.01	79.13	53.35	62.22
Right to organize opposing political communities	57.30	24.60	15.12	62.89	39.09	39.84
Presence of significant opposition that has the opportunity to influence decisions	55.10	20.40	15.02	58.66	32.67	36.38
Complete independence of the courts	65.10	16.20	14.13	51.77	23.42	34.04
Fighting corruption	48.90	13.30	13.13	23.52	20.30	23.78
Transparent government	59.20	13.50	12.94	45.67	25.87	31.40
Government accountability	53.10	13.90	13.93	48.82	26.63	31.26
Freedom of minorities - if available - to self-govern	64.50	25.10	28.36	48.03	40.42	41.28
Electing leaders of central government through free and honest elections	56.70	17.10	15.72	36.12	27.86	30.67
Electing leaders of local government through free and honest elections	56.20	21.00	16.52	35.43	26.91	31.16
Electing powerful representatives to the legislative through free and honest elections	60.20	17.50	16.32	32.38	29.75	31.20

Question	Jordan	Lebanon	Palestine	Morocco	Algeria	Total
Q 201 Women and society						
Girls have the same right to education as boys.	0.20	0.30	0.40	0.79	0.19	0.37
Women have the same right to work as men.	0.60	0.30	0.80	0.98	0.28	0.59
Women have the same right to political action as men.	2.10	0.20	1.39	3.54	0.66	1.57
A woman's children have the right to acquire her nationality that same as men's children have the right to acquire his nationality.	3.10	0.70	2.89	9.06	5.95	4.37
A woman has the right to assume a judiciary position.	1.80	0.30	1.69	2.66	2.27	1.75
A woman has the right to assume the position of Minister.	1.30	0.20	1.69	3.15	1.98	1.67
A woman has the right to assume the position of Prime Minister.	1.50	0.40	2.19	3.84	2.64	2.13
A woman has the right to assume the position of Head of State.	2.20	0.50	1.69	6.00	3.21	2.74
Q 202 Activities of the Council of Deputies/Parliament						
Perform its legislative role effectively	12.30	1.70	3.68	15.85	12.94	9.35
Controls the Government's work effectively	14.20	1.70	4.28	19.59	15.58	11.14
Holds the Government accountable effectively	14.00	1.60	4.78	20.57	18.41	11.97
Q 203 Confidence in going to the courts						
In civil disputes	7.40	3.70	12.74	19.09	8.12	10.22
In financial and economic disputes	7.30	3.10	14.23	21.46	14.73	12.22
In disputes relating to freedoms	11.60	5.10	20.20	24.11	14.73	15.18
Q 204-205 media						
Honest government media	8.40	1.50	5.67	11.61	9.73	7.42
Government media Presents the opinion and the other opinion	10.60	2.40	5.87	13.68	11.05	8.76
Government media Contributes to the acquisition of knowledge	7.60	1.40	5.57	11.42	11.43	7.54
Non-government media Honest	15.90	1.10	6.47	14.76	11.90	10.06
Non-government media Presents the opinion and the other opinion	16.40	0.70	6.57	14.96	12.84	10.33
Non-government media Contributes to the acquisition of knowledge	14.90	0.40	6.17	14.27	14.92	10.20
Corruption						
Q 206 Corruption is common	11.00	1.40	4.88	8.76	3.59	5.91
Q 207 Areas where corruption is the most common	24.00	4.50	10.75	12.40	8.88	12.07
Q 208 Institutions where corruption is the most common						
Courts/Judiciary	34.70	5.10	10.25	16.24	9.35	15.06
Army/Armed forces	40.70	4.30	12.14	100.00	77.62	47.44
Police/Security forces	39.30	4.00	11.34	100.00	82.44	47.95
Traffic police	36.30	3.80	10.05	100.00	81.02	46.77
Education	24.40	3.90	9.05	18.60	12.28	13.64
Customs	36.10	6.40	11.94	100.00	6.61	32.11
Tax	34.60	3.40	12.54	24.41	8.88	16.69
Business community	36.20	7.30	13.73	24.51	10.10	18.29
Central government departments	37.30	7.30	13.53	28.64	25.31	22.46
Local government departments	35.70	6.40	13.13	21.36	18.13	18.94
Parliament	37.50	6.70	15.32	32.19	31.82	24.80
Q 209 Group that contributes the most to the spread of corruption	31.50	6.50	11.44	13.19	10.95	14.67
Q 210 Reasons for the spread of corruption	22.10	5.30	11.14	10.63	8.40	11.48
Q 211 Know of anyone who paid a bribe	6.60	5.80	10.85	4.43	10.95	7.76

Question	Jordan	Lebanon	Palestine	Morocco	Algeria	Total
Q 212 Reason for paying a bribe	79.20	41.00	59.10	29.53	49.10	51.50
Q 213 Know of anyone who used favouritism	5.50	4.20	9.85	4.33	9.35	6.67
Q 214 Reasons for using favouritism	58.10	27.60	45.97	31.10	35.32	39.55
Q 215 Best way to obtain a service	8.10	1.70	6.57	6.20	17.75	8.17
Q 216 Most successful way of avoiding punishment	8.80	2.00	6.37	9.35	20.49	9.53

Q 217 To what extent do you think that .... contributes to fighting corruption?						
Establishing the rule of law	30.30	2.90	5.07	11.02	2.36	10.24
Strengthening government transparency	27.30	2.10	4.58	19.09	3.78	11.30
Enforcing effective government accountability	24.50	1.80	5.17	21.75	5.00	11.59
Elimination of poverty	13.60	0.90	2.59	6.99	2.46	5.28
Ensuring the independence of courts	19.70	1.70	3.58	27.66	4.63	11.42
Strengthening and rigorous enforcement of the sanctions against corrupt people	14.30	1.30	3.28	13.88	2.64	7.05

Q 218 Satisfaction with level of health services						
Government health services	1.00	1.30	0.80	1.18	1.32	1.12
Private health services	9.10	0.30	1.29	8.96	7.55	5.47
Cost of government health services	4.10	0.60	1.29	5.12	3.12	2.85
Cost of private health services	14.30	0.10	3.48	16.83	27.76	12.68

Q 219 Satisfaction with level of education services						
Government education	2.40	2.90	0.90	2.36	3.59	2.44
Private education	8.40	0.90	1.99	8.66	8.97	5.83
Cost of government education	4.70	1.40	1.69	5.02	5.10	3.60
Cost of private education	14.60	0.70	4.88	16.54	27.67	13.05
Q 301 Do you approve (accept) the presence of foreign military bases in						
Your country	3.10	3.30	2.29	3.25	6.23	3.66
Any Arab country	3.50	6.90	3.58	5.02	8.97	5.63
Q 302 Fair solution to the Palestinian problem	13.4	11.90	15.52	4.73	23.32	13.86
Q 303 Satisfaction with the current level of Arab cooperation	8.50	5.40	2.59	5.02	13.98	7.17

Q 304 Ambition for a better level of Arab cooperation						
United Arab currency	9.00	1.40	3.78	10.73	11.90	7.42
A Arab free trade zone	6.80	1.60	2.59	12.11	10.48	6.77
A Arab free citizenship area	7.80	1.50	3.18	11.92	11.24	7.19
Complete political unity	10.40	1.90	2.59	18.70	15.58	9.92
Q 305 Methods which, if implemented, may result in enhancing the scope of freedom						
First method	25.50	1.10	13.73	2.85	1.51	8.84
Second method	51.70	6.70	16.42	5.41	5.48	16.97
Third method	75.30	21.50	25.47	14.27	13.22	29.70

Table A-3 Respondent characteristics, Freedom Survey, 2003 (%)

	Jordan	Lebanon	Palestine	Morocco	Algeria
Residence					
Urban	80.9	67.0	72.0	61.6	70.9
Rural	19.2	33.0	28.0	38.4	29.1
Age					
18-34	49.1	67.2	56.3	62	53.3
35+	50.9	32.8	43.7	38	46.7
Gender					
Male	50.1	51.0	49.5	48.7	50.5
Female	49.9	49.0	50.5	51.3	49.5
Educational level					
Illiterate/read and write	10.5	2.1	2.9	55.2	-
Primary	10.8	5.9	5.9	16.1	-
Basic education	20.5	17.3	12.2	2.1	-
Secondary	35.1	24.7	35.2	21.2	-
College or university student	15.2	22.2	20.8	1.4	-
Completed first university degree	7.0	20.9	19.9	3.5	-
Higher studies	0.9	6.9	3.2	0.6	-

Table A-4 Extent to which respondents considered the elements of freedom as constituents of their concept of freedom, five Arab countries, Freedom Survey, 2003 (%)

Freedom element	Jordan			Lebanon			Palestine			Morocco			Algeria		
	To a large extent	To some extent	Not at all	To a large extent	To some extent	Not at all	To a large extent	To some extent	Not at all	To a large extent	To some extent	Not at all	To a large extent	To some extent	Not at all
Individual freedoms															
Freedom from hunger	69.53	88.59	11.41	56.18	91.96	8.04	52.00	95.98	4.01	83.12	95.58	4.42	72.80	91.97	8.03
Freedom from disease	62.75	85.33	14.67	52.21	89.43	10.56	45.05	94.44	5.56	78.39	95.07	4.92	71.98	90.92	9.08
Freedom from ignorance	76.15	93.42	6.58	69.11	96.09	3.91	60.16	96.27	3.72	87.41	97.22	2.78	79.94	95.30	4.70
Freedom from inadequate income	68.30	91.49	8.50	55.72	94.17	5.82	58.50	96.66	3.34	71.90	92.66	7.34	76.60	94.50	5.51
Freedom from poverty	69.69	92.98	7.02	64.35	94.66	5.34	60.30	97.76	2.23	79.74	91.85	8.14	75.10	93.99	6.01
Social freedoms															
Freedom of thought	76.63	98.37	1.63	79.26	97.79	2.20	70.49	95.54	4.46	88.99	98.57	1.43	86.77	98.28	1.73
Freedom of belief	82.45	95.67	4.33	73.84	98.08	1.91	66.84	95.54	4.46	88.66	96.01	4.00	77.89	94.04	5.97
Freedom of opinion and expression	78.67	99.13	0.88	84.95	97.99	2.01	65.90	97.10	2.91	84.62	96.72	3.28	85.91	99.05	0.96
Freedom of association and organization	61.70	95.17	4.83	63.14	97.38	2.62	46.89	95.65	4.36	66.84	90.08	9.92	68.76	94.12	5.88
Freedom to own property	81.90	97.60	2.40	63.55	92.99	7.01	47.95	95.90	4.11	84.32	95.90	4.11	80.00	97.36	2.65

Freedom element	Jordan			Lebanon			Palestine			Morocco			Algeria		
	To a large extent	To some extent	Not at all	To a large extent	To some extent	Not at all	To a large extent	To some extent	Not at all	To a large extent	To some extent	Not at all	To a large extent	To some extent	Not at all
Freedom of movement within the country	86.43	98.06	1.94	68.18	92.96	7.05	64.26	97.87	2.14	92.83	98.44	1.56	86.45	98.57	1.43
Freedom of marriage	83.64	96.80	3.20	61.47	92.15	7.85	49.95	94.01	5.99	85.40	94.80	5.20	81.95	95.85	4.15
Freedom to engage in economic transactions	72.81	97.18	2.83	53.99	94.05	5.95	51.59	96.10	3.90	71.97	91.41	8.59	73.32	95.28	4.73
Equality before the law	79.61	97.85	2.15	74.67	94.57	5.43	65.76	97.48	2.53	87.28	96.63	3.37	88.39	98.66	1.34
Gender equality	73.51	93.81	6.19	65.56	94.06	5.94	44.34	95.25	4.75	79.73	95.16	4.84	71.80	91.25	8.76

Freedom of organizations and minorities

Freedom element	Jordan			Lebanon			Palestine			Morocco			Algeria		
Independence of the media	63.32	93.41	6.59	60.10	96.58	3.42	51.03	95.98	4.01	66.85	89.18	10.82	77.26	97.38	2.62
Freedom for trade unions and professional associations	58.43	94.00	6.01	57.11	96.44	3.56	41.21	94.45	5.54	68.52	91.45	8.55	71.14	94.72	5.29
Freedom for civil and cooperative organizations	56.42	93.90	6.10	49.33	96.31	3.68	40.76	94.69	5.31	76.60	91.69	8.31	65.09	92.20	7.79
Freedom for religious organizations	69.71	96.86	3.14	55.75	95.47	4.54	49.74	95.14	4.86	66.78	86.62	13.38	55.25	91.85	8.15
Freedom for minorities to use their language	65.35	90.74	9.26	48.18	93.42	6.58	32.30	89.94	10.07	78.96	86.42	13.59	73.06	93.11	6.88
Freedom for minorities to practise their distinctive culture	66.73	92.16	7.83	51.61	94.86	5.14	32.00	89.11	10.89	78.11	85.82	14.18	75.96	94.04	5.96
Freedom for minorities to practise their religious rites	70.65	93.82	6.18	58.06	94.25	5.75	37.08	90.92	9.08	74.70	83.61	16.40	68.01	90.84	9.15
Autonomy for minorities	51.62	83.65	16.35	36.80	83.30	16.70	35.59	88.37	11.64	51.57	65.28	34.71	59.52	85.81	14.19

Political freedoms

Freedom element	Jordan			Lebanon			Palestine			Morocco			Algeria		
Right to form political opposition groups	55.21	89.65	10.35	54.88	93.01	6.99	42.86	94.41	5.59	71.05	87.85	12.15	68.83	93.70	6.30
Existence of a significant opposition able to influence decision-making	55.39	89.36	10.63	58.91	92.52	7.48	50.89	96.21	3.79	68.01	85.06	14.94	68.07	93.36	6.64
Complete independence of the judiciary	74.04	95.47	4.54	72.93	97.48	2.53	63.84	96.18	3.82	60.98	80.05	19.94	81.23	97.32	2.68
Combating corruption	76.08	96.09	3.90	74.52	96.47	3.52	72.32	96.43	3.58	79.81	90.06	9.94	82.22	95.56	4.44
Transparency of governance	72.60	95.89	4.10	66.77	96.06	3.95	66.67	95.97	4.04	80.95	95.52	4.48	82.74	96.45	3.55
Possibility of holding government accountable	73.05	97.34	2.66	72.09	95.85	4.15	64.38	95.84	4.15	69.21	86.94	13.06	85.50	97.02	2.98
Choice of central government leaders through free and fair elections	70.79	93.83	6.17	66.77	96.02	3.99	59.89	94.92	5.08	80.99	95.79	4.21	85.46	98.71	1.29
Choice of local government leaders through free and fair elections	72.01	95.80	4.19	68.44	95.90	4.10	61.00	95.51	4.48	80.15	94.49	5.50	83.23	98.69	1.31
Choice of legislative representatives with effective power through free and fair elections	75.43	96.72	3.28	69.80	95.93	4.08	61.78	94.97	5.03	81.60	95.56	4.44	82.45	97.36	2.64

Table A-5 Extent of enjoyment of the elements of freedom, five Arab countries/territory, Freedom Survey, 2003 (%)

Freedom element	Jordan To a large extent	Jordan To some extent	Jordan Not at all	Lebanon To a large extent	Lebanon To some extent	Lebanon Not at all	Palestine To a large extent	Palestine To some extent	Palestine Not at all	Morocco To a large extent	Morocco To some extent	Morocco Not at all	Algeria To a large extent	Algeria To some extent	Algeria Not at all
Homeland freedoms															
Freedom from occupation	80.57	95.65	4.35	76.50	97.50	2.50	82.82	98.61	1.40	87.51	97.70	2.30	84.55	97.79	2.21
Freedom from military bases	74.82	91.78	8.23	69.49	96.18	3.83	71.28	98.24	1.76	86.90	96.42	3.58	80.36	92.39	7.62
Freedom from foreign influence	80.25	94.76	5.24	80.74	97.49	2.51	66.12	96.71	3.29	77.70	90.80	9.20	72.01	91.78	8.22
Individual freedoms															
Freedom from hunger	28.25	86.99	13.01	8.82	80.42	19.57	8.55	80.85	19.14	50.67	90.46	9.54	40.71	90.95	9.05
Freedom from disease	33.15	90.00	10.00	10.07	81.08	18.92	9.51	83.33	16.67	31.95	86.55	13.44	36.25	89.60	10.40
Freedom from ignorance	43.77	93.80	6.20	19.55	85.20	14.79	16.13	82.86	17.14	35.45	90.80	9.19	45.62	94.78	5.22
Freedom from inadequate income	24.48	83.65	16.35	7.78	76.37	23.64	9.20	78.56	21.44	16.27	77.72	22.28	39.34	93.68	6.33
Freedom from poverty (deprivation from basic human capabilities: health, education, and social and political participation)	25.54	84.84	15.16	9.50	75.93	24.06	10.75	79.33	20.68	21.73	77.24	22.76	37.23	92.55	7.45
Social freedoms															
Freedom of thought	44.11	95.11	4.89	29.02	84.14	15.86	12.32	71.89	28.11	61.87	89.48	10.52	44.11	89.09	10.91
Freedom of belief	69.25	96.16	3.85	35.79	87.00	13.00	26.22	79.88	20.12	60.22	88.95	11.05	43.52	86.33	13.67
Freedom of opinion and expression	39.34	93.89	6.11	21.91	76.69	23.32	8.04	72.23	27.77	39.60	74.98	25.03	25.15	84.05	15.96
Freedom of association and organization	35.91	88.68	11.31	19.92	83.44	16.57	7.30	75.29	24.71	44.05	86.59	13.41	23.46	85.50	14.49
Freedom to own property	72.96	96.41	3.59	43.13	93.84	6.16	24.87	87.10	12.90	71.63	95.40	4.60	45.13	93.37	6.63
Freedom of movement within the country	81.61	98.44	1.56	43.52	95.28	4.72	11.31	69.80	30.20	82.67	98.53	1.46	52.21	95.00	5.00
Freedom of marriage	78.45	97.94	2.07	44.77	95.57	4.43	31.28	90.29	9.72	72.79	95.43	4.57	54.78	93.96	6.04
Freedom to engage in economic transactions	59.13	97.23	2.76	33.47	91.89	8.11	12.70	80.53	19.47	59.97	95.41	4.59	36.62	92.40	7.60
Equality before the law	47.41	90.23	9.77	13.19	78.75	21.25	6.37	78.62	21.38	27.52	69.36	30.65	13.37	72.56	27.43
Gender equality	53.60	92.80	7.20	23.72	93.27	6.73	13.08	87.23	12.77	46.31	90.22	9.78	33.27	86.30	13.70

Freedom element	Jordan			Lebanon			Palestine			Morocco			Algeria		
	To a large extent	To some extent	Not at all	To a large extent	To some extent	Not at all	To a large extent	To some extent	Not at all	To a large extent	To some extent	Not at all	To a large extent	To some extent	Not at all
Freedom of organizations and minorities															
Independence of the media	33.76	88.88	11.12	11.56	74.97	25.03	6.18	73.01	26.98	21.08	70.11	29.90	16.65	78.85	21.14
Freedom for trade unions and professional associations	39.70	92.01	7.98	25.51	89.23	10.77	11.09	79.96	20.04	41.09	90.28	9.72	24.61	86.30	13.71
Freedom for civil and cooperative organizations	45.00	94.29	5.71	29.74	90.56	9.44	12.87	82.24	17.77	61.03	94.59	5.42	34.12	89.85	10.15
Freedom for religious organizations	53.15	92.33	7.67	40.24	92.51	7.48	14.49	80.13	19.88	40.37	78.28	21.72	26.06	82.23	17.77
Freedom for minorities to use their language	73.52	95.96	4.04	58.06	95.87	4.13	23.33	84.94	15.06	87.21	98.88	1.13	50.58	92.81	7.18
Freedom for minorities to practise their distinctive culture	71.83	97.06	2.93	59.65	96.81	3.20	22.36	84.74	15.25	84.71	98.76	1.24	60.95	94.77	5.23
Freedom for minorities to practise their religious rites	74.56	97.98	2.02	59.28	96.31	3.69	27.17	85.63	14.37	77.51	96.58	3.42	45.64	91.18	8.82
Autonomy for minorities	37.16	78.46	21.53	14.24	67.80	32.20	10.49	74.25	25.76	12.04	39.94	60.06	17.13	78.36	21.64
Political freedoms															
Right to form political opposition groups	25.03	82.80	17.20	17.51	75.89	24.11	7.20	75.24	24.76	29.97	74.92	25.09	25.85	88.67	11.33
Existence of a significant opposition able to influence decision-making	24.58	79.35	20.65	13.69	70.95	29.05	7.86	71.62	28.37	16.60	62.30	37.69	15.48	84.09	15.92
Complete independence of the judiciary	53.21	93.05	6.95	12.73	74.03	25.97	8.08	72.23	27.77	22.41	65.55	34.45	12.14	83.85	16.15
Combating corruption	40.12	89.99	10.01	9.63	67.58	32.42	8.27	68.07	31.94	13.22	60.87	39.13	12.95	82.33	17.67
Transparency of governance	43.35	90.57	9.43	9.03	70.77	29.23	5.95	68.58	31.42	28.28	70.95	29.05	13.62	82.65	17.36
Possibility of holding government accountable	33.64	86.60	13.40	8.60	67.50	32.49	5.30	63.56	36.44	12.44	50.08	49.92	14.63	85.69	14.32
Choice of central government leaders through free and fair elections	40.29	79.65	20.35	11.25	72.18	27.81	7.53	74.16	25.83	26.29	72.58	27.42	16.30	84.01	15.99
Choice of local government leaders through free and fair elections	43.24	87.23	12.76	15.19	75.44	24.56	8.92	73.89	26.11	25.20	72.90	27.11	14.77	84.50	15.51
Choice of legislative representatives with effective power through free and fair elections	50.84	91.77	8.23	11.81	72.12	27.88	9.06	73.87	26.13	22.47	73.30	26.70	16.15	84.07	15.94
Homeland freedoms															
Freedom from occupation	56.24	92.37	7.62	15.70	78.11	21.88	10.52	50.16	49.85	72.65	94.15	5.85	57.87	95.78	4.22
Freedom from military bases	50.16	89.33	10.67	15.49	76.96	23.04	12.59	54.14	45.86	58.25	82.27	17.72	64.80	90.23	9.77
Freedom from foreign influence	48.86	86.70	13.30	13.86	71.56	28.44	11.75	59.94	40.06	32.70	69.33	30.67	46.62	90.26	9.73

Table A-6 Perceived change in the enjoyment of the elements of freedom during the five years preceding the survey, five Arab countries Freedom Survey, 2003 (net %)

Freedom element	Jordan			Lebanon			Palestine			Morocco			Algeria		
	Improve-ment	Deteriora-tion	Net change	Improve-ment	Deteriora-tion	Net change	Improve-ment	Deteriora-tion	Net change	Improve-ment	Deteriora-tion	Net change	Improve-ment	Deteriora-tion	Net change
Individual freedoms															
Freedom from hunger	17.79	34.68	-16.89	10.36	46.85	-36.49	7.39	59.54	-52.15	34.37	20.70	13.67	20.69	37.76	-17.07
Freedom from disease	25.24	24.77	0.47	15.81	33.45	-17.64	3.10	46.01	-42.91	44.27	18.02	26.25	27.94	34.29	-6.35
Freedom from ignorance	30.01	18.19	11.82	21.29	31.23	-9.94	23.00	40.68	-17.68	51.33	17.94	33.39	35.46	27.95	7.51
Freedom from inadequate income	12.59	41.98	-29.39	6.87	52.93	-46.06	6.69	60.87	-54.18	24.89	23.55	1.34	15.22	49.26	-34.04
Freedom from poverty	12.11	37.79	-25.68	6.59	48.07	-41.48	11.78	54.92	-43.14	34.73	25.07	9.66	12.52	48.51	-35.99
Social freedoms															
Freedom of thought	25.37	14.89	10.48	13.51	30.40	-16.89	19.41	40.59	-21.18	34.90	20.22	14.68	36.17	22.97	13.20
Freedom of belief	21.06	14.63	6.43	7.69	34.21	-26.52	17.32	37.43	-20.11	28.82	21.61	7.21	21.98	21.61	0.37
Freedom of opinion and expression	23.81	15.62	8.19	7.75	48.93	-41.18	16.91	40.44	-23.53	31.60	20.29	11.31	30.08	29.82	0.26
Freedom of association and organization	20.55	19.81	0.74	7.22	36.88	-29.66	13.40	43.92	-30.52	17.56	29.01	-11.45	23.29	39.43	-16.14
Freedom to own property	24.75	17.31	7.44	12.18	21.77	-9.59	11.80	32.44	-20.64	14.39	31.06	-16.67	32.89	13.23	19.66
Freedom of move-ment within the country	21.51	17.60	3.91	46.53	12.77	33.76	6.49	70.80	-64.31	13.33	19.39	-6.06	25.96	28.60	-2.64
Freedom of mar-riage	23.75	17.11	6.64	19.32	12.76	6.56	13.73	26.12	-12.39	34.43	29.30	5.13	28.73	17.71	11.02
Freedom to engage in economic transac-tions	23.19	17.00	6.19	11.62	29.36	-17.74	8.80	53.98	-45.18	17.97	22.22	-4.25	33.94	17.15	16.79
Equality before the law	16.06	26.18	-10.12	7.72	43.06	-35.34	7.03	53.01	-45.98	21.48	19.91	1.57	13.92	34.74	-20.82
Gender equality	28.69	18.46	10.23	22.57	12.84	9.73	13.18	25.30	-12.12	43.68	14.94	28.74	34.22	15.93	18.29
Freedom of organizations and minorities															
Independence of the media	23.10	18.13	4.97	6.92	45.25	-38.33	11.95	46.46	-34.51	19.24	18.86	0.38	24.07	33.93	-9.86
Freedom for trade unions and professional asso-ciations	21.96	18.43	3.53	9.79	32.20	-22.41	16.04	34.14	-18.10	19.02	21.08	-2.06	24.61	29.94	-5.33
Freedom for civil and cooperative organizations	21.08	14.24	6.84	11.14	24.40	-13.26	18.25	30.70	-12.45	24.57	17.99	6.58	31.71	20.82	10.89
Freedom for religious organiza-tions	19.29	21.73	-2.44	13.73	21.48	-7.75	13.79	43.23	-29.44	19.08	47.59	-28.51	19.48	31.96	-12.48

Freedom element	Jordan			Lebanon			Palestine			Morocco			Algeria		
	Improve-ment	Deteriora-tion	Net change	Improve-ment	Deteriora-tion	Net change	Improve-ment	Deteriora-tion	Net change	Improve-ment	Deteriora-tion	Net change	Improve-ment	Deteriora-tion	Net change
Freedom for minorities to use their language	16.29	12.54	3.75	11.20	9.92	1.28	10.71	26.40	-15.69	31.50	14.17	17.33	58.01	14.00	44.01
Freedom for minorities to practise their distinctive culture	19.71	11.36	8.35	13.39	18.11	-4.72	11.64	26.80	-15.16	19.73	19.05	0.68	42.86	10.91	31.95
Freedom for minorities to practise their religious rites	21.11	8.02	13.09	13.51	18.44	-4.93	11.53	29.38	-17.85	19.81	22.64	-2.83	26.92	18.83	8.09
Autonomy for minorities	14.31	14.06	0.25	5.34	24.43	-19.09	8.19	43.47	-35.28	11.17	16.48	-5.31	18.70	23.93	-5.23
Political freedoms															
Right to form political opposition groups	11.24	24.37	-13.13	8.89	46.15	-37.26	9.73	51.70	-41.97	16.98	22.02	-5.04	21.71	31.47	-9.76
Existence of a significant opposition able to influence decision-making	12.70	24.79	-12.09	5.15	48.62	-43.47	8.67	55.74	-47.07	12.62	22.38	-9.76	17.25	28.61	-11.36
Complete independence of the judiciary	17.90	13.31	4.59	5.01	50.60	-45.59	7.07	56.66	-49.59	13.88	19.59	-5.71	14.30	32.68	-18.38
Combating corruption	16.66	30.56	-13.90	4.96	53.40	-48.44	8.36	65.29	-56.93	22.14	32.56	-10.42	11.49	47.99	-36.50
Transparency of governance	21.64	16.85	4.79	2.66	53.18	-50.52	6.40	64.80	-58.40	17.57	19.93	-2.36	15.29	33.12	-17.83
Possibility of holding government accountable	19.59	22.84	-3.25	3.25	51.68	-48.43	6.13	62.43	-56.30	6.15	22.88	-16.73	19.18	30.24	-11.06
Choice of central government leaders through free and fair elections	13.96	17.97	-4.01	3.74	43.18	-39.44	6.61	52.07	-45.46	25.73	27.43	-1.70	15.45	31.81	-16.36
Choice of local government leaders through free and fair elections	15.48	24.69	-9.21	6.71	42.78	-36.07	6.56	54.35	-47.79	24.54	28.20	-3.66	14.60	33.07	-18.47
Choice of legislative representatives with effective power through free and fair elections	14.84	23.58	-8.74	4.73	46.91	-42.18	6.66	54.46	-47.80	25.04	26.49	-1.45	13.31	32.66	-19.35
Homeland freedoms															
Freedom from occupation	19.64	29.04	-9.40	42.47	16.89	25.58	7.17	72.87	-65.70	19.53	23.83	-4.30	36.07	22.25	13.82
Freedom from military bases	16.41	32.78	-16.37	39.87	17.38	22.49	4.25	66.46	-62.21	14.15	21.54	-7.39	20.74	20.74	0.00
Freedom from foreign influence	14.99	37.65	-22.66	24.88	28.74	-3.86	3.94	57.07	-53.13	20.83	29.62	-8.79	24.74	29.81	-5.07

Table A-7 Most important means of expanding freedom, five Arab countries/territory, Freedom Survey, 2003 (%)

Means of expanding freedom	Jordan	Lebanon	Palestine	Morocco	Algeria	Total
Combating ignorance	5.05	1.62	4.40	5.29	0.00	3.02
Ending unemployment	8.26	1.29	0.00	11.99	19.61	8.58
Eradicating poverty	14.52	0.96	4.40	13.73	11.61	8.62
Freedom of opinion and expression/media	24.06	14.80	9.58	4.22	4.02	9.81
Equality among citizens/ gender equality	5.84	4.91	0.90	7.02	20.76	8.43
Combating corruption	12.60	5.50	9.61	10.96	0.00	7.08
Good governance	3.56	15.02	5.80	5.43	16.71	10.06
Freedom of homeland	0.71	8.15	17.05	0.00	0.00	5.37
Other	25.41	47.75	48.27	41.36	27.30	39.03
Total	100.00	100.00	100.00	100.00	100.00	100.00

Table A-8 Governance and corruption indicators, Arab countries and world regions (weighted by population), 2002

Country/Territory/Region	Representation and accountability	Political stability and absence of violence	Government effectiveness	Rule of law	Control of corruption
Algeria	-0.96	-1.54	-0.59	-0.54	-0.70
Bahrain	-0.74	0.31	0.78	0.92	0.95
Comoros	-0.51	-0.19	-0.84	-0.84	-0.73
Djibouti	-0.69	-0.69	-0.88	-0.51	-0.73
Egypt	-0.87	-0.35	-0.32	0.09	-0.29
Iraq	-2.12	-1.75	-1.64	-1.70	-1.43
Jordan	-0.41	-0.44	0.36	0.33	0.00
Kuwait	-0.29	0.14	0.16	0.81	1.06
Lebanon	-0.54	-0.59	-0.41	-0.27	-0.34
Libya	-1.70	-0.43	-0.87	-0.91	-0.82
Mauritania	-0.67	0.43	-0.16	-0.33	0.23
Morocco	-0.30	-0.14	0.07	0.11	-0.04
Oman	-0.55	0.98	0.69	0.83	1.03
Qatar	-0.52	0.82	0.69	0.84	0.92
Saudi Arabia	-1.40	0.05	-0.05	0.44	0.57
Somalia	-1.51	-1.95	-1.97	-2.05	-1.19
Sudan	-1.71	-1.94	-1.11	-1.36	-1.09
Syria	-1.56	-0.14	-0.57	-0.41	-0.29
Tunisia	-0.83	0.24	0.65	0.27	0.35
United Arab Emirates	-0.47	0.95	0.83	0.95	1.19
West Bank	-1.08	-1.69	-1.04	-0.31	-0.99
Yemen	-0.88	-1.36	-0.87	-1.23	-0.69
Arab countries	-1.10	-0.78	-0.53	-0.44	-0.42
Africa (exc. Arab countries)	-0.70	-0.98	-0.78	-0.86	-0.81
Asia (exc. Arab countries)	-0.56	-0.33	-0.07	-0.20	-0.42
Europe	0.99	0.77	1.05	0.95	0.97
North America	1.34	0.41	1.72	1.71	1.80
Latin America & the Caribbean	0.11	-0.19	-0.25	-0.40	-0.26
Oceania	1.16	0.84	1.27	1.27	1.35
World	-0.28	-0.26	0.03	-0.08	-0.19

ANNEX II. SELECTED DOCUMENTS

I.   Universal Declaration of Human Rights[1]

II.   United Nations Commission on Human Rights Resolution on
        the Question of the violation of human rights in the occupied
        Arab territories, including Palestine (E/CN.4/2004/L.6)

III.   Draft revised Arab Charter on Human Rights (excerpts)

IV.   United Nations Convention against Corruption (excerpts)

V.   Charter for Reform of the Arab Situation (Saudi Arabia)

VI.   Project for Developing the Joint Arab Action Mechanism
        (Yemen)

VII.   Initiative for Developing the League of Arab States (LAS) and
        Activation of the Joint Arab Action Mechanism (Egypt)

VIII.   Sana'a Declaration on Democracy, Human Rights and the Role
        of the International Criminal Court

IX.   Alexandria Charter

X.   Arab Regional Conference on Education for All: Arab Vision
        for the Future (excerpts)

XI.   Tunis Declaration (excerpts)

---

[1] Adopted and proclaimed by General Assembly resolution 217A (III) of 10 December 1948.

I. UNIVERSAL DECLARATION OF HUMAN RIGHTS[2]

PREAMBLE

Whereas recognition of the inherent dignity and of the equal and inalienable rights of all members of the human family is the foundation of freedom, justice and peace in the world,

Whereas disregard and contempt for human rights have resulted in barbarous acts which have outraged the conscience of mankind, and the advent of a world in which human beings shall enjoy freedom of speech and belief and freedom from fear and want has been proclaimed as the highest aspiration of the common people,

Whereas it is essential, if man is not to be compelled to have recourse, as a last resort, to rebellion against tyranny and oppression, that human rights should be protected by the rule of law,

Whereas it is essential to promote the development of friendly relations between nations,

Whereas the peoples of the United Nations have in the Charter reaffirmed their faith in fundamental human rights, in the dignity and worth of the human person and in the equal rights of men and women and have determined to promote social progress and better standards of life in larger freedom,

Whereas Member States have pledged themselves to achieve, in cooperation with the United Nations, the promotion of universal respect for and observance of human rights and fundamental freedoms,

Whereas a common understanding of these rights and freedoms is of the greatest importance for the full realization of this pledge,
Now, therefore,

The General Assembly

Proclaims this Universal Declaration of Human Rights as a common standard of achievement for all peoples and all nations, to the end that every individual and every organ of society, keeping this Declaration constantly in mind, shall strive by teaching and education to promote respect for these rights and freedoms and by progressive measures, national and international, to secure their universal and effective recognition and observance, both among the peoples of Member States themselves and among the peoples of territories under their jurisdiction.

Article 1

All human beings are born free and equal in dignity and rights. They are endowed with reason and conscience and should act towards one another in a spirit of brotherhood.

Article 2

Everyone is entitled to all the rights and freedoms set forth in this Declaration, without distinction of any kind, such as race, colour, sex, language, religion, political or other opinion, national or social origin, property, birth or other status.

Furthermore, no distinction shall be made on the basis of the political, jurisdictional or international status of the country or territory to which a person belongs, whether it be independent, trust, non-self-governing or under any other limitation of sovereignty.

Article 3

Everyone has the right to life, liberty and security of person.

Article 4

No one shall be held in slavery or servitude; slavery and the slave trade shall be prohibited in all their forms.

Article 5

No one shall be subjected to torture or to cruel, inhuman or degrading treatment or punishment.

Article 6

Everyone has the right to recognition everywhere as a person before the law.

Article 7

All are equal before the law and are entitled without any discrimination to equal protection of the law. All are entitled to equal protection against any discrimination in violation of this Declaration and against any incitement to such discrimination.

Article 8

Everyone has the right to an effective remedy

---

[2] Adopted and proclaimed by General Assembly resolution 217A (III) of 10 December 1948.

by the competent national tribunals for acts violating the fundamental rights granted him by the constitution or by law.

Article 9

No one shall be subjected to arbitrary arrest, detention or exile.

Article 10

Everyone is entitled in full equality to a fair and public hearing by an independent and impartial tribunal, in the determination of his rights and obligations and of any criminal charge against him.

Article 11

1. Everyone charged with a penal offence has the right to be presumed innocent until proved guilty according to law in a public trial at which he has had all the guarantees necessary for his defence.
2. No one shall be held guilty of any penal offence on account of any act or omission which did not constitute a penal offence, under national or international law, at the time when it was committed. Nor shall a heavier penalty be imposed than the one that was applicable at the time the penal offence was committed.

Article 12

No one shall be subjected to arbitrary interference with his privacy, family, home or correspondence, nor to attacks upon his honour and reputation. Everyone has the right to the protection of the law against such interference or attacks.

Article 13

1. Everyone has the right to freedom of movement and residence within the borders of each State.
2. Everyone has the right to leave any country, including his own, and to return to his country.

Article 14

1. Everyone has the right to seek and to enjoy in other countries asylum from persecution.
2. This right may not be invoked in the case of prosecutions genuinely arising from non-political crimes or from acts contrary to the purposes and principles of the United Nations.

Article 15

1. Everyone has the right to a nationality.
2. No one shall be arbitrarily deprived of his nationality nor denied the right to change his nationality.

Article 16

1. Men and women of full age, without any limitation due to race, nationality or religion, have the right to marry and to found a family. They are entitled to equal rights as to marriage, during marriage and at its dissolution.
2. Marriage shall be entered into only with the free and full consent of the intending spouses.
3. The family is the natural and fundamental group unit of society and is entitled to protection by society and the State.

Article 17

1. Everyone has the right to own property alone as well as in association with others.
2. No one shall be arbitrarily deprived of his property.

Article 18

Everyone has the right to freedom of thought, conscience and religion; this right includes freedom to change his religion or belief, and freedom, either alone or in community with others and in public or private, to manifest his religion or belief in teaching, practice, worship and observance.

Article 19

Everyone has the right to freedom of opinion and expression; this right includes freedom to hold opinions without interference and to seek, receive and impart information and ideas through any media and regardless of frontiers.

Article 20

1. Everyone has the right to freedom of peaceful assembly and association.
2. No one may be compelled to belong to an association.

Article 21

1. Everyone has the right to take part in the government of his country, directly or through freely chosen representatives.
2. Everyone has the right to equal access to public service in his country.
3. The will of the people shall be the basis of

the authority of government; this will shall be expressed in periodic and genuine elections which shall be by universal and equal suffrage and shall be held by secret vote or by equivalent free voting procedures.

Article 22

Everyone, as a member of society, has the right to social security and is entitled to realization, through national effort and international co-operation and in accordance with the organization and resources of each State, of the economic, social and cultural rights indispensable for his dignity and the free development of his personality.

Article 23

1. Everyone has the right to work, to free choice of employment, to just and favourable conditions of work and to protection against unemployment.

2. Everyone, without any discrimination, has the right to equal pay for equal work.

3. Everyone who works has the right to just and favourable remuneration ensuring for himself and his family an existence worthy of human dignity, and supplemented, if necessary, by other means of social protection.

4. Everyone has the right to form and to join trade unions for the protection of his interests.

Article 24

Everyone has the right to rest and leisure, including reasonable limitation of working hours and periodic holidays with pay.

Article 25

1. Everyone has the right to a standard of living adequate for the health and well-being of himself and of his family, including food, clothing, housing and medical care and necessary social services, and the right to security in the event of unemployment, sickness, disability, widowhood, old age or other lack of livelihood in circumstances beyond his control.

2. Motherhood and childhood are entitled to special care and assistance. All children, whether born in or out of wedlock, shall enjoy the same social protection.

Article 26

1. Everyone has the right to education. Education shall be free, at least in the elementary and fundamental stages. Elementary education shall be compulsory. Technical and professional education shall be made generally available and higher education shall be equally accessible to all on the basis of merit.

2. Education shall be directed to the full development of the human personality and to the strengthening of respect for human rights and fundamental freedoms. It shall promote understanding, tolerance and friendship among all nations, racial or religious groups, and shall further the activities of the United Nations for the maintenance of peace.

3. Parents have a prior right to choose the kind of education that shall be given to their children.

Article 27

1. Everyone has the right freely to participate in the cultural life of the community, to enjoy the arts and to share in scientific advancement and its benefits.

2. Everyone has the right to the protection of the moral and material interests resulting from any scientific, literary or artistic production of which he is the author.

Article 28

Everyone is entitled to a social and international order in which the rights and freedoms set forth in this Declaration can be fully realized.

Article 29

1. Everyone has duties to the community in which alone the free and full development of his personality is possible.

2. In the exercise of his rights and freedoms, everyone shall be subject only to such limitations as are determined by law solely for the purpose of securing due recognition and respect for the rights and freedoms of others and of meeting the just requirements of morality, public order and the general welfare in a democratic society.

3. These rights and freedoms may in no case be exercised contrary to the purposes and principles of the United Nations.

Article 30

Nothing in this Declaration may be interpreted as implying for any State, group or person any right to engage in any activity or to perform any act aimed at the destruction of any of the rights and freedoms set forth herein.

II. UN COMMISSION ON HUMAN RIGHTS RESOLUTION ON THE QUESTION OF THE VIOLATION OF HUMAN RIGHTS IN THE OCCUPIED ARAB TERRITORIES, INCLUDING PALESTINE (E/CN.4/2004/L.6)

COMMISSION ON HUMAN RIGHTS
SIXTIETH SESSION
AGENDA ITEM 8

The Commission on Human Rights,

Guided by the purposes and principles of the Charter of the United Nations and by the provisions of the Universal Declaration of Human Rights,

Recalling Security Council resolutions 242 (1967) of 22 November 1967, 338 (1973) of 22 October 1973, 1397 (2002) of 12 March 2002, 1402 (2002) of 30 March 2002 and 1403 (2002) of 4 April 2002 that called upon both parties to move immediately to a meaningful ceasefire, for withdrawal of Israeli troops and for an immediate cessation of all acts of violence, including all acts of terror, provocation, incitement and destruction,

Guided by the provisions of the International Covenant on Economic, Social and Cultural Rights and the International Covenant on Civil and Political Rights,

Taking into consideration the provisions of the Geneva Convention relative to the Protection of Civilian Persons in Time of War, of 12 August 1949, the provisions of Additional Protocol I thereto of 1977 and the Hague Convention of 18 October 1907, and Annexed Regulations concerning the Laws and Customs of War on Land,

Recalling resolutions of the Security Council, the General Assembly and the Commission on Human Rights relating to the applicability of the Fourth Geneva Convention to the Occupied Palestinian Territory, including East Jerusalem, since the 5 June 1967 war,

Reaffirming the applicability of the Fourth Geneva Convention to the Palestinian territories occupied since the June 1967 war, including East Jerusalem,

Recalling General Assembly resolutions on Israeli violations of human rights in the Palestinian territories occupied since 1967, including East Jerusalem,

Recalling in particular General Assembly resolution 37/43 of 3 December 1982 reaffirming the legitimacy of the struggle of peoples for independence from foreign domination and foreign occupation and for self-determination, by all available means,

Recalling the Vienna Declaration and Programme of Action, adopted in June 1993 by the World Conference on Human Rights (A/CONF.157/23),

Welcoming the report of the Special Rapporteur on the situation of human rights in the Palestinian territories occupied since 1967, Mr. John Dugard (E/CN.4/2004/6 and Add.1), and the report of the Special Rapporteur on the right to food, Mr. Jean Ziegler (E/CN.4/2004/10/Add.2),

Expressing its deep concern at the failure of the Government of Israel to cooperate with the Human Rights Inquiry Commission established pursuant to Commission resolution S-5/1 of 19 October 2000 and its failure to cooperate with other relevant special rapporteurs, particularly Mr. John Dugard,

Gravely concerned at the continued deterioration of the situation in the Occupied Palestinian Territory and at the gross violations of human rights and international humanitarian law, in particular, acts of extrajudicial killing, closures, collective punishments, the persistence in establishing settlements, arbitrary detentions, siege of Palestinian towns and villages, the shelling of Palestinian residential neighbourhoods by warplanes, tanks and Israeli battleships, and incursions into towns, villages and camps to kill innocent men, women and children, as was the case in Jenin, Balata, Khan Younis, Rafah, Ramallah, Gaza, Nablus, Al-Birah, Al-Amari, Jabalia, Bethlehem and Dheisheh and in the Al-Daraj and Al-Zaitoun neighbourhoods in the city of Gaza, and also during recent months in the Rafah and in Al-Shajai'ia neighbourhood in Gaza, as well as during the last Israeli massacres in the Al-Nusseirat and Al-Burreij refugee camps in the centre of the Gaza Strip on 7 March 2004,

Expressing its grave concern at the continued Israeli aggression and the resulting deaths and injuries, mostly among Palestinians, the toll of casualties having increased to over 2,800 martyrs and over 25,000 wounded since 28 September 2000,

Taking note of the reports of the Special Committee to Investigate Israeli Practices Affecting the Human Rights of the Palestinian People and Other Arabs of the Occupied Territories submitted to the General Assembly since 1968, the last of which was A/58/311,

Expressing its grave concern at the continued Israeli refusal to abide by the resolutions of the Security Council, the General Assembly and the Commission on Human Rights calling upon Israel to put an end to the violations of human rights and affirming the applicability of the Fourth Geneva Convention to the Palestinian territories occupied by Israel since 1967, including East Jerusalem,

Convinced that the basis of negotiations and of achieving a just and lasting peace should be Security Council resolutions 242 (1967), 338 (1973) and other relevant United Nations resolutions, including the principle of the inadmissibility of acquisition of territory by war, the need for every State in the area to be able to live in security and the principle of land for peace,

Recalling all its previous resolutions in this respect, the latest of which is resolution 2003/6 of 15 April 2003,

Recalling also the inadmissibility of the acquisition of others' land by force, which constitutes a jus cogens in international law,

Gravely concerned at the construction of the Israeli wall inside the Occupied Palestinian Territory, aimed at expropriating further Palestinian lands by force, with all the drastic consequences that this wall will have on the Palestinian community, namely on its social, economic, educational, health and psychological aspects, and which is destroying any possibility of achieving a genuine peace based on the two-State solution, with an independent Palestinian State and an Israeli State,

Affirming that the construction of this wall on the Palestinian territories constitutes a violation of the right of the Palestinian people to self-determination and hinders the exercise by the Palestinian people of this right,

Recalling in this respect General Assembly resolution ES-10/13 of 21 October 2003,

Recalling also the report of the Secretary-General (A/ES-10/248), which concluded that Israel is not in compliance with the Assembly's demand that "it stop and reverse the construction of the wall in the Occupied Palestinian Territory",

1. Reaffirms the legitimate right of the Palestinian people to resist the Israeli occupation in order to free its land and be able to exercise its right to self-determination, in conformity with the goals and purposes stipulated by the Charter of the United Nations;

2. Strongly condemns once more the human rights violations of the Israeli occupation authorities in the Occupied Palestinian Territory, including East Jerusalem, since 1967;

3. Also strongly condemns the Israeli occupation of the Palestinian territories as being an aggression and an offence against humanity and a flagrant violation of human rights;

4. Further strongly condemns the war launched by the Israeli army, particularly since October 2000, against Palestinian towns and camps, which has resulted so far in the death of hundreds of Palestinian civilians, including women and children;

5. Strongly condemns anew the practice of "liquidation" or "extrajudicial executions" carried out by the Israeli army against Palestinians, a practice which not only constitutes a violation of human rights norms, a flagrant violation of article 3 of the Universal Declaration of Human Rights and of the rule of law, but which is also damaging for the relationship between the parties and therefore constitutes an obstacle to peace, and urges the Government of Israel to respect international law and immediately to put an end to such practices;

6. Strongly condemns once again the establishment of Israeli settlements and other related activities in the Occupied Palestinian Territory, including East Jerusalem, such as the construction of new settlements and the expansion of the existing ones, land confiscation, biased administration of water resources and the construction of bypass roads, which not only constitute grave violations of human rights and international humanitarian law, especially article 49 of the Geneva Convention relative to the Protection of Civilian Persons in Time of War, of 12 August 1949 (the Fourth Geneva Convention) and Additional Protocol I thereto of 1977, according to which such violations are categorized as war crimes, but are also major obstacles to peace, urges the Government of Israel to implement the relevant United Nations resolutions as well as the resolutions of

the Commission on Human Rights relative to the Israeli settlements, and affirms that the dismantling of Israeli settlements constitutes an essential factor for achieving a just, comprehensive and lasting peace in the region;

7. Condemns once again the expropriation of Palestinian homes in Jerusalem, Hebron and the rest of the Occupied Palestinian Territory, the revocation of the identity cards of the residents of East Jerusalem and the policy of imposing fabricated and exorbitant taxes with the aim of forcing Palestinians living in Jerusalem, who cannot afford to pay these high taxes, out of their homes and out of their city, with the aim of Judaizing Jerusalem, and calls upon the Government of Israel to put an end immediately to these practices;

8. Also condemns once again the use of torture against Palestinians during interrogation, as it constitutes a grave violation of the principles of international humanitarian law, of the Convention against Torture and Other Cruel, Inhuman or Degrading Treatment or Punishment and also of article 5 of the Universal Declaration of Human Rights, and calls upon the Government of Israel to immediately put an end to such practices and to bring the perpetrators of these violations to justice;

9. Strongly condemns once more the offensives of the Israeli army of occupation against hospitals and sick persons and the use of Palestinian citizens as human shields during Israeli incursions into Palestinian areas;

10. Also strongly condemns once more the Israeli army of occupation's practices of opening fire on ambulances and paramedical personnel and preventing ambulances and vehicles of the International Committee of the Red Cross from reaching the wounded and the dead in order to transport them to hospital, thus leaving the wounded bleeding to death in the streets;

11. Strongly condemns acts of mass killing of Palestinians at the hands of the Israeli occupation authorities, including the killing of children, such as recently took place in Nablus, Gaza, Rafah, Al-Nusseirat and Al-Burreij and which persist to this day;

12. Also strongly condemns acts that consist of imposing collective punishments, military siege of Palestinian territories, isolating Palestinian towns and villages from each other by military roadblocks used as a trap to kill Palestinians, demolishing houses and levelling agricultural lands, as these practices contribute, together with other factors, to the acts of violence that have prevailed in the region for over three and a half years, and calls upon the Government of Israel immediately to put an end to these practices and to lift its military siege of Palestinian towns and villages and its military roadblocks, and affirms anew that such collective punishments are prohibited under international law, as they constitute grave violations of the provisions of the Fourth Geneva Convention and Additional Protocol I thereto, and also are war crimes;

13. Expresses its grave concern once again at the restriction of the freedom of movement imposed by the Israeli occupation authorities on Yasser Arafat, the democratically elected Palestinian President, in violation of articles 9 and 13 of the Universal Declaration of Human Rights;

14. Strongly condemns campaigns of massive arrests conducted by the Israeli occupation authorities to detain thousands of Palestinians without trial and without any criminal charges having been brought against them, in violation of article 9 of the Universal Declaration of Human Rights and of the provisions of the Fourth Geneva Convention in this respect;

15. Affirms anew that the demolitions carried out by the Israeli occupying forces of at least thirty thousand Palestinian houses, facilities and property constitute grave violations of articles 33 and 53 of the Fourth Geneva Convention and that acts of levelling farmlands, uprooting trees and destroying what is left of the Palestinian infrastructure constitute a form of collective punishment to which Palestinians are subjected, grave violations of the provisions of international humanitarian law and war crimes according to international law;

16. Affirms anew that the Fourth Geneva Convention is applicable to the Palestinian territories occupied by Israel since 1967, including East Jerusalem, and considers any change in the geographical, demographic and institutional status of the city of East Jerusalem from its status prior to the June 1967 war to be illegal and void;

17. Calls once again upon Israel, the occupying Power, to desist from all forms of human rights violations in the Occupied Palestinian Territory, including East Jerusalem, and other occupied Arab territories, and to respect the

principles of international law, international humanitarian law, the Universal Declaration of Human Rights, its international commitments and its signed agreements with the Palestine Liberation Organization;

18. Also calls once again upon Israel to withdraw from the Palestinian territories occupied since 1967, including East Jerusalem, in accordance with the relevant resolutions of the United Nations and the Commission on Human Rights, as a basic condition for achieving a just, lasting and comprehensive peace in the Middle East;

19. Strongly condemns the construction of the Israeli wall inside the Occupied Palestinian Territory, in the West Bank, as it constitutes a new Israeli pretext for the forcible confiscation of further Palestinian lands, it endangers the social, economic, cultural, educational, health and psychological aspects of the lives of hundreds of thousands of Palestinians as well as their familial unity, it prevents Palestinians from having access to their natural resources and it constitutes a major obstacle to achieving a just and lasting peace on the basis of the two-State solution, with an independent Palestinian State and Israeli State, the only solution which guarantees peace and stability in the region, and it also prevents Palestinians from exercising their right to self-determination; and calls on Israel immediately to stop the construction of the said wall and to erase what it has already built of this wall inside the Palestinian territories occupied since 1967;

20. Requests the Special Rapporteur on the situation of human rights in the Palestinian territories occupied by Israel since 1967, to investigate Israel's violations of the principles and bases of international law, international humanitarian law and the Geneva Convention relative to the Protection of Civilian Persons in Time of War, of 12 August 1949, and, in his capacity as a monitoring mechanism, to follow up on the implementation of these recommendations and to report thereon to the General Assembly at its fifty-ninth session and to the Commission on Human Rights at its sixty-first session, until the end of the mandate of the Special Rapporteur as established in Commission resolution 1993/2 A of 1993;

21. Calls upon the relevant United Nations organs urgently to consider the best ways to pro-

vide the necessary international protection for the Palestinian people until the end of the Israeli occupation of the Palestinian territories;

22. Requests the Secretary-General to bring the present resolution to the attention of the Government of Israel and all other Governments, the competent United Nations organs, the specialized agencies, regional intergovernmental organizations and international humanitarian organizations, to disseminate it on the widest possible scale and to report on its implementation by the Government of Israel to the Commission on Human Rights at its sixty-first session;

23. Also requests the Secretary-General to provide the Commission with all United Nations reports issued between the sessions of the Commission that deal with the conditions in which the populations of the Palestinian and other occupied Arab territories are living under the Israeli occupation;

24. Decides to consider this question at its sixty-first session under the same agenda item, as a matter of high priority.

III. DRAFT REVISED ARAB CHARTER ON HUMAN RIGHTS (EXCERPTS)

Article 1 (new article)

In the framework of the national identity of the Arab States and sentiments of belonging to a shared civilization, the present Charter aims to realize the following goals:

a) To place human rights in the Arab States among the most important national interests, such that human rights come to constitute a supreme and fundamental paradigm and exemplar that guides human will in the Arab States, and allows individuals to improve the realities of their lives in accordance with noble human goals.

b) Energizing individuals in the Arab States to strengthen their sense of identity and loyalty to their nation, territorially, historically and in terms of shared interests, together with the dissemination of the culture of human brotherhood, tolerance, and mutual openness to the other, in accordance with the demands of universal principles and values proclaimed in international human rights treaties.

c) Preparing coming generations in the Arab

States to live free and responsible lives in a civil society that is inclusive and based on linking awareness of rights and commitment to duties, governed by the values of equality, tolerance, and justice.

d) Firmly establishing the judicial principle that all human rights are universal, indivisible, inter-related and inter-dependent.

Article 2 (revised Article 1)

a) All peoples have the right to self-determination and control over their own wealth and resources, and have the right to determine through freedom of choice, the type of political system that will govern them, and to maintain freedom of economic and social and cultural development.

b) All peoples have the right to live under national sovereignty and territorial unity.

c) All forms of racism, Zionism, occupation, and foreign control threaten human dignity and constitute fundamental obstacles to the existence of the basic rights of peoples, and it is necessary to condemn all such practices and to work for their eradication.

Article 3 (revised Article 2)

a) Every State Party to this Charter binds itself to guarantee to all individuals under its authority the right to enjoy the rights and freedoms stipulated in this Charter, without discrimination on the basis of origin, colour, sex, language, religious belief, opinion, thought, national origin, social origin, wealth, place of birth, disability, or any other circumstance.

b) The State shall take appropriate steps to guarantee protection from all forms of discrimination on any of the bases stipulated in the preceding paragraph. Likewise it will make all necessary arrangements to realize the aim of securing real independence to enjoy all rights and freedoms stipulated in this Convention.

c) States Parties to the present Convention commit themselves to a course of action that, with all appropriate means and without political suppression, will put an end to discrimination against women; and to take all necessary steps to guarantee and secure the equality of men and women to enjoy all the rights stipulated in this Convention.

Article 4 (revised Article 3)

(a) In exceptional emergency situations that threaten the life of the nation, and which are proclaimed officially, States Parties to this Charter are permitted to take, in the narrowest limits possible given the particular situation, steps in which they are not bound by the obligations pertinent to that situation and stipulated in this Charter, on condition that these arrangements do not contravene the other obligations by which that State is bound under international law, and as long as these arrangements are not of a discriminatory nature, based on origin, colour, sex, language, religion, or social origin.

(b) It is impermissible in any circumstances whatsoever to transgress the following rights which are not subject to derogation or suspension: Article 5 (the right to life); Article 8 (prohibition of torture or cruel, inhuman or degrading treatment or punishment); Article 9 (prohibition of enforced medical or scientific experiment without consent); Article 10 (the banning of any form of enslavement); Article 13 (minimum standards for fair trial); Article 14 paragraph (h) (the right to challenge the legality of arrest or detention); Article 15 (legal definition of crimes and punishments, and non-retroactivity of the law, application of the most appropriate law to the accused); Article 18 (prohibition of imprisonment for non-payment of debts); Article 19 (prohibition on double jeopardy); Article 31 (freedom of thought, identity, and religion); Article 20 (humane treatment of all those deprived of their freedom); Article 22 (recognition of the individual's legal person); Article 27 (the right to return to the homeland); Article 28 (political refugee status); Article 29 (right to citizenship); as it is impermissible to suspend legal guarantees required to protect those rights.

(c) Any State Party to this Charter that implements the right of derogation must inform the other States Parties to the Charter immediately, through the Secretary General of the League of Arab States and the UN Secretary-General, of the specific provisions that it is suspending and the reasons for doing so. And on the date that this suspension ends, it must inform the other States through the same channels.

Source: General secretariat, League of Arab States – United Nations Office of the High Commissioner for Human Rights, 2003.

IV. UNITED NATIONS CONVENTION AGAINST CORRUPTION (EXCERPTS)

PREAMBLE

Concerned about the seriousness of problems and threats posed by corruption to the stability and security of societies, undermining the institutions and values of democracy, ethical values and justice and jeopardizing sustainable development and the rule of law,

Concerned also about the links between corruption and other forms of crime, in particular organized crime and economic crime, including money-laundering, ...

Convinced that corruption is no longer a local matter but a transnational phenomenon that affects all societies and economies, making international cooperation to prevent and control it essential, ...

Convinced that the illicit acquisition of personal wealth can be particularly damaging to democratic institutions, national economies and the rule of law, ...

Article 1

Statement of purpose
The purposes of this Convention are:
(a) To promote and strengthen measures to prevent and combat corruption more efficiently and effectively;
(b) To promote, facilitate and support international cooperation and technical assistance in the prevention of and fight against corruption, including in asset recovery;
(c) To promote integrity, accountability and proper management of public affairs and public property.

Article 5

Preventive anti-corruption policies and practices
1. Each State Party shall, in accordance with the fundamental principles of its legal system, develop and implement or maintain effective, coordinated anti-corruption policies that promote the participation of society and reflect the principles of the rule of law, proper management of public affairs and public property, integrity, transparency and accountability.
2. Each State Party shall endeavour to establish and promote effective practices aimed at the prevention of corruption. ...

Article 6

Preventive anti-corruption body or bodies
1. Each State Party shall, in accordance with the fundamental principles of its legal system, ensure the existence of a body or bodies, as appropriate, that prevent corruption...

Article 7

Public sector
1. Each State Party shall, where appropriate and in accordance with the fundamental principles of its legal system, endeavour to adopt, maintain and strengthen systems for the recruitment, hiring, retention, promotion and retirement of civil servants and, where appropriate, other non-elected public officials:
(a) That are based on principles of efficiency, transparency and objective criteria such as merit, equity and aptitude; ....

Article 12

Private sector
1. Each State Party shall take measures, in accordance with the fundamental principles of its domestic law, to prevent corruption involving the private sector enhance accounting and auditing standards in the private sector and, where appropriate, provide effective, proportionate and dissuasive civil, administrative or criminal penalties for failure to comply with such measures. ...

Article 13

Participation of society
1. Each State Party shall take appropriate measures, within its means and in accordance with fundamental principles of its domestic law, to promote the active participation of individuals and groups outside the public sector, such as civil society, non-governmental organizations and community-based organizations, in the prevention of and the fight against corruption and to raise public awareness regarding the existence, causes and gravity of and the threat posed by corruption. This participation should be strengthened by such measures as:
(a) Enhancing the transparency of and promoting the contribution of the public to deci-

sion-making processes;

(b) Ensuring that the public has effective access to information; …

Article 16

Bribery of foreign public officials and officials of public international organizations

1. Each State Party shall adopt such legislative and other measures as may be necessary to establish as a criminal offence, when committed intentionally, the promise, offering or giving to a foreign public official or an official of a public international organization, directly or indirectly, of an undue advantage, for the official himself or herself or another person or entity, in order that the official act or refrain from acting in the exercise of his or her official duties, …

Article 18

Trading in influence

Each State Party shall consider adopting such legislative and other measures as may be necessary to establish as criminal offences, when committed intentionally:

(a) The promise, offering or giving to a public official or any other person, directly or indirectly, of an undue advantage in order that the public official or the person abuse his or her real or supposed influence with a view to obtaining from an administration or public authority of the State Party an undue advantage for the original instigator of the act or for any other person; ….

V. CHARTER FOR REFORM OF THE ARAB SITUATION (SAUDI ARABIA)

The Arab Kings and Presidents, after reviewing the present Arab situation, and having observed a protracted silence and a nearly incomprehensible acquiescence in events occurring in the Arab region that give an impression of powerlessness and lack of control, impelling some to think little of attacking the Arab nation, thereby damaging its legitimate interests,

Consider that the time has come to rouse the soul of that nation to wakefulness and stimulate its zeal to demonstrate Arabs' capacities, their determination to fortify the vitality of their community and their ability to confront the challenges and dangers arising from

current developments, evolving as they are at a rapid rate, by joining forces to change the bitter situation now being endured by the Arab nation, thereby confirming the words of the Qur'an, "God brings change to a people only when that people changes itself."

In view of the fact that the Joint Arab Action mechanism is in need of seriousness, credibility and commitment to the implementation of duly adopted resolutions, which have been sorely lacking in recent years, the Arab Kings and Presidents recognize the timeliness of a new Arab charter to safeguard the legitimate interests and attain the just objectives of the Arab nation, to build joint Arab action on the strongest and most secure of foundations, rather than on the weakest and most unreliable of foundations as heretofore, and to organize relations between Arab States and guide relations with the States of the world, these aims to be realized through the establishment of clearly defined mechanisms and programmes designed to ensure that resolutions adopted at Arab summit meetings will be duly implemented.

Accordingly, they swear by Almighty God and pledge to their peoples that they will strive firmly and resolutely to safeguard the sovereignty and security of Arab States and the unity of their lands and to build Arab defensive capability, and they affirm that they are prepared to back the Palestinian Authority and support the endurance of the Palestinian people in its occupied homeland, subjected as it is to Israeli policies of oppression, occupation and encirclement.

They renew their adoption of the option of a just, comprehensive peace based on legitimate Arab rights, and they proclaim their resolve to strive for the implementation of the Arab peace initiative together with all the world's peace-loving peoples, deeming that clearly to be the way to a just, comprehensive and lasting peace in the region, which can be attained only by Israel's withdrawal from all the Arab territories occupied in 1967, enabling the Palestinian people to exercise its legitimate and internationally recognized right to establish an independent State on its occupied land, with the holy city of Jerusalem as its capital. They declare that the elements of the Arab peace initiative are the minimum acceptable conditions for entering into normal relations with Israel on the basis of the relevant UN resolutions and pursuant to the authority of the Madrid Conference and the principle of land for peace.

They are persuaded that self-reform and the development of political participation within Arab States are the fundamental starting-points for Arab capacity-building and action to generate the conditions for a comprehensive Arab renaissance, meet the requirements for positive involvement in all areas of the competitive global marketplace, achieve sustainable development, create programmes to encourage innovation and creative thinking, and deal objectively and realistically with rapidly evolving processes of innovation and change in the global economic space, especially as regards the emergence of large economic blocs, the steady growth of globalization, with the challenges and opportunities that it brings in its train, and the constantly accelerating pace of technological progress and the development of information and communication technologies. The Arab world is an important contributor to the process of human cultural development in all its aspects.

They proclaim their categorical rejection of any illegitimate external aggression against any Arab State, their commitment to the resolution of all Arab disputes by peaceful means and the illegitimacy of the use of force between Arab States, and their united opposition to any Arab State that commits aggression against any other Arab State on any pretext and under any circumstances. They harbour enmity toward none; their aim and purpose is to defend their interests and harness their energies in the service of international security and peace.

In view of the fact that a sound economy is the foundation-stone underpinning the strength and prosperity of States, whereas the efforts of Arab States to promote economic cooperation among themselves have lacked seriousness and credibility to date, it is essential to develop a practical plan to complete the final implementation of the Greater Arab Free Trade Area by the end of 2005, with no exceptions or administrative or technical restrictions, and to endeavour to develop a trade policy based on a unified tariff structure with a view to creating a customs union within a period of not more than ten years, as a step toward the establishment of an Arab common market.

VI. PROJECT FOR DEVELOPING THE JOINT ARAB ACTION MECHANISM (YEMEN)

The Republic of Yemen considers that the circumstances surrounding the Arab nation and the Joint Arab Action mechanism imperatively require reformulation of the basis and aims of that mechanism. In the light of more than fifty years of experience of both the positive and the negative aspects of the League of Arab States, we suggest that it is time to transform the League, with all its constituent bodies and institutions, into a new Arab entity to be known as the Union of Arab States, in response to regional and international changes and developments in all areas of politics, economics, social organization, defence, security and culture and in order to enhance regional security in the face of the challenges and dangers imperilling the present and the future of the Arab nation, impeding its progress and preventing it from realizing its aspirations, with a view to achieving the unity of that nation.

PRINCIPLES:

The Republic of Yemen considers that the "Union of Arab States" must be based on a number of essential principles, viz.:
- Respect for the sovereignty of every Arab State and respect for its territorial boundaries and the unity of its national land.
- The right of every State to choose its system of governance.
- Non-interference in the internal affairs of Member States.
- Encouragement for democratic practices, the promotion of democratic institutions and respect for human rights.
- Non-recognition of the seizure of power by force or by extralegal means in any Arab State. Suspension of any such State from membership until such time as legality is restored.
- Establishment of an Arab regional system of security to protect Member States and enable them to participate more effectively in the realization of international security and peace.
- A commitment by Member States to resolve their differences by peaceful means, and to eschew the use of force for settling disputes.
- A commitment to the UN Charter and bilateral treaties between Member States, the

maintenance of international security and stability, and anti-terrorism.

OBJECTIVES:

The Union of Arab States seeks to achieve regional economic integration, considering that development of Member States' shared interests and economic convergence are the true key to political unification, taking into account the importance of a gradual approach in order to enable the Arab nation to bring the Union into being.

ORGANIZATIONAL STRUCTURES AND FRAMEWORK OF THE UNION

Supreme Council of the Union:

The Supreme Council of the Union shall be made up of the Kings, Presidents and Emirs of Arab countries, and shall be the Union's supreme power. It shall be competent to set and adopt general policies, issue executive orders and validate recommendations and resolutions submitted to it by lower councils. The office of President of the High Council of the Union shall be held on a rotating basis for a term of one year.

People's Assembly:

The People's Assembly shall comprise two bodies:
* The Chamber of Deputies;
* The Consultative Council.

The People's Assembly shall be the legislative arm of the Union, enshrining the principle of the right of the Arab peoples to oversee and monitor the institutions of the Union. It shall be formed gradually from existing Parliaments and any other representative bodies in States. Ultimately, it shall be made up of members elected in accordance with agreed standards and conditions. The regulations of the Chamber of Deputies and the Consultative Council shall determine each State's representation and the areas of competence, headquarters site, term and working methods of the body in question.

Council of Heads of Government:

The Council of Heads of Government shall be the executive arm of the Union, and it shall be made up of the Heads of Government of the States of the Union.

Ministerial Councils:

These shall comprise:
* The Council of Ministers for Foreign Affairs of Member States;
* The Council of Ministers of Development, Economic Affairs and Trade (Economic Council);
* The Defence and Security Council;
* Any other Councils that it shall be deemed expedient to add.

The function of these Councils shall be to propose, each in its own area of competence, integrated policies in the framework of more general Union policies, and to monitor the implementation of those policies through executive mechanisms and measures to be established, together with their membership procedures and working methods, by their respective regulations.

Arab Court of Justice

The function of the Court shall be to settle disputes between Member States, and to rule on any matters referred to it in accordance with its regulations, which shall be laid down by the Supreme Council of the Union.
* Commission
* Chamber of Permanent Representatives
* Secretariat of the Union

VOTING

New voting rules have been adopted with a view to achieving the interests of a majority of Member States and the interests of the Arab nation, based on the following principles:
* Acceptance of a new member: unanimous approval required;
* Fundamental issues: a three-quarters majority required;
* Substantive matters: a two-thirds majority required;
* Procedural matters: a simple majority will suffice.

As regards the drafting of the Constitution of the proposed Union of Arab States on the basis of the objectives, principles and working mechanisms outlined above, the Republic of Yemen recommends the establishment of a Ministerial Committee from seven Arab States, to be entrusted with responsibility for preparing the Constitution of the Union. The Committee may enlist the assistance of legal, economic and political experts from the League of Arab States and Member States. The draft Constitution shall be prepared within six months, and shall be submitted to Member States for consideration. It shall subsequently be submitted to the Council of Ministers for Foreign Affairs for approval, and subsequently to a periodic or special summit meeting for signing.

VII. INITIATIVE FOR DEVELOPING THE LEAGUE OF ARAB STATES (LAS) AND ACTIVATION OF THE JOINT ARAB ACTION MECHANISM (EGYPT)

1. Action to clear the air and remove impediments from inter-Arab relations

2. Assumption by the LAS of its role as a primary instrument of the Joint Arab Action mechanism

This would be accomplished through the establishment of a new mechanism within the context of the LAS aimed at achieving the necessary degree of coordination among Joint Arab Action institutions and agencies, including those institutions and agencies that do not come under the LAS umbrella.

3. Containment and resolution of inter-Arab disputes

Means to this end would include:
(a) A dispute prevention, management and settlement mechanism;
(b) Establishment of an Arab Court of Justice.

An Arab Court of Justice would serve as a legal mechanism for resolving inter-Arab disputes, clearing the air and relieving member States of the burden of crisis management, which is incompatible with the logic of Arab solidarity. Its efforts would ease some of the friction in inter-Arab relations and make it easier for Arab States to combine their efforts in dealing with the current Arab situation.

4. Economic projects aimed at achieving Arab integration and fostering private-sector participation

5. Establishment of an Arab Parliament

• With a view to broadening the scope of public participation, enhancing political stability, promoting the concept of the rule of law and strengthening respect for fundamental human rights and democratic values, an Arab Parliament would be established in an effort to put the LAS and the Joint Arab Action mechanism back on track.

• The Arab Parliament might be established through existing Arab representative bodies, directly elected by the people of the member States, or brought into being by some combination of those approaches.

• The main function of the Arab Parliament would be to monitor the work of the organs of the LAS from a political standpoint and to contribute to the drafting of general LAS policies covering all aspects of its work. The Parliament would devise mechanisms, ways and means of performing this political oversight function.

• The Parliament would also monitor the legislative and financial operations of the LAS.

6. Establishment of an Arab regional security system

There are two possible alternatives, or it might be feasible to combine them under an agreed formula:
(a) An Arab Security Council;
(b) An Arab National Security Forum, as an institutional framework for the discussion of all matters which in the view of Arab States might usefully contribute, at a later stage, to the building of a new Arab regional security system.

7. Support for Arab specialized institutions

More active links between those institutions and the LAS would be developed, subject to the condition that the former would retain full jurisdiction in their respective areas of competence and would lose none of their financial or administrative autonomy.

8. Creation of links between the LAS and civil-society institutions

Civil-society institutions would thereby be

enlisted as contributors to the outlook and vision that guide the Joint Arab Action initiative, helping to keep it on track and ensure that it is aware of the fears, aspirations and hopes of ordinary Arab people.

9. Changes to the voting system in organs of the LAS

The system of consensus, which at present is the basis of the voting system in the LAS Council, is regarded as outmoded and inappropriate for the contemporary situation.

10. Use of a method of collective diplomacy in implementing LAS decisions, especially decisions with a bearing on regional and international relations

11. Development of and support for the LAS secretariat

Source: Al-Ahram, Cairo, in Arabic, 8 March 2004.

VIII. SANA'A DECLARATION ON DEMOCRACY, HUMAN RIGHTS AND THE ROLE OF THE INTERNATIONAL CRIMINAL COURT

(a) The principles of democracy and human rights are an important source of and are rooted in beliefs and cultures; these rights are considered an indivisible whole.

(b) Diversity, difference and cultural, civilizational and religious particularities lie at the heart of recognized universal human rights, and must be taken into consideration in understanding the application of democracy and human rights. This diversity should not constitute a source of conflict but, to the contrary, a source of enrichment, and the starting point for dialogue aiming at building bridges for communication and mutual understanding between religions and civilizations.

(c) Democratic governance shall guarantee human rights protection and the welfare of all without discrimination; in particular, the rights and welfare of those sectors which are weak, marginalized or excluded.

(d) Democracy is attained through the establishment of institutions and laws for the practical exercise of democratic conduct at different levels and shall be judged according to the extent to which its principles, standards and values are representative of human rights principles and respect for human rights.

(e) Among the foundations of democratic governance is the existence of a legislature which is periodically elected, represents the citizens fairly and on the basis of popular participation; the constituent bodies of the executive are responsible to and bound by the rules of sound judgement, and an independent judiciary shall guarantee fair trials, protect human rights and freedoms and prevent/punish those who violate them. These fundamental principles are among those that shall guarantee a sound base for democratic performance which safeguards human rights.

(f) It is important to support democratic debate, to encourage participation, and political, democratic development, and to support the exchange of ideas and experience within and among participating States.

(g) Strengthening the democratic architecture and performance, protection of human rights and development of their substance are dependent on overcoming major challenges and threats, which include foreign occupation, defects in the balance between justice and the State, shortcomings in educational systems, and the definition of crimes in ways that are contrary to international law.

(h) The effective application of the rule of law is vital for protection of democracy and human rights, and is founded on an independent judiciary and the principle of separation of powers.

(i) Free and independent media are essential to buttress and protect democratic principles; plurality of the media in giving voice to different opinions and regarding their ownership is a vital component contributing to communicating knowledge and information, achieving participation and accountability and enlightening and forming public opinion, based on appropriate standards and regard for the truth. The media have an important and responsible role in entrenching democracy, and in spreading awareness and knowledge about human rights and their protection.

(j) A soundly based democracy and respect for human rights require guarantees for the right to freedom to set up and be a member of civil-society organizations, providing the appropriate legal framework and environment for their work; this is to strengthen partnership and participation, to organize effective social activism, so that civil society can play its role responsibly within the legal framework and bound by democratic principles and respect for human rights.

(k) The private sector is considered a vital partner in supporting democratic principles and strengthening human rights and has a responsibility to work actively with the State authorities and civil-society institutions in support of efforts aimed at achieving progress in these fields.

(l) The change in the climate of international relations, with increased attention to human rights and the rule of law, and the serious endeavour to put an end to violations of international law, and international human rights law, all demand the activation and development of mechanisms to punish and bring to account the perpetrators of grave crimes and other offences, including war crimes, crimes against humanity, genocide and aggression; all of which should be implemented without using double standards and avoiding their arbitrary application.

IX. ALEXANDRIA CHARTER

The Charter stressed that internal reform must not obscure the importance of a just solution to the Palestinian issue and of the liberation of occupied Arab territory. It also stressed its affirmation of the independence and territorial integrity of Iraq.

Participants called for Arab constitutions to be brought into line with the political systems aspired to by their societies and with international human rights charters. They demanded a separation between the legislative and executive powers and a guarantee of periodic peaceful change of government, the organization of regular free elections, the abolition of imprisonment or detention on grounds of opinion, and the release of prisoners of conscience anywhere in the Arab world whether these have yet to appear before a court or have been sentenced.

Participants demanded the abolition of all exceptional laws and emergency laws, freedom to form political parties and the ratification by Arab countries of the relevant international and Arab charters. They also called for freedom of press and media from government control and freedom for the institutions of civil society.

Participants presented a 22-point programme calling on Arab countries to announce clear plans and timetables for institutional and structural reform and the limitation of the powers of the State as a spur to economic activity and in order to provide an appropriate environment for the work of the private and public sectors. Also included in the programme were calls for the reduction of government bureaucracy, the removal of impediments to investment, the encouragement of privatization, the development of programmes to fund small projects and the adoption of economic policies capable of creating jobs for the five million annual new entrants into the Arab labour market, as well as addressing poverty.

In the area of social reform, participants called for the government to continue to take responsibility for funding and supporting educational institutions while guaranteeing the right of students to practise politics, including the holding of peaceful organized demonstrations, freedom of opinion and its expression, and democratic elections for student unions, plus the implementation of effective policies to guarantee a just distribution of wealth and the various returns on production.

X. ARAB REGIONAL CONFERENCE ON EDUCATION FOR ALL: ARAB VISION FOR THE FUTURE (EXCERPTS)

Based on the discussions and exchanges between conference participants, we affirm:

• That the Arab nation is a responsible partner in world society that is aware of its rights, obligations and responsibilities. The conference believes that the violations of international law and acts of violence and oppression committed in Palestine, Iraq and the Golan and of the threats against Syria by their very nature hamper educational development.

• That development and modernization of education rooted in beliefs, values and identity and responsive to national requirements should be maintained.

• That development and modernization of education should come from within, thus affirming the nation's beliefs, principles and interests while simultaneously taking every precaution to remain open to world thought, to respect the specificities of other peoples, and to welcome human experiences of proven success.

• That development, modernization and reform must encompass the entire world and lead finally to the rule of comprehensive and just peace in accordance with the regulations of international law, respect for human rights everywhere, and the acceptance of justice and law without bias or double stThis vision stresses the importance of the continuous development of academic curricula in terms of philosophy, goals, content and means and styles of teaching and learning. The point of departure for such work should be an attitude to the curriculum that views it as the entry point for the cultivation in the learner of a diversity of styles of thought and for providing him/her with the skills needed to deal, in full awareness, with the challenges of the knowledge society, thus enabling him/her to become a citizen capable of solving problems and contributing effectively to the progress of his/her society and nation. It follows that such a curriculum must place a high value on the role of the learner in the teaching and learning processes while magnifying the importance of the diversification of educational activities in realizing a learning experience of high quality.

Adoption of an authentic form of assessment that stresses the necessity of continuous and comprehensive evaluation of the performance of both students and the teaching system is a fundamental principle on which Arab countries place reliance in the context of the process of education development. Such evaluation deals with learning outputs according to their diverse fields and multiple activities by recourse to a variety of evaluation methods and instruments. Special attention is also paid to talent and to unusually talented students. Under such conditions, evaluation becomes a support and reinforcement for students' capabilities, prescribing treatment for their problems and guaranteeing them paths to excellence and distinction.

The vision also ascribes special importance to model investment in early childhood nurture and care. Here the point of departure should be an attitude that views early childhood as the stage at which children's multiple forms of intelligence are given every opportunity to blossom. This requires that the entire range of psychological, material and educational conditions appropriate for the realization of the unimpeded growth of the child's innate faculties to their maximum potential must be put in place, thus allowing his/her resources, capabilities and energies to blossom, grow and express themselves.

The vision regards illiteracy in all its forms as a grave problem and an impediment to the realization of the desired leap into the knowledge society. Continuous efforts must therefore be devoted to its elimination.

The participation of society at large is considered to be a basic support for the implementation of this vision.

XI. TUNIS DECLARATION (EXCERPTS)

We, the leaders of the Arab States, meeting at the Summit Conference of the Arab League Council in its sixteenth ordinary session held in Tunis, the capital of the Republic of Tunisia;

Committed as we are to the principles upon which the League of Arab States was founded and to the objectives enunciated in its Charter, as well as to the noble universal values spelled out in the United Nations Charter and to all the instruments of international legality;

Taking into account the new world changes and the challenges and stakes they generate;

Determined to pursue efforts in order to strengthen the solidarity and cohesion of the Arab Nation, and to consolidate the Arab ranks, in the service of our primordial causes;

Declare the following:

1. The commitment of all international parties to materialize the principles of international legality and the United Nations resolutions pertaining to the Arab-Israeli conflict, without excluding any of the legal references of the peace process, constitutes the basis for a just, comprehensive and durable settlement to this conflict, in accordance with the Arab peace initiative and in implementation of the "road map". The international community should join its efforts so as to provide the necessary protection for the Palestinian people against the continuing acts of killing and deportation they are enduring, and also to put an end to the policy of assassination perpetrated by Israel against the Palestinian political leaders, to the

siege imposed on the Palestinian people and their leadership, as well as to the aggressions targeting civilians without distinction. Joining these efforts would pave the way for the resumption of peace talks and would enable the brotherly Palestinian people to recover their legitimate rights, including in particular the establishment of their independent State with East Jerusalem as its capital, as well as the evacuation of all the Arab occupied territories, including the occupied Syrian Golan and the Lebanese Shaba Farms.

2. …Convening an international conference aimed at ridding the Middle East region, including Israel, of the weapons of mass destruction.

3. … Support for Iraq's territorial integrity and respect for the sovereignty, independence and national unity of sisterly Iraq, calling upon the Security Council to give a central and active role to the United Nations in Iraq in order to put an end to the occupation and prepare the ground for the transfer of power to the Iraqi people. This will make it possible to establish peace and stability and to launch the process of reconstruction in Iraq.

4. …Solidarity with sisterly Syria in the face of the American sanctions.

We also assert our firm determination:

1. To materialize our common will to develop the system of joint Arab action, through the Tunis Summit resolution to amend the Arab League Charter and to modernize its work methods and its specialized institutions, based on the various Arab initiatives and ideas included in the proposals put forward by the Secretary-General as well as on a consensual and coherent vision.

2. To reaffirm our States' commitment to the humanitarian principles and the noble values of human rights in their comprehensive and interdependent dimensions, to the provisions of the various international conventions and charters, and to the Arab Human Rights Charter adopted by the Tunis Summit, as well as to the reinforcement of the freedom of expression, thought and belief and to the guarantee of the independence of the judiciary.

3. To foster the role of all components of civil society, including non-governmental organizations, in conceiving of the guidelines of the society of tomorrow, by widening women's participation in the political, economic, social, cultural and educational fields and reinforcing their rights and status in society, and by pursuing the promotion of the family and the protection of Arab youth.

4. To consolidate comprehensive development programmes and intensify efforts aimed at promoting educational systems, at disseminating knowledge and encouraging its acquisition, and at fighting illiteracy in order to ensure a better future for the Arab young generations.

5. To achieve economic complementarity among Arab States on the basis of the exchange of benefits and the interdependence of interests, and to endeavour to pursue the upgrading of the Arab economies by entrusting the Economic and Social Council with establishing a joint Arab economic and social action strategy, in such a way as to consolidate the competitiveness of the Arab economy and empower it to establish a solidarity-based partnership with the various economic groupings in the world.

6. To consecrate the values of solidarity and mutual assistance among the Arab States, as part of the Arab anti-poverty strategy adopted by the Tunis Summit, and to mobilize all human potential in the Arab countries in support of their development efforts.

7. To strengthen the bonds of friendship between Arab countries and other countries of the world, and to establish a new approach for solidarity-based cooperation and partnership with them, based on our determination to consecrate dialogue between religions and cultures and to highlight the civilizational and humanist mission of Islam, which calls for disseminating the values of tolerance, concord and peaceful coexistence among peoples and nations, and rejects hatred and discrimination.

8. To reaffirm the commitment of Arab States to pursue their contribution to the international efforts to stand against and combat all forms of terrorism, avoid confusing Islam with terrorism and differentiate between legitimate resistance and terrorism.

9. To call for the holding of an international conference, under the auspices of the United Nations, in order to establish an international code of ethics for the fight against terrorism, while working to tackle the root causes of this phenomenon.

Source: Al-Ahram, Cairo, in Arabic, 24 May 2004.

ANNEX III. LIST OF BACKGROUND PAPERS

ANNEX III. LIST OF BACKGROUND PAPERS
(Author name, paper title, number of pages)

IN ARABIC

- Abdel-Messih, Marie-Thérèse – Freedom in Arab Creative Art, 12.
- Al-Asha'al, Abdallah – Reforming Governance at the International Level and Its Effect on the Arab World, 10.
- Al-Hamdan, Amna Rashed – The Concept of Freedom in Arab Folklore, 10.
- Ali, Ali Abdel Gadir – Freedom from Want: Social Security in Arab Countries, 12.
- Al-Jenhani, Al-Habib – Freedom in Arab History, 9.
- Al-Moneef, Majid Abdallah – Corruption and Development in Arab Countries, 25.
- Al-Nowwab, Nabil – Occupation of Iraq, 6.
- Al-Sayyid, Mustapha Kamel – Parliamentary Governance in Arab Countries, 32.
- Alsowegh, Siham Abdulrahman – Freedom and Education Systems in the Arab East Countries, 22.
- Alwahabi, Amina Lemrini and Khadija Marwazi – Freedom in Educational Curricula, 43.
- Awad, Mohsen – Freedom from Oppression: Civil and Political Rights in Arab Countries, 26.
- Bishara, Azmi – Occupation and Good Governance, 17.
- Bishara, Azmi – Invasion and Occupation of Iraq and the Democratic Political Culture in Arab Countries, 18.
- Chekir, Hafidha – Civil Society in the Arab World: Reality and Prospects, 27.
- Corm, George Antoine – Impasse of Freedom in the Arab World between Foreign Constraints and Internal Factors, 12.
- El-Ati, Jalila – Freedom from Hunger and Malnutrition, Food Safety, 12.

- El-Imam, Mohammed Mahmoud – Reforming Governance at the Pan-Arab Level to Guarantee the Freedom of the Homeland and the Citizens, 9.
- Esber, Khalida Sa'id – Freedom in Creative Arab Literature, 11.
- Farahat, Nour – Freedoms and Human Rights in the Arab Legal Systems, 36.
- Ghubash, Rafia Obaid – Freedom from Illness and Health Security in Arab Societies, 24.
- Guessous, Abdel Aziz – Civil Society and Political Parties in Arab Countries, 27.
- Hafez, Salah El-Din – The Media and Its Role in Protecting Rights and Freedoms, 10.
- Hijazi, Mustafa – A Prerequisite to Freedom and Democracy: Acknowledging the Value of the Human Being, 14.
- Jada'ane, Fehmi – Freedom in the Arab Formal Culture, 32.
- Kana'an, Taher – Political Economy of Freedom and Good Governance for Human Development: Concepts and Analytical Tools, 17.
- Khalil, Abdalla and Mohammad Khalil – Laws Contraining Civil Rights and Freedoms in Arab Countries.
- Kuttab, Jonathan – Christians under Occupation in Palestine, 9.
- Loteh, Mariam Sultan – Political Freedoms in Contemporary Arab Thought, 18.
- Malki, Mhammed – Legal Architecture for Freedom in Arab Countries, 34.
- Osman, Abdelwahab El-Affendi – The Nature of Arab Governance Systems, 10.
- Shaban, Abdel-Hussein – Freedom from Oppression: Civil and Political Rights, 21.
- Zalzal, Marie Rose – Citizenship Rights, 25.

IN ENGLISH

- Kubursi, Atef – Democracy and Development: Cruel Choices and Necessary Conditions, 7.

Annex 4: Statistical Tables on Human Development in the Arab States

Table -1   Human development index

Table -2   Human development index trends

Table -3   Gender-related development index

Table -4   Human Poverty

Table -5   Income poverty and inequality in consumption

Table -6   Population size and distribution

Table -7   Literacy and enrolment

Table -8   Public spending on education

Table -9   Water and sanitation

Table -10   Child health

Table -11   Reproductive health

Table -12   Household and fertility indicators

Table -13   Nutrition

Table -14   Other health indicators

Table -15   Unemployment and child labour

Table -16   Main economic indicators

Table -17   External debt ($ millions)

Table -18   Integration with the global economy

Table -19   Priorities in public spending

Table -20   Women's political participation

Table -21   Gender inequality in education

Table -22   Other indicators on women

Table -23   Press and communications

Table -24   Energy and the environment

Table -25   Armaments and refugees

Symbols used in the tables

..   Data not available.

(.)   Less than half the unit shown.

<   Less than.

-      Not applicable.

A hyphen "-" between two years indicates that the data have been collected during one of the years shown. For example, 1997-2001 indicates that the data is collected during one of the years within the period 1997-2001, i. e. during the year 1997 or 1998 or 1999 or 2000 or 2001.

A slash "/" between two years indicates averages for the years shown. For example, 1997/2001 indicates that the data represents the annual average for the period extending from 1997 till 2001; i.e. the annual average for the years 1997, 1998, 1999, 2000 and 2001.

Table -1

HUMAN DEVELOPMENT INDEX

Country	Life expectancy at birth (years) 2002	Adult literacy rate (% ages 15 and above) 2002	Combined gross enrolment ratio for primary, secondary and tertiary schools (%) 2001/02	GDP per capita (PPP US$) 2002	Human development index (HDI) 2002			GDP per capita (PPP US$) rank minus HDI rank
					Value	Rank within all countries (177 countries)	Rank within Arab countries (20 countries)	
Algeria	69.5	68.9	70	5,760	0.704	108	13	-25
Bahrain	73.9	88.5	79	17,170	0.843	40	1	-4
Comoros	60.6	56.2	45	1,690	0.530	136	16	4
Djibouti	45.8	65.5	24	1,990	0.454	154	20	-21
Egypt	68.6	55.6	76	3,810	0.653	120	14	-12
Iraq	60.7	..	57	..	..	..	..	..
Jordan	70.9	90.9	77	4,220	0.750	90	9	14
Kuwait	76.5	82.9	76	16,240	0.838	44	2	-6
Lebanon	73.5	86.5	78	4,360	0.758	80	8	21
Libyan Arab Jamahiriya	72.6	81.7	97	7,570	0.794	58	5	6
Mauritania	52.3	41.2	44	2,220	0.465	152	19	-25
Morocco	68.5	50.7	57	3,810	0.620	125	15	-17
Occupied Palestinian Territories	72.3	90.2	79	..	0.726	102	11	21
Oman	72.3	74.4	63	13,340	0.770	74	6	-32
Qatar	72.0	84.2	82	19,844	0.833	47	3	-21
Saudi Arabia	72.1	77.9	57	12,650	0.768	77	7	-33
Somalia	47.9	..	..	..	..	..	..	..
Sudan	55.5	59.9	36	1,820	0.505	139	17	-3
Syrian Arab Republic	71.7	82.9	59	3,620	0.710	106	12	4
Tunisia	72.7	73.2	75	6,760	0.745	92	10	-23
United Arab Emirates	74.6	77.3	68	22,420	0.824	49	4	-26
Yemen	59.8	49.0	53	870	0.482	149	18	16

Source: Human Development Report 2004

Table -2

HUMAN DEVELOPMENT INDEX TRENDS

Country	1975	1980	1985	1990	1995	2000	2002
Algeria	0.504	0.554	0.603	0.642	0.664	0.693	0.704
Bahrain	..	0.746	0.779	0.808	0.825	0.835	0.843
Comoros	..	0.479	0.498	0.501	0.509	0.521	0.530
Djibouti	..	..	..	..	0.450	0.452	0.454
Egypt	0.438	0.487	0.539	0.577	0.608	..	0.653
Iraq	..	..	..	..	..	..	..
Jordan	..	0.639	0.663	0.682	0.707	0.741	0.750
Kuwait	0.761	0.776	0.778	..	0.810	0.834	0.838
Lebanon	..	..	..	0.673	0.732	0.752	0.758
Libyan Arab Jamahiriya	..	..	..	..	..	..	0.794
Mauritania	0.339	0.362	0.382	0.387	0.423	0.449	0.465
Morocco	0.429	0.474	0.510	0.542	0.571	0.603	0.620
Occupied Palestinian Territories	..	..	..	..	..	..	0.726
Oman	0.493	0.546	0.640	0.696	0.733	0.761	0.770
Qatar	..	..	..	..	..	..	0.833
Saudi Arabia	0.602	0.656	0.671	0.707	0.741	0.764	0.768
Somalia	..	..	..	..	..	..	..
Sudan	0.344	0.372	0.394	0.427	0.465	0.492	0.505
Syrian Arab Republic	0.534	0.576	0.611	0.635	0.663	0.683	0.710
Tunisia	0.516	0.574	0.623	0.656	0.696	0.734	0.745
United Arab Emirates	0.744	0.777	0.785	0.805	0.803	..	0.824
Yemen	..	..	..	0.392	0.435	0.469	0.482

Source: Human Development Report 2004

Table -3

GENDER-RELATED DEVELOPMENT INDEX

Country	Gender-related development index (GDI) Rank	Value	Life expectancy at birth (years) 2002 Female	Male	Adult literacy rate (% ages 15 and above) 2002 Female	Male	Combined gross enrolment ratio for primary, secondary and tertiary level schools (%) 2001/02 Female	Male	Estimated earned income (PPP US$) 2002 Female	Male	HDI rank minus GDI rank
Algeria	89	0.688	71.1	68.0	59.6	78.0	69	72	2,684	8,794	-2
Bahrain	39	0.832	75.8	72.4	84.2	91.5	82	77	7,961	23,505	-2
Comoros	108	0.510	62.0	59.2	49.1	63.5	41	50	950	1,699	0
Djibouti	..	..	47.0	44.8	55.5	76.1	20	28	..	..	..
Egypt	99	0.634	70.8	66.6	43.6	67.2	72	80	1,963	5,216	-1
Iraq	..	..	..	..	..	..	..	..	..	..	..
Jordan	76	0.734	72.4	69.6	85.9	95.5	77	76	1,896	6,118	-2
Kuwait	42	0.827	78.9	74.8	81.0	84.7	81	71	7,116	20,979	-1
Lebanon	64	0.755	75.0	71.8	81.0	92.4	79	77	2,552	8,336	2
Libyan Arab Jamahiriya	..	..	75.3	70.7	70.7	91.8	100	93	..	..	..
Mauritania	124	0.456	53.9	50.7	31.3	51.5	42	46	1,581	2,840	0
Morocco	100	0.604	70.3	66.6	38.3	63.3	52	61	2,153	5,354	0
Occupied Palestinian Terr.	..	..	73.9	70.7	..	..	81	78	..	..	..
Oman	68	0.747	74.3	70.9	65.4	82.0	63	62	4,056	18,239	-7
Qatar	..	..	75.3	70.4	82.3	84.9	84	79	..	..	..
Saudi Arabia	72	0.739	73.6	71.0	69.5	84.1	57	58	3,825	18,616	-9
Somalia	..	..	..	..	..	..	..	..	..	..	..
Sudan	115	0.485	57.0	54.1	49.1	70.8	34	39	867	2,752	-4
Syrian Arab Republic	88	0.689	73.0	70.5	74.2	91.0	57	62	1,549	5,496	-3
Tunisia	77	0.734	74.8	70.7	63.1	83.1	75	74	3,615	9,933	-2
United Arab Emirates	..	..	77.3	73.2	80.7	75.6	72	65	..	..	..
Yemen	126	0.436	60.9	58.7	28.5	69.5	37	66	387	1,274	-5

Source: Human Development Report 2004

Table -4

HUMAN POVERTY

Country	Human poverty index (HPI-1) Rank within 95 developing countries	Value (%)	Probability at birth of not surviving to age 40 (% of cohort) 2000-05	Adult illiteracy rate (% ages 15 and above) 2002	Population without sustainable access to an improved water source (%) 2000	Children under weight for age (% under age 5) 1995-2002
Algeria	43	21.9	9.3	31.1	11	6
Bahrain	..	..	4.0	11.5	..	9
Comoros	49	31.4	18.1	43.8	4	25
Djibouti	55	34.3	42.9	34.5	0	18
Egypt	47	30.9	8.6	44.4	3	11
Iraq	..	..	..	..	..	..
Jordan	7	7.2	6.6	9.1	4	5
Kuwait	..	..	2.6	17.1	..	10
Lebanon	14	9.5	4.3	13.5	0	3
Libyan Arab Jamahiriya	29	15.3	4.5	18.3	28	5
Mauritania	87	48.3	30.5	58.8	63	32
Morocco	56	34.5	9.4	49.3	20	9
Occupied Palestinian Territories	..	..	5.2	..	14	4
Oman	50	31.5	5.0	25.6	61	24
Qatar	..	..	5.1	15.8	..	6
Saudi Arabia	30	15.8	5.2	22.1	5	14
Somalia	..	..	..	..	..	..
Sudan	51	31.6	27.6	40.1	25	17
Syrian Arab Republic	25	13.7	5.7	17.1	20	7
Tunisia	39	19.2	4.9	26.8	20	4
United Arab Emirates	..	..	3.4	22.7	..	14
Yemen	67	40.3	19.1	51.0	31	46

Source: Human Development Report 2004

Table -5

INCOME POVERTY AND INEQUALITY IN CONSUMPTION

Country	Population below national poverty line 1992-2000 (%)			Population below income poverty line $1 a day 1990-2000 (%)	Population below income poverty line $2 a day 1990-2000 (%)	Share of consumption (%)			
	National	Urban	Rural			Poorest 10%	Richgst 10%	Richest 10% to poorest 10%	Gini index
Algeria	12.2	7.3	16.6	<2	15.1	2.8	26.8	9.6	35.3
Bahrain	15	..	..	..	..	..	..	..	..
Comoros	..	..	..	..	..	..	..	..	..
Djibouti	45.1	..	86.5	..	..	..	..	..	..
Egypt	22.9	22.5	23.3	3.1	43.9	3.7	29.5	8.0	34.4
Iraq	45	..	..	..	..	..			..
Jordan	11.7	..	..	<2	7.4	3.3	29.8	9.1	36.4
Kuwait	11	..	..	..	..	..	..	..	..
Lebanon	19	..	..	..	..	..	..	..	..
Libyan Arab Jamahiriya	..	..	..	..	..	..	..	..	..
Mauritania	50.0	30.1	65.5	25.9	63.1	2.5	29.5	12.0	39.0
Morocco	19.0	12.0	27.2	<2	14.3	2.6	30.9	11.7	39.5
Occupied Palestinian Terr.	..	..	..	..	..	..	..	..	..
Oman	17	..	..	..	..	..	..		..
Qatar	11	..	..	..	..	..	..	..	..
Saudi Arabia	21	..	..	..	..	..	..	..	..
Somalia	..	..	..	..	..	..	..	..	..
Sudan	..	..	..	..	..	..	..	..	..
Syrian Arab Republic	22	..	..	..	..	..		..	..
Tunisia	7.4	3.5	13.1	<2	6.6	2.3	31.5	13.4	39.8
United Arab Emirates	3	..	..	..	..	..	..	..	..
Yemen	41.8	30.8	45.0	15.7	45.2	3.0	25.9	8.6	33.4

* The Gini index measures inequality over the entire distribution of income or consumption. A value of 0 represents perfect equality, and a value of 100 perfect inequality.

Source:

Human Development Report 2004

World Bank: http://www.worldbank.org/data/wdi2004/pdfs/table2-5.pdf

Mohammed Bakir, Measuring Poverty in the Countries of the Economic and Social Commission for Western Asia, UN ESCWA, Amman, 1996.

Table -6

POPULATION SIZE AND DISTRIBUTION

Country	Estimated population (thousands) 2004	Sex ratio (males per 100 females) 2004	Average annual rate of change of population (%) 2000-2005	Urban population (% of total population) 2003	Population less than 15 years (% of total population) 2004	Population density (people per sq. km) 2002
Algeria	32,339	102	1.67	59	32	13
Bahrain	739	135	2.17	90	29	983
Comoros	790	101	2.83	35	42	263
Djibouti	712	99	1.58	84	43	30
Egypt	73,389	100	1.99	42	34	67
Iraq	25,856	103	2.68	67	41	55
Jordan	5,613	108	2.66	79	37	58
Kuwait	2,595	151	3.46	96	26	131
Lebanon	3,708	96	1.56	87	28	434
Libyan Arab Jamahiriya	5,659	107	1.93	86	30	3
Mauritania	2,980	98	2.98	62	43	3
Morocco	31,064	100	1.62	57	31	66
Occupied Palestinian Territories	3,685	104	3.57	71	46	..
Oman	2,935	134	2.93	78	37	8
Qatar	619	172	1.54	92	26	55
Saudi Arabia	24,919	116	2.92	88	39	10
Somalia	10,312	99	4.17	35	48	15
Sudan	34,333	101	2.17	39	39	14
Syrian Arab Republic	18,223	102	2.38	50	37	92
Tunisia	9,937	101	1.07	64	27	63
United Arab Emirates	3,051	185	1.94	85	25	38
Yemen	20,732	103	3.52	26	48	35

Source:

UNSD: http://unstats.un.org/unsd/demographic/products/socind/population.htm

UNICEF: http://www.unicef.org/files/Table6_english.xls

World Bank: http://www.worldbank.org/data/wdi2004/tables/table1-1.pdf

Table -7

LITERACY AND ENROLMENT

Country	Adult literacy rate (% ages 15 and above)		Youth literacy rate (% ages 15-24)		Net primary enrolment ratio (%)		Net secondary enrolment ratio (%)		Tertiary students in science, math & engineering (% of all tertiary students)
	1990	2002	1990	2002	1990/1	2001/2	1990/1	2001/2	1994-1997
Algeria	52.9	68.9	77.3	89.9	93	95	54	62	50
Bahrain	82.1	88.5	95.6	98.6	99	91	85	81	..
Comoros	53.8	56.2	56.7	59.0	57	55	..	..	..
Djibouti	53.0	..	73.2	..	31	34	..	17	..
Egypt	47.1	55.6	61.3	73.2	84	90	..	81	15
Iraq	..	..	..	..	..	91	..	..	..
Jordan	81.5	90.9	96.7	99.4	94	91	..	80	27
Kuwait	76.7	82.9	87.5	93.1	49	85	..	77	23
Lebanon	80.3	..	92.1	..	78	90	..	..	17
Libyan Arab Jamahiriya	68.1	81.7	91.0	97.0	96	..	..	..	..
Mauritania	34.8	41.2	45.8	49.6	35	67	..	15	..
Morocco	38.7	50.7	55.3	69.5	57	88	..	31	29
Occupied Palestinian Territories	..	..	..	..	..	95	..	81	10
Oman	54.7	74.4	85.6	98.5	69	75	..	68	31
Qatar	77.0	84.2	90.3	94.8	89	94	70	78	..
Saudi Arabia	66.2	77.9	85.4	93.5	59	59	31	53	18
Somalia	..	..	..	..	..	..	..	..	..
Sudan	45.8	59.9	65.0	79.1	43	46	..	..	..
Syrian Arab Republic	64.8	82.9	79.9	95.2	92	98	43	39	31
Tunisia	59.1	73.2	84.1	94.3	94	97	..	68	27
United Arab Emirates	71.0	77.3	84.7	91.4	100	81	58	72	27
Yemen	32.7	49.0	50.0	67.9	52	67	..	35	6

Source:

UNICEF: http://www.unicef.org/files/Table5_english.xls

Human Development Report 2004

Table -8

PUBLIC SPENDING ON EDUCATION

Country	Public expenditure on education				Public expenditure on education by level (% of all levels)					
	As % of GDP		As % of total government expenditure		Pre-primary and primary		Secondary		Tertiary	
	1990	1999-2001	1990	1999-2001	1990	1999-2001	1990	1999-2001	1990	1999-2001
Algeria	5.3	..	21.1	..	..	..	..	..	..	..
Bahrain	4.2	..	14.6	..	..	..	45.8	..	..	..
Comoros	..	..	..	..	42.4	..	28.2	..	17.3	..
Djibouti	..	..	10.5	..	58.0	..	21.7	..	11.5	..
Egypt	3.7	..	..	..	..	..	..	..	..	..
Iraq	..	..	..	..	..	..	..	..	..	..
Jordan	8.4	4.6	17.1	20.6	..	51.7	62.4	48.3	35.1	..
Kuwait	4.8	..	3.4	..	53.4	..	13.6	..	16.0	..
Lebanon	..	2.9	..	11.1	..	..	..	..	..	..
Libyan Arab Jamahiriya	..	2.7	..	..	..	17.8	..	14.2	..	52.7
Mauritania	..	3.6	..	..	33.3	54.5	37.7	31.4	24.9	14.1
Morocco	5.3	5.1	26.1	..	34.8	48.0	48.9	51.5	16.2	0.3
Occupied Palestinian Territories	..	..	..	..	..	..	..	..	..	..
Oman	3.1	4.2	11.1	..	54.1	36.4	37.0	51.4	7.4	1.8
Qatar	3.5	..	..	..	..	..	..	..	..	..
Saudi Arabia	6.5	..	17.8	..	78.8	..	..	..	21.2	..
Somalia	..	..	..	..	..	..	..	..	..	..
Sudan	0.9	..	2.8	..	..	..	..	..	..	..
Syrian Arab Republic	4.1	4.0	17.3	11.1	38.5	..	28.2	39.2	21.3	..
Tunisia	6.0	6.8	13.5	17.4	39.8	33.3	36.4	45.0	18.5	21.7
United Arab Emirates	1.9	..	14.6	..	..	51.9	..	46.4	..	..
Yemen	..	10.0	..	32.8	..	..	..	..	..	..

Source: Human Development Report 2004

Table -9

WATER AND SANITATION

Country	% of population using improved drinking water sources 2000			% of population using adequate sanitation facilities 2000		
	total	urban	rural	total	urban	rural
Algeria	89	94	82	92	99	81
Bahrain	..	..	..	..	..	..
Comoros	96	98	95	98	98	98
Djibouti	100	100	100	91	99	50
Egypt	97	99	96	98	100	96
Iraq	85	96	48	79	93	31
Jordan	96	100	84	99	100	98
Kuwait	..	..	..	..	..	..
Lebanon	100	100	100	99	100	87
Libyan Arab Jamahiriya	72	72	68	97	97	96
Mauritania	37	34	40	33	44	19
Morocco	80	98	56	68	86	44
Occupied Palestinian Territories	86	97	86	100	100	100
Oman	39	41	30	92	98	61
Qatar	..	..	..	..	..	..
Saudi Arabia	95	100	64	100	100	100
Somalia	..	..	..	..	..	..
Sudan	75	86	69	62	87	48
Syrian Arab Republic	80	94	64	90	98	81
Tunisia	80	92	58	84	96	62
United Arab Emirates	..	..	..	..	..	..
Yemen	69	74	68	38	89	21

Source: UNICEF: http://www.unicef.org/files/Table3_english.xls

Table -10

CHILD HEALTH

Country	Under-5 mortality rate (Per 1000 live births)		Infant mortality rate (Per 1000 live births)		Immunized one year old children (%) 2002		
	1960	2002	1960	2002	TB	polio3	measles
Algeria	280	49	164	39	98	86	81
Bahrain	160	16	110	13	..	98	99
Comoros	265	79	200	59	90	98	71
Djibouti	289	143	186	100	52	62	62
Egypt	282	41	189	35	98	97	97
Iraq	171	125	117	102	93	84	90
Jordan	139	33	97	27	..	95	95
Kuwait	128	10	89	9	..	94	99
Lebanon	85	32	65	28	..	92	96
Libyan Arab Jamahiriya	270	19	159	16	99	93	91
Mauritania	310	183	180	120	98	82	81
Morocco	211	43	132	39	90	94	96
Occupied Palestinian Territories	..	25	..	23	96	97	94
Oman	280	13	164	11	98	99	99
Qatar	140	16	94	11	99	96	99
Saudi Arabia	250	28	170	23	98	95	97
Somalia	..	225	..	133	60	40	45
Sudan	208	94	123	64	48	40	49
Syrian Arab Republic	201	28	136	23	99	99	98
Tunisia	254	26	170	21	97	96	94
United Arab Emirates	223	9	149	8	98	94	94
Yemen	340	107	220	79	74	69	65

Source:

UNICEF: http://www.unicef.org/files/Table1_english.xls

UNICEF: http://www.unicef.org/files/Table3_english.xls

Table -11

REPRODUCTIVE HEALTH

Country	People with HIV/AIDS (% ages 15-49) 2003	People with HIV/AIDS (% women among adults) End of 2001	Pregnant women who received prenatal care (%) 1996	Deliveries attended by skilled attendant (%) 1996	Maternal mortality ratio (per 100,000 live births) around 2000	Length of maternity leave
Algeria	0.1	..	58	77	140	14 weeks
Bahrain	0.2	..	96	94	28	45 days
Comoros	..	..	69	74	480	14 weeks
Djibouti	..	..	76	79	730	14 weeks
Egypt	<0.1	10	53	46	84	50 days
Iraq	..	..	59	54	250	60 days
Jordan	..	..	80	87	41	10 weeks
Kuwait	..	..	99	99	5	70 days
Lebanon	0.1	..	85	45	150	40 days
Libyan Arab Jamahiriya	0.3	16	100	76	97	50 days
Mauritania	0.6	..	49	40	1000	14 weeks
Morocco	0.1	15	45	40	220	12 weeks
Occupied Palestinian Territories	..	..	..	..	..	..
Oman	0.1	15	98	92	87	..
Qatar	..	..	100	97	7	40-60 days
Saudi Arabia	..	..	87	90	23	10 weeks
Somalia	..	..	40	2	1100	14 weeks
Sudan	2.3	56	54	86	590	8 weeks
Syrian Arab Republic	<0.1	..	33	67	160	75 days
Tunisia	<0.1	..	71	90	120	30 days
United Arab Emirates	..	..	95	96	54	45 days
Yemen	0.1	15	26	16	570	60 days

Source:

UNSD: http://unstats.un.org/unsd/demographic/products/indwm/table3b.htm

UNSD: http://unstats.un.org/unsd/demographic/products/indwm/table5c1x.htm

Human Development Report 2004

Table -12

HOUSEHOLD AND FERTILITY INDICATORS

Country	Average house-hold size 1991-1994	Households headed by women (%) 1991-1994	Contraceptive prevalence rate among married women (%) 1991-2002	Fertility rate (births per woman) 1991-1995	Fertility rate (births per woman) 2000-2005	Births per 1000 woman for the age group 15-19 years 2000-2005
Algeria	7.0	11	52	4.1	2.8	16
Bahrain	5.6	..	62	3.4	2.7	18
Comoros	6.2	25	21	5.8	4.9	59
Djibouti	6.6	18	..	6.3	5.7	64
Egypt	4.9	13	56	4.0	3.3	47
Iraq	7.3	..	14	5.7	4.8	38
Jordan	6.9	..	53	4.9	3.6	27
Kuwait	6.5	5	50	3.2	2.7	31
Lebanon	4.8*	12.5*	61	2.8	2.2	25
Libyan Arab Jamahiriya	..	..	40	4.1	3.0	7
Mauritania	..	..	8	6.1	5.8	104
Morocco	6.0	15	50	3.6	2.7	25
Occupied Palestinian Territories	..	..	..	6.5	5.6	94
Oman	7.0	..	24	6.5	5.0	66
Qatar	5.6	..	43	4.1	3.2	20
Saudi Arabia	7.4	..	32	5.8	4.5	38
Somalia	..	..	1	7.3	7.3	213
Sudan	6.3	13	8	5.3	4.4	55
Syrian Arab Republic	6.0	..	36	4.6	3.3	34
Tunisia	5.4	11	60	3.1	2.0	7
United Arab Emirates	..	..	28	3.8	2.8	51
Yemen	5.8	12	21	7.8	7.0	111

* Data for 1997 according to Household Living Condition Survey 1997.

Source:

UNSD: http://unstats.un.org/unsd/demographic/social/childbr.htm

World Women 2000: http://unstats.un.org/unsd/demographic/ww2000/table2b.htm

Central Administration of Statistics, Household Living Condition Survey 1997, Statistical Studies No. 9, Republic of Lebanon, February 1998.

Table -13

NUTRITION

Country	Infants with low birth weight (%) 1998-2002	% of under-fives suffering from 1995-2002			% of households consuming iodized salt 1997-2002	Iron deficiency cases among women (%)	Under nourished people (thousand) 1999
		underweight	wasting	stunting			
Algeria	7	7	3	18	69		2000
Bahrain	8	11	5	10	..	37	..
Comoros	25	34	12	42	82	..	..
Djibouti	..	24	13	26	..	70	..
Egypt	12	14	5	21	28	24	2000
Iraq	15	18	6	22	40	51	6000
Jordan	10	6	2	8	88	29	..
Kuwait	7	13	11	24	..	..	..
Lebanon	6	3	3	12	87	27	..
Libyan Arab Jamahiriya	7	6	3	15	90	..	..
Mauritania	42	42	13	35	2	..	..
Morocco	11	11	4	24	41	35	2000
Occupied Palestinian Territories	9	5	3	9	37	..	..
Oman	8	28	13	23	61	38	..
Qatar	10	..	2	8	..	..	..
Saudi Arabia	11	17	11	20	..	..	1000
Somalia	..	33	17	23	..	..	..
Sudan	31	24	..	..	1	..	7000
Syrian Arab Republic	6	8	4	18	40	..	1000
Tunisia	7	5	2	12	97	31	..
United Arab Emirates	15	17	15	17	..	..	..
Yemen	32	61	13	52	39	..	6000

Source:

UNICEF: http://www.unicef.org/files/Table2_english.xls

UNICEF, The State of Children and Women in the Middle East and North Africa, 2001

Table -14

OTHER HEALTH INDICATORS

Country	Expectation of lost healthy years at birth (years) 2002		Tuberculosis cases (per 100,000 people) 2002	Malaria cases (Per 100,000 people) 2000	Physicians (per 100,000 people) 1990-2003	Health expenditure per capita (PPP US$) 2001	Prevalence of smoking (% of adults) 2000	
	Male	Female					Women	Men
Algeria	7.9	9.6	51	2	85	169	44	7
Bahrain	7.9	10.1	68	..	169	664	..	..
Comoros	7.8	9.6	121	1,930	7	29	..	..
Djibouti	6.1	7.4	1,161	715	13	90	..	..
Egypt	7.4	8.8	38	(.)	218	153	35	2
Iraq	10.3	11.6	..	..	..	..	..	..
Jordan	9.0	10.9	6	3	205	412	48	10
Kuwait	8.2	10.6	53	..	160	612	30	2
Lebanon	8.4	10.4	15	..	274	673	46	35
Libyan Arab Jamahiriya	8.1	10.5	20	2	120	239	..	..
Mauritania	6.9	8.2	437	11,150	14	45	..	..
Morocco	9.4	11.9	100	(.)	49	199	35	2
Occupied Palestinian Territories	..	..	38	..	84	..	..	..
Oman	8.3	11.1	13	27	137	343	16	2
Qatar	8.2	10.0	70	..	220	782	..	..
Saudi Arabia	8.6	11.0	59	32	153	591	22	1
Somalia	6.9	8.1	..	..	..	..	..	..
Sudan	7.8	9.4	346	13,934	16	39	24	1
Syrian Arab Republic	8.5	10.5	54	(.)	142	427	51	10
Tunisia	8.2	10.3	26	1	70	463	62	8
United Arab Emirates	7.8	10.9	26	..	177	921	18	1
Yemen	10.8	11.5	145	15,160	22	69	60	29

Source:

Human Development Report 2004

WHO, The world health report 2004: http://www.who.int/whr/2004/annex/topic/annex4.xls

Table -15

UNEMPLOYMENT AND CHILD LABOUR

Country	Unemployment rate (%) 1999-2001			Child labour (5-14 years) 1999-2001 (%)						
	Total	Male	Female	Total	Male	Female	Urban	Rural	Poorest 20%	Mother with no education
Algeria	29.8	33.9	29.7	..	..	..	..	..	..	..
Bahrain	6.2	4.2	2.0	5	6	3	..	..	..	5
Comoros	..	..	..	27	27	28	28	27	32	29
Egypt	9.2	5.6	22.6	6	6	5	3	8	12	8
Iraq	..	..	..	8	11	5	6	12	12	9
Jordan	14.5	13.4	20.8	..	..	..	..	..	..	..
Kuwait	0.8	0.8	0.6	..	..	..	..	..	..	..
Lebanon	..	..	..	6	8	4	..	..	..	13
Morocco	11.6	11.6	12.5	..	..	..	..	..	..	..
Occupied Palestinian Territories	31.3	33.5	17.1	..	..	..	..	..	..	..
Saudi Arabia	4.6	3.9	9.1	..	..	..	..	..	..	..
Somalia	..	..	..	32	29	36	25	36	38	35
Sudan	..	..	..	13	14	12	7	19	25	16
Syrian Arab Republic	11.7	8.3	24.1	..	..	..	..	..	..	..
Tunisia	14.9	..	..	..	..	..	..	..	..	..
United Arab Emirates	2.3	2.2	2.6	..	..	..	..	..	..	..
Yemen	11.5	12.5	8.2	..	..	..	..	..	..	..

Source:

UNICEF: http://www.unicef.org/files/table9 english.xls

ILO: http://laborsta.ilo.org/

Department of Statistics, Jordan: http://www.dos.gov.jo/sdb_pop/sdb_pop_a/index_o.htm

Table -16

MAIN ECONOMIC INDICATORS

Country	GDP per capita (PPP US$)		Gross domestic product 2002		GDP per capita annual growth rate (%) 2001-2002	Average annual change in consumer price index (%) 2002	Official development assistance received (US$ millions) 2002
	Highest value during 1975-2002	Year of highest value	US$ billions	PPP US$ billions			
Algeria	6,190	1985	55.9	180.4	2.5	2.2	361
Bahrain	17,170	2002	7.7	12.0	..	-0.5	..
Comoros	2,140	1985	0.3	1.0	..	..	..
Djibouti	..	..	0.6	1.4	..	2.7	..
Egypt	3,810	2002	89.9	252.6	1.1	..	1,286
Iraq	..	..	..	..	..	19.3	116
Jordan	5,100	1987	9.3	21.8	2.0	1.8	534
Kuwait	29,180	1975	35.4	37.8	-3.3	0.6	5
Lebanon	4,520	1997	17.3	19.4	-0.3	..	456
Libyan Arab Jamahiriya	..	..	19.1	..	..	..	10
Mauritania	2,220	2002	1.0	6.2	0.8	3.9	355
Morocco	3,810	2002	36.1	112.9	1.6	2.8	636
Occupied Palestinian Territories	..	..	3.4	..	..	..	..
Oman	13,710	2001	20.3	33.8	-2.3	-0.7	41
Qatar	..	..	17.5	..	..	1.6	..
Saudi Arabia	23,980	1977	188.5	276.9	-1.8	-0.6	27
Somalia	..	..	..	..	..	..	194
Sudan	1,820	2002	13.5	59.5	3.3	..	351
Syrian Arab Republic	3,630	1998	20.8	61.5	0.3	1.0	81
Tunisia	6,760	2002	21.0	66.2	0.6	2.8	475
United Arab Emirates	47,790	1975	71.0	..	-5.0	2.9	4
Yemen	870	2002	10.0	16.2	0.5	11.9	584

Source:

World Bank: http://www.worldbank.org/data/wdi2004/tables/table1-1.pdf

ILO: http://laborsta.ilo.org/

Humman Development Report 2004

Iraq Central Statistical Organization, Baghdad.

Table -17

EXTERNAL DEBT ($ MILLIONS)

Country	Total external debt 1990	Total external debt 2002	Long-term debt 1990	Long-term debt 2002	Public and publicly guaranteed debt 1990	Public and publicly guaranteed debt 2002	Private nonguaranteed external debt 1990	Private nonguaranteed external debt 2002
Algeria	28,149	22,800	26,688	21,362	26,688	21,255	0	107
Bahrain	..	..	..	..	..	..	..	..
Comoros	..	..	..	..	..	..	..	..
Djibouti	..	..	..	..	..	..	..	..
Egypt	33,017	30,750	28,438	27,282	27,438	26,624	1,000	658
Iraq	..	..	..	..	..	..	..	..
Jordan	8,333	8,094	7,202	7,076	7,202	7,076	0	0
Kuwait	..	..	..	..	..	..	..	..
Lebanon	1,779	17,077	358	14,530	358	13,829	0	701
Libyan Arab Jamahiriya	..	..	..	..	..	..	..	..
Mauritania	2,113	2,309	1,806	1,984	1,806	1,984	0	0
Morocco	25,017	18,601	23,860	16,913	23,660	15,001	200	1,912
Occupied Palestinian Territories	..	..	..	..	..	..	..	..
Oman	2,736	4,639	2,400	3,451	2,400	1,979	0	1,471
Qatar	..	..	..	..	..	..	..	..
Saudi Arabia	..	..	..	..	..	..	..	..
Somalia	2,370	2,688	1,926	1,860	1,926	1,860	0	0
Sudan	14,762	16,389	9,651	9,539	9,155	9,043	496	496
Syrian Arab Republic	17,259	21,504	15,108	15,849	15,108	15,849	0	0
Tunisia	..	..	..	..	..	..	..	..
United Arab Emirates	7,690	12,625	6,880	12,027	6,662	10,641	218	1,386
Yemen	6,352	5,290	5,160	4,563	5,160	4,563	0	0

Source: World Bank: http://www.worldbank.org/data/wdi2004/pdfs/Table4_16.pdf

Table -18

INTEGRATION WITH THE GLOBAL ECONOMY

Country	Trade in goods (% of GDP) 1990	Trade in goods (% of GDP) 2002	Ratio of commercial service exports to merchandise exports (%) 1990	Ratio of commercial service exports to merchandise exports (%) 2002	Growth in real trade less growth in real GDP % points 1990-2002	Gross private capital flows (% of GDP) 1990	Gross private capital flows (% of GDP) 2002	Gross foreign direct investment (% of GDP) 1990	Gross foreign direct investment (% of GDP) 2002
Algeria	36.6	53.5	3.7	..	−0.5	2.6	..	0	..
Bahrain	..	..	..	..	..	..	..	..	..
Comoros	..	..	..	..	..	..	..	..	..
Djibouti	..	..	..	..	..	..	..	..	..
Egypt	36.8	18.8	138.4	208.3	−2.1	6.8	6.6	1.7	0.8
Iraq	41.2	..	..	..	..	..	..	..	..
Jordan	91.1	82.8	134.4	53.7	−2.6	6.3	7.8	1.7	0.9
Kuwait	59.8	68.9	15	8.9	..	19.3	18.9	1.3	0.5
Lebanon	106.5	43.3	..	..	−2.5	..	..	..	..
Libyan Arab Jamahiriya	64.2	87.1	0.6	..	..	7.3	..	0.9	..
Mauritania	84.1	76.8	3.0	..	−1.2	48.8	..	0.7	..
Morocco	43.3	54.2	43.9	51.7	2.7	5.5	3.3	0.6	1.4
Occupied Palestinian Terr.	..	..	..	..	..	..	..	..	..
Oman	77.7	84.6	1.2	3.1	..	3.8	5.0	1.4	0.2
Qatar	..	..	..	..	..	..	..	..	..
Saudi Arabia	58.6	56.4	6.8	7.0	..	8.8	13.9	1.6	0.5
Somalia	26.7	..	..	..	..	..	..	..	..
Sudan	4.1	26.5	35.9	2.5	5.8	0.2	7.5	0	4.6
Syrian Arab Republic	53.7	51.8	17.6	26.7	3.6	18.0	16.8	0	1.5
Tunisia	73.5	77.7	44.7	38.3	0.3	9.5	10.6	0.6	3.8
United Arab Emirates	101.8	..	..	..	..	..	..	..	..
Yemen	46.9	58.4	11.8	4.0	3.1	16.2	3.6	2.7	1.1

Source: Word Bank: http://www.worldbank.org/data/wdi2004/tables/table6-1.pdf

Table -19

PRIORITIES IN PUBLIC SPENDING

Country	Public expenditure on education (% of GDP)		Public expenditure on health (% of GDP)		Military expenditure (% of GDP)		Total debt service (% of GDP)	
	1990	1999-2001	1990	2001	1990	2002	1990	2002
Algeria	5.3	..	3.0	3.1	1.5	3.7	14.2	7.5
Bahrain	4.2	..	..	2.9	5.1	3.9	..	..
Comoros	..	..	2.9	1.9	..	..	0.4	1.9
Djibouti	..	..	..	4.1	6.3	..	3.6	2.0
Egypt	3.7	..	1.8	1.9	3.9	2.7	7.1	2.3
Iraq	..	..	..	..	..	..	..	..
Jordan	8.4	4.6	3.6	4.5	9.9	8.4	15.6	6.3
Kuwait	4.8	..	4.0	3.5	48.5	10.4	..	..
Lebanon	..	2.9	..	..	7.6	4.7	3.5	12.7
Libyan Arab Jamahiriya	..	2.7	..	1.6	..	2.4	..	..
Mauritania	..	3.6	..	2.6	3.8	1.9	14.3	6.6
Morocco	5.3	5.1	0.9	2	4.1	4.3	6.9	10.2
Occupied Palestinian Territories	..	..	..	..	..	..	..	..
Oman	3.1	4.2	2.0	2.4	16.5	12.3	7.0	8.6
Qatar	3.5	..	..	2.2	..	..	..	..
Saudi Arabia	6.5	..	..	3.4	12.8	9.8	..	..
Somalia	..	..	..	..	..	..	..	..
Sudan	0.9	..	0.7	0.6	3.6	2.8	0.4	0.2
Syrian Arab Republic	4.1	4.0	0.4	2.4	6.9	6.1	9.7	1.2
Tunisia	6.0	6.8	3.0	4.9	2.0	..	11.6	6.8
United Arab Emirates	1.9	..	0.8	2.6	6.2	3.7	..	..
Yemen	..	10.0	1.1	1.5	8.5	7.1	3.5	1.7

Source: Human Development Report 2004

Table -20

WOMEN'S POLITICAL PARTICIPATION

Country	Seats in parliament held by women (% of total) 1997-2004		Year women received right to stand for election	Year first woman elected or appointed to parliament	Women in government at ministerial level (% of total) 1998	Women in government at sub ministerial level (% of total) 1998
	Lower or single house	Upper house or senate				
Algeria	6.2	19.4	1962	1962	0	10
Bahrain	0	15	1973	—	0	1
Comoros	..	..	1956	1993	7	0
Djibouti	10.8	..	1986	2003	0	3
Egypt	2.4	5.7	1956	1957	6	4
Iraq	..	..	*1980	*1980	0	0
Jordan	5.5	12.7	1974	1989	2	0
Kuwait	0	..	—	—	0	7
Lebanon	2.3	..	1952	1991	0	0
Libyan Arab Jamahiriya	..	..	1964	..	..	..
Mauritania	3.7	5.4	1961	1975	4	6
Morocco	10.8	1.1	1963	1993	0	8
Occupied Palestinian Territories	..	..	..	..	..	..
Oman	–	..	—	—	0	4
Qatar	–	..	—	—	0	0
Saudi Arabia	0.0	..	—	—	0	0
Somalia	..	..	..	..	0	0
Sudan	9.7	..	1964	1964	0	0
Syrian Arab Republic	12.0	..	1953	1973	8	0
Tunisia	11.5	..	1957,1959	1959	3	10
United Arab Emirates	0	..	—	—	0	0
Yemen	0.3	..	1967	1990	0	0

Source:

World Women 2000: http://unstats.un.org/unsd/demographic/ww2000/table6a.htm

Inter-Parliamentary Union: http://www.ipu.org/wmn-e/classif.htm

Human Development Report 2004

Human Development Report 2000 (for Iraq when * is used)

Table -21

GENDER INEQUALITY IN EDUCATION

Country	Adult literacy 2002		Youth literacy 2002		Net primary enrolment		Net secondary enrolment		Gross tertiary enrolment	
	Female rate (% ages 15 & above) 2002	Female rate as % of male rate 2002	Female rate (% ages 15-24) 2002	Female rate as % of male rate 2002	Female ratio (%) 2000/01	Ratio of female to male 2000/01	Female ratio (%) 2000/01	Ratio of female to male 2000/01	Female ratio (%) 2000/01	Ratio of female to male 2000/01
Algeria	59.6	76	85.6	91	94	0.97	64	1.06	..	..
Bahrain	84.2	92	98.9	100	91	1.01	86	1.12	28	1.86
Comoros	49.1	77	52.2	79	50	0.84	..	..	1	0.73
Djibouti	..	..	..	..	30	0.77	13	0.63	1	0.80
Egypt	43.6	65	66.9	85	88	0.96	79	0.95	..	..
Iraq	..	..	..	..	..	..	..	..	..	..
Jordan	85.9	90	99.5	100	92	1.01	81	1.03	31	1.02
Kuwait	81.0	96	93.9	102	84	0.99	79	1.05	32	2.58
Lebanon	..	..	..	..	89	0.99	..	..	48	1.14
Libyan Arab Jamahiriya	70.7	77	94.0	94	..	..	..	..	61	1.09
Mauritania	31.3	61	41.8	73	65	0.96	13	0.83	1	0.27
Morocco	38.3	61	61.3	79	85	0.93	28	0.83	9	0.80
Occupied Palestinian Terr.	..	..	..	..	95	1.01	83	1.06	30	0.98
Oman	65.4	80	97.3	98	75	1.01	68	1.00	10	1.67
Qatar	82.3	97	95.8	102	94	0.98	80	1.06	34	2.69
Saudi Arabia	69.5	83	91.6	96	57	0.92	51	0.93	26	1.49
Somalia	..	..	..	..	..	..	..	..	..	..
Sudan	49.1	69	74.2	88	42	0.83	..	..	6	0.92
Syrian Arab Republic	74.2	82	93.0	96	96	0.95	37	0.91	..	..
Tunisia	63.1	76	90.6	93	97	0.99	·69	1.04	21	0.97
United Arab Emirates	80.7	107	95.0	108	80	0.97	74	1.05	..	..
Yemen	28.5	41	50.9	60	47	0.66	21	0.46	5	0.28

Source: Human Development Report 2004

Table -22

OTHER INDICATORS ON WOMEN

country	Economic activity rate (%) 1986-2001		Self employed (%) 1995-2002		Women among administrative and managerial workers (%) 1985/1997	Year of ratification of the Convention on the Elimination of All Forms of Discrimination against Women	Whether national plan of action provided to the UN Secretariat
	Male	Female	Men	Women			
Algeria	47	7	..	..	6	1996	Yes
Bahrain	65	24	..	..	21	2002	Yes
Comoros	..	..	..	..	..	1994	..
Djibouti	..	..	19	16	2	1998	..
Egypt	69	20	31	17	16	1981	Yes
Iraq	74	10	..	..	13	1986	Yes
Jordan	73	13	..	..	..	1992	Yes
Kuwait	83	43	..	..	5	1994	Yes
Lebanon	..	..	..	..	..	1997	Yes
Libyan Arab Jamahiriya	..	..	..	..	..	1989	..
Mauritania	..	..	..	..	8	2001	..
Morocco	78	26	23	5	..	1993	Yes
Occupied Palestinian Territ.	66	10	32	9	..	..	..
Oman	59	13	..	..	..	..	Yes
Qatar	93	28	..	..	1	..	Yes
Saudi Arabia	80	15	..	..	..	2000	..
Somalia	..	..	..	..	..	..	..
Sudan	75	29	..	..	..	..	Yes
Syrian Arab Republic	82	24	37	6	3	2003	Yes
Tunisia	73	24	25	14	9	1985	Yes
United Arab Emirates	92	31	..	..	2	..	Yes
Yemen	81	2	49	63	..	1984	Yes

Source:

UNSD, World Women 2000: http://unstats.un.org/unsd/demographic/ww2000/table5d.htm

UNSD, World Women 2000: http://unstats.un.org/unsd/demographic/ww2000/table5e.htm

Table -23

PRESS AND COMMUNICATIONS

Country	Press Freedom Barometer*	Deaths of journalists and media workers 1990-2002	Daily news paper (per 1000 people) 1998-2000	Telephone mainlines (per 1,000 people) 2002	Cellular sub-scribers (per 1,000 people) 2002	Internet users (per 1,000 people) 2001
Algeria	Noticeable problems	107	27.3	61	13	16
Bahrain	Noticeable problems	0	..	261	579	246
Comoros	Noticeable problems	0	..	13	0	4
Djibouti	Difficult situation	0	..	15	23	7
Egypt	Difficult situation	0	31.2	110	67	28
Iraq	Very serious situation	11	..	30	..	..
Jordan	Noticeable problems	0	75.5	127	229	58
Kuwait	Noticeable problems	4	..	204	519	106
Lebanon	Noticeable problems	6	..	199	227	117
Libyan Arab Jamahiriya	Very serious situation	0	..	118	13	23
Mauritania	Difficult situation	0	..	12	92	4
Morocco	Noticeable problems	0	28.3	38	209	24
Occupied Palestinian Territories	Noticeable problems	0	..	87	93	30
Oman	Noticeable problems	9	..	92	183	71
Qatar	Noticeable problems	0	..	286	433	113
Saudi Arabia	Very serious situation	0	..	151	228	65
Somalia	Difficult situation	17	..	..	..	..
Sudan	Difficult situation	0	..	21	6	3
Syrian Arab Republic	Very serious situation	0	..	123	23	13
Tunisia	Very serious situation	0	19.0	117	52	52
United Arab Emirates	Noticeable problems	0	..	291	647	313
Yemen	Difficult situation	0	..	28	21	5

* The Press Freedom Barometer has five levels: good situation, satisfactory situation, noticeable problems, difficult situation and very serious situation.

Source:

Reporters Without Borders: http://www.rsf.fr/rubrique.php3?id_rubrique=43

International Federation of Journalists: http://www.ifj.org/pdfs/safetyapp2.pdf.

UNESCO: http://stats.uis.unesco.org/eng/TableViewer/Wdsview/dispviewp.asp?ReportId=27

Human Development Report 2004

Table -24

ENERGY AND THE ENVIRONMENT

Country	Electricity consumption per capita (kilowatt-hours)		Carbon dioxide emissions per capita (metric tons)		Framework Convention on Climate Change	Kyoto Protocol to the Framework Convention on Climate Change	Convention on Biological Diversity
	1980	2001	1980	2000			
Algeria	381	866	3.5	2.9	●		●
Bahrain	4,784	10,350	23.4	29.1	●		●
Comoros	26	26	0.1	0.1	●		●
Djibouti	416	286	1.0	0.6	●	●	●
Egypt	433	1,129	1.1	2.2	●	○	●
Iraq	..	..	..	..	..	..	..
Jordan	366	1,507	2.2	3.2	●	●	●
Kuwait	6,849	15,309	18.0	21.9	●		●
Lebanon	1,056	3,025	2.1	3.5	●		●
Libyan Arab Jamahiriya	1,588	4,021	8.8	10.9	●		●
Mauritania	60	61	0.4	1.2	●		●
Morocco	254	569	0.8	1.3	●	●	●
Occupied Palestinian Territories	..	..	..	..			
Oman	847	5,119	5.3	8.2	●		●
Qatar	10,616	16,677	56.3	69.5	●		●
Saudi Arabia	1,969	6,018	14.0	18.1	●		●
Somalia	..	..	..	..	..	..	..
Sudan	47	81	0.2	0.2	●		●
Syrian Arab Republic	433	1,528	2.2	3.3	●		●
Tunisia	434	1,106	1.5	1.9	●	●	●
United Arab Emirates	6,204	13,948	34.8	21.0	●		●
Yemen	...	164	..	0.5	●		●

● Ratification, acceptance, approval, accession or succession

○ Signature

Source: Human Development Report 2004

Table -25

ARMAMENTS AND REFUGEES

Countries	Conventional arms imports (US$ millions at 1990 prices)		Total armed forces 2002		Refugees, excluding Palestinian refugees (thousands) 2003	
	1994	2003	Thousands	Index (1985 = 100)	By country of asylum	By country of origin
Algeria	156	513	137	80	169	4
Bahrain	10	(.)	11	382	0	(.)
Comoros	..	..	..	..	0	(.)
Djibouti	(.)	(.)	10	327	27	(.)
Egypt	1,976	504	443	100	89	1
Iraq	..	..	..	..	..	..
Jordan	5	258	100	143	1	1
Kuwait	37	21	16	129	2	(.)
Lebanon	13	(.)	72	413	3	19
Libyan Arab Jamahiriya	(.)	(.)	76	104	12	1
Mauritania	27	(.)	16	`185	(.)	26
Morocco	131	(.)	196	132	2	1
Occupied Palestinian Territories	5	(.)	..	..	0	326
Oman	173	14	42	143	0	(.)
Qatar	10	10	12	207	(.)	(.)
Saudi Arabia	991	487	200	319	241	(.)
Somalia	..	..	..	..	..	..
Sudan	(.)	(.)	117	207	328	567
Syrian Arab Republic	44	15	319	79	4	16
Tunisia	32	(.)	35	100	(.)	2
United Arab Emirates	554	922	42	97	(.)	(.)
Yemen	4	30	67	104	62	1

Source: Human Development Report 2004